WHEN
CRIME
PAYS

WHEN CRIME PAYS

MONEY AND MUSCLE IN

INDIAN POLITICS

MILAN VAISHNAV

Yale UNIVERSITY PRESS

New Haven and London

Yale University Press books may be purchased in quantity for educational, business, or promotional use. For information, please e-mail sales.press@yale.edu (U.S. office) or sales@yaleup.co.uk (U.K. office).

Set in Sabon type by Newgen North America.
Printed in the United States of America.

Library of Congress Control Number: 2016945528
ISBN 978-0-300-21620-2 (cloth : alk. paper)

A catalogue record for this book is available from the British Library.
This paper meets the requirements of ANSI/NISO Z39.48-1992 (Permanence of Paper).

10 9 8 7 6 5 4 3 2 1

For Sheba, who endured

Contents

Part III

Preface

India's 2014 general election was the largest democratic exercise ever undertaken. On nine separate polling days staggered over six weeks, 554 million voters queued up at more than 900,000 polling stations to cast their ballots in favor of one of 8,251 candidates representing 464 political parties.

While the numbers were overwhelming, so too was the verdict. For the first time in three decades, Indians delivered a majority of seats in the lower house of Parliament (known as the Lok Sabha) to a single political party—the opposition Bharatiya Janata Party (BJP). The stunning result was the product of deep-seated disenchantment with the ruling Indian National Congress (INC), whose second term in office was marked by a slowing economy and besmirched by a series of sordid corruption scandals, as well as the personal and professional appeal of former Gujarat Chief Minister Narendra Modi, who led the BJP campaign.

Modi's record in Gujarat was far from untarnished; in the early months of his tenure, violence between Hindus and Muslims left more than 1,000 people dead, and the state government appeared either unwilling or unable to stem the bloodshed. Nevertheless, Modi's tenure in the state was marked by a galloping economy, the fastest growing among India's states. On the whole, his twelve-year rule in Gujarat was, in the minds of many voters, synonymous with prosperity, development, and good governance—qualities that exit polls suggested were at the forefront of voters' minds in 2014. At a time of widespread consternation over the fate of India's economy and the quality of the country's administration, large sections of the electorate viewed Modi to be the right man to get India's house in order.

The resounding victory for Modi and the BJP, the stunning repudiation of the incumbent Congress Party, and the rhetorical emphasis on *vikas* (development) during the campaign led many analysts to dub the 2014 campaign India's "good governance" election. So it was curious that the very same election produced a parliament in which one-third of its members were facing ongoing criminal prosecution. One in five newly elected members of Parliament (MPs) disclosed at least one pending case involving serious criminal charges—charges that, if a conviction were obtained, would merit real jail time.

These facts raise a number of uncomfortable questions about how free and fair democratic elections and widespread illegality can comfortably coexist. This book addresses those questions, using the world's largest democracy as a test case. To be clear, this nexus is not unique to India, but a thorough examination of the Indian experience can shed light on the dozens of other democracies where criminality and corruption are deeply entrenched, from Pakistan to the Philippines.

Any explanation of complex social realities, such as the criminalization of politics, can rarely be boiled down to a single root cause. To try to simplify matters, I argue throughout the book that it is useful to think of criminal politicians existing within an electoral marketplace. As with any market, the marketplace for criminal politicians comprises both supply (politicians) and demand (voters). Of course, these factors are highly contextual, varying substantially even within a single country. To be clear, the term "criminal politicians" refers to politicians who have been named in ongoing criminal cases, even if a court of law has not conclusively established their guilt. Criminal politicians often have a reputation for engaging in illegal activity, but they may not have been convicted (yet) of criminal transgressions.

Individuals with criminal reputations have long been associated with politics in India, but amid a changing electoral environment in which uncertainty and competition have both intensified, over time they have moved from the periphery to center stage. Once content to serve politicians, criminals gradually became politicians themselves. In taking the electoral plunge, they have not acted on their own. Just as markets feature intermediaries who match buyers with sellers, political parties have embraced and promoted candidates with criminal links, drawn to their deep pockets at a time when the cost of elections has exploded and party organizations have atrophied. Loophole-ridden campaign finance laws have been no match for the torrent of undocumented cash that those with criminal ties are able to marshal.

Money helps grease the wheels, but voters too often have a rational incentive to back politicians with criminal reputations. In places where the rule of law is weak and social divisions are rife, politicians can use their criminality as a signal of their ability to do whatever it takes to protect the interests of their community—from dispensing justice and guaranteeing security to providing a social safety net. What the Indian state has been unable to provide, strongmen have promised to deliver in spades. What this means in practice is that voters are not necessarily blind to the predilections of the political class: many voters vote for politicians *because,* rather than *in spite,* of their criminal reputations.

The argument I have sketched out above is not a straightforward one to make, given the sensitive nature of the issues at hand. To overcome this hurdle, this book adopts an eclectic approach, drawing on a wide diversity of rich source material from India's complicated and colorful democracy.

The foundation of this book is a unique database of candidate disclosures that have been submitted to the Election Commission of India (ECI) and digitized by various civil society organizations. For those who are interested, I have made this database publicly available through my personal website. The database contains detailed information on the criminal and financial attributes of nearly 60,000 candidates from 35 state and two national elections held between 2003 and 2009. In addition, I compiled data on the 8,000-plus candidates contesting the 2014 national election to demonstrate the contemporary relevance of the issues presented here. The data are not perfect (I discuss some of their salient features, including shortcomings, in subsequent chapters), but they are an important source of reference material.

Another significant source came from fieldwork in India. Between 2008 and 2014, I interacted with dozens of journalists, politicians, party officials, and ordinary voters in the states of Andhra Pradesh, Bihar, Delhi, and Gujarat.

In Bihar, I conducted fieldwork during the 2010 state assembly elections, which involved following electoral campaigns of state legislative candidates across three districts (analogous to counties in the United States). I was fortunate to observe the campaigns of several candidates with serious criminal reputations, studying the interactions that took place between candidates, voters, and political parties on the campaign trail. I also collaborated with the Delhi-based Centre for the Study of Developing Societies (CSDS) on a post-election survey of more than 2,000 voters in Bihar. As a state that has long had the dubious distinction of electing significant numbers of politicians implicated in criminal activity, the Bihar experience was central to developing the theory of criminal candidacy presented in this book. By observing subsequent elections in Andhra Pradesh and Gujarat, two states chosen to demonstrate the geographic reach of the crime-politics nexus, I was able to test how well the theory traveled to other settings.

Fieldwork around the 2012 Gujarat elections also helped clarify my thinking on the role of money in politics. This research primarily consisted of interviews with academics, businesspeople, civil society representatives, election officials, and journalists. To add granularity to my thinking on the financial aspects of electioneering, I followed the campaign of an aspirant to state office in Andhra Pradesh, as the region headed for election in 2014. Throughout this period, I also made several trips to Delhi to gather additional material drawn from conversations with politicians, party workers, journalists, officials at the ECI, and several scholars and activists working on electoral politics.

Wherever possible I have drawn from collaborative research being done with other scholars whose findings pertain to the subject matter. With various colleagues, I have been working on a number of subjects relevant to this book, ranging from an exploration of India's election finance regime and a historical analysis of the ECI, to a survey of the social and political attitudes of a broad cross section of ordinary Indians.

This book is also informed by a wide array of secondary source material, culled mainly from the work of scholars who have examined diverse aspects of Indian politics as well as from journalists who have pounded the pavement. As a comparative political scientist, I have looked far and wide for illuminating voices, examples, and illustrations.

There are myriad implications of this book for India, and for democracies around the world. Unlike many countries in the West, India embarked on its democratic journey without first possessing capable institutions of governance. Whereas many advanced industrialized democracies built strong states over centuries before embarking on a process of political liberalization, India instituted universal franchise from the outset, operating under the constraints of a relatively weak institutional framework. Over time, as the stresses of political, economic, and social change have grown, the country's institutional framework has proven too frail to cope. The resort to suspected criminals in politics has to be understood through this larger prism of the state-building enterprise—an endeavor many developing countries also find themselves struggling with at present.

Over time, many Indian voters—faced with a state unable to service their needs—have looked to those who can. Viewed in this light, politicians with criminal records are not symptomatic of a failure of the democratic process. Instead, malfeasant politicians and popular accountability can in fact be compatible (although surely not free of adverse consequences). This means that contrary to the widely held belief that "sunlight is the best disinfectant," raising the level of transparency regarding the nexus between crime and politics will not be sufficient to stamp out this link.

The good news is that an understanding of this marketplace and how it behaves can help us grapple with the public policy ramifications and suggest possible remedies. In the short run, reformers must revamp how elections are funded and tackle the most egregious cases of illegality indulged in by politicians. But in the long run, there is no substitute for building up the capacity of the state to expand its writ while simultaneously taming its worst excesses. Put somewhat more provocatively, the problem with the Indian state is not that it is too big; it is that it is big in all the wrong places. Contrary to popular lamentations that India's developmental performance remains burdened by an unruly democracy while that of its Chinese neighbor, unencumbered by the constraints imposed by popular consent, has been able to rapidly develop, India's democracy is not, in fact, the difficulty.

Rather, what India lacks is a state that can keep pace with popular aspirations.

In India's boisterous democracy, the debate over the role of crime in politics is raging ahead—although our understanding of the underlying drivers is still inchoate. The humble ambition of the present study is to help nudge that process along.

Acknowledgments

As with many first books, this one began its life as a doctoral dissertation—written for a degree in political science at Columbia University. The idea for the dissertation came from Devesh Kapur, a brilliant scholar of India, whom I am lucky to call an advisor, colleague, friend, and mentor. Even though Devesh was at the University of Pennsylvania, I cajoled him into working with me on the project. Maria Victoria Murillo had all the qualities of an ideal dissertation advisor—patience, a sense of humor, and very high standards. I am grateful for her constant willingness to exchange ideas, read drafts, and provide moral support. Despite being in high demand by his many students, Macartan Humphreys made time to share his unique insights and sharp comments.

At Columbia, I benefited from the advice and counsel of many professors and friends. Above all, I thank Andy Gelman, Lucy Goodhart, Guy Grossman, John Huber, Virginia Oliveros, Laura Paler, Kelly Rader, Cyrus Samii, Mark Schneider, and Pavithra Suryanarayan. Phil Oldenburg is due special thanks for sharing his encyclopedic knowledge of India with me on a regular basis, as is Neelanjan Sircar for being an ever-present sounding board. Obtaining some of the data required for this book was no simple task, but Diego Fulguiera's computer science wizardry made it much easier. Thanks also to the team at Innovaccer for additional assistance.

Although this book began at Columbia, it took its present shape at the Carnegie Endowment for International Peace, where I have happily spent the last four years. Carnegie's former president, Jessica Mathews, was supportive of this project from the get-go and current president Bill Burns graciously extended that support. I owe special thanks to Ashley Tellis, George Perkovich, and Frederic Grare for providing a wonderful intellectual home in Carnegie's South Asia Program. Molly Pallman and Rachel Osnos have been the glue (and the fun) that has kept our program humming. Along the way, I have borrowed copious brain cells from friends in Carnegie's Democracy and Rule of Law Program, namely, Tom Carothers, Rachel Kleinfeld, and especially Sarah Chayes. I am also grateful to the Carnegie Endowment for allowing me to reproduce material (coauthored with Devesh Kapur) that previously appeared in the 2014 Carnegie edited volume, *Getting India Back on Track: An Action Agenda for Reform.*

Before joining Carnegie, I spent a wonderful year as a doctoral fellow at the Center for Global Development (CGD). I will never have a boss quite like Nancy Birdsall, who has been my biggest champion. Thanks to Todd Moss, Michael Clemens, and Justin Sandefur for being terrific colleagues. My first stint at CGD was in 2003–5, when I had the pleasure of working with Jeremy Weinstein, to whom goes the credit and/or blame for my deciding to pursue a PhD.

The research done for this book was made possible with the help of a large cast of characters. I consider myself very lucky to have worked with a series of excellent research assistants, beginning with Owen McCarthy at CGD and continuing with Will Hayes, Danielle Smogard, Alec Sugarman, Reedy Swanson, and Reece Trevor at Carnegie. They were equal partners in every respect. Saksham Khosla and Aidan Milliff ably helped me push this book across the finish line.

In 2008 I was a visiting researcher with the Lokniti program at CSDS in New Delhi. Thanks to Sanjay Kumar for hosting me and to Banasmita Bora for being a wonderful guide to Delhi. The following year I spent time as a visitor with the Accountability Initiative at the Centre for Policy Research in New Delhi courtesy of the indefatigable Yamini Aiyar. E. Sridharan and Ruchika Ahuja of the University of Pennsylvania Institute for the Advanced Study of India have been immensely helpful during my many trips to Delhi.

Jeff Witsoe, my guru on all things Bihar, helped me plan my research there in 2010, and his work on criminality significantly shaped my own thinking. Sanjay Kumar, Akhilesh Kumar, and Sanjay Pandey were terrific guides to the local political scene. Thanks to Zaheeb Ajmal, Rakesh Ranjan, Rakesh Kumar, Mukesh Kumar Rai, and especially Sanjay Kumar of Lokniti for help with data collection. I am grateful to Howard Spodek for sharing his unique insights on Gujarat as well as Mahesh Langa, Mona Mehta, and Navdeep Mathur for their help in Ahmedabad. In Andhra Pradesh, I owe an enormous debt to the candidate described here as "Sanjay," who allowed me to shadow him on the campaign trail. Thanks also to Sanjay's campaign team for their cooperation.

Many of the findings reported in this book were a result of, or inspired by, research collaborations with a number of friends and colleagues, including Reuben Abraham, Sanjoy Chakravorty, Devesh Kapur, Rajiv Lall, Pratap Bhanu Mehta, Suyash Rai, Megan Reed, Nasra Roy, Neelanjan Sircar, Danielle Smogard, E. Sridharan, Reedy Swanson, Sandip Sukhtankar, and Mahesh Vyas. Of course, any errors found in these pages are my own.

Many others have shared their friendship, scholarship, and expertise out of the goodness of their hearts. For this, I am grateful to Rikhil Bhavnani, Jennifer Bussell, Kanchan Chandra, Simon Chauchard, Jagdeep Chhokar, Christophe Jaffrelot, Rob Jenkins, Francesca Jensenius, Madhav Khosla, M. R. Madhavan, Akshay Mangla, Govind Mohan, Irfan Nooruddin, Ananth Padmanabhan, S. Y. Quraishi, Arvind Subramanian, Tariq Thachil, Ashutosh Varshney, Steven Wilkinson, and Adam Ziegfeld.

Some of the underlying papers upon which this book is based benefited from comments received at numerous seminars and conferences. Thanks to Taylor Boas, Miriam Golden, Christopher Haid, Stuti Khemani, Beatriz Magaloni, Peter Van der Windt, and Sanjay Ruparelia. For constructive feedback, I am grateful to seminar participants at Brookings India/University of Chicago, Brown University, Center for Global Development, Centre for Policy Research, Columbia University, U.S. Foreign Service Institute, Georgetown University, Johns Hopkins School of Advanced International Studies, New York University, Princeton University, University of Southern California, University of

Pennsylvania, and World Bank 1818 Society. I also received useful feedback from participants at prior annual meetings of the American Political Science Association and Midwest Political Science Association.

This project received generous financial support from the Smith Richardson Foundation, without which it would not have been possible. I am especially thankful for the support and advice of my program officer, Allan Song. Several institutions affiliated with Columbia University helped support this work; they include: the Graduate School of Arts and Sciences, Department of Political Science, Center for International Business and Education Research, and Earth Institute. The Center for the Advanced Study of India at the University of Pennsylvania stepped in with critical funding when it was badly needed. Finally, I was fortunate to receive a doctoral dissertation improvement grant from the National Science Foundation (SES #1022234).

My agent, Kathleen Anderson of Anderson Literary Management, championed this book from the very beginning. At Yale University Press, it has been a pleasure to work with Jaya Aninda Chatterjee, who has been a fantastic editor. Eliza Childs provided superb guidance on the final text. I am also grateful to the team at HarperCollins India, above all Somak Ghoshal and Karthika VK.

Two anonymous reviewers provided incisive comments on the manuscript, for which I am sincerely appreciative. Devesh Kapur, Madhav Khosla, Neelanjan Sircar, and Ashley Tellis gave all, or part, of the manuscript a thorough read.

This book project has relied implicitly, and sometimes explicitly, on the aid and succor of close friends and family. I owe special thanks to Jatin and Jyoti Desai, Tani Sanghvi and Ajay Shah, Jasu and Indu Sanghvi, and the entire Desai-Vaishnav clan, especially Dilip and Pragna Desai and Mona and Ranjeet Vaishnav for their help in Mumbai.

On the home front, I have been blessed to count on Chester and Saône Crocker; Rennie and Kai Anderson; and Rebecca Crocker for good cheer. Not to be outdone, my nieces and nephews, Tala, Caleb, Avey, and Milo Anderson and Ella and Rosa Sagarin, have kept me on my toes. There is not a day that goes by that I do not miss Rafe Sagarin, whose example was—and is—an inspiration. I owe a special debt to Anand Vaishnav, not least for bringing Madhavi Chavali, Kavya, and Manali into our family. My parents, Mahendra and Sukeshi Vaishnav, were good to never once to ask when my book was going to be finished.

People say writing a book is like giving birth. While that may be true, it is no match for the joy one feels in actually bringing new (animate) lives into this world. When they finally hold this book in their hands, Asha and Farrin will hopefully understand what their dad was doing typing on his computer all that time. Their presence, along with that of my canine offspring Cleo, helped me realize that all the typing really could wait. I owe special thanks to Elisa Avalos for all of her help over the years.

My biggest debt is to Sheba Crocker, who at this point deserves not only an honorary doctorate but also coauthorship of this book. From patiently indulging my incessant book-related babble to editing chapters and managing our lives when I had to travel, she has been a perfect partner in every respect. It is to her that this book is dedicated.

Abbreviations

AAP	Aam Aadmi Party
ABS	Akhil Bharatiya Sena
ADR	Association for Democratic Reforms
AITC	All India Trinamool Congress
BJP	Bharatiya Janata Party
BPL	Below Poverty Line
BSP	Bahujan Samaj Party
CAG	Comptroller and Auditor General
CBI	Central Bureau of Investigation
CIC	Central Information Commission
CPI	Community Party of India
CPI(M)	Communist Party of India (Marxist)
CSDS	Centre for the Study of Developing Societies
DMK	Dravida Munnetra Kazhagam
ECI	Election Commission of India
FIR	First Information Report
FSLRC	Financial Sector Legislative Reforms Commission
G20	Group of 20
GDP	Gross Domestic Product
IAC	India Against Corruption
IAS	Indian Administrative Service

INC	Indian National Congress
IPC	Indian Penal Code
JD(U)	Janata Dal (United)
LJP	Lok Janshakti Party
MLA	Member of the Legislative Assembly
MP	Member of Parliament
NGO	Non-Governmental Organization
OBC	Other Backward Class
OMC	Obulapuram Mining Company
PIL	Public Interest Litigation
QED	Quami Ekta Dal
RJD	Rashtriya Janata Dal
RSS	Rashtriya Swayamsevak Sangh
RTI	Right to Information
SAD	Shiromani Akali Dal
SC	Scheduled Caste
SP	Samajwadi Party
ST	Scheduled Tribe
TADA	Terrorist and Disruptive Activities (Prevention) Act
TDP	Telugu Desam Party
YSR	Y. S. Rajasekhara Reddy
UPA	United Progressive Alliance
WHO	World Health Organization

Note to Readers

Throughout the book, I quote prices in terms of Indian rupees. For the convenience of readers, I also express these quantities in terms of U.S. dollars, using the exchange rate (as of December 2015) of approximately 66 rupees per one U.S. dollar. Readers should be aware that this conversion does not take inflation into account, thus underestimating the present value of historical prices cited herein.

I

1 Lawmakers and Lawbreakers
The Puzzle of Indian Democracy

IN JULY 2008, New Delhi was abuzz with rumors of the impending collapse of the country's governing coalition. In the dead of a typically sultry Indian summer, the ruling United Progressive Alliance (UPA) government was staring down the prospect of a no-confidence vote over its controversial bill to strengthen civilian nuclear cooperation with the United States. If the government lost the vote—which pundits suggested was eminently plausible—it would be forced to hold early elections.

Given the stakes and the simmering controversy over the deal, which had many high-profile detractors even from within the ruling alliance, the government feared the worst. To avoid defeat, it turned for help to an unexpected source: the bowels of the country's most notorious jails. Inside those cells sat six MPs who, though charged or convicted for serious crimes, still retained crucial votes that could tip the balance on the floor of Parliament.[1]

Forty-eight hours before the vote and with little fanfare, the government furloughed six of the nation's most prominent suspected lawbreakers—collectively facing over 100 cases of kidnapping, murder, extortion, arson, and more—so that they could fulfill their constitutional duties as lawmakers.

One of the six temporarily sprung parliamentarians was Ateeq Ahmed, a Samajwadi Party (SP) legislator from the northern state of Uttar Pradesh with a conspicuous handlebar moustache and a penchant for safari suits. Ahmed's alleged dalliance with crime began as a young boy when he and his friends racked up extra money stealing coal from trains passing through their Allahabad neighborhood.[2] Having reportedly established his credentials as a petty criminal, Ahmed leveraged his small-time racket into a lucrative business selling railway scrap metal, intimidating rival contractors into submission in order to bag government tenders.[3]

Flush with cash, an army of loyal foot soldiers, and a reputation as a fierce local power broker with limited patience, Ahmed was soon inducted into the world of politics, where he won five consecutive state elections from 1989 to 2002. Judging by the lengthy list of criminal cases in which he stood accused, Ahmed was equally proficient at running a criminal enterprise as he was conducting constituency service.[4] Locals marveled at his weekly *durbar* (a Persian term for a monarch's court), where Ahmed, one ear pressed to his mobile phone and the other taking in requests for constituency service, would mutter orders to his personal assistant or stenographer.[5] The party headquarters in which Ahmed would hold forth often bore closer resemblance to an armory than an administrative office, the walls impressively lined with imported automatic weaponry.[6] Yet Ahmed's canny ability to efficiently process requests filed by his constituents—from covering the costs of a funeral to mediating a dispute between neighbors—earned him plaudits from constituents as well as grudging praise from many bureaucrats, whose painfully slow response times stood in unfavorable contrast.[7]

When Ahmed made the jump to national politics, he sought to bequeath his local seat to his younger brother, Ashraf. A rival candidate, Raju Pal, had other designs, defeating Ashraf in a closely fought special election. The election was about gangland dominance as much as achieving political power, although one could be excused in failing to distinguish between the two. One observer euphemistically noted that "the status of a legislator would have helped both Ahmed and Pal to advance their other, not strictly, political interests."[8] Within months of the election, Pal was gunned down in broad daylight on Allahabad's main thoroughfare. Ateeq was jailed in connection with the crime, but not before he masterminded Ashraf's win over Pal's widow in the next election.[9]

Joining Ahmed on temporary bail in July 2008 was Pappu Yadav, of the Lok Janshakti Party (LJP), whose physical stature was matched only by the length of his rap sheet.[10] An imposing man fond of bragging that there was no jail in his home state of Bihar whose insides he had not seen, Yadav was once described as having "the physique of a baby elephant and the reputation of a raving, stampeding one."[11]

Yadav was an unabashed, self-styled mafia don, openly referred to by supporters and opponents as a *bahubali* (strongman). As a child, Yadav was largely left to his own devices; his parents were reportedly members of an obscure cult whose ritual dance involved snakes, knives, and human bones.[12] Absent parental supervision, Yadav reportedly spent his free time getting into trouble: extorting local businesses, engaging in black market deals, and working as a hired gun for local gangs in Bihar's Kosi region. Once when cops arrested Pappu after one of his many criminal escapades, the local administration made him wear a plaque around his neck that read "I am Pappu Yadav, a thief" and paraded him around town.[13]

Yadav came of age at a time of great social churning in his home state, especially among the Yadavs—a populous, mid-ranking agrarian caste to which he belonged and that had long suffered in the shadows of upper-caste dominance. Buoyed by his community's rising ambitions, Yadav sensed an opening and transitioned into politics, assuming the mantle of his caste-mates' chief protector.[14] Stories did the rounds that while Bihar was bathed in darkness, Yadav's stomping grounds had access to a steady supply of power. With just one phone call from the strongman, community doctors would provide free healthcare to local residents.[15] In Yadav's constituency, an aphorism began making the rounds: *Rome Pope ka, Saharsa Gope Ka* (Rome belongs to the pope, Saharsa [a district in the Kosi region] belongs to the Gope—the latter a synonym for the Yadav caste).

The gamble paid off. Yadav won his first election to Bihar's state assembly at the age of 23. As his political star rapidly rose, he encountered numerous stumbling blocks, not least of which was a lifetime conviction for the murder of Ajit Sarkar, a rival politician who had the gall to run against (and defeat) Yadav in the late 1990s. Three months after Sarkar's stunt, he was murdered in cold blood. So great was Yadav's political base that, even after he was locked up, he successfully fielded his wife, Ranjeet, in his stead. When asked by a reporter what it was like to be married to a *bahubali*, Ranjeet replied flatly: "He has been in jail more than he has been in home."[16] She was not exaggerating. I once inadvertently typed "Pappu Yadav Bihar" into Google Maps (as opposed to the search engine) and was given directions to Beur Jail, the grimy high-security prison where he was serving time.

But when Yadav's conviction was unexpectedly thrown out in 2013 thanks to irregularities in the prosecution's case, hundreds of his supporters showered him with flowers and handed out sweets at the gates of his prison. Upon his release, Yadav penned a tell-all memoir, *Drohkaal Ke Pathik* ("A solo traveler during a time of rebellion"), which documented his turbulent rise to political prominence. Political parties swooned and vied for his affection; invitations to his glitzy post-release book party in Delhi were secured by a veritable who's who of leaders from half a dozen political parties.[17] Within one year, Yadav and his wife were once more members of Parliament—the body's only husband-wife couple. It was Yadav's fifth election to the lower house of Parliament.

Yet perhaps the most notorious of the jailed politicians to be given a momentary reprieve that July was Bihar's Mohammed Shahabuddin of the Rashtriya Janata Dal (RJD), who at that point had spent more of his political career inside jail than outside it. Since his days as a sharp-shooter for a local gang, which earned him the nickname "Shaahabu-AK" (in honor of his favorite weapon, the AK-47), Shahabuddin had been named in nearly three dozen criminal cases, ranging from extortion to murder and kidnapping.[18] The son of a stamp-paper vendor, Shahabuddin had developed a personal animus against Leftist fringe parties whose fighters routinely targeted the landlords and business-people Shahabuddin was hired to protect.[19] "Shaahabu-AK" was not the type to take provocations lying down. Tens of activists and workers associated with the Left disappeared or were allegedly murdered during the peak of Shahabuddin's reign in Siwan district.[20]

As his profile rose, Shahabuddin picked up another moniker: the "Saheb (or master) of Siwan."[21] Beginning in the 1990s, when he first dipped his toes into the world of electoral politics, Shahabuddin had established a parallel administration in Siwan district that functioned virtually independent of the state government. In fact, many argued Shahabuddin's rule *was* the state administration. Before opening shops, business owners would seek his blessing and counsel; doctors would routinely receive instructions from the MP about the rates they could charge patients; even the police used to ask permission before moving in areas controlled by the leader. According to one account, the MP's "phone call to any government officer . . . was a non-negotiable order."[22]

When the police finally mustered the courage to confront Shahabuddin, the result was a seven-hour gun battle that left 14 dead; Shahabuddin miraculously got away.[23] Eventually the MP was arrested and jailed, yet he managed to obtain a "medical leave," which placed him in Siwan's Sardar Hospital, where he enjoyed not a room or a floor but an entire ward to himself. A plaque near the front entrance of the hospital bore the words "Built by Mohammed Shahabuddin."[24]

The fear that gripped the minds of many residents when the name Shahabuddin was uttered was often tinged in equal measure with respect—especially when the leader used threats, and on occasion actual force, to whip the lethargic bureaucracy into shape. Before him, "we had only potholes in the name of a road here," claimed one Siwan resident. "Colleges had closed because there was no money . . . doctors never turned up on time . . . but now everything works."[25] Another resident, lamenting Shahabuddin's incarceration, said of the former MP, "He was 99 percent good, but people only speak of the 1 percent."[26] As the politician was fond of asking journalists who sought an interview with him, "Do you think I would win election upon election if I were such a figure of dread?"[27]

Ahmed, Yadav, and Shahabuddin made for a colorful trio, but when they landed in Parliament the morning of the crucial no-confidence vote, they were accompanied by three more MPs who had also been passing time behind bars. This illustrious group included Afzal Ansari, jailed on murder charges for conspiring with his brother to pump more than 400 bullets into the car of a political rival; Suraj Bhan Singh, a lawmaker who was convicted for shooting a farmer with whom he had a long-standing land dispute; and Umakant Yadav, who was behind bars facing charges for forcibly occupying a parcel of land he coveted and fraudulently registering it in his name.[28]

In the end, the UPA government barely survived the no-confidence motion, and having carried out their parliamentary duty, the six furloughed MPs were promptly returned to jail. Reading the newspaper in a poorly air-conditioned library in New Delhi the morning after the vote, I was struck by the scarce coverage the jailed lawmakers merited in the country's leading dailies. The previous evening I had caught a glimpse of the antics in Parliament on cable television, and so I was surprised that there were but fleeting mentions of the absurdity of MPs being carted in from prison, casually discussed in passing along with the ailing MP who had to be wheeled in on a gurney, the lawmaker who had to be urgently flown back from America where he was having knee replacement surgery, and the MP whom the government courted by promising to name an airport after his father.

Whatever press the jailed lawmakers did receive was swiftly and thoroughly overshadowed by a second scandal associated with the no-confidence vote. Just minutes before voting was to commence, three opposition lawmakers disrupted the proceedings by holding up wads of cash—reportedly upwards of 30 million rupees (or a little over $450,000)—which they alleged government legislators had given to them in an attempt to buy their support.[29] The situation on the floor of Parliament had gotten so out of control that one television channel felt compelled to cut away, beaming in shots of Mother Teresa and Calcutta instead.[30] And just like that, the "cash for votes" scandal was all the rage, and the fleeting reprieve the jailed lawbreakers received was nothing more than a distant memory for the Indian polity.

TROUBLING FACTS

Although the Indian press had moved on to the next story, I had not. The oddity of watching lawmakers being escorted from jail to Sansad Bhavan (Parliament House), what one prime minister referred to as a "temple of democracy," stuck with me.[31] Naively at the time, I wondered whether the jailed lawbreakers were an exception in the world's largest democracy or perhaps representative of a deeper malaise. The more digging I did, the murkier India's politics became.

As outlandish as it seems, the incarcerated lawmakers who were brought from jail to cast their votes on the floor of Parliament were far from the only elected representatives implicated in some kind of criminal wrongdoing. Of the 543 members elected to the Lok Sabha in 2004, nearly one-quarter faced pending criminal cases before the courts.[32] To be clear, these were cases and not convictions; it can take years, if not decades, for a case to wind its way through India's sluggish judicial system and reach a resolution. Furthermore, not all of these cases involved the sorts of charges that had swirled around Ateeq Ahmed or Pappu Yadav; many involved minor charges, such as unlawful assembly, libel, or trespass. It was not unheard of for politicians in India to be charged with such things as their careers progressed; after all, the "politics of protest" was intrinsic to the country's own struggle for independence from the British Empire, and so it was to some extent woven into its political fabric.[33]

Yet, leaving such minor infractions aside, 12 percent of parliamentarians faced cases of a serious nature.[34] Many of these involved alleged crimes like murder or attempted murder, physical assault, and kidnapping. These charges were of a qualitatively different and decidedly more dramatic nature—and significantly harder to explain away by falling back on the routine expression of civil disobedience in Indian political life (see Appendix A for a detailed discussion of the distinction between "minor" and "serious" criminal charges).

These disconcerting details about India's politicians emerged as a result of a 2003 order by the Supreme Court of India, mandating that candidates seeking elected office publicly disclose information about their criminal records. As I pored over tens of thousands of these disclosures spanning the past decade, several truths about India's murky politics became abundantly clear, and they illustrate just how widespread the marriage of crime and politics has become.

First, the share of elected officials in India with pending criminal cases has been increasing, not decreasing, over time (figure 1.1). This is in spite of the fact that, as a result of the Supreme Court's mandate that candidates must disclose their criminal antecedents, general awareness about the private lives of politicians has grown. Indeed, today it is possible for an ordinary Indian to simply send a text message to a civil society organization to electronically receive, within a matter of seconds, biographical details of the candidates contesting local election.[35] According to data compiled by the Association for Democratic Reforms (ADR), a good-governance watchdog, 24 percent of MPs elected in 2004 faced criminal cases (12 percent faced charges of a serious nature). This figure grew to 30 percent in 2009 (15 percent serious) and climbed to 34 percent (21 percent serious) in 2014.[36]

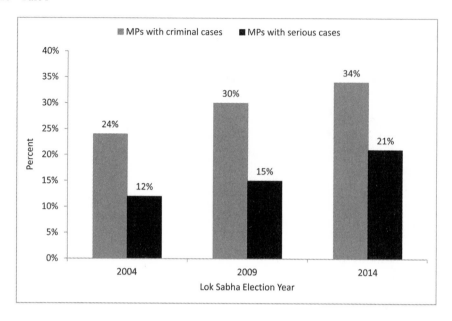

Figure 1.1. Share of Lok Sabha MPs with pending criminal cases, 2004–14. (Data from Association for Democratic Reforms, various years)

Second, the geographic reach of politicians under serious criminal scrutiny is widespread and not restricted to any single region of the country. MPs with pending criminal cases are found in virtually all parts of the country (figure 1.2). Their widespread prevalence across space defies any neat explanations that focus on regional "cultures of corruption" or a tight relationship with relative poverty or backwardness. For instance, some scholars speak of an India that is divided into a relatively backward north and a more progressive, wealthier south.[37] Previous explanations in this vein have predominantly portrayed the relatively underdeveloped north as the source of criminality in politics—an assumption that is belied by the widespread popularity of "bad politicians" (shorthand for politicians involved in illegal or unethical behavior) in both north and south.

Third, the prevalence of elected leaders who face some kind of criminal scrutiny is not restricted to the national political arena alone. As of early 2014, 31 percent of India's elected state legislators (members of

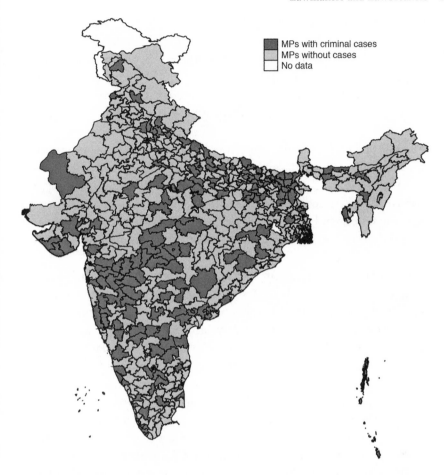

MPs with criminal cases
MPs without cases
No data

Figure 1.2. Distribution of Lok Sabha MPs with pending criminal cases, 2014. (Author's map based on data from Association for Democratic Reforms, 2014)

the legislative assemblies, or MLAs) faced pending criminal cases, with 15 percent falling into the serious category. While there has been no systematic analysis of local governments, anecdotal evidence suggests that local tiers of governance too are hardly free of criminality.[38]

Furthermore, the severity of the charges that have been leveled against India's political class is striking. Looking back at all state and national elections held between January 2004 and September 2013, one comprehensive analysis found that candidates racked up nearly

14,000 discrete charges judged to be of a "serious" nature. During this period, candidates standing for election disclosed 4,357 distinct murder-related charges lodged against them. There were 68 separate allegations of rape and more than 450 other charges involving crimes against women. Other popular categories of alleged crimes involved robbery and dacoity (1,004) and cheating, forgery, and counterfeiting (3,039).[39]

Finally, candidates linked to crime appear to have a hefty electoral advantage. Based on data from the three most recent general elections—in 2004, 2009, and 2014—a candidate with a criminal case was, on average, almost three times as likely to win election as a candidate who faced no cases. And of those facing cases, the "win rate" of candidates with serious charges, in turn, is marginally higher than those who face only minor charges.[40]

These cardinal facts about India's democracy, although little known back in 2003 when candidates first began disclosing their criminal antecedents, soon earned much broader national—and international—attention. Politicians with lengthy rap sheets were memorialized in Bollywood films like Anurag Kashyap's *Gangs of Wasseypur* and dissected in such international literary hits as the Booker Prize–winning *The White Tiger* by Aravind Adiga and Katherine Boo's best-selling portrait of a Mumbai slum, *Behind the Beautiful Forevers.*

Over the next several years, the "criminalization" of India's political class would become a standard talking point whenever elections were in the offing. In democracies the world over, elections often acquire a sort of habitual rhythm as time goes on. In India, one facet of this rhythm is the spate of news headlines before elections about the dubious biographical details of politicians who aspire to elected office. Once voting is over and the results are announced, a second wave of stories about the criminal records of those who are actually elected pours forth.[41]

From the *Times of India* to the *New York Times,* headlines like "In India's Politics, Jail Time Is a Badge of Honor," "India's Jailbirds Win Elections," and "Criminals Flourish in Indian Elections" have become commonplace. Citing the numbers of elected officials facing criminal inquiries is now just another fact one tosses out when describing contemporary India; it seemingly rolls off the tongue as easily as declaring that the country has 29 states or a $2 trillion economy.

A PUZZLING COEXISTENCE

These stylized facts, while interesting and important in their own right, raise larger questions about the symbiosis of crime and politics in democratic nations. In many ways, it remains a puzzle how democratic elections and large numbers of elected officials tied to illegal activity can comfortably coexist. After all, democratic theory suggests that one of the crucial functions of elections is to provide a reliable channel through which voters can weed out badly behaving politicians.[42] Indeed, a key distinction between democratic and nondemocratic systems is the fact that in the former, voters can utilize the ballot box to punish lawmakers who betray the public trust.[43] If, however, candidates tied to wrongdoing are rewarded, rather than rejected, through relatively free and fair electoral processes, it means something is amiss either in the functioning of democracy or in common conceptual understandings of how democracy works.

This book asks—and tries to answer—five fundamental questions about the perplexing cohabitation of criminality and democratic politics. In particular, the focus of this inquiry is on the symbiosis of *serious* criminality and electoral democracy, rather than on criminal activity in a general sense. It is precisely the grave nature of the alleged transgressions of India's politicians that makes this nexus so mystifying.

First, what incentives do individuals with serious criminal reputations have to take part in the electoral sphere? It is not immediately obvious why someone with a track record of running afoul of the law would actively seek a role in everyday democratic politics. In countries ranging from Nigeria to Thailand, criminals or strongmen operate at the peripheries of political life, but they often leave the politicking to the professionals, that is, to the career politicians. What are the underlying factors that make elections in India fertile ground for criminals to try their hand as politicians?

Second, why do political parties select candidates with serious criminal records? In most modern democracies, including India's, parties play the essential role of screening and selecting candidates to elected office. One might reasonably expect that parties would hesitate to recruit candidates linked to criminality for fear of being tainted or tarnished in the eyes of voters. Yet often parties appear to compete with one another to embrace candidates under criminal scrutiny.

Third, although elections have been typically viewed as an opportunity to "throw the rascals out," might voters have sound reasons for actually keeping the "rascals" in? Individuals with serious criminal records might have private incentives to stand for election, and parties may have reasons for giving them a platform, but that does not necessarily compel voters to support them on Election Day. This is especially true in countries where elections are deemed reasonably free and fair. Given that voters often have a choice between candidates with criminal records and those without, it is something of a mystery why they would actively prefer the former. Are voters inadvertently endorsing criminal representatives, or can an affirmative case be made for voters to elect these candidates?

Fourth, to the extent the involvement of criminally linked individuals in electoral politics is deemed undesirable, what are the public policy instruments reformers can wield in order to limit, if not eliminate, the entrenched position of tainted politicians? Theoretically, an array of reformist actors, ranging from civil society activists to the media and the judiciary, can be mobilized to tackle the creeping "criminalization" of politics. But knowing which policy levers to pull in order to contain their proliferation crucially depends on the identification of underlying drivers. If a lack of information explains why voters support politicians with criminal records, the resulting policy response might focus on raising popular awareness. If, however, the root cause lies elsewhere, information provision alone might be an inadequate, if not inappropriate, solution.

Fifth, what are the implications of the presence of criminal politicians for democracy and accountability? Many have argued that if democratic elections produce large numbers of elected leaders with dubious biographies, this is—by definition—symptomatic of a breakdown in the chain of popular accountability. But if politicians tied to criminal activity are elected, and often reelected, it raises the prospect that some semblance of democratic accountability remains intact. What, if anything, can the Indian experience tell us about the challenges facing other developing democracies?

WHY INDIA?

The answers to these questions are obviously much larger in scope than the study of any one nation, yet there can be payoffs to looking for answers within a single democracy in order to fully grapple with their nuances. India, in particular, presents an interesting case for contemplating these questions.

For starters, as the largest democracy in the world, India is home to one-quarter of the world's voters. With one-sixth of the earth's humanity residing within its borders, India's size alone makes it a worthy case for studying the interactions between crime and politics. If answers to these probing questions on crime and democracy can be found in India, that will go a considerable way to shaping the public's broader understanding.

But the reasons to pay careful attention to India go beyond size considerations: India is not only the world's largest democracy, it is also the most enduring democracy in the developing world. As the number of low-income democracies continues to grow (including many that, like India, are both low-income and multiethnic), India's experience can provide lessons to an expanding set of developing-country peers. Because if criminality can thrive in a democracy as established as India, what are the prospects for fledgling democracies that remain unconsolidated?

Moreover, by focusing on India, researchers stand to benefit from analyzing several sources of rich, credible data on elections—chief among them are the data collected by the independent, highly professionalized ECI. Since 2003, candidates contesting state and national elections in India must submit, at the time of their nomination, judicial affidavits detailing not only their criminal records but also their financial assets and liabilities. This public disclosure regime, coupled with the sheer number of elected posts, provides unparalleled opportunities for detecting patterns in the biographical profiles of democratically elected representatives. Candidate disclosure requirements are not unique to India, but in more than half the countries where they are required, filings are not publicly available.[44] In India, however, both candidates in the electoral fray as well as the eventual winners must reveal detailed information about themselves.

Finally, India's federal system of governance means that it is, in actuality, far more than a single case study. India comprises 29 states and 7 union territories (or areas administered directly by the central government). Some states, such as Uttar Pradesh and Maharashtra, have populations on par with the most populous countries in the world.[45] India has 543 elected members of Parliament (plus another nearly 250 indirectly elected members) and more than 4,000 elected state politicians. Grafted on to these subnational units is tremendous variation on key economic, political, and social characteristics. Indeed, due to its size, diversity, and population, it is often said that India's federal democracy has more in common with the European Union than with the United States.[46] Yet India is, of course, a unified entity rather than a disparate amalgamation of countries. The ability to slice and dice it into a much larger number of smaller entities is a major boon to researchers because it allows them to easily compare and contrast internal units. This book takes advantage of this unique democratic laboratory.

LESSONS BEYOND INDIA

While the aim of this book is to analyze debates about crime and politics within the context of India's democracy, its findings are relevant far beyond India's borders. Indeed, as a diverse array of scholars has documented, India has plenty of company when it comes to individuals with dubious biographies playing an active role in electoral politics.

Brazilians, for instance, have coined a Portuguese phrase to describe a politician who is known to run afoul of the law yet perceived to function as an effective representative: "*rouba, mas faz*" (He robs, but he gets things done). According to one study, the former ethically challenged mayor of the city of São Paulo, Paulo Maluf, was so brazen as to use maluf@masfaz.com as his personal e-mail address.[47]

Elsewhere in Latin America, outlawed paramilitary groups and other criminal organizations in Colombia have used their extensive political connections and deep pockets to get their members elected to local and national political office.[48] In Southeast Asia, a tradition of "godfathers" (known as *chao pho* in Thailand) tied to criminal activity plays a leading role in regional politics.[49] In democracies such as Jamaica and Nigeria, candidates for public office compete not on the basis of ideas and policy platforms but on their connections to criminal gangs.[50] As Kenya was preparing for its national election in 2012, commentators remarked that Deputy Prime Minister (and presidential candidate) Uhuru Kenyatta actually stood to gain from the fact that the International Criminal Court had indicted him for engaging in crimes against humanity.[51]

Even in the United States of America, the world's oldest democracy, it is not unheard of for candidates to thrive politically despite past run-ins with the law. For instance, convicted felon Edwin Edwards campaigned in the 1991 Louisiana gubernatorial race (against notorious white supremacist David Duke) on the slogan: "Vote for the crook. It's important." Edwards won the race by more than 20 percentage points. Of the "unapologetically corrupt" former four-term governor, one admirer warmly recalled: "We all knew he was going to steal . . . but he told us he was going to do it."[52] From former Massachusetts governor James Michael Curley—who served not one but two jail terms—to the convicted ex-mayor of the District of Columbia, Marion Barry, criminal rap sheets have not always been a barrier to higher office.[53] Of course, Marion Barry and Mohammed Shahabuddin are very different politicians, yet they may be responding to similar motivating factors. Understanding what is generalizable and what is unique about India's democratic evolution can be hugely illuminating.

THE MARKETPLACE FOR CRIMINALITY

To preview what lies ahead, this book has five principal findings, each a response to the five central questions posed above. One of its core premises is that it helps to think about politicians, of all types, operating within an electoral marketplace.

Of course, elections and markets are not completely analogous.[54] Indeed, one could argue that markets possess a number of underlying characteristics that are rarely, if ever, found in everyday electoral politics. For instance, economic markets typically consist of arm's-length transactions between independent agents. In a truly free market, buyers and sellers can enter and exit the marketplace with relative ease and information about prices is ubiquitous. Politics often departs significantly from these core tenets. Politics is about the structure of power. Actors do not always behave independently and information asymmetries often crop up. Furthermore, status considerations matter a great deal; indeed, voters, politicians, and parties are all embedded within larger social realities.

These caveats notwithstanding, there is a utility to the market analogy. In elections, there are buyers (voters) and sellers (parties and politicians). As with any market, there are underlying supply and demand factors at work. The idea of supply can be disaggregated into two components: the decision of individuals to make themselves available as candidates, and the selection of candidates by political parties. Without the backing of parties, candidates in most democracies struggle to make it on their own. The demand comes from the voters. Faced with a particular constellation of candidates on offer, voters express their demand for their preferred choice through the ballot box. At the end of the day, elections determine the precise location where supply and demand meet. All actors in the electoral marketplace presumably behave in their own self-interest, much like profit-seeking firms and bargain-seeking consumers. Politicians known for their criminal conduct too must live and die by this market test.

From Criminals to Candidates

One of the fundamental requirements of any marketplace is that there must exist at least two parties willing to make a transaction. Before getting to why voters might buy what criminal candidates have to offer, one must ask why criminal candidates are willing to sell their wares to the electorate.

Although commentators often speak of the criminalization of Indian politics as a new phenomenon, the interplay between crime and politics actually has deep historical roots. Over time, however, there has been a qualitative shift in the nature of their engagement. In the immediate post-independence period, politicians often relied on "criminal elements"—a catchall term for ruffians, strongmen, thugs, and mercenaries—for electioneering. By the late 1970s and early 1980s, the phenomenon of criminals contesting elections as *candidates* was commonplace. Within a few decades, the tables had turned.

The weakening of the hegemonic Congress Party and the corresponding growth of multiparty competition, organizational decline within political parties more generally in the face of a deepening of identity politics, the decay in the rule of law, and the collapse of India's election finance regime pulled such individuals into the electoral realm.

While these "pull" factors speak to the political opportunity made available to individuals with criminal records, there was also an important factor pushing them to contest elections. As electoral uncertainty increased within rising levels of political fragmentation, criminals sought to vertically integrate their operations, cutting out the politician middleman in order to maximize control over their own survival and protection. By this time, having functioned as prominent local power brokers who were thoroughly embedded within their local communities, criminals had accumulated considerable social capital; entering the lucrative world of politics allowed them the possibility of reaping greater social and financial rewards on this initial investment.

Welcome to the Party

Just as markets feature intermediaries who help to match buyers with sellers, political parties perform a similar function in an electoral marketplace. In fact, it is hard to think of any truly vibrant democracy anywhere on the planet where political parties do not mediate relations between voters and politicians. True, individuals might have their own incentives to enter politics, but the question naturally arises: why do parties recruit candidates with known criminal backgrounds? Even if one cynically assumes that most criminal cases aspiring candidates face are politically motivated, one might think that parties would still hesitate to embrace implicated candidates out of a fear that they will be punished at the polls. Given this, why do parties find it in their interest to facilitate the supply of criminally suspect candidates into the electoral market?

Money is a core reason parties are attracted to politicians with dubious backgrounds. Election costs in India have risen considerably over the years as the size of the population has ballooned and the competitiveness of elections has grown. This resource crunch has compelled all political parties to innovate in their desperate search for financial "rents." While these campaign funds are raised to cover the exorbitant costs of elections, undoubtedly some portion of these resources end up lining the pockets of party leaders.

In parties' struggles to identify reliable sources of funding—a partial reflection of the decline in their organizational strength—they have increasingly placed a premium on candidates who can bring resources into the party and will not drain limited party coffers. Candidates who are self-financing are not only able to cover their own campaign costs; they might also be in a position to pay their parties for the privilege of running and thereby subsidize lesser-endowed candidates. When it comes to campaign cash, candidates willing to break the law have a distinct advantage: they both have access to liquid forms of finance and are willing to deploy them in the service of politics. In some cases, money comes from illicit, rent-seeking business activities; in others, it comes from deep-rooted patronage networks or simple extortion. Either way, parties value "muscle" (serious criminality, in Indian parlance) because of the money that comes along with it.

Voting with Eyes Open

In order to maximize their financial objectives, it makes sense that parties might cut deals with questionable characters who have access to ample in-hand resources. Yet this is only half of the story. Irrespective of what parties might feel, an explanation based on money alone does not fully clarify why voters are willing to vote for candidates who face serious criminal cases. Returning to our marketplace analogy, what is driving the demand for criminal candidates?

Scholars who have studied the connection between malfeasance and democratic politics have often assumed that voters do not willingly support tainted candidates but instead do so inadvertently due to a lack of information. In a poor country such as India, for example, it is highly plausible that many voters make their decisions on Election Day with a heavy dose of ignorance about the qualifications of their local candidates. If this were the case, the election of suspected criminal candidates would be incidental rather than a genuine expression of latent demand.

Despite the plausibility of this "ignorant voter" scenario, it turns out that voters in India—including those who are reasonably well-informed—often have very rational reasons for supporting candidates with criminal reputations. Beyond money, in contexts where the rule of law is weak and social divisions are highly salient, politicians can often use their criminality as a badge of honor—a signal of their credibility to protect the interests of their community and its allies, casting themselves as modern-day Robin Hoods operating in a polarized society. The allure of politicians with criminal reputations is, thus, a by-product of the institutional failings of Indian democracy to meet the needs of its citizenry in between elections.[55]

What the interaction of deep social cleavages and weak rule of law means in practice is that voters might vote for politicians expressly because of their criminal reputations. This possibility turns the conventional argument about a lack of information on its head: voters can have access to credible information and still decide to support candidates linked to crime. In some sense, the popular appeal of political strongmen should not be surprising given the widely known struggles of the Indian state to catch up with the aspirations brought about by the democratic, economic, and social changes the country has experienced in recent decades. When the state is either unable or unwilling to fulfill its core obligations vis-à-vis its citizenry, the latter will naturally begin looking for alternatives.

Reforming the System

Although the electoral success of politicians linked to crime can have very real downsides in terms of broader social welfare, the existence of a marketplace for criminal politicians suggests that perhaps democracy is working as it should. After all, the marketplace for politicians associated with wrongdoing only works when both buyers and sellers come together to strike a deal. However, it does not mean that policymakers must meekly accept the status quo. On the contrary, there are many reasons why the existence of such a market should deeply concern them. But if mitigating the phenomenon of criminal politicians is their goal, there is a wide array of potential remedies policymakers can embrace and democratic reformers can support. When governance failures, not a lack of information, are to blame for keeping the criminal-politician marketplace humming, policymakers must turn to a very specific set of policy remedies. These include quickening the wheels of justice in India, building the state's capacity to efficiently deliver basic goods and services, and freeing the economy from the shackles of state control.

Oftentimes, advocating for "governance reform" is misinterpreted as a kind of pessimistic fatalism: institutions are notoriously sticky so overhauling them is, at best, a multigenerational task. While addressing the deep roots of India's governance failures is a long-term enterprise, there are many actions reformers can take that would make a difference in the short run on such issues as shutting down loopholes in how campaign finance is regulated or improving the level of transparency and inclusion within political parties. However, reformers must pursue short-term remedies with caution; while politicians tied to criminal activity might make a mockery of the rule of law, the cure should not be worse than the disease. In erecting barriers to criminal entry into politics with the intention of "cleansing" democracy, there is scope for actually engaging in antidemocratic activity (for instance, by contravening the principle of the presumption of innocence).[56]

Implications for Democracy and Accountability

The value of any book such as this one lies not simply in the light it can shed on any one case but also in how it can shape—however modestly—conventional thinking about broader political phenomena. The key takeaways of this book have implications for popular conceptions of the relationship between democracy and accountability.

For starters, a commonly held view is that the political success of bad politicians in democratic countries is symptomatic of a breakdown in the standard chain of democratic accountability. What this book shows is that, under certain conditions, malfeasant politicians and accountability are compatible. Granted, this form of "democratic accountability" is often partial, imperfect, and counterintuitive. Yet it offers a corrective to the narrative that voters, and parties, are saddled with malfeasant politicians.

Another important takeaway is that there are limits to what greater transparency can offer in terms of improving governance. Just as scholars err in automatically assuming that coexistence of allegedly corrupt or criminal lawmakers and democracy is evidence of a grave accountability failure, they often move too quickly in pointing the finger at information asymmetries as the likely culprit. The findings of this book suggest that while transparency might be a worthy cause to pursue on its own terms, it is not necessarily the proximate driver of the rise of bad politicians.

A final implication is that the selection of candidates with criminal records varies considerably in response to local incentives. In an attempt to simplify complex matters, we often paint with a broad brush when talking about a country's political elites; most of us are guilty of doing this on a regular basis. For instance, one often hears such statements as "Italian politicians are corrupt," "America's representatives are self-serving," or "India's legislators are criminals." What this book shows is that the market for criminal politicians responds to highly contextualized factors of supply and demand, which can vary substantially even within a single country. For instance, although India is a multiethnic democracy, the salience of social cleavages is not uniformly distributed across the entire country. In some cases, due to historical or institutional factors, mobilization on ethnic lines is weaker, which diminishes the relevance of politicians with criminal records (some of whom use these divisions to bolster their own standing).

This final insight provides some intuition for why India's electoral marketplace for criminal politicians has settled into a kind of equilibrium, to borrow another concept from the economics discipline. No doubt, politicians with criminal backgrounds remain important political actors in India, yet they have not successfully captured the electoral system as a whole. Candidates suspected of serious crimes often fail to win elections and, in many cases, are not even on the ballot. As the various supply and demand drivers suggest, the electoral relevance of candidates with criminal records is conditional on the presence (or absence) of a set of underlying conditions.

OUTLINE OF THE BOOK

My inquiry into the underbelly of India's democracy is divided into three parts. Part I continues with a brief recap of the evolution of India's political economy up to the present day, providing useful context for the book's later discussion of the marketplace for India's criminal politicians.

Part II examines the key supply and demand drivers underlying this marketplace. I begin first by examining the historic roots of India's crime-politics nexus to understand why criminals sought to enter the electoral domain, the first step in injecting supply into the market. To understand why parties recruit, rather than reject, candidates with serious criminal antecedents, I delve into the skyrocketing costs of elections and the financial challenges parties must endure.

Although money is part of the equation, it alone cannot explain how the marketplace functions or fully account for voter demand. In contrast to conventional arguments about ignorant voters, I show how even well-informed voters might seek out candidates with criminal records, particularly in contexts where social divisions run deep.

Part III of the book looks to the future, focusing on the broader implications of this research. It begins by asking and answering the "so what" question: what remedies do reformers have at their disposal to address the nexus between crime and politics? In response, I outline a detailed agenda of priority, short-term actions and long-term reforms, which the private and public sectors can get behind. I conclude by stepping back from the case at hand to discuss the lessons India's democracy might hold for other developing countries embarking on their own democratic journeys.

2   The Rise of the Rents Raj
India's Corruption Ecosystem

ON THE MORNING of September 5, 2009, major media organizations in Delhi received a series of bizarre news reports from local outlets across the state of Andhra Pradesh claiming that as many as 122 people had died of shock or committed suicide in the preceding 48 hours under sketchy circumstances.[1] The trigger underlying these alleged mass casualties, it turned out, was not one of the usual suspects—drought, indebtedness, natural calamity, or rebel violence—but rather a spontaneous reaction to the unexpected death of a local politician.

The politician in question was Y. S. Rajasekhara Reddy (commonly known as YSR), the incumbent chief minister of Andhra Pradesh, a coastal state in the southern half of India known for centuries as the country's "rice bowl," and more recently for its capital city of Hyderabad, home to a sizeable chunk of India's booming information technology industry.

On the morning of September 2, YSR and a few close aides embarked on a trip from the capital city to the southern district of Chittoor to attend a village meeting. The helicopter ferrying the chief minister was flying in a dangerous rainstorm, and the pilots, blinded by the deluge, veered dangerously off course—eventually colliding with a cliff and smashing the chopper into thousands of shards strewn across the Nallamalla forests below.[2]

Upon hearing of YSR's death, dozens of his faithful supporters ended their lives, such was their love for their leader. "YSR dedicated his life to people, I am dedicating my life to him," read a suicide note one young follower penned right before ending his life with a vial of pesticide.[3] According to one longtime political observer, YSR "was one of the most fascinating and powerful political figures to arrive [in India] in the past decade."[4] Judging by the over-the-top responses to his sudden passing, this sentiment was widely shared.

YSR hailed from Kadapa, a district in Andhra's Rayalaseema region. Often described to the uninitiated as the "Wild West," Rayalaseema is a parched expanse of land far removed from the sleek glass structures of Hyderabad's office parks or the brilliant green fields of the Godavari basin. Of the three regions of Andhra Pradesh—Telangana and Coastal Andhra being the other two—Rayalaseema is considered the most backward when judged against most standard socioeconomic indicators.[5] When I mentioned to a friend in Hyderabad that I was curious about visiting the region, he snorted: "You can certainly go. But do you want to come back?" Notwithstanding its harsh reputation, an article written in 1999 about life in Rayalaseema reassures visitors that "a stranger visiting the area has nothing to fear, even during an election." It ends with the unhelpful caveat "unless s/he is caught in a crossfire. . . ."[6]

Rayalaseema politics has long been dominated by warring "factions," or armed gangs, whose leaders are a modern-day hybrid of feudal lords and warlords. The British colonial authorities referred to these men as "poligars," and their leaders were known as "Reddys," which today is one of the dominant castes in the state.[7] Rayalaseema's clan style of governance was organized around the Reddys' singular dominance. Noted one local observer, "Everything turns around the [Reddy's] primary interest: the leader's preeminence in the village, his honour, his writ, his word."[8] Although the level of local violence is not as severe as it was in previous decades, internecine disputes between dueling factions persist today.[9]

YSR's father, Raja Reddy, was one such faction leader—a strongman known for taking matters into his own hands, like the time he witnessed a robbery taking place in the local market and, wanting to teach other would-be thieves a lesson, allegedly doused the thief in kerosene and burned him alive for all to see.[10]

On the basis of his tough-as-nails reputation, Raja Reddy was hired to manage a local barite mine, which became his passport to wealth and influence. Eventually claiming outright ownership of the mine, Reddy rocketed to prominence in Kadapa, grooming his son to join politics to ensure that the family business would be protected. YSR first contested state elections in 1978, later making the jump to national politics in 1989, all the while maintaining an unblemished election scorecard. Indeed, YSR regularly won election with solid two-thirds majorities. The succession from father to son was abruptly completed in 1998 when Raja Reddy, returning to his farmhouse late one day, was killed by a bomb supposedly planted by a rival faction leader.[11]

Underwritten with funds from the family's lucrative mining operations and emboldened by his dominant position among the Reddys of fractious Rayalaseema, YSR successfully transformed his village factions "into full-fledged instruments of political and economic domination at the highest level."[12] Here was a man who was perceived by his supporters—and, crucially, by his detractors as well—to be a leader who would do anything to protect his loyal following, "even if it meant stepping beyond the bounds of law and government."[13] In the words of K. Balagopal, an author and human rights activist, people in Kadapa came in one of two types: with YSR or against YSR.[14]

YSR achieved his big political breakthrough in 2004 when the Congress Party trounced the incumbent Telugu Desam Party in the Andhra state elections, finally catapulting him into the chief minister's chair. In office, YSR reimagined himself as a mass leader with a markedly softer edge than he displayed during his climb to prominence, a rise Balagopal claimed was "accompanied by more bloodshed than that of any other politician in the state."[15] Although he may have moderated his image once he rose to the state's top job, YSR did not fully turn his back on his bare-knuckles brand of politics: those who dared oppose him personally, or the Congress Party in Andhra more generally, were said to be financially or physically harassed.[16]

YSR occupied the chief minister's chair until his sudden death in 2009. His rule is hard to characterize because it combined several disparate (even contradictory) elements: "populist giveaways, smelly deals that converted politicians into millionaires, fiscal prudence and economic freedom," topped with unabashed personal enrichment.[17] This mishmash was held together by his reputation as a no-holds-barred, somewhat autocratic leader; his rule was an amalgamation of "crony capitalism and a caudillo-style leadership."[18] Strong chief ministers have never gone down well with the overly centralized Congress Party, but one close observer stated of the party brass: "as long as the suitcases of money were coming, they were happy" with YSR.[19]

The focal point of alleged corruption during YSR's time in office was his son, Jagan Mohan Reddy, a charismatic and ambitious though soft-spoken young man then in his mid-thirties. Jagan fashioned himself a hotshot entrepreneur, starting or investing in multiple companies in sectors as diverse as hydroelectric power, cement, real estate, and the media.[20] According to police documents, Jagan and his father used the latter's office to carry out a massive "pay to play" operation: businesses seeking favors from the state, namely land allotments, would agree to invest in Jagan's businesses in exchange for favorable treatment by the YSR government.[21]

This alleged quid pro quo—the exchange of state patronage for business investment—served Jagan exceedingly well. In 2004, when YSR first became chief minister, Jagan's assets were estimated to be a modest 919,951 rupees (around $14,000). Within five years, his wealth had exploded: according to his own disclosures, Jagan was worth more than 730 million rupees in 2009 ($11 million). By 2014, his net worth was north of 4.1 billion rupees ($62 million).[22]

The firms who invested in Jagan's assorted companies fared pretty well too. They were given highly prized land at throwaway prices, unencumbered by routine regulatory hassles, according to an examination carried out by India's chief auditor. In auditor speak, the allocation of land by YSR's government during 2006–11 "was characterized by grave irregularities, involving allotment on an ad hoc, arbitrary, and discretionary manner" to provide favored entities lucrative land at very cheap rates "without safeguarding the financial and socio-economic interests of the state."[23] The auditor reported that the alleged sweetheart deals deprived the state treasury of billions of dollars in foregone revenue.[24]

After YSR's death, a succession battle ensued within the Congress Party. Jagan, the brash young heir to the throne, was denied his father's political inheritance, sparking a split in the Andhra branch of the party. Jagan led an open rebellion and, not coincidentally, was slapped with serious corruption charges.[25] Jagan alleged that the charges were manufactured by Congress in order to "malign [his] image and to defame [the] late Dr. YSR's legacy and to keep [his] family away from [his] people."[26] In fact, these charges did nothing to diminish Jagan's standing and may have done the opposite; in a special 2011 by-election to fill his father's seat, Jagan won the race by the biggest margin in the state's history (521,000 votes). Although he would later spend 16 months in jail awaiting trial, Jagan rejoined politics upon getting bail, winning a seat in the Andhra state assembly in 2014 with nearly 70 percent of his constituency's vote.[27]

Today, Jagan remains one of India's richest politicians. Although he failed to lead his party to power in the 2014 Andhra election, he serves as leader of the opposition in the state assembly and his ambition remains unbowed. "There are two things nobody has ever done: to stay alive after death, and to have your picture in every man's house," Jagan once told an interviewer. "Every poor man should have a picture of you in their house. That is a dream."[28]

INDIA'S MISSING TRANSFORMATION

According to allegations levied by federal prosecutors, the rise of the father-son duo of YSR and Jagan Reddy is an apt example of what the fusion of muscle power, personal riches, crony capitalism, and natural resource rents can achieve in contemporary Indian politics. To come to grips with the role "muscle," or serious criminality, plays in contemporary Indian politics, one has to understand the larger ecosystem of corruption and (mis)governance that prevails.

And to understand how India got to this place, one first needs to recognize the impressive transformations the country has experienced, especially over the last quarter century, when it comes to domestic politics, the economy, and social relations. These transformations, which are still unfolding, have redefined the traditional India narrative in fairly fundamental ways.[29]

Where the story traverses from good news to bad is the quality of governance, where the status quo truly has prevailed. By and large, India's institutional firmament has not experienced the rejuvenation— caveats and all—that marks these other three areas. The gap between the capacity of the state to fulfill its most basic obligations and the rising aspirations of 1.25 billion Indians means that India's government has been often left in the dust, struggling to catch up.

This is not an entirely novel infirmity. The historian Ramachandra Guha has referred to India as "the most recklessly ambitious experiment in history."[30] It is, in the words of philosopher John Dunn, "the most surprising democracy there has ever been: surprising in its scale, in its persistence among a huge and . . . still exceedingly poor population, and in its tensile strength in the face of fierce centrifugal pressures."[31] Never before had a country established and sustained democracy with universal franchise at such a low level of per capita income.[32] By design then, India experienced the traditional state-building process in reverse order: unlike Europe, for instance, India instituted full democracy and *then* set about building a state. Much of the West did precisely the opposite. As a result, underdeveloped institutions have been the Achilles' heel of Indian democracy from the outset.

However, the dilemma of India's anemic institutions has been brought into starker relief in recent years as the aspirations of the Indian citizenry have grown thanks to the forces of globalization, rapid economic growth, and concomitant social change. As popular aspirations have increased, so have the state's responsibilities—revealing a larger chasm between the promise and reality of democratic governance.

The precise nature of India's institutional weakness deserves closer scrutiny, for appearances can be deceiving. The Indian state is regularly lambasted for being too burdensome, too big, and too unwieldy, often leading analysts to prescribe a thorough scaling down. But a slash-and-burn approach is likely to fail, because the central paradox of the Indian state is that it is overbureaucratized in procedural terms but badly undermanned in personnel terms.

As successive Indian governments have failed to rectify this state of affairs, an unfortunate mismatch between tectonic democratic, economic, and social shifts, on the one hand, and India's woeful state of governance, on the other, has been exposed—paving the way for rent-seeking and corruption. Over the last two decades, during the apogee of India's domestic transformation amid institutional stasis, three major sources of "rents" have emerged as the principal by-products of big-ticket, "grand" corruption: regulatory, extractive, and political.[33] Like circles on a Venn diagram, the categories each have their own foundations but also overlap (figure 2.1). It is the third—political rents—that is the explicit focus of this book, but it is important to understand that it is not the only form of rent-seeking gaining ground in India today, and

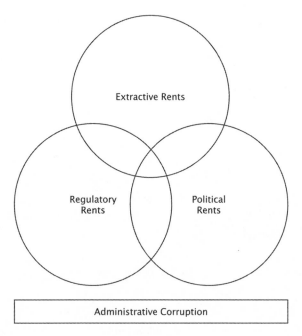

Figure 2.1. Ecosystem for grand corruption in India.

that the three are connected in many ways. These three manifestations of grand corruption are supported by a foundation of underlying administrative, or "petty," corruption—a much older, preexisting condition.

THREE TRANSFORMATIONS

When one pauses to consider India's journey since independence, it is easy to be awestruck by the changes that have transformed India's political economy. Across three dimensions—politics, economics, and social relations—the India of today looks markedly different than the India of seven decades ago.

Politics

The first transformation worth noting involves the country's politics. Feeding off the reservoir of nationalist goodwill it accumulated as the party of independence, the Congress Party dominated India's political

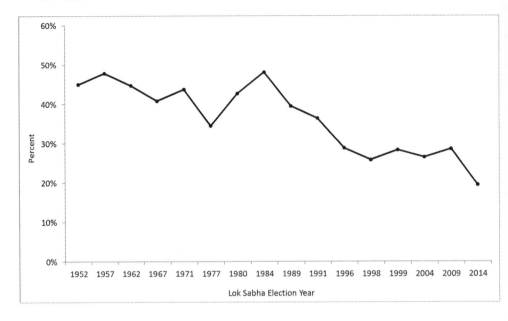

Figure 2.2. Congress Party vote share in Lok Sabha elections, 1952–2014. (Author's calculations based on data from Election Commission of India)

scene in the first several decades after 1947. To be fair, there was a spirited opposition to the dominant party, but it was deeply divided— its influence on politics largely limited to influencing factional disputes within the Congress. Hence, the Congress was able to dominate national politics even though it never once won a majority of the popular vote in a national election (figure 2.2). The heady early years of the republic became known as the Congress "system," to borrow a phrase coined by political scientist Rajni Kothari.[34] The party was not only the preeminent party in India but also arguably the preeminent *political institution* in the country—playing a more significant role than even the institution of Parliament itself, according to the scholar James Manor.[35]

Two decades after independence, the Congress system began to exhibit serious signs of strain. In 1967, the party suffered a series of electoral losses at the state level, which marked the beginning of the unraveling of its political hegemony. After 1967, Congress would maintain power in Delhi but a much more competitive multiparty system took root in the states thanks to the rise of a motley group of regional, caste-based parties. The brief exception to Congress rule at the center was a short-lived period of opposition control between 1977 and 1979. In the wake of fierce antigovernment protests Prime Minister Indira Gandhi massively overreached by imposing a 21-month period of emergency rule between 1975 and 1977. When fresh elections were eventually called, voters summarily tossed Congress out, only to bring the party back in just a few years thanks to the opposition's foibles. By 1980, Indira Gandhi was prime minister once more, but the Congress balloon was gradually deflating.

Three trends—political fragmentation, deepening competition, and continued Congress decline—converged in the late 1980s to break open the political system in an unprecedented manner (figure 2.3). Beginning in 1989, Indian politics would become synonymous with coalition politics. After clinging to power for decades, Congress ceded its monopoly on power in Delhi and lost its prized status as the "pole against which every political formation is defined."[36]

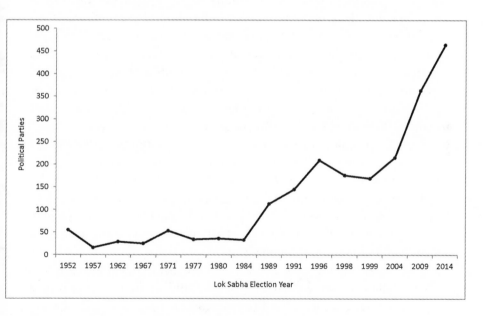

Figure 2.3. Number of political parties contesting Lok Sabha elections, 1952–2014. (Data from Election Commission of India)

The political winds of change in India revolved not simply around the identity of the party, or parties, in power but also the configuration of competition itself. The growth of regionally oriented parties, coupled with structural economic changes, also helped to shift the center of political gravity away from Delhi and toward the states. As politics became more decentralized, India's states asserted their primacy as the key venues for political contestation.[37]

Economics

India's economic trajectory closely tracked its political evolution. Independent India began its economic journey saddled with the legacy of nearly a century of British colonial rule.[38] As Devesh Kapur has noted, at the start of the eighteenth century, India's share of overall global income was roughly between one-fifth and one-quarter. At the dawn of independence, India's share had dipped to a meager 3 percent.[39] In light of the country's colonial subjugation, the realities of India's abject poverty, and in line with prevailing state-led economic theories of development, the government under India's first prime minister, Jawaharlal Nehru, pursued a statist orientation in its economic policy. While India's external posture was actually quite liberal in many respects, Nehru presided over a highly planned economy at home that placed strict controls on and conveyed a deep-seated suspicion of private sector activity. India's political elites granted instruments of the state, rather than markets, primary control over the allocation of resources.[40]

Propelled by the state's guiding hand, India's economic performance in the 1950s and early part of the 1960s was actually quite respectable. Between 1951 and 1965, India experienced an average annual gross domestic product (GDP) growth of 4.3 percent (figure 2.4). Nonetheless, the temptations of manipulating bureaucratic controls for political gain proved too immense for Nehru's eventual successor, daughter Indira Gandhi.[41] Faced with a slowing economy, buffeted by external shocks, and besieged by mounting corruption scandals, Indira responded to a political challenge on her right flank by doubling down on the stifling state-led model, using myriad instruments of state power to squeeze India's corporate sector and marginalize the opposition. India's decent, if not impressive, economic growth would slump over the next fifteen

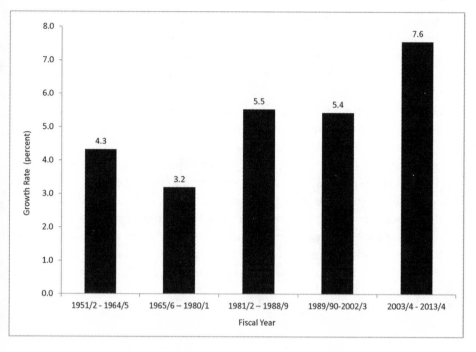

Figure 2.4. Average annual GDP growth, 1951–2014, measured in constant 2004–5 prices. (Author's calculations based on data from Central Statistical Organisation, Government of India)

years: between 1965 and 1981, GDP growth clocked in at just above 3 percent.[42]

Two oft-repeated tropes came to define this era of India's economic development. The first was the "Hindu rate of growth," a phrase coined by the economist Raj Krishna to describe the way India's social and economic characteristics had locked the country onto a disappointing economic trajectory.[43] The second was the "License Raj," the watchword used to describe the ponderous system of government licenses, permits, clearances, and permissions that businesses above a certain size had to obtain in order to actually do any business. This complex web of regulation controlled not only who could be in business but what, how, how much, where, and when business could be undertaken.

When Indira Gandhi reemerged as prime minister in 1980, she began to align herself closer to private sector interests in an effort to revitalize the foundering economy. Under her watch and that of her successor, son Rajiv Gandhi, India undertook a series of pro-business reforms in the 1980s, granting more space for the indigenous private sector. A balance-of-payments crisis in 1991 empowered reformers to take drastic steps to reorient India's economic model, both domestically as well as with the external world. These pro-market reforms reduced trade barriers and opened India up to foreign capital.[44]

The fruits of India's liberal economic reforms were considerable. In the decade of the 2000s, the economy's annual growth rates often touched double digits, second only to China among the world's major economies during this period. In a marked shift, India had abandoned its decades-long dalliance with socialism and moved toward a more market-friendly approach that brought it squarely into the global marketplace. The "triumph of liberalization," as economist Arvind Panagariya has dubbed it, produced remarkable material gains for the country in relatively short order.[45]

Society

A third transformation involves social relations. Historically Indian society has been highly stratified thanks to the entrenched nature of the Hindu caste system, a ranked system of social hierarchy that has structured social order on the subcontinent for centuries. Caste, dominant within Hinduism but present in other religious communities as well, has colored nearly all forms of social life, from shaping occupational choices, to determining spousal selection, to regulating prosaic forms of basic social interaction. Caste is, of course, not the only cleavage that structures the wide diversity of everyday social interactions, but it has arguably been the most powerful and pervasive of these cleavages.

Our modern understanding of caste is heavily shaped by the way in which the British Raj repackaged it for modern consumption and deployed it to effective use as a tool for maintaining order in the colonial period. At its core, the caste system consists of four overarching categories known as *varnas,* listed in order of ritual status from high to low: *Brahmins* (priests), *Kshatriyas* (warriors), *Vaishyas* (merchants), and *Shudras* (backward castes). While these ritually based categories retain salience in contemporary India, albeit at a diminishing rate, caste has also assumed a distinctly political manifestation. The Indian state has used the divisions inherent in the caste system as a basis for developing affirmative action schemes, employment and educational quotas, and even political reservation. The government formally recognizes three groups on the basis of their caste identity: Scheduled Castes (SCs or Dalits, and formerly referred to as "Untouchables"); India's tribal communities, known as Scheduled Tribes (STs); and Other Backward Classes (OBCs), a vast group initially defined mainly as not belonging to any other category. Upper castes, made up of Brahmins and other elite castes, make up the fourth community—although not formally recognized by the government as a discrete category.[46]

While there is no clear mapping between caste and class, the upper castes have traditionally comprised the best-off segments of society, occupying the most sought-after jobs in the public and private spheres. Perhaps not surprisingly, then, it is the upper castes that have historically dominated political life in India, although there has been significant regional variation.[47] For instance, in parts of south India where anti-Brahminical movements gathered steam during the colonial period, upper castes have largely been bit players in politics. In the northern "Hindi belt" states, in contrast, upper castes enjoyed political superiority for far longer.

Over time, even in the north, caste groups situated toward the lower rungs of the hierarchy began asserting themselves, no longer content to live in the shadow of those deemed to be superior in ritualistic terms. The lower castes mobilized, launched political parties, and contested the glass ceiling under which they toiled—spurred by Congress's failure to adequately represent lower-caste interests. Propelled by gradual improvements in economic status, the lower castes successfully pushed back against elite domination.

The genuine opening up of the economic and political systems in India further fueled the awakening of the backward castes and other disadvantaged groups. This "silent revolution" irrevocably altered the makeup of India's political class.[48] In India's first general election in 1952, 65 percent of north Indian ("Hindi belt") MPs hailed from the upper or intermediate castes; by 2004, their share was cut to 40 percent (figure 2.5).[49] For the first time in India's history, OBCs and Dalits

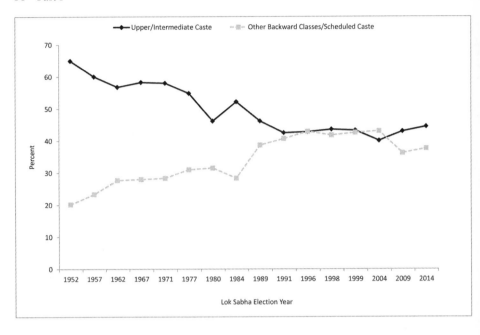

Figure 2.5. Caste identity of Hindi belt Lok Sabha MPs, 1952–2014. (Data from Christophe Jaffrelot and Sanjay Kumar, eds., *Rise of the Plebeians? The Changing Face of Indian Legislative Assemblies* [New Delhi: Routledge, 2009]; Christophe Jaffrelot and Gilles Verniers, "The Representation Gap," *Indian Express,* July 24, 2015)

(SCs) had a greater share of north Indian MPs in the Lok Sabha than the upper/intermediate castes. By 2009, the two groupings would again switch position, but India's representative picture stood irrevocably transformed.[50]

In contemporary India, while caste has not disappeared, in many contexts it now functions more as a marker of difference than of hierarchical rank.[51] Although social biases still loom large, there have been quantum improvements in the economic and political lives of the traditionally disadvantaged lower castes. A vivid study of the well-being of Dalits by a team of researchers led by Devesh Kapur and Chandra Bhan Prasad found massive shifts in the status of India's lowest castes in the period after 1991. From asset ownership to grooming practices and eating habits, Dalits have notched impressive gains over the past two and a half decades.[52] While the success of low-caste politicians has not always easily translated into material gains for their communities, research has found that political power wielded by members of the lower segments has had an influence on the psychology of caste relations, reducing discriminatory behaviors.[53]

Unfinished Business

In reviewing the meaningful transformations marking India's political, economic, and social landscapes, one must not overstate the case. The remarkable change India has experienced uncomfortably coexists with a great deal of continuity.

Regarding the economy, while some of the worst excesses of the License Raj have been dismantled, many remain and new manifestations have cropped up. There has been liberalization in product markets but much less progress in factor markets (such as land, labor, and capital). Private investment in India is still stymied by a raft of regulations and permits that can depress even the most gung-ho entrepreneur, and state-owned enterprises remain dominant in many lucrative sectors of the economy, from mining to petroleum.

Politically, there can be no doubt that voters today have an expanded menu of parties and candidates to support. Yet, as two astute observers of Indian politics noted, the opening up of robust multiparty competition "has not led to greater and more meaningful political choices for the citizen."[54] Parties have, by and large, not distinguished themselves on the basis of programmatic policies or divergent ideologies. Internally, parties remain the province of a small coterie of elite bosses, often a single political family or just one charismatic individual.

The declining relevance of status markers in society has also not followed a linear path. Discrimination remains a mighty challenge for Indian democracy in myriad ways—whether in the labor, housing, or even marriage market.[55] Inequality in opportunity, as well as outcomes, also remains a major public policy concern. Across a broad range of metrics, from educational attainment to wages and consumption expenditure, there is evidence of "clear disparities in virtually all indicators of material well-being" over the 2000s, largely breaking along caste lines.[56] While status hierarchies built around caste may have diminished, research shows that inequalities remain deeply entrenched.[57]

INSTITUTIONAL STAGNATION

Arrayed against the backdrop of multiple remarkable, if incomplete, alterations to India's domestic landscape, the lack of change that characterizes India's institutional core is all the more striking. Of the many challenges that confront India's democracy, governance is arguably the most vital.[58]

Before proceeding, it is important to separate the evaluation of the durability of India's democracy from its effectiveness. Any discussion on India must acknowledge the admirable fact that India's post-independence democracy has shown surprising resilience against formidable odds. Despite its diversity, poverty, population, and sprawling size—and in contrast to the predictions of many analysts—India has thrived both politically and economically.[59] With the exception of the brief period of emergency rule under Indira Gandhi, India has remained fully committed to a democratic form of government. According to the 2008 State of Democracy in South Asia Survey, India's citizens stand out as being the most consistent in their support of democracy (and opposition to nondemocratic forms of governance) of all their South Asian peers.[60] As a form of governance, democracy enjoys widespread legitimacy as the only game in town.

Although the resilience of India's democracy is thus rarely called into question, the ability of Indian democracy to deliver for its citizens is in doubt. Despite impressive rates of economic growth, many of India's poorest lack access to basic forms of social protection. Perhaps as a consequence, India's populace has not perceived the country's economic rise as unambiguously positive.[61] A 2014 Pew survey found that 70 percent of Indians felt that the gap between rich and poor was a "major challenge" for the country."[62] The state's ability to deliver basic public goods, raise adequate revenue, provide security, and enforce the rule of law is badly wanting. In the words of Ashutosh Varshney, "India's democracy has become Janus-faced. Political power is used at the time of elections to please citizens. Between elections, it is often used to treat citizens in an unfeeling manner."[63]

The state's inability to carry out its essential sovereign functions is historically rooted. As Francis Fukuyama has pointed out, unlike China, India never had a centralized state that concentrated power and effectively deployed it to penetrate and thoroughly reshape society. The British Raj, despite its tyrannical underpinnings, ruled India with a relatively light footprint and never fully conquered the subcontinent, having followed a policy of indirect rule in a substantial portion of the region.[64]

The failure of the state to keep up with India's rapid transformations points to two important realities. First, as the economist Lant Pritchett has argued, India defies easy categorization: it neither lives up to its reputation as the poster child for booming growth and development in the third world nor belongs in the category of weak and failing states in which some of its conflict-ridden South Asian neighbors are often placed. Rather, Pritchett argues, India is best thought of as a "flailing state"—one in which certain elite institutions function at a high level but are surrounded by political and administrative failures that impede overall developmental progress. The government can conduct elections for over 800 million voters, but it can't stop millions from dying every year due to a lack of access to proper sanitation facilities.[65] The government can provide one billion people with a unique biometric identification number, but it struggles to enforce basic legal contracts. This duality has been a defining feature of independent India; it is what Lloyd and Susanne Rudolph once referred to as the paradox of the "weak-strong" state.[66]

There is a second reality, however, one that has received far less attention. In many ways, the Indian state suffers from an identity crisis: its presence is oppressive in places where it should not be, and it is nearly absent in places where it should.[67] The end result is two distinct pathologies: India has far too much procedure, and far too few personnel.[68]

This state of affairs has resulted in all sorts of suboptimal outcomes. Although more than three-quarters of India's banking system is controlled by the public sector, tens of millions of rural Indians lack access to basic banking facilities. On several indicators of socioeconomic well-being, such as malnutrition, India fares unfavorably even when compared to the poorest countries of the world. Yet India does not suffer from a lack of food production; rather, half of the food grains procured by the government intended for subsidized ration shops never reach their final destination.[69] As one scholar put it, "Like Sisyphus the Indian state appears condemned to incessantly launch poverty programs and then with little to show for its efforts begin the process all over again."[70]

Excessive Procedure

Despite proclamations to the contrary, many of the bad habits and customs of the License Raj remain deeply entrenched in India. Indeed, what frustrates those who interact with the Indian state the most is the incessant red tape its bureaucracy dispenses and the seemingly endless ways in which it inserts itself into people's ordinary lives. The courts regularly opine on issues that are not matters of law, the police harass students for posting messages critical of political leaders on Facebook, and opening a simple checking account at a bank can require a battery of forms and approvals from multiple agencies.

The quintessential example of the suffocating nature of the Indian bureaucracy is its regulation of private business activity. Each year, the World Bank carries out an exercise to rank countries on how onerous their requirements are for businesses wishing to start operations. In the 2016 edition of this "Doing Business" index, India ranked 130th out of 189 countries. This was marginally below the South Asia regional average (128/189) but well beneath fellow BRICS economies, Russia (51), South Africa (73), China (84), and Brazil (116). Among "lower middle income nations," the category to which India belongs, it ranked just below war-torn West Bank and Gaza and just ahead of Egypt. For instance, in Mumbai obtaining a construction permit involves 40 discrete procedures that take, on average, 147 days at an expense equal to one-quarter of the overall project cost.[71]

Given India's historically fraught relationship with private capital, perhaps focusing on the business environment is unfair. Yet such realities persist in even the most mundane aspects of day-to-day life, such as obtaining a driver's license. A team of economists that followed 822 applicants in Delhi who were looking to get their driver's license found that Indian bureaucrats artificially restricted the number of licenses given and created excessive red tape in order to secure bribes. Many applicants paid bribes and/or sought private agents to assist them in their quest. What is even more troubling about this are the social costs; nearly three-quarters of those who successfully obtained a license did not actually take the written examination and almost two-thirds failed an independent driving test.[72] Unsurprisingly, India has among the highest number of road deaths in the world.

A plethora of comparable examples could be mentioned, ranging from the surreal (regulations on the color and type of pen to be used when making notations on government files) to the inexcusable (the lengths to which impoverished households must go to obtain a Below Poverty Line card).[73] Indeed, India's stifling regulatory burdens have become the stuff of legend. The economist Bibek Debroy wonderfully documented the poignant example of the Uttar Pradesh Association of Dead People (Uttar Pradesh Mritak Sangh), established to convince the Indian bureaucracy that many of its members were much alive, despite being ruled dead according to official government records. At one point, the association was said to have more than 20,000—living, but pronounced dead—members.[74]

Insufficient Personnel

Given India's extreme overbureaucratization, there is a widely held view that the powers of India's public authorities must be dramatically curbed. It is hard to quibble with those who advocate curtailing the worst excesses of the state, especially where the state's heavy-handed role distorts economic and social freedoms. Yet here one must separate bureaucratic *proceduralism* from bureaucratic *personnel*.

Due to endemic shortfalls in human resources, the capacity of the Indian state to perform its essential functions is wholly inadequate. Although this runs counter to the popular perception of a bloated bureaucracy desperate to be cut down to size, the problem with the Indian state is not that it is too big; it is that its functioning is too bureaucratic. To be sure, the weak capacity of the Indian government is only partially about having the requisite number of warm bodies—it is also about having personnel with the rights skills and training *in the right places*. Nevertheless, employing adequate personnel is a necessary, though perhaps insufficient, starting condition.

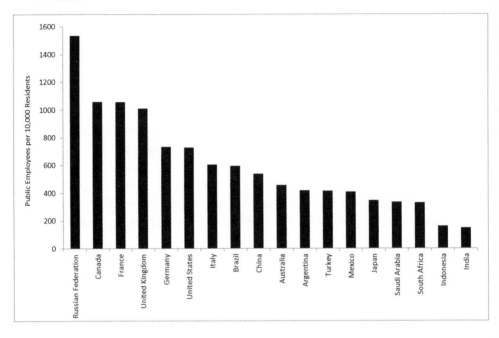

Figure 2.6. Public employment in G20 countries, 2010. (Data as of 2010 or most recent year available from International Labor Organization, Saudi Arabia's Ministry of Economy and Planning, China's National Bureau of Statistics, World Bank)

Despite the fact that politicians regularly treat public sector employment as a method for rewarding supporters and trading favors, India has one of the lowest rates of per capita public sector employment of any Group of 20 (G20) country (figure 2.6).[75] For every 10,000 residents, India has approximately 146 public employees. On the opposite end of the spectrum, Russia has more than ten times as many government employees on a per capita basis, and the United States has five times as many employees relative to its population.

Furthermore, while it is true that public sector employment in India —across all levels of government—nearly doubled between 1971 and 1991, that number has steadily declined since then, to around 17.6 million in 2012 (figure 2.7). In a major committee report, the Indian government revealed that, as of January 2014, central governmental departments faced as many as 729,000 outstanding vacancies.[76] While

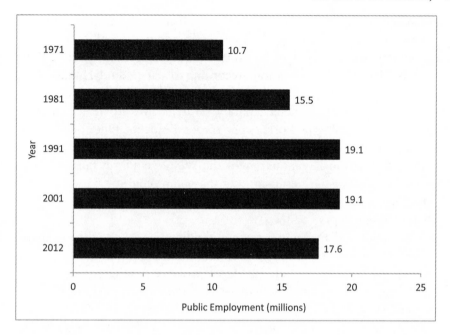

Figure 2.7. Trends in public employment in India, 1971–2012. (Data from Economic Survey of India, various years)

some of these positions could potentially be filled by temporary workers and others could be eliminated altogether, it is clear that adequate staffing is a serious challenge for the public sector.

Sovereign Failures

The combination of excessive proceduralism and human capital shortfalls hampers the Indian state's ability to perform even its most essential sovereign functions. Taxation, for instance, is one of the most vital functions of the modern nation-state since it provides the resource base upon which all else is built. Despite the government's desperate need to raise revenues to cover the costs of an expanding welfare state, just over 32 million people in a country of 1.2 billion pay income tax.[77] Ironically, alongside a burdensome tax regulatory regime (India ranks 157th in the world when it comes to the ease of paying taxes, according to the World Bank) sits a dramatic shortage in the number of government tax collectors. In 2012 the Income Tax Department disclosed that it faced a shortfall of nearly 20,000 personnel.[78]

Similar problems plague the state's ability to provide basic public goods, like health or education. According to a 2014 study, India's density of allopathic doctors, nurses, and midwives (11.9 per 10,000 residents) is roughly half the benchmark set by the World Health Organization (WHO) of 25.4 workers per 10,000 residents. Once one factors in quality (based on medical qualifications), Indian health worker coverage drops to just one-quarter of the WHO standard. Furthermore, there are great disparities in coverage based on geography; for instance, the density of health care providers is nearly ten times larger in urban than rural settings.[79]

Protecting Indians from foreign and domestic security threats is another area where there is a human resources crisis. Despite major internal security concerns—from Maoist violence to religious extremism and organized criminal activity—the domestic-oriented Intelligence Bureau struggled with more than 8,000 vacancies (as of March 2013), equivalent to 30 percent of its sanctioned strength.[80] When terrorists launched a series of coordinated, simultaneous attacks on Mumbai on November 26, 2008, the response of local security forces was hampered by the fact that many of the bulletproof vests officers were outfitted with were of poor quality, the end result of a shoddy procurement deal.[81] When a terrorist's bombs went off in West Bengal in 2014, officers from the National Investigative Agency, India's premier counterterrorism bureau, had to hail cabs to the scene of the crime because they lacked enough cars.[82]

The entire spectrum of India's rule of law institutions—from the police to the courts and prisons—are desperate for renewed investment. India has the lowest rate of police officers per capita—122.5 per 100,000 people—of any G20 member state, and the police vacancy rate stands at 25 percent.[83] In the United States, there are 108 judges per million citizens, compared with a mere 12 per million in India. Here too, many positions that are officially sanctioned are not filled; more than one-third of the higher judiciary and one-quarter of judges on subordinate courts are simply not in place due to unfilled vacancies (as of mid-2015) (figure 2.8). The result is a mind-boggling backlog of 31.2 million cases facing the courts.[84]

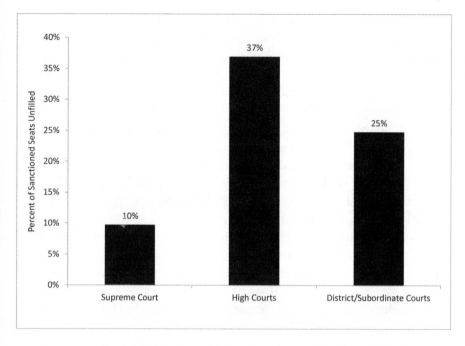

Figure 2.8. Vacancies in India's judiciary, 2015. (Data from the Supreme Court of India as of September 30, 2015, for the Supreme Court, and June 30, 2015, for district/subordinate courts)

In many instances, human resource shortfalls are compounded by failures of allocation. For instance, despite India's woeful police-to-population ratio and widespread enforcement failures, the police force it does have is preoccupied with nonessential activities. In the wake of the horrific 2012 Delhi gang rape, it came to light that of the roughly 84,000 police officers working in Delhi, only about 39,000 actually do routine police work. The remaining 45,000 officers are tasked with "VIP security" duty or mundane office work.[85]

GOVERNANCE DEFICIT

Thus, over time, a gap has opened up between the rapid political, social, and economic change and stagnant quality of India's institutional firmament. After growing at a modest clip for much of its post-independence history, economic growth surged in the last quarter century. Politics became significantly more fragmented and decentralized, and new groups found political voice. Just in the last two decades, India added more people than its entire population at the time of independence. Even reasonably decent state institutions would have come under considerable stress thanks to the rapid changes underfoot. With decaying institutions, however, India's governance deficit painted an even more striking contrast to the dramatic changes underfoot. This contrast is not altogether unfamiliar.

In his 1968 book, *Political Order in Changing Societies,* political scientist Samuel Huntington warned of the negative repercussions for countries that found themselves burdened with a state unable to keep up with the pressures of modernization. Huntington was writing at a time of considerable turmoil in the developing world, when the frequency of military coups, prolonged insurgencies, and civil strife were on the uptick. His diagnosis was remarkably simple but compelling: "The primary problem of politics is the lag in the development of political institutions behind social and economic change."[86] One of the by-products of this mismatch Huntington points to, not surprisingly, is corruption. While elements of Huntington's account fit India's dilemma quite well, the dynamics of India's institutional shortcomings also shape the corruption environment in very distinctive ways.

Weak Institutions and Corruption

Three things link India's institutional stasis and corruption.

First, the rampant bureaucratic proceduralism that has survived the supposed dismantling of the License Raj has provided bureaucrats—and, crucially, the politicians who oversee them—with ample leverage to manipulate the thicket of state controls in the service of narrow private interests. State actors have wide discretionary authorities that they can use and abuse with impunity. The discretion available to those in power increases the financial rewards to holding (and retaining) office, thus increasing the costs individuals are willing to endure to achieve power. Hence, the excessive regulatory intensity of the Indian state gives political incumbents a great many levers to manipulate policy in exchange for private benefits.

Second, the relative incapacity of the state, due to shortages in the quantity and quality of government personnel, has left the public sector severely outmatched in its oversight function. The understaffed and underfunded government is incapable of adequately regulating the vastly more complicated and diverse economic environment it faces following the country's economic takeoff. This limits the state's ability to control rent-seeking and, in conjunction with stifling regulation, allows actors who want to fleece the state to get away with it.

Third, excessive proceduralism and gaps in capacity interact to inhibit the state's ability to provide the basic public goods necessary to meet the demands of a growing, increasingly aspirational population. This shortcoming creates political space for private actors to perform these functions, but these private actors do not always act with the general welfare in mind. The very failure of the Indian state to deploy its authority ends up further contributing to governance failures.

Modernization and Corruption

Modernization—and this is where Huntington's insights are germane to India's current predicament—compounds the problems emanating from this institutional misalignment.[87] Indeed, one should not underestimate the profound changes rapid rates of social and economic development can have on a country's domestic fabric.

For starters, modernization creates new sources of wealth and power in society, and the owners of that wealth often try to use this money to achieve greater political power. Conversely, groups situated closer to the bottom rungs of society—awakened by a realization of the potential for social and economic mobility—begin clamoring for more recognition. In many instances, the historical record suggests that such groups will trade their mobilizing potential for material incentives.[88]

Moreover, modernization multiplies the functions any government must undertake. Rapid economic growth requires the creation of new infrastructure (e.g., ports, road, and railways), a larger social safety net, and an enhanced role for the state in regulating economic activity. This expansion of the state's role creates a new set of interactions between the state and society—which themselves create the potential for engaging in malfeasance.[89]

Lastly, modernization entails multiple processes of dynamic economic growth—urbanization, increasing literacy, and so on—which involve a reordering of values in society. Modern societies, in contrast to feudal ones, begin to create separation between one's "public role and private interest," in Huntington's words. New norms are established, and then diffused, about what is right and what is wrong in the political sphere.[90]

Modernization and Corruption, Indian Style

The set of conditions Huntington identifies to describe the interplay between modernization and corruption in a context of weak institutions describes, with a few modifications, the facts of the India case pretty well.

First, there has been substantial wealth creation in India, especially after economic activity began to pick up in the 1980s and 1990s, leading to truly rapid growth in the decade of the 2000s. The growth in the ultra-rich during this time has also been phenomenal. According to an analysis by Michael Walton and Aditi Gandhi, in the mid-1990s India was home to only two billionaires, worth a combined $3.2 billion. By 2012, India boasted 46 billionaires worth more than $175 billion. As a share of GDP, the wealth belonging to India's billionaires blossomed from just 1 percent in the mid-1990s to as high as 22 percent in 2008 before falling to 10 percent in 2012 following the global financial crisis.[91] In 2014, for the first time ever, India's 100 richest individuals were all billionaires, collectively worth around $346 billion.[92] This class of high net worth individuals, and the corporations they represent, have skillfully used their financial clout to shape policy on a range of matters—from influencing regulatory policy to limiting foreign competition—and sectors, from telecommunications to petrochemicals.[93]

While this period of India's development has been associated with a rise in income inequality, those at the bottom of the pyramid have also considerably improved their lot, although there is still a long way to go. In 1993–94, the government of India estimated that 45.3 percent of Indians were living below the poverty line, accounting for slightly more than 400 million people. By 2011–12, the share of poor had declined to just under 22 percent, or 270 million Indians.[94]

In line with Huntington's argument, the desire for economic fulfill-
ment has created opportunities for patronage and clientelism, which
allows for the transfer of material benefits from the elites to the masses.
Democratic and social transformations have also raised the expectations of ordinary voters, whose aspirations are often thwarted by political institutions that are unable to deliver. The search for credible
governance has opened the door for ordinary Indians to seek out representatives who will look out for their interests, even if they short-circuit
the official system to get things done. Thus, the corrupt politician becomes "the crutch that helps the poor navigate a system that gives them
so little access" in the first place.[95]

Second, the process of rapid economic growth has provided greater
scope for rent-seeking, as Huntington rightly observed.[96] As University
of Chicago economist turned governor of the Reserve Bank of India Raghuram Rajan has argued, Indians have not necessarily become more
corrupt, but rather "the opportunities for corruption have increased
due to higher growth."[97]

As societies industrialize, the economic pie expands considerably;
governments grow in line with the demands on them and the focus of
development moves from agriculture to commerce and industry. The
latter typically require large government contracts or permissions
to build modern infrastructure, creating processes that are vulnerable to corruption. As India's poorest states have moved along this
spectrum, they have become hotbeds for more, not less, corruption.
As political scientist Pratap Bhanu Mehta once remarked about the
poor Indian state of Bihar, which has long had a reputation for widespread corruption: "There is a cruel joke that has an element of truth
in it: Bihar's problem was not too much corruption, it was too little
corruption."[98]

Third, while the conceptual separation between the public and private sphere is not all that new in India, there is now a much greater
awareness of the private actions of public servants and elected officials.
As independent India has evolved, the availability of information on
the behavior of public officials has greatly improved, thanks to rising
incomes and improved literacy, a more competitive media marketplace,
and legal reforms such as the Right to Information (RTI) Act (under
which any citizen can petition the state for information deemed to be
in the public interest). Now, more than ever before, there is greater

reporting on corruption; after all, where there is more sunlight one is likely to see more dirt.[99]

The growth of the media is an important component of this changed environment. In 2006, according to one estimate, 296 million Indians were newspaper readers. That number grew to 340 million in 2012.[100] The growth in television news outlets has been even more striking, from just nine stations in 2000 to 122 in 2010.[101] Of course, increasingly in India, as in many parts of the world, the primary conveyor belts of information are not "old media" like newspapers and television but "new media" that can be accessed via the Internet. In a comparative sense, Internet connections are still something of a rarity in India: by December 2014, approximately 270 million Indians had an Internet subscription. This implies a rate of 21.6 subscribers per 100 residents (the comparable figure in Brazil for 2013 was 51.6).[102] While this number remains small, it is growing fast—but nowhere as fast as the growth of mobile phones. India went from having zero mobile phone subscribers in 1994 to 975 million a little more than a decade later, in

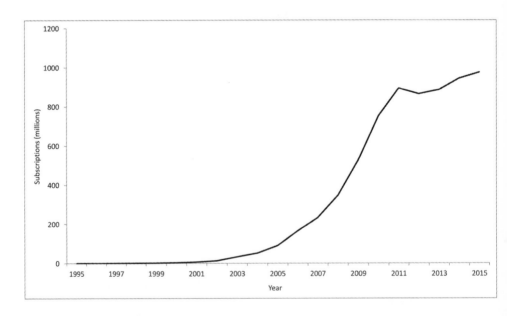

Figure 2.9. Mobile phone subscriptions in India, January 1995–June 2015. (Data from World Development Indicators, 2014; Telecom Regulatory Authority of India, 2015)

June 2015 (figure 2.9).[103] This information environment has no doubt brought more corruption allegations and suspected transgressions to the forefront.

Huntington's framework, which rings true in so many ways, does have at least one clear shortcoming, and it is one other scholars have focused on as well. The idea that a misalignment between modernization and institutional quality leads to negative developmental outcomes (such as corruption) comes across as overly deterministic; in such a model, even the most idealistic, reform-oriented politicians would be ultimately frustrated by a political system unable to change or adapt.

Yet any country's struggles—India's included—are fundamentally about the choices individuals make.[104] Structural arguments leave very little room for human agency. This is an important caveat to Huntington's thesis, but it does not mean that structural factors do not matter; rather, it is best to think of them as providing the larger opportunity structure for corruption to thrive (or not). The later discussion on India's marketplace for criminality will bring into sharp focus the role human agency plays.

GRAND POSSIBILITIES FOR GRAND CORRUPTION

Of course, corruption is far from a recent phenomenon in India. After all, as far back as the fourth century BC the philosopher Kautilya famously wrote, "Just as it is impossible not to taste the honey or the poison that finds itself at the tip of the tongue, so it is impossible for a government servant not to eat at least a bit of the King's revenue."[105] Entire libraries could be filled with treatises on the causes and consequences of corruption in modern India (or indeed in many other countries).

But while corruption is hardly new, the *nature* of corruption has changed in recent years. "Petty" or low-level administrative corruption has long been endemic in India—but as India has progressed, the scope for "grand" corruption has increased. "Grand corruption" refers to corruption that involves high-level elected officials and can have systemic effects on economic and political outcomes.[106] Examples include vested interests paying for large-scale regulatory or legal favors, the payment of kickbacks for lucrative licenses, or the exertion of influence through illicit political finance.

"Petty corruption," by contrast, typically involves a low-level functionary soliciting a bribe from a citizen or taking payment for allowing illegal access to public benefits. It is grand corruption that has received a particular boost from the failure of India's institutions to keep up with the pace of political, economic, and social change, and it is manifested by three types of rents: regulatory, extractive, and political.[107]

Regulatory Rents

In the years following India's path-breaking economic reforms of 1991, reform proponents argued that liberalization would substantially address India's corruption affliction. After all, liberal reforms were meant to get the government out of the way, unburden the private sector, and harness the "animal spirits" of free-market capitalism. Despite reformers' best intentions, corruption has actually thrived in the wake of reform.

But it is not the reforms per se that are to blame for the rise in corruption. To the contrary, corruption has mainly thrived in those areas where the state still plays a domineering role or where the state has opened up the sector but failed to institute sound regulatory institutions in the wake of liberalization. This has led some to suggest that what India suffers from is more akin to "crony socialism" than "crony capitalism."[108]

The economic reforms India managed to carry out freed businesses from some of the worst excesses of the License Raj era, such as industrial licensing, but three problems arose from the liberalization push. First, many key sectors of the economy remained essentially unreformed. In sectors ranging from higher education to power and mining, the state remained the dominant player and private participation was minimal or nonexistent. As Raghuram Rajan put it, the reforms left the public sector occupying the "commanding heights."[109] In these areas, the state was able to abuse its virtual monopoly to engage in rent-seeking for the benefit of the political class and free of competitive pressures.

Detailed research studying the impact of India's industrial de-licensing, the rolling back of one of the central elements of the License Raj, has found that these reforms left the dominance of large incumbents

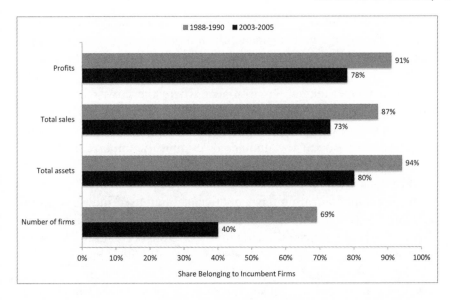

Figure 2.10. Economic dominance of incumbent firms, 1988–2005. "Incumbent firms" are defined as state-owned enterprises and private firms incorporated before 1985. (Data from Laura Alfaro and Anusha Chari, "India Transformed: Insights from the Firm Level 1988–2007," *India Policy Forum* 6 [2009]: 153–224)

—many of which are state-owned enterprises—largely unchallenged (figure 2.10).[110] Thus in 2005, nearly a decade and a half after India's "big bang" economic reforms, as much as three-quarters of the economy was still in the hands of state firms and long-standing private firms born before the mid-1980s.[111]

Second, the Indian state was unable (or unwilling) to address issues of regulatory capture. As with many countries making the transition from a state-controlled to a market-based economy, India found itself trapped in a "partial reform equilibrium."[112] In many sectors, powerful incumbents exploited their political connections amid the unique window of economic opening to entrench their own favorable positions while stymieing further reform that would introduce competitive pressures and, hence, limit their market power. This was a result of what Rajan calls an "unholy alliance" between elements of the political class and shady, aggressive entrepreneurs he dubs *"the connected"* (italics in original).[113]

Deregulation introduced a rash of new, predominantly small firms, while at the same time entrenching the importance of powerful incumbent firms. Although political connectedness is not the only driver, this evidence is consistent with the notion that liberalization "may have created a winner-take-all environment where the largest firms drive out" competition, hollowing out the middle.[114] For example, research shows that Indian firms operating in industries that are relatively concentrated (in terms of the number of established important players) have been more successful at preventing the entry of foreign firms, who might pose a competitive threat.[115]

In the pre-liberalization days, politicians often used India's onerous regulatory environment to engage in decentralized bribe taking. Back then, firms paid politicians to circumvent onerous regulation. The 1991 reforms liberalized markets—yet without establishing robust legal and regulatory checks and balances. In the post-liberalization era, firms have gone from trying to evade the rules to trying to rewrite them in their favor.[116]

It is perhaps no surprise that of the Indian billionaires Walton and Gandhi study, 43 percent of them (accounting for 60 percent of overall billionaire wealth) are connected to "rent-thick" sectors, or sectors where the state's role in granting licenses and permissions remains intensive. Such industries include real estate, infrastructure, construction, mining, telecom, cement, and media.[117] A 2011 survey by accounting firm KPMG ranked sectors according to business perceptions of the prevalence of corruption. This ranking correlates exceptionally well with regulatory intensity, or "rent-thickness."[118]

But there was a third, almost opposite, infirmity. At the same time the state could (or would) not fend off regulatory capture, it also itself engaged in predatory behavior with abandon. As is typical with many economic reforms, "the withdrawal of the state in one form . . . necessitated its reappearance in another."[119] Patronage opportunities did not disappear; they merely relocated. There is plenty of evidence to suggest that the greatest exchange of favors between firms and politicians exists in sectors of the economy where the regulatory intensity of the state is highest. This is not necessarily an India-specific observation but a more generalizable pattern validated by the Indian case.[120]

For instance, in research undertaken with the economist Sandip Sukhtankar, we set out to document the biggest public corruption scandals that were uncovered between the years 2000 and 2014. Most of the scams we identified involved simple embezzlement by a senior government official or politician or bribes paid by firms to obtain lucrative government contracts or licenses. There was also an obvious correlation with sectors where the state exercised a heavy regulatory hand. For instance, 35 percent of the scams we documented were in the mining and land sectors.[121]

Extractive Rents

The second type of grand corruption that has taken off involves rents stemming from natural resource or extractive industries.[122] Typically, corruption here involves the discretionary allocation of public resources to private (or other public) players for their development and/or refinement. The economist Arvind Subramanian has further classified extractive rents into three subcategories: "terrestrial" rents, derived from the allocation of land or resources located above ground; "subterranean" rents, drawn from the allocation of rights to coal mining and oil and gas exploration, which take place below ground; and "ethereal" rents, from the allocation of telecommunications spectrum.[123]

Land is essential to agriculture, manufacturing, mining, real estate and construction, and large infrastructure—the sectors that constitute the lifeblood of modern, industrial economies. Because of land's intrinsic role in the growth process, its lucrative nature, and the state's fundamental role in setting the conditions for how land markets in India operate, there is ample scope for malfeasance. As scholar Pratap Bhanu Mehta has written, "The discretionary power the state has with respect to land is the single biggest source of corruption" in India.[124]

India's byzantine system of land regulation, which dates back to colonial-era statutes, provides ample opportunity for politicians and bureaucrats to grant discretionary access to land. As the Indian economy gathered strength in the 2000s and the size of the upwardly mobile classes grew, there was a mad dash to acquire land—for residential buildings and commercial real estate, as well as for industrial and manufacturing-related activities. Nearly every deal involves intense interaction with the state, which tightly regulates supply.[125]

One of the most memorable recent cases of cronyism when it comes to land is the case of the Adarsh Housing Society, a tony apartment complex located in one of the most expensive sections of South Mumbai. The Adarsh building was ostensibly constructed for the purpose of housing widows of soldiers who had fought in the 1999 Kargil War with Pakistan and other Ministry of Defense personnel. Instead, thanks to the connivance of several of the state's leading politicians, bureaucrats, and regulators, flats within the complex were distributed among themselves and their cronies.

In addition to using the complex as a vehicle for political patronage, the politicians and bureaucrats responsible for Adarsh openly flouted an untold number of land, zoning, and environmental rules and regulations to get the project done. The scam, which created a political uproar in the state of Maharashtra and even forced the sitting Congress chief minister to resign in 2011, became a symbol of the sleaze and corruption that characterize many land deals consummated across India. An independent investigation into what the media began calling "Mumbai's Tower of Shame" called the plot "a shameless tale of blatant violations" that reflected "greed, nepotism and favouritism" on the part of several former chief ministers and cabinet ministers of the state.[126] Yet most politicians implicated in the scheme got off scot-free. After initially refusing even to entertain the report, the state government—forced to act under mounting pressure—set its sights on complicit bureaucrats, thereby absolving their political masters. Asked years later about this decision, the former chief minister of Maharashtra stated plainly: "If I had sent them [the politicians] to jail, it would have hit the party organisation. . . . The party would have split. Nobody articulated that openly then. Neither could I."[127]

The dash to control land was restricted not only to the land itself but also access to the resources that lay beneath the surface, which produce what Subramanian has referred to as subterranean rents. As domestic and Chinese demand for raw materials intensified, and commodity prices skyrocketed, mining and quarrying became hugely lucrative.

The land and natural resources sector was left virtually untouched by the reforms of the early 1990s, not necessarily due to venal motivations but at least in part because few could foresee at the time how well India's economy would take off and, hence, how important the allocation of natural resources would be in later years. The end result of the toxic mixture of oppressive regulation, regulatory incapacity, and ill-defined rules for allocation created new space for corruption.

Within ten years, India had moved from the "License Raj" to the "Resource Raj."[128]

One of the most prominent poster children for the Resource Raj is the son of a tribal farmer hailing from one of India's poorest states. Madhu Koda was a quietly ambitious politician from the eastern state of Jharkhand, home to an estimated 40 percent of the nation's known mineral wealth and 30 percent of its coal reserves.[129] Koda's risky gambit to launch a rebellion against his state's BJP government in 2005 resulted in a fractious scrum, out of which he emerged as the new chief minister at the ripe old age of 35.[130]

Koda executed this maneuver only after he had secured the lucrative mining portfolio, which he held onto after becoming the state's chief executive. Within a few years, Koda allegedly created an international mining empire worth billions of dollars built on a complex foundation of kickbacks, suspicious *hawala* (informal money transfer system commonly found in South Asia) transactions, secret Swiss bank accounts, fraudulent shell companies, and lavish offshore investments.[131] Koda was finally arrested in December 2009 on money-laundering charges and a special CBI court framed corruption charges in the case in July 2015.[132]

According to one account, Koda and his aides would compile a list of companies that had applied for mining licenses, invite their representatives to his residence, and then grant licenses to companies based on the size of the bribes they promised.[133] In one instance, Koda is said to have cleared 48 mining licenses in less than one hour.[134] As for existing mines, it was rumored that Koda and politicians loyal to him would receive up to a 25 percent cut of the mining companies' financial turnover in exchange for continued support.[135]

But all of this money needed a home that would avoid detection. So large chunks of cash allegedly moved informally, sometimes in suitcases ferried by bus or train, often winding their way across country to Mumbai to be channeled into shell companies located in tax havens. By the time his alleged mining racket came undone, Koda had reportedly plundered roughly one-fifth of his state's annual revenue, according to law enforcement sources.[136]

One of the most hotly debated scams of the recent era, however, involves the allocation of telecommunications spectrum and the generation of ethereal rents. After the government liberalized the once-closed telecommunications sector to private players in the 1990s, the sector—especially the wireless component—witnessed explosive growth. Mobile telephony surged, as did the revenues of leading telecom providers in the early 2000s (see figure 2.9).

To facilitate the introduction of "2G," or second-generation technology, the government announced its intention in 2007 to award new telecom licenses and spectrum allocations. However, the rules for allocation had not yet been determined. Enter A. Raja, the union minister for telecommunications. Raja was a prominent leader of the Dravida Munnetra Kazhagam (DMK), a political party in the state of Tamil Nadu and member of the ruling coalition in New Delhi, and a favorite of the DMK's octogenarian leader, M. Karunanidhi.[137] The telecom ministry was a "DMK post," a position the Congress Party (as leader of the ruling alliance) ceded to the party as part of its power-sharing arrangement. Without the support of smaller parties such as the DMK, the Congress did not have the numbers to sustain a parliamentary majority.

Irrespective of the policy morass in Delhi, Raja himself had very clear designs for how licenses should be awarded, if federal authorities are to be believed. According to the Central Bureau of Investigation (CBI), rather than auctioning off licenses to the highest bidder, his ministry adopted a first-come, first-served policy.[138] If the ministry had truly followed a first-come, first-served policy, based on a set of transparent requirements, perhaps Raja's decision could have been defended. But what followed instead was an arbitrary muddle. With very little warning, the Department of Telecommunications announced that it would stop accepting applications for new licenses on October 1, 2007. Without justification, on January 10, 2008, it retrospectively revised the deadline to September 25, 2007. That same January afternoon, at 2:45 to be precise, the Department added an additional wrinkle: if applicants wished to preserve their current standing in the license queue, they would have to show up at the ministry between 3:30 and 4:30 that very day with bank guarantees worth 16.5 billion rupees (or a quarter of a billion U.S. dollars).[139] This had all the makings of an inside job.

It was only a matter of time before the "2G scam" earned the attention of India's law enforcement and anticorruption authorities. The comptroller and auditor general (CAG) found that of the 122 licenses handed out by Raja's ministry in 2008, 85 were given to companies that were ineligible to receive them—at 2001 prices to boot. These 85 firms had "suppressed facts, disclosed incomplete information and submitted fictitious documents" in order to win licenses, the auditor alleged.[140] Many were real estate companies with zero telecommunications experience but with ready access to millions of dollars in cash. After winning the lucrative licenses, these firms immediately turned around and sold them to legitimate operators for a much higher price, reaping massive windfall gains overnight.

In February 2011 Indian prosecutors ordered the arrest of A. Raja (along with DMK leader Karunanidhi's daughter, Kanimozhi, herself an MP) and several others on corruption charges. Their criminal cases are still ongoing.[141] Although the allegations have not yet been proven, anticorruption investigators also suspect that Raja received a handsome bribe (channeled via a television station owned by the Karunanidhi family) as a result of his ministerial machinations.[142] Raja also stands accused of acquiring "disproportionate assets" while serving as an MP.[143]

Political Rents

The third and final pillar of grand corruption has to do with India's political and electoral system, which will be covered in detail later in the book. But it suffices to say that politics is the linchpin that holds India's corrupt ecosystem in equilibrium. There are two primary aspects of the political system that are relevant to this discussion.

The first is the nature of political finance in India, which is opaque, highly dependent on undocumented cash, and utterly corrupt. As subsequent chapters will show, the ineffectual regulation and monitoring of how politics in India is financed both allows for the continuation of policies which do not benefit the public interest and explicitly props up corruption in the other domains.

For instance, political finance serves as the glue that holds together India's dubious system of regulating land, lubricating the well-oiled machine that benefits land sharks, builders, and politicians. As previously discussed, politicians (and the bureaucrats they control) exercise considerable discretion over the acquisition and allocation of land and what the land is ultimately used for. This provides politicians with a steady supply of favors they can dole out to prospective builders and developers, who must come with hat in hand to politicians for policy and regulatory favors.[144] There is a good reason, therefore, for India ranking 183rd (out of 189 countries) in the ease with which firms can obtain a construction permit.[145]

Oftentimes, politicians will use their regulatory leverage to demand a cut of the builders' investment; one prominent member of the Legislative Assembly (MLA, or state legislator) in Gujarat, for instance, was known to demand a 5 percent "silent equity" stake in any new development built within his constituency.[146] Come election time, politicians need to amass large war chests to cover the costs of campaigning, and, here, their builders (who are often their business partners) are expected to funnel cash back to the campaign.[147] What helps grease the wheels of this quid pro quo is the construction industry's heavy reliance on cash, which makes it a perfect venue for such laundering.[148]

In research carried out with Devesh Kapur, we actually found hard evidence of this quid pro quo by studying fluctuations in the consumption of cement. Given that builders rely heavily on cash and frequently lack adequate sources of bank financing, one would expect that firms in the real estate and construction industries will experience a short-term liquidity crunch as elections approach because of their need to re-route funds to campaigns as a form of indirect election finance, thereby momentarily reducing their consumption of cement (an indispensable ingredient in modern construction). Indeed, that turns out to be exactly what the data reveal.[149] The month elections are taking place cement consumption exhibits a statistically significant decline. This effect is stronger for state elections (it is India's state governments that regulate land), urban states, and in more competitive elections.[150] Undoubtedly, this transaction of cash for favors imposes a short-term cost on builders, but the exchange brings long-term benefits in terms of future goodwill, which is vital for commercial success.

The interplay between politicians and builders highlights two aspects of how money in Indian politics works. The first is that money serves to bankroll politics; politicians and political parties are beholden to vested interests that can organize and deploy sizeable amounts of largely undocumented cash. But while money greases the wheels of politics, political office can also be used to generate large quantities of money. Once ensconced in power, India's politicians have many lucrative levers they can wield to make money for themselves, their families, and their associates.[151]

The second aspect of corruption in politics is the extent to which criminality intersects with, and resides within, the political sphere. While criminality cannot be simply reduced to corruption in the traditional sense of the word, politicians associated with criminal activity are inextricably tied to corruption on two accounts. First, they acquire political status on the basis of their ability to manipulate the state to divert benefits to a narrowly defined community (often violating the legal norms that exist on paper). Second, such politicians cultivate their own criminal reputations and perpetuate the corruption and subversion of the state to consolidate their own political success.

One quintessential example of such a politician is Raghuraj Pratap Singh, commonly known as "Raja Bhaiya," a man whom one journalist described as having successfully maintained "a life in politics coterminous with a life in crime" for over two decades.[152] Since first entering politics in 1993, Raja Bhaiya has won election to the Uttar Pradesh state assembly five consecutive times representing the constituency of Kunda.

A member of the royal family of the onetime Bhadri princely state in Pratapgarh, Raja Bhaiya has allegedly traded on his ancestral lineage, landlord roots, Rajput (Hindu upper caste) bona fides, and criminal reputation to seize, and to maintain, a hold over local politics. In each of his five electoral victories, he has won no less than 65 percent of his constituency's vote, a remarkable achievement in a country with intensely competitive elections. In the poetic words of one local resident, *Raja Bhaiyya ke ishare ke bina ek patta bhi nahi hilta* (Not even a leaf can flutter without Raja Bhaiyya's permission).[153]

Raja Bhaiya is not the first member of his family to come under a cloud of criminal scrutiny. His father, Uday Pratap Singh, had also earned the reputation as a feared gangster in Uttar Pradesh politics, at one time reportedly racking up as many as 34 criminal cases— including charges of violating the Terrorist and Disruptive Activities (Prevention) Act (TADA).[154]

As someone who is seen as a protector of the Rajputs, an influential vote bank, Raja Bhaiya has played an outsized role in his state's complex caste politics. Indeed, he has been named a minister in the

Uttar Pradesh state government on five separate occasions. When Raja Bhaiya was invited to join the cabinet as food minister in the Samajwadi Party government elected to office in 2012, observers saw it as an effort by the ruling party to "mollycoddle the Rajputs."[155]

Raja Bhaiya was also given additional charge of the prisons portfolio in 2012. Having spent his fair share of time behind bars pending various criminal trials, one could say he was uniquely suited to this role. At the time of his latest election (in 2012), Raja Bhaiya faced no fewer than eight criminal cases, including allegations of kidnapping, attempted murder, and dacoity. For many years, it was rumored that Raja Bhaiya stocked a lake on his property with live crocodiles, to which he would threaten to feed his enemies if they crossed him. Despite the number of charges filed against him, Raja Bhaiya has yet to be convicted of a serious crime.[156] His criminal rap sheet, far from deterring electoral support, helped to consolidate it because it conveyed the impression that Raja Bhaiya is capable of going to great lengths to do what it is necessary to protect his constituents' interests.[157]

In addition to wielding a potent mix of strong-arm tactics and caste politics to construct an impressive political base, Raja Bhaiya also used his position and his alleged criminal support structure to simultaneously substitute for, *and* subvert, the state apparatus. Asked why he has been able to monopolize political power in his area, Raja Bhaiya once explained: "Anyone can say he is your representative. And occasionally, he will tar a stretch of road, or add a few streetlights, or get a new well dug. . . . What the people need is someone to intercede for them when they get into trouble with the police; someone to speak on their behalf to government *babus* [bureaucrats] and get their work done. Someone to solve their problems."[158]

The ability to substitute for the state gives politicians backed by serious criminal reputations an authority and legitimacy to take advantage of the state as well. According to an investigation into the activities of Uttar Pradesh's food ministry, as much as $14.5 billion in food grain intended for poor beneficiaries was looted in the decade of the 2000s.[159] Between 2004 and 2007, a former aide to Raja Bhaiya told *Bloomberg* that he collected $200,000 per week from local officials implementing the food scam under Raja Bhaiya's watchful eye.[160]

The Bedrock of Administrative Corruption

Any discussion of grand corruption in India would be incomplete without at least a mention of the endemic system of administrative corruption that has existed in India and persists to the present day. This provides the foundation for high-level malfeasance and illegality, operating through at least three channels.[161]

The first involves officials charging fees or soliciting bribes for providing citizens with basic government services that they are eligible to receive, embodied in the distribution of drivers' licenses in Delhi or the targeting of certain households for Below Poverty Line (BPL) cards. One study found that 75 percent of households surveyed in rural Karnataka paid a bribe to get a BPL card. The incidence of misallocation was on the order of one in every two households in the state.[162]

The second involves collusion between public and private actors, such as companies paying bribes to government officers in order to bypass fines and regulations or win government contracts. For instance, a 2014 survey of global economic crime by the accounting firm PricewaterhouseCoopers found that the industry reporting the greatest degree of procurement fraud was government/state-owned enterprises.[163] This corruption need not involve the complicity of politicians, but anecdotal evidence suggests that it typically does. Indeed, it is an integral piece of the vertical patron-client relationship. The incentive for bureaucrats to comply with a politician's desire is, in part, financial—compliant bureaucrats may receive a percentage of any private payments, sending some portion upward to the politician. Alternatively, noncompliant bureaucrats may find themselves victim to a politician's ability to arbitrarily transfer them for reasons not related to performance—a sword hanging over any bureaucrat's head.[164]

One egregious example is the recent case of Haryana Indian Administrative Service (IAS) officer Ashok Khemka, who had the audacity to investigate and later cancel questionable land deals involving Robert Vadra, the son-in-law of Congress Party president Sonia Gandhi. Although Khemka's allegations were later independently confirmed by a report of the CAG, the officer's willingness to stamp out corruption came at a considerable cost.[165] In response to Khemka's actions on the Vadra deal, the Congress government of Haryana charged the officer with professional misconduct, a charge that was later dropped.[166]

Khemka's commitment to probity has come at a substantial professional cost; he has been transferred 46 times thus far in his 22-year career.[167] This "Transfer Raj" is what helps keep this peculiar social contract between politician and bureaucrat intact.[168]

A final form of administrative corruption involves embezzlement. This is what Prime Minister Rajiv Gandhi had in mind when he once famously claimed that only 15 percent of benefits disbursed by the government of India actually reach the poor.[169] The remaining 85 percent is siphoned off along the way. Also common is the practice of bureaucrats collecting a salary while shirking their official responsibilities. An extensive survey of government schools in 2006 found that 25 percent of schoolteachers were absent when researchers randomly showed up at their schools. In 2014, when the researchers repeated the experiment, very little had changed; this time, the rate of absenteeism stood at 23 percent.[170]

VENN DIAGRAM OF GRAND CORRUPTION

Atop a foundation of administrative corruption, the three modalities of "grand" corruption—regulatory, extractive, and political—provide a snapshot of the governance challenges India faces and offer a context for the larger ecosystem in which the country's struggles with political criminality are situated. Yet a critical element of this ecosystem is the interaction among the various pillars.

As Raghuram Rajan has pithily summed up: "The poor need the savvy politicians to help them navigate through rotten public services. The politician needs the corrupt businessman to provide the funds that allow him to supply patronage to the poor and fight elections. The corrupt businessman needs the politician to get natural resources cheaply. And the politician needs the votes of the poor, who are numerous enough to assure him reelection, no matter how much an idealistic middle class may rail. Every constituency is tied to the other in a cycle of dependence, which ensures the status quo prevails."[171]

The alleged exploits of the father-son duo of YSR and Jagan Reddy aptly demonstrate several of these overlaps. YSR's emergence was steeped in the muscular politics of Rayalaseema, further fueled by his access to financial resources and boosted by his control over natural resource extraction. The corrosive regulatory environment which mediated relations between the state and private capital allowed YSR, if prosecutors and India's top auditor are to be believed, to trade regulatory and policy favors in exchange for "investments" (i.e., bribes), which were then allegedly channeled into the vast business empire overseen by Jagan Reddy.[172]

YSR was also instrumental in giving an early break to another set of Reddys (no relation), the sibling trio of Janardhana, Karunakara, and Somashekara Reddy, another family success story seemingly intertwined with the three pillars of grand corruption. The Reddy brothers hail from Bellary in the state of Karnataka, which borders Andhra to the west. Janardhana, the most ambitious of the trio, was an entrepreneur who struck up a friendship with YSR.[173] Despite possessing zero experience in the mining sector, Janardhana started his own venture in iron ore extraction, the Obulapuram Mining Company (OMC), to chase the profits stemming from increasing Chinese demand and newly relaxed export controls. Thanks to these changes, the price of iron ore skyrocketed from a measly $17 per metric ton to $130 in 2010, making even bit players in the industry overnight successes. "People who had no knowledge of mining but who had money or muscle power" rushed to join the mining race, using shovels, pick-axes, and an unclaimed bit of land to set up shop.[174]

Late to the game, the brothers had missed out on the Bellary boom, where the mining universe became quickly saturated, but Janardhana convinced his old friend YSR to grant OMC licenses in a neighboring district on the Andhra Pradesh side of the border. Flush with cash, the brothers' ambitions quickly grew, and they soon sought a more formal engagement in politics to protect and multiply their investments.

In 1999, the brothers threw in their lot with the BJP, supporting the party financially. In 2008, in part thanks to the brothers' largesse, the BJP won 110 seats in the Karnataka state election, an impressive showing but short of an outright majority. By reportedly paying off independent candidates 250 million rupees ($3.8 million) each to switch their affiliations to the BJP and promising them lucrative government posts, the Reddy brothers emerged as kingmakers.[175] When asked about the brothers' intervention, Janardhana Reddy hardly denied these allegations: "We asked [the independent legislators] and they answered positively. And God has given us enough. We are only sharing what we have."[176] In addition to winning seats in the Karnataka state legislature, two of the brothers were selected to join the cabinet. A fourth, honorary "brother"—B. Sriramulu—was awarded the health ministry.

From that day forward, the BJP government in Karnataka owed its allegiance to the Reddy brothers.[177] According to allegations made by anticorruption investigators, the brothers wasted no time in exploiting their leverage, barging into the Bellary mining market to facilitate the illicit mining and transport of iron ore and extorting or coercing those who stood in their way.[178] In the words of the anticorruption ombudsman who eventually brought the Reddy brothers' various exploits to light, "That district had become the Republic of Bellary. It is not part of India."[179] The brothers amassed fabulous wealth and were not bashful about openly flaunting it. They built a sixty-room mansion, bought several helicopters, and imported expensive foreign cars. Janardhana allegedly even purchased a throne made of gold for their palatial home.[180] Even after literally moving the state border to expand their Andhra mining operations beyond the terms of their license, the brothers acted with impunity under the permissive gaze of both the Andhra Pradesh and Karnataka governments.[181]

Those in government who could have stopped them were either bought off or incompetent.[182] Instead, the government just granted more and more mining licenses. When Karnataka government agencies did attempt a crackdown on illegal mining, the brothers launched a fierce rebellion, threatening to pull down the BJP government unless the harsh policies were reversed and the offending ministers sacked. The chief minister of the state, the veteran politician B. S. Yeddyurappa, was forced to hastily call a press conference, during which he openly sobbed, apologizing "to the people of the state for this situation." Soon enough, the Bellary brothers got their way and Yeddyurappa got to keep his job.[183]

When companies refused to share a cut of their illegal mining profits with OMC, the brothers allegedly responded fiercely.[184] About Janardhana Reddy, one investigative journalist mused: "Those he hates, he crushes. . . . He has spent much time with political toughies who can bludgeon their way through. This makes him think like a street fighter. He is able to scare people."[185] In the 2008 state election, Sriramulu (the honorary brother) was twice arrested: first for allegedly burning a rival candidate's car and then later on reports that he assaulted a Congress worker.[186] One local resident remarked, "Politics is dirty in India, but it is dirtiest here in Bellary."[187]

YSR's death removed one of the brothers' key patrons, and shortly thereafter the Karnataka anticorruption ombudsman released a damning indictment of the brothers' illicit mining racket.[188] Janardhana was charged with orchestrating the illicit mining ring but, as of November 2015, was still awaiting trial.[189] Yet, the brothers hardly seem chastened. Somashekara, who is under investigation for trying to bribe a judge overseeing his brother's bail application, told a reporter: "Yes, my brother mined illegally, but everybody did it openly at that time.... When [he] went to jail, the goddess of wealth left thousands of Bellary homes too."[190]

NARROWING OUR SIGHTS

The failure of India's public institutions to keep pace with the dramatic political, economic, and social transformations under way has led to severe gaps in governance. The end result of this disjuncture has been a proliferation of grand corruption—a malaise made up of a diverse array of regulatory, extractive, and political rent-seeking activities. With this context in mind, Part II hones in on this third and final domain, or how corruption and crime are manifest in the realm of democratic politics.

II

3 Criminal Enterprise
Why Criminals Joined Politics

"GOD BROUGHT ME into this profession," proclaimed Arun Gawli, sporting a white Gandhian *topi* (hat) that so many Indian politicians regularly don.[1] The year was 1997 and Gawli was still adjusting to his new incarnation as aspiring politico and head of a budding new political party, the Akhil Bharatiya Sena (ABS). Headgear notwithstanding, Gawli was no ordinary *neta* (politician). Known as the "Daddy" who ruled Dagdi Chawl, a slum in the heart of teeming Mumbai once home to many of the city's blue-collar mill workers, Gawli was one of the most feared gangsters in India's "Maximum City."

The son of migrants from central India who traded life in rural Madhya Pradesh for metropolitan Mumbai, Gawli dropped out of primary school to work as a milkman so that he could support his impoverished family in the big city. Hailing from a family of country shepherds, Gawli struggled to find his way in Mumbai, but he eventually found his place toiling among the city's mills, where he hooked up with a local gang charged with protecting goods being smuggled to Mumbai by the notorious mobster Dawood Ibrahim.[2] Gawli quickly moved up the ranks, making a name for himself as a force to be reckoned with in the central Mumbai lanes of Byculla. Following an internecine gangland spat, Gawli went from serving Dawood Ibrahim to allegedly ordering hits on the mobster's men.

In no time, Dagdi Chawl became ground zero for Mumbai's notorious underworld. From his fortress-like compound, Daddy dispensed patronage, protection, and even justice to local residents. Journalists who came to interview Gawli wrote of the hundreds of men and women—unemployed youth, aging widows, aspiring gangsters, and established politicians—who queued up on a daily basis in front of the iron gates of Gawli's compound just for a few minutes of face time in the hopes of being showered with Daddy's munificence.[3] They came seeking building permits, ration cards, welfare payments, employment—all things the state was meant to provide but was either unable or unwilling to.

As Gawli's stature grew, the Shiv Sena—an influential regional political party—brought him into their fold. The Sena was founded in the late 1960s as a platform for espousing the rights of native Maharashtrians, many of whom chafed at the influx of migrants who had relocated to Mumbai in search of economic opportunity. Founded by media-savvy former news cartoonist Bal Thackeray, the Sena quickly emerged as a political force in Mumbai and other urban centers in the state thanks to the popularity of its "sons of the soil" propaganda and the network of social service provisions its cadres established to serve destitute locals.[4]

Even while functioning as a mainstream political party, the Sena instilled within its members an organizational ethos of "direct action," a euphemism for threatening force and occasionally using it. Gawli's arrangement with the Sena was never well defined, but in media interviews he sketched the basic understanding: "The *netas* come to the underworld during elections. To fix voters. They also come for funds. Since they seek help they also have to help when it comes to fixing the police."[5] Thackeray, in turn, openly claimed Daddy as the party's mascot: "If they [Muslims] have Dawood, we [Hindus] have Gawli. These [referring to Gawli and fellow gangster Amar Naik] are *amchi muley* [our boys, in Marathi, the local vernacular]."[6]

Eventually, Gawli was put behind bars for his misdeeds. When the police came to Dagdi Chawl to arrest him, Gawli was hiding inside the drawer of a bed, gun in hand.[7] While in jail in the late 1990s, Gawli and the Shiv Sena abruptly parted ways. As to why, rumors of all sorts made the rounds: that Gawli had ordered the murder of several Shiv Sena lawmakers, including a godson of Bal Thackeray's; that Thackeray grew wary of Gawli's rising prominence; and that Daddy had outgrown his existence as a mere hired gun in the employ of overbearing political masters.[8]

For decades (if not longer), mafia groups in Mumbai had maintained links to politics, although the biggest dons typically chose to live on the periphery of the electoral spotlight rather than on its center stage. After severing ties with the Shiv Sena, Gawli broke with tradition and floated the ABS as his personal vehicle for seizing political power. The party's ideology was unclear; its primary objectives seemed to be to counter the Shiv Sena while providing Gawli a means to promote his personal interests. Explaining his foray into politics, Gawli stated that he was only doing "what the public demanded" and that, like any good servant of the people, he "had no choice but to bow to their desire."[9] In a more honest moment, Gawli would admit to a more selfish motivation: protection. "I am not afraid of any rival," he once remarked to a journalist. "My only fear is that the police may get me."[10] Having decided to join active politics, Gawli quickly mimicked the Sena's modus operandi of setting up a network of *shakhas* (branches), often directly adjacent to the Sena's own operations, from which he and his party-mates could dispense social services and burnish their credentials as selfless Robin Hoods.[11]

After a series of frustrating failures in local elections, Gawli managed to get his eldest daughter, Geeta, elected to the Mumbai municipal corporation in 2002. He finally hit pay dirt himself when he won election to the Maharashtra state assembly in 2004, representing urban Chinchpokli. Gawli's wife, Asha, was his campaign manager and effectively represented her husband's constituency in his stead; he spent much of his term in jail on murder charges.[12] "Violence and non-violence have their own place in society," Gawli once remarked. "It all depends on the situation."[13]

Gawli's political rags-to-riches story reads more like a screenplay for a summer Bollywood blockbuster than the bio-sheet of a rising politician.[14] Yet within just a few years, Gawli successfully completed a surprising transition from gangster hired by politicians, who was booked in more than three dozen criminal cases involving murder and extortion, to a political player in his own right. In making this leap, Gawli was far from alone. One government commission after another convened over the past few decades has lamented the well-trodden career transition from lawbreaker to lawmaker; a 2002 government of

India white paper noted that it was a "disgrace" that "several hardened criminals who may have many cases of murder, rape and dacoity against them are actually occupying the seats" in Parliament and the various state assemblies.[15]

What explains the sudden change of heart experienced by Gawli and others like him who traded on their criminal reputations to run for political office? Why did criminals with lengthy rap sheets, who were once content to contract with political parties but remain squarely in the background, take the plunge and enter the political foreground?

WHERE DO CRIMINAL POLITICIANS COME FROM?

Throughout this book, I conceive of electoral politics as functioning as a marketplace for politicians. As with any market of any type, there are both supply and demand factors at work. Politicians, much like firms, wish to "supply" their wares to voters, the consumers who have some "demand" for the goods and services politicians are offering.

Though the analogy is imperfect, the market metaphor serves as a useful framing device to understand why the appeal of politicians linked to criminality endures. But before getting to what motivates demand on the part of voters for candidates linked with crime, it is important to explore why individuals associated with crime choose to take the electoral plunge in the first place.

Many analysts of contemporary India treat the association of criminals and politics as a new phenomenon. In actuality, individuals tied to criminal activity have been active in Indian politics from the early days of the republic. Indeed, the historical record is replete with evidence of politicians using "antisocial" or "lumpen" elements in the earliest elections following independence. At some point, however, the power dynamic seems to have shifted; criminals decided to run for office themselves. Therefore, what is new is the precise nature of the connection between criminals and politics.

Surprisingly, social scientists have not, by and large, grappled with the puzzle of the entry of criminals into politics. Instead, many existing analyses of the cozy links that developed between criminals and politics in India have a "black box" quality to them; a certain configuration went into the black box of Indira Gandhi's tenure in the 1970s and out of the other end emerged a new arrangement where criminals appeared ascendant in the electoral domain.[16]

A closer examination suggests there were two sets of factors responsible for injecting a supply of criminals into electoral politics at this precise stage of India's history: "pull" factors, or structural forces that created a certain enabling environment, and "push" factors, or the immediate influences on the behavior of criminals. To the extent scholars have focused on the evolving nexus of crime and politics in contemporary India, their explanations have largely centered on pull factors. These factors range from the breakdown of the Congress Party's ossified patronage networks, to rising, unmet social demands often expressed through the prism of caste or identity politics, and to the hollowing out of public sector institutions, or what one scholar has called a "crisis of governability."[17]

All of these explanations have merit. Large structural changes in the political system did in fact open up political space for individuals of dubious repute to take up a starring role in electoral politics in the absence of effective mediating institutions. One crucial pull factor many scholars have missed—or, at the very least, underemphasized—is the collapse of India's election finance regime.

However, these accounts gloss over the precise motivations that pushed criminals, once content to live on the fringes of electoral politics, to stand for elections directly. Drawing on the marketplace analogy, I argue that one way of understanding the rise of criminals in India's politics is to conceptualize them as behaving like private firms seeking to "vertically integrate" their operations.

Two caveats before I proceed: throughout the chapter, I cite statistics (largely drawn from reports published by the ECI) on electoral incidents involving breaches of law and order, violence, or malpractice as proxies for the spread of criminality in politics. Strictly speaking, these are analytically separate concepts. But because there is a dearth of detailed data on the personal characteristics of India's politicians before the mid-2000s, these data are immensely useful. However, the reporting of incidents is often impressionistic and should be taken as illustrative of a blossoming nexus between crime and politics.

In addition, the data on electoral incidents, while deeply troubling, must also be seen within the proper context. On the one hand, the rising tide of electoral violence and allegations of fraud represents a debasement of the democratic process. Such occurrences raise questions about how "free and fair" elections in India have been in the decades since independence. On the other hand, when viewed in the context of India's gargantuan elections, these incidents account for a small minority of cases. Furthermore, these illegal acts also reflect the reality of increased political contestation, especially on the part of previously disadvantaged groups, who coalesced around new parties representing their interests. Many of these groups had been practically, if not legally, disenfranchised in previous eras.[18]

HEGEMONY, INTERRUPTED

Before delving into the nexus of crime and politics, a cursory review of the evolution of India's electoral politics after 1947 is helpful. Political scientist Yogendra Yadav has argued that Indian politics since independence has experienced three distinct phases, or "electoral systems" (see figure 3.1).[19] Each system—1952 to 1967, 1967 to 1989, and 1989 to the present—is characterized by a unique configuration of political power and format of political competition. These phases, it turns out, serve as useful milestones for tracking the rise of criminal politicians.

To quickly recap, the years between 1952 and 1967 comprise the first electoral system, when the Indian polity was firmly under the grip of the Congress Party. It was the heyday of the famed Congress system. In the second phase—from 1967 to 1989—the Congress-dominated system morphed into a more competitive multiparty system. The third phase, beginning in 1989 and lasting until the present, marks the era of coalition politics in Delhi and the increasing primacy of the states as the primary venues for political contestation. In this most recent iteration, democratic mobilization greatly expanded to include castes and communities who had been previously marginalized, or what Yadav has referred to as the "creolization" of democracy.[20]

Most analyses of the interplay between crime and politics focus on the third and most recent phase. However, the story really begins much earlier. Though implementing some of the world's largest democratic elections—under considerable constraints—was an immense achievement, the earliest days of India's electoral democracy were also crucial

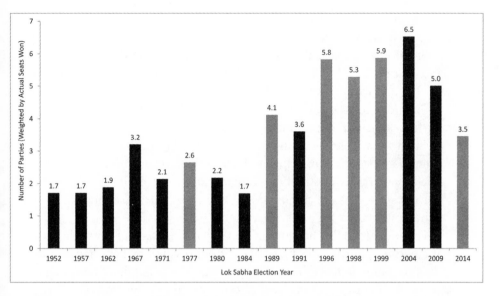

Figure 3.1. Effective number of parties in Lok Sabha elections, 1952–2014. Dark-shaded bars indicate Congress Party rule. (Author's calculations based on data from the Election Commission of India; Sanjay Kumar, "Regional Parties, Coalition Government and Functioning of Indian Parliament: The Changing Patterns," *Journal of Parliamentary Studies* 1, no. 1 [June 2010]: 75–91)

in giving rise to the rapport between crime and politics. Indeed, there is evidence to suggest that parties and politicians were reliant on criminal elements for electoral purposes from the very first elections (and perhaps even before).[21]

"An Act of Faith"

Standard accounts of independent India's first elections in the 1950s are understandably marked by the warm glow of the heady years following India's emancipation from Britain. The period following the British departure saw India tick off a number of crowning achievements: the incorporation of hundreds of princely states (semi-sovereign entities the British never directly controlled) and the unification of what is recognized today as modern India; the successful drafting and ratification of a progressive constitution; and, of course, the execution of India's first general election in 1951–52.

The creation of an independent ECI was enshrined in Article 324 of the constitution, which endowed it with relative independence from political interference. Yet the commission itself existed only on paper and literally had to be constructed from the ground up. In its efforts to plan and carry out India's first elections, the commission was aided by a leader of tremendous capacity in the form of Sukumar Sen, an oft-forgotten but important figure in Indian democracy who served as India's first chief election commissioner.[22] Jawaharlal Nehru, as the country's first prime minister and a true believer in the commission's role in integrating and unifying India, also took it upon himself to bolster the stature of the commission in the early years, granting it ample latitude in organizing polls.[23]

The most readable account of Sen's thankless task of preparing for, and carrying out, India's first elections is provided by historian Ramachandra Guha in his book, *India after Gandhi*. Guha describes in vivid detail the enormity of the task faced by Sen and his colleagues and the extraordinary pressure he was under from Nehru and his government to carry out elections at the earliest possible date. Guha refers to the first general election as "an act of faith"; indeed, Sen himself had described the landmark polls in exactly such terms. The commission's own narrative report reflecting on the 1951–52 general election is an inspiring read, further enhanced by the fact that the report did not come out until 1955, three years after the elections—a testament to the shoestring budget and limited manpower the commission had at its disposal.[24]

The first general election resulted in a landslide victory for the Congress. The party won 364 of 489 seats in Parliament, capturing 45 percent of the vote. The second largest party, the Communist Party of India (CPI), won a paltry 16 seats. Beyond the numerical significance of the victory margin, the successful execution of free and fair elections was of even greater symbolic importance for the fledgling democracy.

Yet India's first landmark election was not without its blemishes; indeed, there were scattered reports of Congress politicians contracting with local strongmen in the very early days of the republic. Politicians allegedly relied on criminal or "antisocial" elements to coerce opponents, mobilize supporters, stuff ballot boxes, distribute clientelistic goods and handouts, and staff election campaigns, among other duties.[25] In the 1951–2 general election, the ECI estimated that roughly

80 polling stations witnessed "minor breaches of law and order" and recorded 1,250 poll "incidents," the vast majority of which (over 65 percent) had to do with the impersonation of voters.[26] Polling was adjourned in 93 cases and had to be resumed at a later date on account of improprieties, ranging from the tampering of ballot boxes to coercive violence.[27] Overall, these were relatively isolated incidents; the polling stations where law and order breaches were reported accounted for less than 1 percent of all polling places.

The Congress System

India's inaugural general election kicked off the first phase of India's electoral politics. Given the role the Congress played spearheading India's independence movement, the party transcended the traditional boundaries that typically circumscribe the role of ordinary political parties. As such, it was accorded a kind of legitimacy that fed a widespread sense in the polity that "only Congress could be trusted" to run the country's affairs.[28] It served as *the* crucial link between the state and the citizenry at large.

While the constitution may have created the legal framework for holding India's raucous democracy together, "the real cement was provided by the Congress."[29] In terms of ideological appeal, Congress functioned as a classic "big tent" political party; it occupied "not only the broad center for the political spectrum, but most of the left and right as well."[30] As such, it left little room for opposition parties to maneuver. Furthermore, Congress was the only political organization in existence that had the ability to reach all four corners of the country.[31] In terms of the degree of its institutionalization, Congress was not only an outlier as far as India was concerned; scholar Steven Wilkinson writes that it was "one of the best-institutionalized political parties in any colony at independence."[32]

To perpetuate its position of preeminence, the "Congress Raj" presided over a top-down brand of politics in which the Congress hierarchy essentially co-opted local notables or "bosses" who could exert power in their local constituencies.[33] This power was derived from multiple sources—economic, social (namely, caste-based or ethnic), as well as coercive in some instances. Congress's extensive local network, coupled with the uniqueness of its principled top-level leadership and the reservoir of nationalist goodwill it enjoyed, allowed it to nurture a heterogeneous social coalition with many contradictory impulses. During this period of dominance, Congress behaved at the ground level like a political machine that one scholar claimed "would have warmed the heart of legendary Chicago Mayor Richard J. Daley"—albeit one that was less organized and coherent.[34]

Despite Congress's catchall appeal and the economic resources its patronage networks could marshal, violence—whether actualized or threatened—did play a minor role. In 1957, the first instances of "booth capturing" were recorded in India. In its most essential form, booth capturing literally refers to the practice of politicians employing physical force to manipulate elections by commandeering polling booths and dictating the vote.

The process of booth capturing involved several steps, beginning with the pre-election contracting of "muscle" by politicians and the procurement and transfer of arms or other weaponry to the contracted muscle. Politicians reportedly exchanged pledges of protection from the state in return for perpetrating electoral fraud. Often the next step in the process involved influencing officials on election duty to strategically place booths in select locations within a candidate's electoral constituency.[35] Sometimes government officials on election duty were also bribed to omit selected names from the voter lists. The day of the election, local "influencers" hired by politicians would mobilize or suppress turnout as needed and engage in the "management" of election booths.[36]

The first recorded instances of alleged booth capturing occurred in the village of Rachiyari in Bihar's Begusarai district, where Congress is believed to have pioneered the use of criminals in the electoral process.[37] It is alleged that a group of upper-caste Bhumihars intimidated Yadav voters in the village so that they could cast votes for their favored candidate on their behalf.[38] Begusarai was the stomping grounds of Kamdev Singh, one of the most notorious criminals-for-hire and a feared gang leader employed by the Congress Party to engage in booth capturing, who rose to political prominence in the 1960s and 1970s.[39]

In Bihar, as in many other parts of rural India, many upper-caste landowners had developed systems of institutionalized coercion and repression that they would wield—often through the hiring of "toughs"—to control peasants who were in their employ.[40] These landowners were often powerful members of the rural elite and formed close alliances with Congress, in which state patronage was exchanged for the votes of villagers beholden to the landlords. This feudal setup was tailor-made for the deployment of muscle during elections.[41]

Over the next several decades, booth capturing evolved to encompass all manner of electoral malpractice and trickery. Such practices included stuffing ballot boxes, employing violence to intimidate voters, locating polling booths in a candidate's stronghold, or simply dividing up control of the booths among rival factions. For instance, booth capturing did not always entail, nor can it be easily reduced to, the use of force. When booth capturing occurred peacefully, typically a dominant caste group (or a group vying for dominance) would prevent voters from rival groups from voting, manage police and polling booth agents, or vote on behalf of disenfranchised voters.[42]

The incentive for the criminals was not just monetary, in terms of payments from politicians and parties to do their bidding; it was also about self-preservation. In exchange for doing the politician's dirty work, criminals received protection from the state and a direct line to state patronage in terms of contracts, tenders, and giveaways.[43] This quid pro quo preserved an equilibrium in which all parties stood to gain, but it was a delicate balancing act—one vulnerable to political shocks.

The Congress System Breaks Down

During the era of Congress hegemony, politicians were firmly in the driver's seat; criminals were the hired guns, and they rarely stood for elections themselves. As electoral competition stiffened and the Congress Party's organizational foundations began to deteriorate, this dalliance started to spread to other parties.

The mid-1960s were a tumultuous period for the Congress, thanks to the disastrous rout India suffered at the hands of China in the 1962 war, ongoing economic woes and concerns over corruption, and the deaths, in quick succession, of Prime Ministers Jawarhalal Nehru in 1964 and Lal Bahadur Shastri in 1966. In the wake of Shastri's death, Nehru's daughter, Indira Gandhi, assumed the prime ministership. Although Indira would come to be remembered as an authoritative, even authoritarian leader, at the time she was perceived to be a figurehead who could be remote-controlled by a group of Congress state bosses (collectively known as the "Syndicate"). In the minds of Congress insiders, Indira was a placeholder—a politician who would appeal to the masses and could capitalize on Nehru's personal legacy but who ultimately would defer to the wishes of the Syndicate on most matters of politics and policy.

It was in this context that Congress suffered a devastating series of political defeats in the states in 1967. While electoral challenges to Congress began much earlier in southern India, northern India was still seen as its impregnable citadel. That perception changed in 1967, as Congress was thrown out of office for the first time in the north Indian heartland states of Bihar and Uttar Pradesh and sustained losses in West Bengal and the southern states of Kerala and Tamil Nadu. By July 1967 two-thirds of the country no longer lived under Congress Party rule.[44] In the national election held that year, Congress too suffered a serious setback. Having won 361 out of 494 seats in the 1962 election, Congress won just 283 out of 520 seats in 1967.

One consequence of the weakening of the Congress machine was a rapid increase in the exercise of sheer political opportunism in the form of political defections—politicians deserting one party to join another.[45] According to one estimate, there were 542 cases of defections between India's first and fourth general elections; in one year alone (1967), more than 438 MLAs (state legislators) defected from one party or another.[46] As a result of this political promiscuity, 32 state governments fell between 1967 and 1971 and as many as half of India's MLAs had changed party affiliations at least once by March 1971. On average, at least one politician changed parties each day and one government fell each month.[47]

The second consequence of a weakened Congress was the influx of individuals connected to criminality into mainstream electoral politics. The resort to criminality was spurred on not just by the fracturing of the vaunted Congress system but also by the widespread organizational decay in the political arena. James Manor, for example, has argued that politicians of all stripes recruited criminals during this period because they could not adequately maintain transactional links to important social groups. As the efficacy of traditional tactics of top-down control gradually diminished, parties struggled to mediate citizen demands in ways that satisfied the desires of voters. With the formal party system exhibiting signs of strain, space opened up for a new set of actors—

namely, local power brokers who were "professional managers" or, simply, fixers—to fill the vacuum. As Rajni Kothari noted, this change in the prevailing political order was no freak accident, but the result of sustained institutional deterioration.[48]

Organizational Decline of Parties

Echoing Samuel Huntington's argument about modernization, Manor further disaggregates the decay into two distinct components: the growing organizational weakness in party structures, and the "demand overload" faced by parties in the face of intense social mobilization and an "awakening" on the part of the lower castes.[49]

The Congress Party's internal organization, which had yielded a string of electoral victories, showed significant signs of strain as genuine multiparty competition intensified and its revered political leadership either passed away or struck out on their own. The party's dominance heavily relied on its ability to distribute the resources it accumulated by controlling the state to its varied constituencies in return for political fealty.[50] As its organizational coherence faded, the party's distributional ability eroded as well. Organizational considerations, intraparty democracy, and party loyalty fell victim to political expediency and "winnability" in a desperate attempt by Congress to maintain its grip on power. As a consequence, Congress increasingly relied on coercive or criminal elements to project some semblance of institutional authority and to prevent challenges from below. Some have gone so far as to suggest that the Congress devolved into a "mercenary organization."[51]

The Congress apparatus, which operated like a well-oiled machine in the years after independence, was badly in need of a tune-up if not an outright overhaul. As the organization foundered, Indira Gandhi ignored calls to right the ship and instead chose to plow ahead. Corruption, internal factionalism, and disputes—both ideological and identity based—gradually came to dominate party affairs, and the internal procedures the party had deployed skillfully in the past to diffuse such tension were no longer up to the task under its new leadership.[52]

While the indiscipline and internal factionalism within the Congress has been well documented,[53] these pathologies were further exacerbated by a leadership, especially during Indira's rule, that sacrificed party building for short-term political expediency. In seeking to establish direct contact with the masses via a populist electoral strategy, Gandhi saw little need to invest in a robust party organization. The resultant decline in party structures led to the "indiscriminate recruitment of dubious activists in the quest for power."[54]

But what was true of Congress could also apply to the emergent opposition, which also demonstrated ample "incapacity to develop solid party structures."[55] Parties across the board grew increasingly detached from concerns of the common man and overly reliant on a single charismatic leader. Of this affliction, scholar K. C. Suri writes: "There cannot be any 'number two' in the party. . . . There is very little scope for disagreement with, or criticism against the party boss. . . . They are like modern princes."[56] Such organizational shortcomings were not unique to Congress but were endemic across the political spectrum.

The second ingredient that contributed to the organizational decline of political parties was the political awakening experienced by those at the bottom of the social pyramid.[57] In India's first electoral system, Congress had impressively managed to defuse the full expression of ethnic and caste identity in politics through its accommodationist proclivities, even though the party itself was thoroughly dominated by individuals belonging to the elite castes. Although the social awakening of the lower castes occurred at different times in different parts of the country, the 1960s witnessed the widespread assertion of the lower castes for greater political voice. This agitation was greatest among the middle peasants (mainly OBCs), many of whom had benefited from land reforms. These groups saw a yawning gap between the economic power they had accumulated since 1947 and that of their political representation.[58] Resentful of this chasm, they were no longer willing to have their "superiors"—the upper castes and the erstwhile landed elites—dictate for whom they should cast their vote.

To some degree, it was only a matter of time before the hodgepodge social coalition underpinning Congress began to sag under the weight of its internal contradictions. Unfortunately, new forms of (largely identity-based) social mobilization, used by both Congress and new electoral competitors, were motivated by short-term political benefits and control over state power rather than programmatic politics. As political scientist Pratap Bhanu Mehta notes, "such mobilizations, instead of throwing up genuine well-organized and disciplined grass roots movements, usually throw up demagogues," resulting in a decline in the quality of political representation.[59]

From the perspective of democratic inclusion, the broadening of political participation and the diffusion of political power was obviously a positive trend. But the newfound assertiveness of previously marginalized communities occasionally morphed into declining deference to established authority structures (which, to be fair, often used repressive tactics) and a willingness to resort to extralegal means in the pursuit of social justice.

Doubling Down on Criminal Elements

The organizational shortcomings exhibited by Congress and rising social assertiveness opened the floodgates to the forging of closer linkages between politicians and criminals. As journalist Prem Shankar Jha writes of Congress, "To win elections party leaders began to rely more and more on musclemen who would physically 'capture' voting booths, stuff the ballot boxes with ballot papers stamped in favour of the candidate who had employed them, intimidate entire caste and community groups, and physically prevent them from going to the polling booth to cast their vote."[60]

Opposition parties resorted to similar strategies in order to counter Congress and break through the barriers that stood between them and state power. Non-Congress opposition parties, often representing lower-caste interests that felt increasingly disenfranchised, were compelled to fight fire with fire, thus further entrenching the competitive recourse to criminality in the political firmament.

The ECI noted in its official report on the 1967 election that the tension that existed prior to the election, involving occasional bursts of violence, was unprecedented in the fifteen years since India's first national election. After relatively calm polls in 1962, the ECI documented violence in several states five years later, which prompted re-polls to be called in several instances. One independent analysis found 474 cases of reported violence in the two months leading up to elections.[61] Bihar alone accounted for around one-fifth of all election violence. While this tally was head and shoulders above the number of incidents documented elsewhere, numerous other states recorded significant amounts of election-related unrest, from Andhra Pradesh and Assam to Madhya Pradesh and Maharashtra.[62] Beyond violence, there is evidence other forms of malfeasance were also on the rise. In Kerala, the commission reported a massive increase in the number of rejected ballot papers—an outcome consistent with rigging—for mysterious reasons that it admitted were "not easy to spot."[63]

In subsequent state elections held in 1968, the commission documented a "comparatively large number of complaints about intimidation and coercion" from the Hindi belt states of Uttar Pradesh and Bihar, the latter of which saw violence sparked by "turbulent mobs" occurring around polling booths.[64] Many analysts point to intensifying electoral violence in the late 1960s as an important inflection point. To explain the changes in, and consolidation of, criminal and political power, one political analyst wrote that following Bihar's assembly election in 1969 winning elections now meant that "the ballot must be backed by the bullet."[65]

DEINSTITUTIONALIZED DEMOCRACY

Following the electoral setback of 1967, simmering tensions within the Congress Party apparatus eventually boiled over. There was tremendous dissension within the leadership ranks as to how the party could right itself after its series of electoral debacles in order to regain its past glory. The rift between the Syndicate and Indira Gandhi further deepened because Indira believed that the prime minister, not the party, should direct the policies of the government. To make matters worse, the two sides also disagreed vehemently as to the content of those very policies, with a left-right ideological disagreement coloring the party's internal deliberations.[66]

These internal disagreements prompted a major split in the Congress Party in 1969. In the aftermath of this division, Indira Gandhi championed a new kind of plebiscitary politics that minimized the role of the party apparatus and established direct links between herself and the voter. After winning a slender majority in 1967 while suffering setbacks and disaffection in several states across the country, Gandhi faced an uphill battle in the 1971 general election. In fact, the 1971 election was actually supposed to be held the following year in 1972; Gandhi called early elections in an effort to nationalize the poll and break the link between state and national elections, which would allow her to minimize the relative influence of state and local factors in the minds of voters. By de-linking state and national elections, Gandhi "was, in effect, asking voters to put aside the performance of state MLAs and even of the individual MPs in serving their constituencies and to vote instead on the basis of national issues."[67] Holding separate elections would also have the effect of vastly increasing the cost of elections (which is discussed in greater detail below).

By lurching markedly to the left in terms of economic policy (campaigning famously on a pledge of *garibi hatao,* or "abolish poverty") and brandishing personalistic appeals (later pithily summed up by Devakanta Barua's quip, "Indira is India and India is Indira"), Gandhi led Congress to a massive victory in 1971. The electoral landslide further emboldened her efforts to convert the party into a cult of personality. In the aftermath of the election, Gandhi acted swiftly and confidently to consolidate her power. For instance, she moved to ensure that Congress state leaders would no longer be selected on the basis of grassroots support, but rather on their personal loyalty to her.[68] Traditionally, following elections in which Congress emerged victorious, each state unit of the Congress Party would propose the name of its chosen chief minister; after 1971, state units simply deferred to the wishes of the "high command," shorthand for Indira herself. In the five years between March 1972 and March 1977, Gandhi dismissed as many as fourteen chief ministers, including twelve from her own party.[69] To facilitate this meddling, Indira Gandhi formally suspended internal elections within the Congress.[70]

In terms of its relations with the states, the Congress-led central government adopted a much more interventionist stance in the 1970s. The Congress under Indira cunningly worked to topple opposition governments, a strategy that further subverted democratic institutions.[71] Under Article 356 of the constitution, the center has the authority to suspend the rule of state governments in exceptional circumstances (such as the collapse of a coalition government) and impose central rule, known as "President's Rule." Under Indira Gandhi, the Congress Party used this provision with abandon in order to shape local political outcomes.[72] In the first fifteen years of the republic (1952–67), the center invoked Article 356 just ten times. In the subsequent nine years from 1968 to 1976, it imposed President's Rule twenty-five times (figure 3.2).[73]

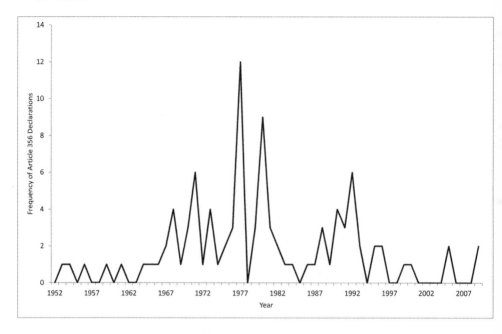

Figure 3.2. Frequency of President's Rule (Article 356), 1952–2009. (Data from Anoop Sadanandan, "Bridling Central Tyranny in India," *Asian Survey* 52, no. 2 [March/April 2012]: 247–69)

Repeated central intervention and the blatant disregard for states' rights would, among other things, plant the seeds for the separatist violence and disorder that India would witness later on in several crucial states.

Entrenched Muscle Power

In a context of increasingly personal rule and mounting social and political tension, the patterns of employing muscle power in elections, which blossomed in the 1960s, became more entrenched in the following decade. According to the Election Commission, the 1971 general election witnessed a significant amount of turbulence. The commission had to order fresh polls in 66 cases where open booth capturing was detected, primarily in Bihar but also in Haryana, Jammu and Kashmir, Nagaland, Orissa, and Uttar Pradesh. The geographic variation should dispel the popular perception that the practice of criminals working hand in glove with politicians was exclusively a Hindi belt phenomenon.

Similar developments were recorded in the eastern state of West Bengal. The 1967 state election in Bengal brought to power a coalition government headed by the Communist Party of India (Marxist)—or CPI(M)—only to be dismissed shortly thereafter by the Congress central government. When fresh elections were called in 1969, the CPI(M) again formed the government, only to be ousted once again by Congress in cahoots with defectors from the ruling coalition.

In both the 1971 general election and the 1972 state election, West Bengal witnessed large-scale political thuggery (often referred to as *goondagiri* in Hindi).[74] Indeed, although the ECI singled out political violence in Bihar, the minister of state in the Home Ministry K. C. Pant told Parliament in April 1971 that Bengal actually topped the list of electoral violence (1,027 discrete incidents, or nearly half of the national total by the ministry's count). Bihar, according to Pant, clocked in at third, "bested" by Tamil Nadu and followed closely by Andhra Pradesh.[75]

Paradoxically, the steps Gandhi took to bolster her own position in the short term helped to weaken and destroy whatever vestiges of party structure and internal democracy Congress still clung to.[76] While Gandhi's tactics had long alienated many within the party, her machinations now manufactured considerable resentment among the populace. Indeed, within a few years, anti-Congress sentiment was once again raging, thanks to the unfulfilled promises of the Indira myth, economic travails, and the rise of a confrontational political movement led by opposition leader Jayprakash Narayan, who called for "total revolution."

Deepening electoral strife, coupled with rising social demands and the decline of Congress and, more generally, political parties, set the stage for a more active role for criminals in politics. Two additional pull factors also contributed to the evolving relationship between crime and politics: the continuing breakdown of law and order and the collapse of the election finance regime.

Centralized Powerlessness

Since the late 1960s in particular, the Indian state's capacity to effectively deliver services, adjudicate disputes, and protect its citizens had badly eroded. For starters, the institutional base that India had inherited from the British, upon which it had further built under Nehru's leadership, could not keep up with India's growing population and social mobilization in the absence of adequate investment or proper care and nurturing from India's political leaders. To make matters worse, in seeking to establish a direct link with the masses, Indira Gandhi sought to stir up mass political mobilization without investing in the "requisite institutional mechanisms to satisfy their demands."[77] The result was a combination of centralization and powerlessness.[78]

Within Congress, ideology and party service were replaced by personal loyalty as the most important selection criteria. Gandhi imported many of the same strategies in dealing with the institutions of governance. Rather than reaffirming the autonomy of the Indian state, she pushed for the civil administration, the police, and the judiciary to be directly answerable to her. As Lloyd and Susanne Rudolph noted, "The independence, professional standards and procedural norms of the Parliament, courts, police, civil service and federal system gave way to centralization based on personal loyalty."[79] The advent of a "committed bureaucracy"—where political neutrality was dismissed in favor of partisan loyalty—greatly weakened the "steel frame" India's rulers inherited from the British.[80]

The deinstitutionalization of the police was of particular relevance to the growing criminalization of politics. The political class's growing reliance on criminals, gangs, and assorted toughs posed a complex quandary for the politicians because they had to find ways of awarding protection to such nefarious characters in exchange for their cooperation. This meant, above all, that the police had to be neutralized. The chosen solution was to ramp up political control of the police and remove any semblance of a firewall between the people making the laws and those actually implementing them. As with other aspects of the state apparatus, India's political leaders decided to prioritize partisanship over professionalism in making appointments.

To be fair, the police had been under great stress even before Indira's time. But the decades of the 1960s and 1970s pushed the force to new lows. Under Indira, one scholar wrote, the police became "deeply involved in partisan politics: they are preoccupied with it, penetrated by it, and now participate individually and collectively in it."[81]

Not all blame should be placed at the door of the central government, however. Under the Indian Constitution, law and order is a state subject so there is considerable scope for regional governments to shape and influence the police. Sadly, state politicians adopted a largely similar stance to the police as the center; many state chief ministers held onto the home ministry portfolio precisely because that ministry has oversight of the police.[82] Across all levels of government, the "substitution of party control of the police for the rule of law became a matter of high policy."[83]

"Mastanocracy"

The breakdown in law and order, and the corresponding politicization of the state apparatus, blurred the line between violence and legitimate democratic tactics. What transpired was nothing less than the partial privatization of the coercive functions of the state.[84] The growth of the Shiv Sena of Bal Thackeray, for instance, took place in this context. In its original incarnation, the Sena was expressly nonpolitical in that it did not participate in elections; it was a nativist social movement premised on the belief that Maharashtra belonged to native Maharashtrians, not migrants from other states.[85] Over time, it morphed into a political organization with statewide appeal. The Sena perfected the art of simultaneously engaging in "institutionalized politics, violent street-level agitation, and informal networking and local brokerage."[86] Earning "respect" through violence was an essential part of the Sena's repertoire; as one MLA told the scholar Thomas Blom Hansen, "Thackeray has told us that you should be polite and talk to the person, but if he does not talk and shows you the law, there is also nature's law and I can use it—that is to hammer the person."[87]

In other parts of the country, like rural north India, caste-based gangs exploited the breakdown in law and order to leverage their ability to serve as effective public goods providers to gain electoral traction.[88] Many of these groups arose in opposition to violent left-wing extremist groups, such as the Naxalites, which the state was unable or unwilling to combat. The Naxalites too had their allied political formations that were highly active in electoral politics.

In West Bengal, growing violence and lawlessness created a situation of "Mastanocracy," or rule of the *mastans* (gangs), which were one part of a larger nexus between thugs, politicians, and the police.[89] Even in the south, which is commonly perceived to be less prone to such thuggery, the decline of India's framework of public institutions led to a discernible rise in the use (and abuse) of "ruffians" in everyday politics.[90] In Kerala, which is an outlier in India on account of its remarkable human development indicators (which are on par with many advanced industrial democracies), violence between Left parties and forces aligned with Congress was openly practiced hand in hand with routine electoral tactics.[91]

In these (and in many other) instances, the police operated in close coordination with criminal groups. Because politicians were deeply involved with both sides, the result was a nexus between the police, politicians, and criminals.

THE DAWN OF "BLACK MONEY"

As the maintenance of law and order began to fray, another pernicious development was also gathering steam: the influx of "black money" into politics. Indeed, the collapse of India's election finance regime, which has to date been somewhat underemphasized, constitutes a fourth pull factor responsible for the entry of criminals in politics.[92]

Rise of Corporate Financing

In its pre-independence incarnation, the Congress Party was primarily financed by membership contributions with supplemental assistance from some of India's big business houses that supported the nationalist struggle. In fact, the close relationships between business titans like G. D. Birla and Mahatma Gandhi have been amply documented. Birla was widely considered to be the "foremost financier of the Congress party [sic] for over two decades before Independence."[93] Notwithstanding such close ties, by most accounts business was responsible for a relatively small segment of the party's overall coffers before 1947.[94]

After independence, Congress—and its competitors—required additional funds to finance costly election campaigns. Under law, there were limits on how much candidates could spend in any given election, although these restrictions were of questionable effectiveness given the limited monitoring capacity of the ECI and ambiguities in the law. Following India's second general election, the commission itself noted that legal loopholes essentially vitiated the de jure campaign finance regime, as "a candidate can easily evade the objectives of the law if he is so inclined."[95]

While membership dues remained the bedrock of party finances in the early post-1947 era, over time they covered a shrinking share of parties' overall outlays, which grew in concert with rising democratic mobilization and political competition. In light of this democratic expansion, "elections could not simply be held, they had to be fought."[96] One scholar estimated that election expenses may have grown as much as tenfold between 1957 and 1962.[97] Politicians, in turn, turned to business with increasing frequency to cover their financial shortfall.[98]

Under the Representation of the People Act, which codified India's election finance regime, corporations could contribute to parties (with a few caveats) as long as they declared their donations. The Congress, befitting its dominance in the early post-1947 period, collected the lion's share of the donations. According to one source, in 1966–67 Congress received more than thirty times as much in corporate contributions as the second largest recipient, the market-friendly Swatantra Party.[99]

The situation came to a head in the late 1960s as Parliament, the courts, and many intellectuals expressed concern that cozy ties between business and politics were unduly influencing the policymaking process. As early as 1964, the government-appointed Santhanam Committee warned of collusion between businessmen and politicians and the resulting adverse implications for India's system of election finance.[100] This, in turn, produced calls to ban corporate donations to parties altogether. Congress, which had been the prime beneficiary of such largesse, stood to lose from such stringent regulation, but Indira Gandhi had several ulterior motives for supporting such a move.

For starters, Indira was deeply suspicious of the power the Syndicate continued to wield in organizing and collecting funds for the party from business. Cutting off the flow of funds would also cut the Syndicate bosses down to size. Second, in the wake of the Congress split in 1969 and Gandhi's move to the ideological left, Indira worried that big business was slowly but surely gravitating toward the conservative faction of Congress as well as to the opposition Jana Sangh and Swatantra Parties.[101] Finally, as a public relations ploy, what better way to blunt calls for cracking down on corruption than to—superficially, at least— appear tough on cronyism in politics?

Ban on Corporate Donations

In 1969, with Indira's blessing, Parliament amended the Companies Act to impose a total ban on corporate giving to political parties. The move was part of a larger attempt to put business in its place and reassert the primacy of the state. In quick succession, Gandhi nationalized India's banks and its domestic coal industry and imposed sweeping new restrictions, such as the Monopolies and Restrictive Trade Practices Act and the Foreign Exchange Regulation Act, on business.[102] In spite of the ban on donations, Indira calculated that big business would still be compelled to donate to Congress even after the ban, albeit covertly, given Congress's ability to discipline businesses that refused to play ball. The aim of the ban, as one author put it, was not to *ensure* the Congress a "secure and above-board source of funds in the future, but to *cut off* the flow of funds to its rivals."[103]

By making corporate donations illegal, Indira essentially eliminated the most important *legal* source of funds for elections. Without providing an alternative campaign finance mechanism (such as state funding), Gandhi's decision—far from abolishing the link between business and politics—effectively pushed campaign finance underground.

The ban, combined with new restrictions on business, led to the proliferation of black money in the political system. Indeed, the period after 1969 came to be known—in the memorable words of Stanley Kochanek—as the era of "briefcase politics."[104] The intensified License Raj policies that placed strict controls on private business activity helped spur the creation of a parallel economy, in which undocumented money sloshed around with the hope of evading detection, as firms sought to avoid high taxes and circumvent overregulation.[105] They also provided a new and useful lever for government to trade permissions, licenses, and clearances in exchange for under-the-table campaign donations.[106] One of Indira Gandhi's biographers later noted that "donation" was actually a euphemism for extortion; there was a clear quid pro quo in which businesses were threatened with stiff penalties if they failed to comply with the demands of Congress bagmen.[107] The situation had deteriorated to such an extent that "ministers deliberately talked publicly about nonexistent government plans to nationalize or regulate a particular industry or trade with the intention of creating nervousness" among the private firms concerned.[108] To avert such a possibility, firms reluctantly opened up their wallets.

The long-term consequence of Gandhi's short-sighted decision to ban corporate donations was to set parties off on a competitive search for underground financing, which further drove them into the embrace of individuals and organizations of "dubious character, including a very large number of extortionists and racketeers."[109] In one fell swoop, the move greatly empowered criminal networks and entrepreneurs who were major players in the growing black economy and had the means to readily aggregate and distribute cash without detection.[110] "The bigger the criminal, the more black money he had, the more he gave to the party, the greater his influence," wrote one observer.[111] In short order, "lawbreakers of all sorts entered into a special relationship with the political leaders of Congress and progressively all other political parties."[112] The push toward black financing was further given a boost by a 1975 legislative change that formally excluded third party spending from the limits placed on candidates (although in practical terms, this had been going on for many years).[113]

Relegalization: Too Little, Too Late

Many years later, recognizing the folly of Indira Gandhi's decision to ban corporate contributions, the Congress government of Rajiv Gandhi amended the Companies Act in 1985 to once again legalize corporate giving. Unfortunately, the damage had already been done. In the intervening years, corporations had grown accustomed to providing donations "in the black" and even came to value the benefit of such contributions since incumbents could easily use the state's discretionary authority to punish a firm that had donated to a political rival. Keeping donations secret allowed firms to play their cards close to their chest, protecting themselves from possible political retribution. The intricate system of black money contributions "had become so entrenched that there was no incentive for business groups to come above board."[114]

There is evidence to suggest that Rajiv Gandhi was genuine in his desire to reform India's corrupt political system. In a famous speech delivered at an event commemorating the centenary of the Congress Party, he lambasted the state of the party and the cronyism it both initiated and helped to perpetuate. "We talk of the high principles and lofty ideals needed to build a strong and prosperous India. But we obey no discipline, no rule, follow no principle of public weal. Corruption is not only tolerated but even regarded as the hallmark of leadership. Flagrant contradiction between what we say and what we do has become our way of life."[115]

Unfortunately, there was a large gap between Rajiv Gandhi's rhetoric and reality. Under his leadership, Congress operatives further innovated in their attempts to obtain new sources of political finance that could supplement whatever funds could be gathered by shaking down domestic businesses. The opening of the Indian economy in the 1980s and 1990s not only had salutary effects on the domestic growth rate but also brought renewed interest in the Indian market from foreign multinational firms as the number of contracts eligible for foreign bidding grew. Foreign interests, eager to gain a foothold in India's vast market, became a much sought after source for "donations." In fact, one report suggests that domestic business titans were initially quite perplexed as to why the demand for political contributions appeared to be in decline. The answer, it seemed, was that parties were rushing to take advantage of new opportunities to raise money from abroad.[116] Foreign side payments had the added benefit of circumventing the Indian financial system entirely and thus rendering detection much more difficult.

CHANGING OF THE GUARD

As the electoral process became more hazardous and the relationship between money and politics grew more opaque, a qualitative shift in the relationship between criminals and politicians occurred in the mid to late 1970s, during the heyday of Indira Gandhi. The Congress Party's reliance on muscle power had made criminal entrepreneurs an "integral element of political control" in many parts of the country.[117] By the end of the 1970s, those who had previously engaged in criminal activity on behalf of politicians now decided to directly contest elections, no longer content to concede the spotlight to traditional party elites.

Existing narratives about why this switch took place do not fully explain why. The pull factors identified in the previous sections were clearly important pieces of the overall story, as was the politically traumatic nearly two-year period of emergency rule between 1975 and 1977. But an important push factor—which I call "vertical integration"—has not been adequately explored.

The Black Box of Existing Explanations

A typical example of the vague narrative summarizing the shifting power dynamics between criminals and politicians comes from a commission established by the government of India to review the functioning of the country's political system. The commission's report, issued in 2001, states: "A stage has now [been] reached when the politicians openly boast of their criminal connections. . . . Earlier in the 1960s, the criminal was only content to play . . . second fiddle to the politician to enable him [to] win the election and in turn to get protection from him. The roles have now reversed. It is the politician now, who seeks protection from the criminals. The latter seek direct access to power and become legislators and ministers."[118]

Numerous accounts highlight a similar shift but stop short of providing a fully developed explanation for the change. For instance, Robert Hardgrave and Stanley Kochanek discuss how politicians in India in the past would recruit *goondas* (thugs) in order to gain electoral advantage. Yet, after a point, criminals themselves occupied center stage; "the nexus among politicians, local police, bureaucrats, and criminals has in fact 'criminalized' politics," they write. "In some constituencies, where once the politicians hired the goondas, the goondas have become the politicians."[119] In both popular discourse and the scholarly literature regarding India, politicians associated with criminal activity are often referred to as *goondas*. In truth, *goonda* does not quite capture the figure of the criminal politician; a more apt name (in Hindi) is *dada*, a figure who operates more like a "godfather" or leader of *goondas*. While many criminals may have started out as *goondas*, by the time they possess real political power they have morphed into *dadas*.[120]

Former top civil servant S. S. Gill has argued that the entry of criminals into politics "was a logical corollary of using them to gain political power. If the criminals could put others in power, they were bound to use the same violent methods to get into positions of power themselves." To this end, he quotes a state-level politician with criminal ties who captures this evolution nicely: "Those whose feet we used to touch, are now touching our feet. We captured booths for them, now we are in power."[121]

The Emergency

Most, if not all, accounts suggest that one key triggering event that may have helped tip the balance of power was the brief period of emergency rule. In 1975, the president of India—acting on the advice of Indira Gandhi—declared a state of emergency, which suspended the constitution and centralized an unprecedented degree of power in the hands of the prime minister and, by extension, a small group of political and bureaucratic insiders. The Emergency, which lasted less than two years, involved curbs on freedom of expression, arbitrary detention and arrest, overt political pressure on the judiciary, and the further politicization of the state and represented the nadir of political sycophancy within the Congress.[122]

The Emergency was in many ways the culmination of a decades-long process of hollowing out of the state apparatus. The debasement of state authority and the politicization of virtually every tier of government further infused politics with individuals harboring criminal ties. As the internal democratic structures of the Congress were progressively eliminated, the party began to resemble a pyramid-like organization responsible only to the very top. Loyalty to Indira and Sanjay Gandhi (Indira's younger son and closest political adviser) took precedence over all other criteria.[123] It was during the height of the emergency period that a raft of political cronies tied to Congress—less charitably described as *goondas* and linked especially with Sanjay—became important power brokers in the party. This brief period saw the sharp rise of what came to be called "Sanjay culture" in India, which refers to the young Gandhi's induction of many criminals and thugs into positions of leadership in the Congress.[124] Over time, it has become shorthand for the marriage of crime and politics.

Congress was voted out of office in 1977 after Indira called surprise elections and brought an end to the Emergency, but it would once again climb to power in 1980 following the collapse of the brief rule by the Janata government. Congress underwent another split following the

Emergency with the largest faction renamed Congress(I); the "I" stood for "Indira"—a telling detail about the state of the party.

Although politics was churning at a rapid clip, the shift of criminals to the forefront of politics gained unstoppable momentum.[125] The Emergency may well have served as a proximate trigger for a more direct incorporation of criminals in the electoral mainstream. But this brief nondemocratic interregnum came on the heels of trends that had been building up for many years. Furthermore, the Emergency itself does not adequately explain why criminals felt the need to become politicians themselves, having toiled successfully in the service of politicians for several decades.

Vertical Integration

To understand what propelled this change in strategy among criminals, it is important to look at the human motivations that pushed them more squarely into the electoral domain. Returning to the marketplace analogy, I argue that criminals adopted a strategy of "vertical integration," a concept popularized by the Nobel economist Oliver Williamson. Vertical integration refers to the "substitution of internal organization for market exchange," or the merging together of two businesses that are at different stages of production.[126] Think, for example, of an auto manufacturer that decides to make its own tires in-house rather than contract with a third party to manufacture them.

When do firms operating in a competitive marketplace typically seek to vertically integrate their operations? According to Williamson, when markets work well, there is typically little need for firms to prefer internal supply to the external contracting of goods and services. But when markets fail to work efficiently—for example, when contracts are incomplete, ambiguous, or lack finality—firms might shift production in-house, thus vertically integrating. It turns out that this is roughly the position criminals working with politicians in India found themselves in during the 1970s.

When Congress was the dominant player in Delhi and in the states, there was little doubt about which party would be returned to power once elections were over. Of course, there was electoral competition in most parts of the country, but there were few viable players other than

Congress. Thus, from a criminal's perspective, working as an agent for hire for Congress made eminent sense. Criminals demanded money and protection in exchange for helping politicians with their work during the height of election season and were virtually guaranteed employment for the next go-round after their candidate was elected. In other words, Congress could credibly commit to upholding its political contracts, and criminals were accordingly rewarded after the election.

However, incentives began to shift once the era of Congress hegemony gave way to greater fragmentation. Between 1951 and 1966, incumbent state governments were virtually guaranteed reelection; during this fifteen-year period, the incumbent reelection rate stood at 85 percent. As a result, there was a semblance of political stability and predictability in electoral markets. That changed in subsequent decades: between 1967 and 1979, incumbents won reelection just 54 percent of the time.[127]

At this stage, criminals faced a complex dilemma. Thanks to the uncertainty stemming from greater electoral competition, they were no longer able to rest easy knowing that the party that employed them would remain in power. Congress was, in other words, no longer the only game in town. This shift drastically increased the uncertainty associated with contract negotiations. In the event that Congress lost an election, a criminal in the employ of the party would have to negotiate a new "contract" with the party in power and would be at an obvious bargaining disadvantage. Alternatively, the criminal could try to negotiate multiple contracts with parties, but this would, if nothing else, complicate decision making. The danger, of course, was that the criminal would be left out in the cold, vulnerable to the retributive whims of the state that he had previously been protected from. Any *ex ante* promises of protection were now "too tenuous to guarantee their safety."[128]

The pursuit of protection was a crucial objective for aspiring criminal politicians. Candidates charged with engaging in illegal activity first sought elected office because they feared the reach of the state, and politics offered a promising mechanism for evading prosecution. While politicians in India do not have formal immunity from criminal prosecution, officeholders can rely on the trappings of office to delay or derail justice, such as the power to transfer public officials.[129] In the words of the Supreme Court of India, the slow motion of justice "becomes much slower when politically powerful or high and influential persons figure as accused."[130]

The protection criminally linked candidates seek is not only from the state—in some cases it is from their rivals. The politicization of state institutions means that the state does not act as an entirely neutral arbiter. This lack of impartiality allows politicians to manipulate the state according to their whims, leaving those outside government vulnerable to state crackdown. In pockets of the country, there is anecdotal evidence that some criminal politicians contest elections where their rivals have decided to do the same, reducing elections in these constituencies to a choice between rival criminal politicians.[131]

In the wake of uncertainty prompted by chaotic "client-shifting," a rational solution to this challenge was for criminals to move from outsourcing political protection to doing it in-house. In other words, the solution rested in becoming politicians themselves. By directly contesting elections, criminals could reduce the uncertainty associated with negotiating (and renegotiating) contracts with politicians, all the while retaining the benefits they had previously depended on Congress to deliver.

Bypassing politicians and directly contesting elections was a natural response by criminals not only to political market failures but also to obvious status concerns. Many politically savvy criminals eventually realized that, having worked in the service of politicians to win elections, they had accumulated enough local notoriety to contest elections directly. Over time, criminals had acquired a considerable amount of social capital as a result of their ethnic bona fides, their reputation as fixers, their access to resources, and their roots within local communities. This social capital gave criminal entrepreneurs useful leverage they could now exploit in the political realm.[132]

The alleged gangster Ashok Samrat, who contested elections in north Bihar, summed it up best: "Politicians make use of us for capturing the polling booths and for bullying the weaker sections. . . . But after the elections they earn the social status and power and we are treated as criminals. Why should we help them when we ourselves can contest the elections, capture the booths and become MLAs and enjoy social status, prestige and power? So I stopped helping the politicians and decided to contest the elections."[133]

Once the vertical integration process took hold, it was difficult for it to be undone. Criminals now had both the status and the power; having invested in building up their local electoral machinery, they found that the costs of reversal far outweighed the benefits, particularly as electoral uncertainty further intensified.

If criminals decided to take the electoral plunge and become full-fledged politicians in their own right, it begs the question: why did criminals-cum-politicians tie up with political parties rather than strike out on their own and contest elections as independents? There are several possible answers. For starters, although party labels in India possess very little programmatic content, parties are still connected to distinct leaders, families, ethnic groups, and social bases. Aspiring candidates can tap into these networks to expand their appeal beyond their own narrow support bases. Although political parties may not have clearly distinct views on, say, the welfare state, that does not mean that party labels are devoid of meaning. It is entirely possible that these labels also have some normative appeal for potential candidates as well.

Second, in a country with high rates of poverty and illiteracy, party symbols hold great weight; they serve as an important visual cue through which millions of voters connect to electoral politics. As such, the historical legacy of parties matters a great deal in Indian democracy. To this day, many voters support Congress, for instance, because their families have done so since the days of the independence struggle. The available evidence suggests that the party imprimatur remains vital for maintaining electoral relevance. Of the 4,300 MPs elected between 1977 and 2014, a mere 1.4 percent (or 82 in total) were independent candidates. Given that independents accounted for over 56 percent of all candidates, their lack of electoral success is even more striking.[134]

WAGGING THE DOG

In the post-Emergency period, a whole class of hired agents who once served politicians now *were* the politicians. "Gone are the days when the gangsters were a pawn in the hands of politicians. The position is practically reversed today," wrote one observer. "It is no longer the dog that wags the tail but the tail that is wagging the dog."[135] Examples of the role reversal abound. As one scholar notes, "The criminalization process cuts across various states, political parties and ideologies."[136]

In Bihar, Suryadeo Singh was once a powerful mafia leader who ran a protection racket in Dhanbad, the hub for India's coal mafia. Singh and his associates successfully captured the state-controlled coal mining operations in the region through a combination of luck, grit, political connections, and sheer coercive power.[137] By virtue of his position, Singh became a key financier for the Janata Party, but he eventually outgrew this limited role. In 1977, Singh won assembly elections on a Janata Party ticket and became a close confidant of Chandrashekhar, who later went on to serve briefly as prime minister.[138] In 1984, Singh was the Janata Party candidate in the Lok Sabha election and a sitting member of the Bihar legislative assembly. At the time of the election, he faced no fewer than 17 murder charges, and the state police deemed him to be too dangerous to let him set foot in his home district.[139] He was arrested in 1988 on charges of murder, rioting, and extortion but was later released. The man who put him in jail, the deputy commissioner of Dhanbad, was not so lucky. For the crime of incarcerating Singh, he was promptly transferred from his post.[140]

Around the time Arun Gawli shot to political prominence in Mumbai, scores of small-time crooks and gangsters employed by politicians emerged as politicians in their own right across Mumbai and the state of Maharashtra. Although the connection between organized crime and political parties in Mumbai began in the late 1970s, propelled by a lucrative smuggling racket, this fusion broke new ground with the rise of the Shiv Sena.[141] In the words of one close observer: "The popularity of *sainiks* [foot soldiers/volunteers] as brokers and protectors owes much to their image of being violent, ruthless, aggressive defenders of the common man by means of employing the common man's only strength—his strength in numbers—and his language—fists and muscles—in order to assert his rights vis-à-vis the establishment."[142] Not surprisingly then, "several well-established gangsters, major slumlords, and *dadas* ran on a Shiv Sena ticket" in the 1980s and 1990s.[143]

In Gujarat, another son of the textile chawls was enjoying a similar rise to prominence in the 1980s. The infamous bootlegger Abdul Latif (known simply as "Don Latif") operated in urban Ahmedabad, running a crime syndicate—financed by illicit liquor smuggling—that doubled as a Muslim protectorate in the ethnically tense metropolis. Gujarat was, and is, a dry state, making liquor a prized commodity. Politicians, including at least one former chief minister of Gujarat, Chimanbhai Patel, reportedly protected Latif from the law in exchange for support from the city's Muslim community and illicit cash infusions.[144] After the communal riots of 1985, Latif and his associates organized an emergency social services network to assist the rehabilitation of Muslim riot victims.[145] Latif, armed with dirty money, then traded on his image as a social worker to catapult into mainstream politics. In jail on charges of inciting riots, Latif contested and won election to five separate wards in the city's 1987 municipal poll.[146] To the police, Latif was an antisocial element, but to his poor, urban constituents, he was a local Robin Hood, who stood ready to assist the unemployed, parents who could not provide dowries, or widows who lost their husbands.[147]

In southern Andhra Pradesh, as the case of YSR illustrated, political competition took place not between parties but between gang-like factions.[148] One notorious "factionist" who emerged from this milieu was Paritala Ravi.[149] Inspired by the Naxalite insurgency, Ravi's family was actively involved in resisting the landed aristocracy in southern Andhra. After Ravi's father illegally occupied the property of a well-known landlord with Congress ties, he was brutally hacked to death, triggering a bitter dispute between the opposing families that would play out over the next several decades and would eventually claim the lives of two generations of family members on both sides.[150]

The two sides left no stone unturned in their attempts to exterminate one another, planting bombs in cars, ice cream carts, and even televisions in order to gain the upper hand.[151] Ravi went underground and joined the Naxalites. He soon emerged as one of the most powerful leaders in the region, a self-made faction leader, distinguishing him from the many feudal landlords who held sway in this part of Andhra. Along the way, Ravi accumulated 54 serious criminal cases, 16 of which involved murder; it was for good reason that he was once described as "the most feared person in Anantapur district."[152] In 1994, the Telugu Desam Party (TDP) recruited Ravi to run for office.[153] Ravi won handily and was immediately made a minister in the state government. Ravi would repeat his electoral victories in 1999 and 2004, winning his three elections with an average of 63 percent of the vote. Shortly after securing reelection in 2004, Ravi was brutally murdered, gunned down in broad daylight on the steps of the TDP party office in Anantapur.[154]

Post-Emergency Fallout

The criminal-to-candidate transition was accompanied by a marked increase in the incidence of coercive violence around elections. The 1980 Lok Sabha election brings this out clearly. During the brief two-year period of Janata rule following the Emergency, Sanjay Gandhi allegedly mobilized a corps of pro-Congress "storm-troopers and street-fighters" to stymie the Janata government. By the time of the general election, Sanjay made sure that the most loyal among these *goondas* were given tickets to contest elections in exchange for their services while the party was in opposition.[155] The election in Uttar Pradesh, Sanjay's home turf, proved a perfect opportunity for the Congress scion to put this motley crew to work. Sanjay Gandhi's antics in the 1980 election helped crystallize earlier trends that heralded closer cooperation between crime and politics: "Politics became attractive to those unscrupulous enough to subvert, by corruption and violence, the procedures and institutions designed to protect civility and a government of laws."[156] The new recruits into the party, handpicked by Sanjay, were "often young men on the make, of dubious provenance, some with criminal records"—all of whom professed a loyalty to the Gandhi family rather than any Congress ideology.[157]

As troubling as Sanjay's antics were, Congress was hardly the only party willing or able to play dirty. One journalistic account of the 1980 election in western Uttar Pradesh found "electoral fraud, perpetrated in practically every constituency" in the region.[158] "Though rigging is nothing new" in the area, the author wrote, "the scale of unbridled rigging and booth capturing" carried out by all three major parties in the election was "unprecedented." The election machinery was thoroughly cowed by antisocial elements; as one polling officer explained, he was given two choices by local *goondas:* "milk with cream" (offered to a guest) or "milk with turmeric" (typically offered to an injured person to heal wounds).[159] From north Bihar, another correspondent wrote that "elections in this region rank amongst the premier cottage industries . . . as democracy recedes into smudgy limbo" and the "local brand of intrigue-ridden and caste-based hooliganism appears in sharper focus as a political reality." In sum, the 1980 election was a "contest of muscle, social status and male dominance."[160]

Just four years later, as India went to the polls following the assassination of Prime Minister Indira Gandhi, the ECI reported that polling in 264 polling stations (across 53 constituencies) was "vitiated" due to factors such as "miscreants scaring away polling personnel, snatching away ballots papers/ballot boxes, rigging, prevention of voters belonging to weaker sections from reaching polling stations," among others.[161] Unfortunately, the ECI ceased publishing detailed, narrative reports on elections after the 1984 poll. Yet it is possible to piece together a picture from more recent elections on the basis of what other scholars have documented.

Booth capturing was said to have reached "serious proportions" in at least twelve states in the 1989 Lok Sabha election, particularly in Andhra Pradesh, Bihar, and Uttar Pradesh.[162] Whereas re-polls (due to improprieties) took place in only 65 booths during the 1957 election, that number shot up to 1,670 in 1989. Bihar on its own saw 1,046 re-polls in 1991 and another 1,273 in 1996. As one MLA stated at the time, "Unless you have one hundred men with guns you cannot contest elections in Bihar."[163] The rise in politically motivated murders was also astonishing. In the 1984 parliamentary election, 33 people were killed in Bihar, as were 28 others in state elections that year. In state elections in 1985, another 63 people were murdered in the run-up to the polls. In the difficult 1989 general election, Bihar witnessed 60 election-related deaths.[164]

According to a police report obtained by the newsmagazine *India Today,* there were 35 MLAs in the state of Uttar Pradesh (out of a house of 425) with criminal records in 1984. This number grew to 50 in 1989 and more than doubled to 133 in 1991. By 1993, there were 148 MLAs who either had run-ins with the law in the past or were wanted by the police for harboring connections with mafia groups. This number grew modestly to 152 in 1996; a pre-election report assembled by the Uttar Pradesh police stated that there were upwards of 55 gangs in the state patronized by political parties ahead of the polls.[165] By 2002, the tally stood at 207 (while the overall strength of the house actually declined to 403).[166] The number of criminally suspect legislators dipped in 2007 before rebounding in 2012, when their number stood at 181 (figure 3.3).

The scope of the problem was so immense that the government of India commissioned Home Secretary N. N. Vohra to conduct a study into the growing crime-politics nexus. While Vohra's 1993 report was never publicly disclosed, a leaked summary provides the gist of the

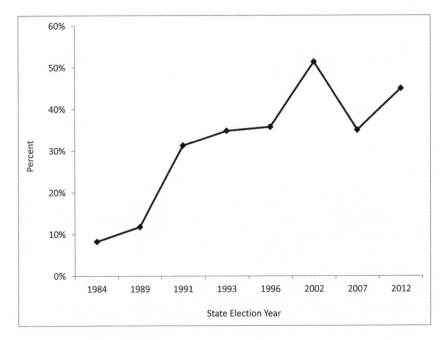

Figure 3.3. Uttar Pradesh MLAs with pending criminal cases, 1984–2012. (Data from Association for Democratic Reforms; Subhash Mishra, "A Criminal Record," *India Today*, November 1, 2004)

report. The report pulls no punches in assessing the magnitude of the criminalization of politics:

> There has been a rapid spread and growth of criminal gangs, armed senas, drug Mafias, smuggling gangs, drug peddlers and economic lobbies in the country which have, over the years, developed an extensive network of contacts with the bureaucrats/Government functionaries at the local levels, politicians, media persons and strategically located individuals in the non-State sector. In certain States, like Bihar, Haryana and UP, these gangs enjoy the patronage of local level politicians, cutting across party lines and the protection of governmental functionaries. Some political leaders become the leaders of these gangs/armed senas and, over the years, get themselves elected to local bodies, State Assemblies and the national Parliament. Resultantly, such elements have acquired considerable political clout.[167]

In September 1997, India's chief election commissioner publicly declared that, of the nearly 14,000 candidates in the fray in the 1996 general election, about 1,500 candidates possessed criminal records of one sort of another. More than half of the total came from just two states—Bihar and Uttar Pradesh—but many other large states, such as Andhra Pradesh and Maharashtra, were also well represented. It was later reported in the media that at least 40 MPs with criminal records actually emerged victorious, while an additional 700 MLAs (out of 4,120) from the various state assemblies were under criminal scrutiny.[168]

Adaptation to the Marketplace

Paradoxically, at the same time that the number of suspected criminals standing for elections rapidly grew, the frequency and intensity of electoral malpractice began to suddenly reverse course. According to one source, the number of violent incidents declined from 3,363 in 1991 to 2,450 in 1998, and the number of deaths linked to elections dropped from 272 in 1991 to 65 in 1998 and 32 in 1999.[169]

The improvement in the sanctity of polls is due in large measure to the reassertion of authority by the ECI. The commission's resurgence was part and parcel of a larger trend, which saw the reinvigoration of "referee" institutions that place restraints on the exercise of political power. As Devesh Kapur has observed, referee institutions (such as the CAG, ECI, and the presidency) were allowed space to regenerate precisely because India's fragmented politics prevented any one party from dominating the political space. Faced with such a reality, most parties found it in their self-interest to have a credible umpire to keep an eye on its rivals, even if that meant submitting to greater scrutiny.[170]

In reinvigorating its regulatory authority to curb the worst of India's poll-related excesses, leadership would also prove crucial, especially that of the hardheaded T. N. Seshan. In the early to mid 1990s, Seshan infused the role of India's chief election commissioner with the missionary zeal of a democratic crusader, seized with the fear that ordinary Indians were losing faith in the institution of the Election Commission specifically and the democratic process in general. Since the early 1960s, the Election Commission had tried to get parties and politicians to abide by a "Model Code of Conduct," a voluntary set of principles meant to guide the conduct of candidates, parties, and incumbent governments during election time, with little success.[171]

By dint of his personality, Seshan transitioned from championing the code to actually implementing it, leveraging the moral voice of the commission and the reach of the news media to publicly shame politicians and parties who crossed him. In addition to reinvigorating the model code, the commission also took a number of complementary steps to safeguard the electoral process, from switching from paper ballots to electronic voting machines less susceptible to capture, to coordinating with the Home Ministry to deploy security forces to protect polling booths, and to enhancing local-level surveillance and monitoring capacity through the creative use of technology.[172]

As successful as the Seshan-led crackdown on electoral malpractice was, it failed to eliminate criminality in politics; rather, it merely altered its outward manifestation. As booth capturing and brazen intimidation at the polling booth declined, criminal politicians adapted their operating procedures accordingly. This is important to note because, as is discussed in greater detail later, criminality in politics cannot be reduced to coercion or the perpetration of violence alone. In many cases, these may be manifestations of the criminalization of politics, but it would be inaccurate to conclude that candidates with criminal reputations only win elections by virtue of violent antidemocratic acts.

As overt forms of violence receded in elections, the role of money in politics grew exponentially in the 1990s, thanks, in part, to the increasing competitiveness of elections. Criminals had an advantage in this regard because they had both greater access to funds and the means to raise them (more on this in the following chapter). Thus, while criminals became less reliant on overt uses of force, they (and the parties that supported them) doubled down on the use of "money power" in elections. Indeed, a survey of more than 200 MLAs from five states conducted in 1996 found that 82 percent believed politics was more corrupt than before; 68 percent stated that the situation will get worse in the future, and—ironically—these politicians held "politicians" themselves most responsible for this bleak outlook.[173]

Another reason criminals were able to adapt to the new realities imposed by the Election Commission is because they became integrated with the state apparatus over time. They soon had other levers of power with which to shape politics and election outcomes other than resorting to fraud or employing outward expressions of force or malpractice. In addition, there were limits on how far the writ of the Election

Commission could travel. As one villager once told me in Bihar on the eve of that state's 2010 election, "The Election Commission may control the polling booths, but it is not present in the villages." This lack of overarching institutional oversight implied that politicians freely do a number of things to influence elections, including intimidating voters in their localities, distributing money, or sending more subtle signals of force and power. As K. Balagopal has written, threats made in advance of the election can be cashed in once elections are over, by which time Seshan and his colleagues are back in Delhi, and their jurisdiction over local circumstances is nil.[174]

As discussed in Chapter 1, by 2014 the extent of criminality in the Lok Sabha and the various state assemblies reached record levels. And suffice it to say that the nexus of crime and politics is alive and well in India, notwithstanding the efforts by the Election Commission to tackle some of the most brazen forms of electoral malpractice and violence.

Three Routes for the Criminalization of Politics

Thus far, I have treated the recruitment of criminals into politics as synonymous with the criminalization of politics. To be fair, this approach is an oversimplification, and it is worth briefly discussing why. The "criminalization of politics" actually describes three distinct, albeit related, political processes. The first is what has been covered thus far: individuals who initially gained notoriety as criminals but who eventually entered the electoral domain and became entrenched within the contemporary party system.

The criminalization of politics also entails a second process, which is when individuals who had no previous ties to illegality resort to such activity in order to obtain or preserve political power. This trajectory is, anecdotally, quite common. Such individuals were first and foremost politicians but later developed links with criminals or obtained serious criminal records of their own because they became corrupted by the system or desired an advantage over their opponents. Typically, these politicians developed connections to criminals who could be a source of election finance and/or contracted with muscle power to further a political or electoral objective. While such officials entered office free of any criminal associations, the positions they held precipitated their involvement with criminals and other unsavory elements. The difference between this pathway and the standard narrative of parties recruiting "criminals" is that while politicians may have developed criminal ties or picked up serious criminal cases, this development occurred *after* joining politics.

The third and final process contributing to the criminalization of politics is the wholesale conversion of criminal organizations into political entities. Here, criminal groups or gangs that were not previously electorally focused transformed themselves into political parties in order to capture power. This pathway is unique and quite rare. Political scientist James Manor cites the Shiv Sena of Maharashtra as the only such organization to have attained widespread electoral success.[175]

However, there are several other examples of smaller players making this jump. In Bihar, leaders of the Ranvir Sena, a militia formed to protect the interests of the upper-caste, landed Bhumihar community, joined electoral politics in the 1980s to further the agenda of their caste group, which at its core was to perpetuate their centuries-old social dominance in south and central Bihar and to defend itself against violent Naxal attacks. Leaders of the militia openly fused violent tactics and electoral politics in an effort to consolidate support from the Bhumihars and allied groups, counteracting lower-caste communities who opposed them through intimidation. While the Ranvir Sena did not form its own party, it built alliances with existing formations. The precise partisan affiliations mattered little; both the militia leaders and the political operators were driven by sheer opportunism. Given their political clout, members of the Ranvir Sena came to function as "subcontractors hired by the political and administrative wings of the state to enforce the dominance of the state" in society."[176]

Another example comes from neighboring Uttar Pradesh, where Afzal Ansari, one of the six temporarily sprung MPs who was brought to vote on the no-confidence motion in Parliament in the summer of 2008, and his brother Mukhtar Ansari launched a political party in 2010 known as Quami Ekta Dal (QED). The Ansari brothers are influential politicians in the eastern region of Uttar Pradesh known as Purvanchal, a swath of northern India that has been the stage of a violent struggle between rival gangs, each headed by a politician. The Ansaris are said to control one of the most influential factions, who openly (and often violently) feud over lucrative contract work, known as *thekadari*.[177]

In the past, the brothers cycled through both the Bahujan Samaj Party and the Samajwadi Party, the two biggest regional parties in Uttar Pradesh, until their alleged criminal exploits began to create headaches for the party leadership. The siblings responded by launching their own party; Afzal acts as party president, and Mukhtar and another brother, Sibgatullah, serve as MLAs in the Uttar Pradesh assembly.[178] "If someone calls me a 'mafia don,' it makes no difference," Mukhtar told the author Patrick French. "Can they name one person I have attacked who comes from a weaker section? I have always fought against the powerful, I have taken power from them."[179] In another interview, Ansari put it this way: "Anyone I killed got what they deserved but it's not like I killed a boatload of people. . . . If anyone troubles the poor, I will murder them."[180]

Although these three pathways are analytically distinct, the underlying factors discussed here to explain the criminalization of politics still pertain—although the precise sequence of events varies somewhat in each.

THE ORIGIN OF SUPPLY

The nexus of crime and politics, far from a product of the recent past, has deeply historical roots in India. It is the present balance of forces between criminals and politicians, where the two identities have become thoroughly fused, that is of more recent vintage.

Although the fusion of crime and politics often gets discussed as a purely north Indian phenomenon, it has far more diverse roots. Clearly, north India does boast a fair amount of criminality in politics, but the phenomenon extends to most parts of the country. One reason for this geographic stereotyping might have to do with the outsized influence of Bollywood, the hub of Hindi-medium cinema. But, in fact, *goondagiri* is a recurring theme across linguistic and cultural settings.[181]

This chapter has outlined the first step in understanding the electoral marketplace for criminals: the motivations of criminals to join active politics. But the supply of criminals into politics cannot be reduced to the decisions of these individuals alone, for this leaves out the calculations of a key intervening actor: political parties. The next chapter will review their role in injecting supply into the marketplace.

4   The Costs of Democracy
How Money Fuels Muscle in Elections

"IT IS TOO hot for campaigning, sir," the aide explained. "We will take our lunch and then try again in the late afternoon." It was 104 degrees in the shaded area of the porch where I was sitting and the aide's words provided a welcome reprieve.[1]

Elections were only two weeks away in this predominantly rural constituency located in the southern state of Andhra Pradesh.[2] On this particularly scorching day, I had come to spend some time with a candidate who was standing for elections to the Andhra state assembly. Due to the relentless heat this time of year, candidates would visit constituents first thing in the morning before breaking around ten or eleven, at which point the sun's glare became unbearable. They would resume again in the late afternoon, when the worst had passed, and stay out as late as their bodies could stand it before collapsing.

Fortunately for me, I was scheduled to accompany the candidate in his well-air-conditioned SUV for his afternoon and evening engagements. The candidate, whose identity I agreed not to reveal but will call "Sanjay," was a newcomer to politics. Sanjay was well educated, quite wealthy by Indian standards, and had several years' experience in the private sector. Despite his parents' qualms and his wife's protestations, he had decided to take the plunge into electoral politics.

"This has been a great experience," Sanjay told me in the car as we drove to a nearby village for a rally, "but my wallet does not agree with me." We both laughed before he continued, "This election is costing me between $1.5 and $2 million." Doing the math in my head, I figured his estimate was in the ballpark of thirty to forty times the legal limit state assembly candidates could spend (roughly $47,000) under Indian law. Sanjay went on to explain that most of the money was his own or his family's—as a newcomer, he could not rely on big corporate donations, and his party was not much help either. His unique background and personal wealth had made him an attractive candidate, and so he had no problems securing a nomination.

Now, however, he was literally paying the price—handing out an unending stream of cash to media houses for advertising, to workers for food and liquor to keep them motivated, and occasionally to the wayward government officer on election duty for a sweetening bribe. In fact, at one of Sanjay's rallies I attended later in the week, the proceedings were interrupted by a probing government officer on election duty who was tasked with ensuring the candidate had the proper permissions. Within minutes, the officer disappeared, and I turned to Sanjay's campaign manager to find out what had happened. "We will settle this later directly with him," he whispered. "This is election season so everyone is looking for their cut."

Sanjay estimated that three-quarters of his total election expenditure would take place in the final 48 to 72 hours of campaigning, when trusted members of his team would fan out across the constituency handing out wads of cash and liquor to voters in the constituency as inducements. Sanjay's story was a familiar one; politicians in India are notorious for distributing all manner of goodies in the run-up to Election Day. To get around Election Commission strictures, candidates have come up with ingenious workarounds. In Sanjay's case, rather than risk distributing actual bottles of alcohol—which could raise unnecessary suspicion—campaign workers provided households with vouchers (that looked like innocent scraps of paper) for free booze that they could redeem at local liquor outlets.[3] For most households, country hooch would suffice. For influential notables or well-to-do residents, the campaign was compelled to gift name brand liquor.[4]

I was dubious whether this type of "vote buying" was actually effective. In 2010 I had met a voter in Bihar who, mistaking me for a politician, desperately asked me to buy his vote. When I asked him how

much he required, he admitted that one party had already given him
100 rupees. So if I gave him money too, would he vote for me, I asked?
He let out a devilish grin and confessed he takes money from all candidates but then votes for whomever he wishes on the actual day.

I relayed this story to Sanjay and he nodded approvingly. "If money
is distributed, voters might give you a chance. But if money is not distributed, you are finished," he said. It was difficult, if not impossible,
to secure an airtight quid pro quo, but the money and goodies were a
sign of goodwill and largesse. Politicians like Sanjay held out hope that
if they gave more money than the next guy, norms of reciprocity would
kick in and voters would feel obliged to vote "the right way."

When we reached the village rally, I was introduced to a man who
had previously contested state elections in the area but was now campaigning for Sanjay. I asked the man why he chose not to run again; he
rubbed his thumb and forefinger together, making the universal gesture
for cash. "I just finished paying off the last one," he said with a laugh.
Without going into detail, I casually mentioned my conversation with
Sanjay about campaign costs. "That's nothing," he remarked. "The
man who is running for the parliamentary seat from this area is spending several times as much."

Later that night, when we returned to Sanjay's party office after a
series of exhausting though exhilarating rallies, I asked him why he
decided to get into politics. He responded by citing all the usual reasons
one would expect: public service, a desire to help people, a belief he
could better represent the constituency than the incumbent. But given
the huge expenses, was the financial investment worth it? "If I am lucky
enough to win, next time, I'll need even more money," he lamented,
already pondering his potential reelection expenses. "How does one
remain honest and succeed in politics in this country?" he wondered
aloud.

Before departing Sanjay's constituency, I spent some time with one
of the young men tasked with handling the large amounts of cash Sanjay's campaign would distribute on the eve of elections. The boy, whose
parents were longtime friends of the candidate's, described to me the
intricate network of cash distribution he would play a small role in
facilitating. The constituency was divided into five segments and for
each segment, the candidate had entrusted one family member or close
associate with the responsibility of providing "goodies" on the eve of
voting. Each of the five "block" leaders, in turn, had five deputies, and

so on. The boy was one such deputy, but for someone entrusted with so much responsibility he appeared deeply uninterested in politics, telling me that he was doing it only as a favor since Sanjay was a close family friend. When I asked him if he ever thought of joining politics, his response was swift: "No way." Politics was a dirty game, he said, and money was having a corrosive effect.

A few weeks before I arrived in Andhra, the state held local body elections, and the boy was asked by another politician friend of the family to help in the final days of the campaign. The candidate he was tasked with helping had come up with a clever plan to win votes: rather than handing out cash to voters, he would distribute free cell phones. The phones were worth several hundred rupees, but the candidate had ordered in bulk and hence received a huge discount from his supplier. The ploy backfired, the boy explained, because most voters already had a mobile phone and had no use for a second one. Furthermore, voters felt the candidate was behaving like a cheapskate. The rival candidate in the area who stuck to traditional cash handouts won handily. Whether money had anything to do with the candidate's loss was impossible to verify, but it was immaterial; there was a *perception* that it cost him the election. "Local elections now cost what state elections used to five years ago. State elections now cost what national elections used to. Where does it stop?" he asked. The role of "money power," as it's often called in India, had clearly colored the boy's impressions of politics—and not in a good way.

But the influx of money into politics was doing more than disillusioning young people; it was also shaping who steps forward to enter politics (and who does not) in the first place. Before heading to the local airport to catch a flight out of town, I paid one last visit to Sanjay in his makeshift party office. I regaled him with stories the young boy had told me—stories, of course, that Sanjay had already heard. I promised Sanjay I would return in several months if he won his election. "If I win," Sanjay daydreamed, "maybe I will run for member of Parliament in five years." He paused, smiling, "But to do that, I'll have to become a billionaire first."

BEYOND WINNABILITY

The previous chapter demonstrated that criminals first joined electoral politics for a variety of factors, not least of which was their desire to vertically integrate their operations in an attempt to guarantee their self-preservation. But understanding the supply of certain types of candidates in the electoral marketplace in any modern democracy—including India's—requires one to consider not just the incentives of aspirant politicians but also those of political parties as well. As political scientist Paul Brass has noted, "In every modern polity, and in every polity which aspires to modernity, political parties are the indispensable link between the society and the institutions of government."[5] Parties are, in short, the "mechanism through which power is organized and exercised in a democracy."[6] Therefore, any explanation that focuses exclusively on the self-selection of candidates renders parties redundant, which is out of sync with the essential gate-keeping function they fulfill.[7]

Whatever criminals' precise motivations might be to contest elections, it is not immediately obvious why political parties play along. After all, it seems natural to assume that parties might shrink from selecting candidates linked to criminality out of concern for their reputation. Any compelling exploration of the factors influencing the supply of criminals into the electoral marketplace, therefore, has to grapple with the question: why do parties recruit "muscle," or candidates known to have serious criminal backgrounds?

In India, parties across the political spectrum nominate candidates who have criminal cases pending against them to the highest political office (figure 4.1). If one were to look at India's five most popular parties, based on the combined number of parliamentary seats they won in 2004, 2009, and 2014, it is clear that criminality in politics is widespread. While there is some variation in the prevalence of candidates with criminal cases across parties, this is not an issue facing any one political party or type of party.

India's two truly national parties, the Bharatiya Janata Party (BJP) and Indian National Congress (INC), both select a fair number of parliamentary candidates with pending cases, between 14 and 11 percent, respectively, who face serious cases. The Samajwadi Party (SP) of Uttar Pradesh and the All India Trinamool Congress (AITC) of West Bengal, both single-state parties, figure in this list, as does the ideologically driven Communist Party of India (Marxist) (CPI[M]).[8]

In one sense, the answer to why political parties in India nominate candidates with criminal backgrounds to stand for election is painfully obvious: because they win. Across the last three general elections, if one were to pick a candidate out of a hat, he or she would have—on

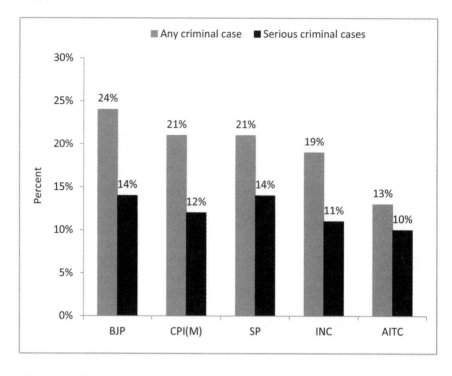

Figure 4.1. Party nomination of Lok Sabha candidates with pending criminal cases, 2004–14. (Author's calculations based on affidavits submitted to the Election Commission of India by candidates contesting the 2004, 2009, and 2014 parliamentary elections)

average—a 6 percent chance of coming out on top (figure 4.2). Compare this with a candidate who boasts at least one criminal case: he or she has a nearly 18 percent chance of winning.

The differences in state elections are slightly smaller but still stark: "clean" candidates (e.g., those who do not face pending criminal cases) have a 9.5 percent probability of winning whereas candidates with criminal cases have a roughly 22 percent chance—more than twice as large.[9] Granted, this simple comparison does not take into account numerous other factors, such as a candidate's age, education, partisan affiliation, or type of electoral constituency. Nevertheless, the contrast is marked. Indeed, if one were to disaggregate parliamentary candidates facing "serious" charges (those charges, such as assault or murder, which are clearly not tied to a politician's normal job description), the divergence is marginally greater: compared to a 6 percent win rate for "clean" candidates, the win rate for candidates facing a charge of any

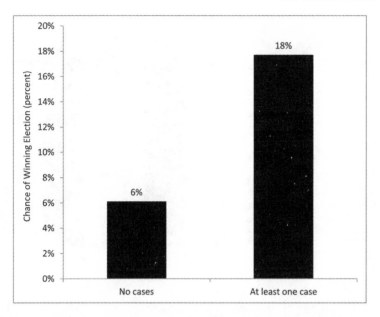

Figure 4.2. Criminal case status and electoral success in Lok Sabha elections, 2004–14. (Author's calculations based on affidavits submitted to the Election Commission of India by candidates contesting the 2004, 2009, and 2014 parliamentary elections)

type is just above 17 percent while the rate for candidates facing cases involving serious charges is 18 percent (figure 4.3). At the state level, whereas candidates without cases have a 9.5 percent chance of winning election, this probability increases to 19 percent for candidates with minor cases and 23 percent for those implicated in serious cases.[10]

To say that parties pick "winnable" candidates begs the question: what is it that makes them winnable? It turns out that a key factor motivating parties to select candidates with serious criminal records comes down to cold, hard cash. In a context of costly elections, weakly institutionalized parties, and an ineffectual election finance regime, parties are likely to prioritize self-financing candidates who do not represent a drain on finite party coffers but can instead contribute "rents" to the party. For these purposes, rents mean not only illicit financial transfers but also the ability of candidates to cover the expenses of contesting elections and bring in resources for the party. Implicitly, self-financing candidates also free up resources coveted by party elites. And, it turns out, individuals associated with criminal wrongdoing have both deep

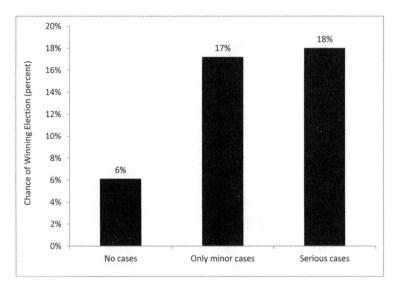

Figure 4.3. Severity of criminal case status and electoral success in Lok Sabha elections, 2004–14. (Author's calculations based on affidavits submitted to the Election Commission of India by candidates contesting the 2004, 2009, and 2014 parliamentary elections)

pockets and the willingness to invest resources in the service of politics (figure 4.4).

Based on a wide array of evidence, it seems that the rent-seeking motivations of parties in India explain their dalliance with suspected criminal candidates exceptionally well. Findings from previous research, as well as my own interviews with politicians in India, confirm this connection: parties place a premium on muscle because it often brings with it the added benefit of money. Exploiting a new source of information, the candidate affidavits, to look into these previously opaque connections provides further confirmation. Data drawn from nearly 70,000 aspirant candidates in India over the last decade substantiate the claim that money and muscle are inexorably linked (see Appendix A for more information on the candidate data).

Venturing into parties' inner motivations for embracing criminal candidates adds an important dimension to the understanding of the supply-side considerations at play in the marketplace for criminal poli-

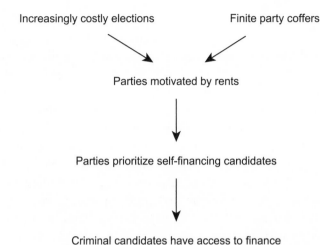

Figure 4.4. How financial pressures faced by parties create demand for criminal candidates.

ticians. Candidates do not just present themselves to the electorate; in most democracies they enter the fray under the banner of a political party. In turn, parties, select candidates on the basis of hardheaded political calculations.

RENTS AND RECRUITMENT

In most modern democracies, parties play a vital gate-keeping role, carefully choosing the candidates who appear before voters. As important screeners, however, it is not immediately obvious why parties would knowingly throw their weight behind corrupt, incompetent, or low-quality candidates typically referred to as "bad politicians." Yet evidence from a range of democracies suggests that parties are quite often in cahoots with many such individuals.[11]

Why parties welcome such characters into their fold remains a mystery. Curiously, most studies treat the issue of bad politicians as a given. In other words, they assume that parties lack agency: they are simply empty vessels saddled with the burden of undesirable politicians. Thus, the question of bad politicians is framed primarily as an allocation decision: party bosses have a stable of bad politicians, and they must decide how to apportion them across electoral districts. For instance, one strand of thinking suggests that parties, once encumbered with bad politicians, will allocate them to less electorally competitive environments in order to preserve their "good" candidates for contestable elections to attract swing voters.[12] Interestingly, some scholars have argued the exact opposite: that parties are more likely to select bad politicians in highly competitive—or "politically extreme"—contexts where parties are more desperate for a leg up and willing to take a gamble.[13] In exceptionally competitive races, parties might be willing to recruit candidates who can use coercion to dampen opposition turnout. Other studies claim parties will send their bad politicians to economically poor places or areas where voters are poorly informed (and hence cannot discern between good and bad types).[14]

While these studies acknowledge the role of political parties in candidate selection, parties appear to function as little more than glorified conveyor belts. Furthermore, they implicitly assume that a candidate's bad behavior is a liability, rather than a potential asset, for a political party. As such, they are unable to provide a compelling explanation for why parties might actively recruit bad politicians, something they regularly do in India. Fundamentally, they cannot answer the question of what bad politicians bring to the table or what their comparative advantage might be. Parties might allocate bad politicians to competitive or electorally safe districts, to poor or low-information places, but why even bother recruiting them in the first place?

The Mother's Milk of Politics

One does not have to stretch one's imagination very far to get a grip on why parties might willingly embrace candidates with unsavory biographies. In all democratic societies, a party's primary job is to contest (and win) elections. Virtually every aspect of elections—from advertising to polling, and from voter sops to large rallies—requires money, typically vast amounts of it. American politician Jesse Unruh said it well when he famously claimed that "money is the mother's milk of politics."

Where elections are costly and the rule of law is weak, parties are often motivated by rents, defined as an economic payoff where the ultimate beneficiary incurs no costs in producing that payoff. In other words, money that comes without strings attached. It is access to these rents that might motivate parties to recruit bad politicians in the first place. Economist Timothy Besley formalized this relationship between bad politicians and rent-seeking, arguing, "If rents are earned by parties as well as successful candidates, and protection of those rents is dependent on selecting bad politicians with little public service motivation, then the party may have an interest in putting up bad candidates."[15]

When economists think of rents, they typically think of illicit acts of corruption, but a more expansive definition of rents could also encompass Besley's hypothesis. Take election finance, for instance. Because elections cost money, parties often have to use money from their own coffers to subsidize candidates' expenditures. But if a candidate is able to independently finance his own campaign, he no longer constitutes a drain on party funds. The result is a positive rent in the sense that the party has more money to spend on other activities.

The financial rents parties collect can be directed toward legitimate purposes, like covering the costs of campaigning, as well as illegitimate ones, like lining the pockets of party bosses and their family members. In the first instance, the money a candidate is able to bring in on his own acts as a cross-subsidy, either explicitly or implicitly, of lesser-endowed candidates. A self-financing candidate who covers the costs of his campaign, thereby freeing up party resources for other candidates who really need party funds, is providing an implicit subsidy.

If candidates provide funds to the party itself, it can also act as an explicit subsidy of other candidates contesting under the party's banner. Furthermore, there is nothing to stop crooked party leaders from pocketing some of the rents they extract from self-financing candidates for themselves. This could take the form of party bosses simply skimming money off the top or actually requiring that well-resourced candidates provide funds directly to the party for the privilege of running under its aegis. In either scenario, self-financing candidates improve the fiscal position of parties.

Wealthy, self-financing candidates are not only attractive to parties, but they are also likely to be more electorally competitive. Because contesting elections is an expensive proposition in most parts of the world, a candidate's wealth is a good proxy for his or her electoral viability. As one scholar of politics in the United States put it, "Private wealth can be a distinct asset to a legislative career, particularly in entrepreneur-ial political systems where candidates must raise their own campaign resources."[16]

If parties are truly motivated by rents, it could lead to an influx of candidates with questionable backgrounds but who have access to re-sources and are willing to deploy these resources in the service of poli-tics. As icing on the cake, such candidates might also have no qualms about engaging in run-of-the-mill corruption on behalf of parties, ei-ther contributing ill-gotten gains to party coffers or helping to protect the party's illicit wealth.

Supporting Conditions

The likelihood that rent-seeking parties might be drawn to wealthy, bad politicians increases when two supporting conditions are in place. A party's rent-seeking motivation is potentially strengthened by the fact that elites often dominate party recruitment, especially in devel-oping democracies or in underinstitutionalized party systems.[17] When intraparty democracy is weak—that is, where parties lack primaries or effectively empower elites to handpick candidates—selection can be a highly opaque, connections-driven process. "Where candidate selection is structured to maximize the power of party elites," Besley writes, "this process could allow bad candidates . . . to use their influence."[18]

Furthermore, if ideology is not a significant factor in the political system in question, this reduces the qualification requirements of pro-spective candidates. This is especially likely in developing democracies, where there is ample evidence that ideology plays a minimal role as a screening mechanism for parties and voters. Political economist Phil Keefer has observed that in young or poor democracies "political party development and other indicators of credibility in political systems are often weak. Parties have little history and no identifiable positions on issues." Where parties do not rely on a prospective candidate's ideo-logical proclivities as a litmus test, opportunistic candidates gain an advantage.

FINANCING ELECTIONS IN INDIA

The rent-seeking logic sketched out above jibes nicely with the reali-ties of contemporary Indian politics. The financial pressures of elections in India, as Chapter 3 showed, have grown considerably over the years. At the same time, parties have struggled to find legitimate sources of funding, reflecting a general decline in their organizational strength. Consistent with the supporting conditions thought to lead to an influx of opportunistic candidates with deep pockets, most political parties in India lack any semblance of intraparty democracy. By and large, parties are top-down enterprises that function with minimal input from the masses. Furthermore, ideological considerations are largely an after-thought, with politicians switching parties with relative abandon. In such an environment, those with the deepest pockets have ready access to political power.

Soaring Election Costs

Five underlying structural factors have contributed to the rising costs of elections in India. First, the country is home to one out every six people on the planet, or 1.25 billion residents according to 2013 data. By the year 2022, the United Nations projects that India will surpass China as the most populous country on the globe. As India's popula-tion has grown, the size of political constituencies has ballooned. The average parliamentary constituency in 1952, when India held its first post-Independence election, had fewer than 400,000 voters; in 2014, each parliamentary constituency was home to roughly 1.6 million vot-ers, on average (figure 4.5). The growth in the size of the electorate over time has meant that candidates have to spend more money on electioneering as they seek to reach and woo an ever-larger pool of potential supporters.

Second, there has been a marked increase in the competitiveness of Indian elections. In the 1952 general election, 55 parties took part; in 2014, 464 parties entered the fray. This surge in political competition began in the 1980s—the number of parties contesting elections jumped from 38 in 1984 to 117 in 1989. The decline of the Congress system and the dawn of the coalition era in Delhi incentivized the growth of regional parties, whose leaders recognized that they could wield consid-erable influence in the formation of governments with a relatively small number of seats in Parliament.[19]

As the number of parties seeking—and winning—representation in Parliament has steadily increased, so has the competitiveness of elec-tions. By 2009, the average margin of victory in a parliamentary contest

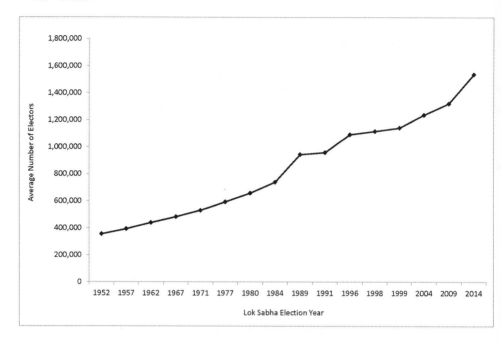

Figure 4.5. Average size of electorate in Lok Sabha constituencies, 1952–2014. (Author's calculations based on data from the Election Commission of India)

registered at 9.7 percent, the thinnest margin since independence (figure 4.6). In 2014, elections actually were less competitive (average margins reached 15 percent), but it is not yet clear if this is a reversal or merely a statistical anomaly. Either way, it contrasts with the 32 percent average margin of victory in the 2012 United States congressional elections or the 18 percent margin of victory in Britain's 2010 parliamentary elections. Competition adds significantly to electoral uncertainty, meaning that parties find it increasingly difficult to calculate the returns to every rupee spent. In this environment, the incentive is always to spend more.

Third, and perhaps less discussed, is the fact that the scope of elections has increased dramatically over the last two decades. The Seventy-Third and Seventy-Fourth Amendments to the Indian Constitution (1992–93) formally established a three-tier system of democratic governance at the local level, meaning that India's democratic patchwork went from having a little over 4,500 elected positions to nearly 3 million virtually overnight. Political parties field candidates at all three levels, even at the

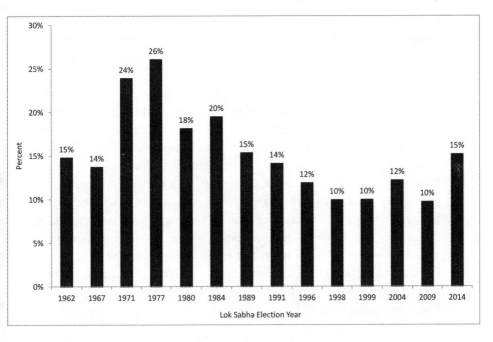

Figure 4.6. Average margin of victory in Lok Sabha elections, 1952–2014.
(Author's calculations based on data from the Election Commission of India)

village level where formal partisan affiliations are prohibited (though regularly brandished). Each election, in turn, requires campaign resources. State-level politicians have been openly reluctant to devolve real power to the local level, remaining content to use the new third tier of governance as a supply chain for lower-level functionaries, or "brokers," as well as for election funds.[20] For their part, candidates in local elections compete for proximity to higher-ups (and their resources) on the political food chain. But the interdependence flows in both directions; state- and national-level politicians also must help fund the campaigns of these local officials or risk alienating their grassroots organizational base.

Fourth, state and national elections in India now occur on independent political calendars. This was largely the result of Indira Gandhi's decision to call an early national election in 1971, motivated by a short-term desire to separate state-level issues and vote banks from national ones.[21] The decision had long-term ramifications, however, as it led to separate fundraising cycles for state and national elections. As a consequence, parties and politicians were forced to collect money more frequently, and contributors could no longer get away with a one-shot gift for "elections."

Finally, the expectations of Indian voters for election "freebies" has increased as parties have engaged in a competitive bidding process. For many decades, it was standard practice for candidates to offer voters free bags of rice or grain, country liquor, or small sums of cash in advance of elections as positive inducements.[22] As political competition has surged, India has experienced vote-buying inflation: voters' expectations for what they can extract from parties has risen, and parties have tried to outdo one another with increasingly lucrative pre-election "gifts." As one major party candidate from Bihar told a news reporter ahead of key state elections in 2015: "Five years ago, 151 rupees was considered a decent amount as [a] gift. . . . Now if you give anything less than 501 rupees, you face ridicule and therefore, run the risk of losing potential voters."[23]

Ineffectual Regulation

The reality of increasingly expensive elections has occurred against a backdrop of very weak regulation of election finance.[24] These regulations, many of them well-intentioned, have often had counterproductive, even perverse impacts on the electoral system.[25] In the previous chapter I discussed some of the broad trends in the regulation of funds for elections. At a microlevel, the ECI places strict limits on candidates' campaign expenditures. The expenditure ceiling is a maximum of 7 million rupees (or $106,000) and 2.8 million rupees ($42,000) for parliamentary and assembly elections, respectively (although the precise limit varies by the size of the state). Any expenditure by a third party (to include political parties) in connection with a candidate is attributed to the candidate, but third parties can spend without limit on promoting the "party's program."[26] At present, there is no system of public financing of elections, short of the government providing tax incentives and limited giveaways (for poll materials) and television time for recognized parties on the basis of past performance.

In terms of contributions, there are no limits on individual contributions, while tax-deductible corporate contributions are capped at

7.5 percent of the company's average net profits for the preceding three years. Foreign contributions are prohibited under Indian law.[27] Following the conclusion of elections, candidates have 30 days to disclose their detailed campaign expenditures, but parties face no such requirement. Parties are required to disclose all contributions greater than 20,000 rupees ($300), but do not need to maintain records of contributors below this threshold.

Some of these regulations may appear reasonable on paper, but in practice they have resulted in a great many perversities.[28] For starters, the candidate spending limits prescribed under law are laughably small, even though they were revised upwards as recently as 2014. Next, because parties face no limits on their expenditure on the "party program," and because the line between party and candidate-focused spending is often blurred, the effective cap on candidate spending is actually moot, rendering candidate expenditure "meaningless and almost never adhered to."[29] This is a problem the ECI acknowledged as far back as 1962: "The fact that the expenses incurred by the political parties on the electioneering campaign of individual candidates or groups of candidates do not require to be included in the accounts of the latter, makes the prescribed maxima quite unreal and meaningless."[30] One MP from Andhra Pradesh allegedly told a U.S. diplomat in 2009 that the spending limit imposed by the Election Commission was a "joke," claiming that he planned to spend his entire limit for the general election on Election Day alone.[31]

Furthermore, because parties only need to disclose contributions greater than 20,000 rupees, donors who wish to preserve their identity while contributing large sums of money can divide and disguise large donations in a number of smaller contributions. In fact, one of the oldest tricks in the book is for savvy donors to make a large number of donations, each worth no more than 19,999 rupees. Finally, parties are not required to submit independently audited accounts to the Election Commission, which means that their internal numbers need not add up.

The end result of this disarray is that the election finance regime in India today is farcical. There is a widely acknowledged gap between candidates' stated expenditures and reality. Former BJP prime minister Atal Bihari Vajpayee famously captured this fact when he remarked, "Most legislators embark on their parliamentary career with a gross lie

—the false election returns which they submit."[32] Politicians regularly lambaste the strict limits on their campaign expenditure for being unreasonably low, yet candidates still report falling far short of this cap in post-election finance disclosures. According to one independent analysis, winning candidates from the 2014 parliamentary election reported spending 58 percent of the authorized limit on average. Of these MPs, 33 percent declared spending less than 50 percent of the legal limit in their constituency.[33] Even more troubling, many candidates do not comply with the requirement to file expenses, banking on the fact that once the election is over officers on temporary election duty will have returned to their day jobs.[34]

One academic who once embedded himself into the campaigns of several MP candidates seeking election in rural Uttar Pradesh reported that the "statutory limit of election expenses for candidates has no sanctity whatsoever."[35] Another study carried out in the early 1990s, with state legislators from five states, reported that MLAs spent well over twenty times the legal limit on elections.[36] An independent audit of a representative sample of 25 parliamentary constituencies in 1999 found that viable candidates spent more than five times the amount allowed by election authorities. The authors concede that even this was a serious underestimate since it did not include "underhand or non-visible" items of electoral expenditure."[37] Economist Arun Kumar carried out a similar exercise during the 1998 election. Not only were candidates' reported expenditures typically well above the respective limits, they were also orders of magnitude smaller than what Kumar himself estimated they spent. For instance, in one urban constituency in north India, a candidate estimated he spent around 4 million rupees ($61,000) for the election when Kumar roughly calculated he had spent nearly 33 million rupees ($500,000).[38]

In fact, according to some estimates, candidates contesting local elections often exceed the spending limits for much more consequential state and national elections. One 2013 news report, citing the views of political money managers, estimated that a municipal councilor's election in a major metropolitan city runs between 3 and 5 million rupees ($45,000 to $76,000), with the upper bound exceeding the spending limits in parliamentary elections. The report estimates the cost of a state election at around 10 to 50 million rupees ($150,000 to $760,000) and a parliamentary election at between 100 and 250 million rupees ($1.5 million to $3.8 million).[39]

Another study placed the total expenditure on India's 2014 general election around $5 billion. Although estimating the true cost of elections is impossible given the opacity of campaign spending, assuming this figure is in the ballpark, it would make the 2014 polls one of the most expensive elections ever held, second only to the 2012 presidential election in the United States.[40]

Hollowed-Out Parties

As the costs of elections have grown, political parties in India have simultaneously experienced a decline in their organizational effectiveness.[41] As illustrated in the previous chapter, this decline is not unique to political parties; India's political institutions across the board witnessed a progressive weakening stemming from Indira Gandhi's personalistic rule of the 1970s.

In broad terms, parties in India do not function as mass membership organizations, as they do in many advanced democracies. The possible exceptions are the Left parties, such as the CPI(M), and the BJP, which serves as the political wing of the Rashtriya Swayamsevak Sangh (RSS), a Hindu nationalist cultural and volunteer organization. For most parties, data on party membership are hard to come by, but anecdotal evidence suggests that the figures swell immediately before elections but are otherwise of dubious value.[42] As one commentator noted, "There does not seem to be any relationship between a party's membership and its capacity to spend."[43] Most parties do not report or even maintain proper records on their membership, an oversight that is symbolic of their internal shortcomings.[44]

With weak membership norms, party leaders struggle mightily to leverage their organizations to raise funds to cover operating costs and the costs of electioneering. However large (or small) the membership figures are in reality, party membership dues are a negligible contributor to overall party coffers. The BJP, for instance, charges a nominal annual membership fee of 1 rupee (in 2015, this is less than $.02). After two years in the party, members can apply for "active membership," which requires a 100 rupee donation ($1.5). The Congress Party charges an annual membership fee of 5 rupees ($.08) for up to five years, while the newly established Aam Aadmi Party charges 10 rupees ($.15).[45]

The "Iron Law" of Oligarchy

The German sociologist Robert Michels, in his famous 1911 treatise on the nature of political parties, argued that the control of a party apparatus by a small clique of elites, or oligarchs, was an "iron law" of any democratic organization. Faced with the pragmatic necessities of decision making and governing, oligarchic control over parties was, to a certain extent, inevitable.

Of course, not all parties are oligarchic to the same extent. Internal party democracy exists on a continuum across democratic countries. On one end of the spectrum are democracies like the United States, where party elites wield significant power but are constrained by internal party structures as well as primary elections. On the other side of the spectrum are countries that have democratic structures on paper that largely serve as window dressing; they exist to placate party members and civil society but have no real authority.

India, unfortunately, is situated toward the latter extreme. This is true for both established parties, which have experienced serious organizational decay over time, and for newer parties, which have not dedicated themselves to the hard work of creating enduring party structures. Most political parties in India today are elite-driven outfits, with ultimate power residing within the hands of a select few.[46] By and large, this is by design; party elites are intrinsically more interested in accumulating and protecting their own political power rather than building well-institutionalized organizations. This top-down architecture maximizes the discretionary power of party elites, offering little political space for the aspirations or views of the rank-and-file membership. One observer writes that in India, the internal structure of parties is "generally autocratic and oligarchic. . . . The uppermost crust of the party organization tends to form a ruling group, isolated from the mass of workers."[47]

The lack of intraparty democracy infects political parties of all stripes, including prominent national parties like the Congress and BJP.[48] For instance, neither party's constitution contains any detailed information on the candidate nomination process.[49] State parties, however, are perhaps most prone to this vulnerability as they often resemble little more than personal fiefdoms. Most regional parties in India function as "single-leader parties without substantial organizational networks," where the absence of organization is "compensated by the projection of the leader as a demi-god."[50] The political scientist Kanchan Chandra recalls visiting the state president of one well-known regional party and requesting a list of his party's office-bearers. The official turned indignant upon being asked to disclose "classified" information, barking, "Why should I give my party's inside information to you?"[51]

When it comes to selecting candidates, the preferences of party elites play an outsized role in choosing candidates. Party primaries in India do not exist, and although parties often possess very detailed, decentralized procedures for candidate selection, in practice the party often authorizes the party leader to select its slate of candidates.[52] Using objective criteria on the degree of decentralization in party nomination procedures, political scientists Adnan Farooqui and E. Sridharan found that India lies on the "centralized" extreme; its major parties rate as "completely centralized" or "near-completely centralized" compared to other countries, with the national party leadership given the final say for all nominations.[53]

One immediate consequence of the lack of intraparty democracy is nepotism or "dynastic politics," which is rampant in Indian politics. In an elite-dominated environment, families have become substitutes for weak party organizations, with "the proximity of blood ties" serving as a readymade chain of command.[54] Of the 543 MPs elected in 2014, between one-fifth and one-quarter hail from political families, depending on the measure used.[55] This figure is a slight decline from 2009 (29 percent) but roughly on par with 2004 levels (21 percent).[56] Many critics of India's hereditary politics tend to direct their fire at the Nehru-Gandhi dynasty, which has controlled the Congress Party for much of the past one hundred years.[57] But family politics cannot be reduced to any single party; many parties operating at the national and state levels exhibit dynastic tendencies.[58]

Indifference to Ideas

Together with internal party democracy, ideology is largely an afterthought in Indian politics. By the absence of ideology, I am referring to the fact that there is no single issue-based dimension along which parties can be neatly organized, such as a simple left-right (liberal-conservative) spectrum. "Ideologies like socialism or liberal democracy . . . make no sense to this generation of politicians," Sumanta Banerjee wrote in 2004 of India's political class. "Whichever party gives them [candidates] that slot of power is good enough."[59] Ideology then has taken a backseat to more pragmatic considerations.

Since there is no ideas-based criterion to gain entry into a given political party, politicians can seamlessly move between parties as free agents. To a significant extent, party recruitment and nomination is based on sheer opportunism. "The rise of leaders within political parties is not, in a single instance, dependent on persuading party members of the cogency of your ideas," according to Pratap Bhanu Mehta.[60] Rather, aspirant candidates gain traction with parties based on social connections and leaders' assessments of their "winnability." There are few permanent friends or enemies in Indian politics; as one author noted, "It is possible for practically everyone to cohabit with practically anyone else in the pursuit of power."[61]

In a politics free of ideology, ideas are neither a barrier to entry into a party nor to exit. Large-scale party defections were commonplace well into the 1980s. In one well-known case in 1979, one minister from the state of Assam defected three times in less than 36 hours.[62] Parliament eventually passed a law in 1985 to curb the defection of sitting legislators, but the law does not apply to politicians who switch party alliances at the time of elections. Indeed, party switching continues to be rampant.[63]

Although India's anti-defection law was originally intended to curb party fragmentation and the proliferation of factionalism within parties, it only further strengthened the hand of party elites and diminished the relevance of individual legislators. Hence, it simultaneously weakened internal party democracy and exacerbated the absence of ideology. One reason parties do not necessarily traffic in new ideas is because ordinary rank-and-file members have very little incentive to do so since upward mobility within parties is severely constrained.

While ideology of a programmatic sort is virtually absent, it is present in a very different (noneconomic) sense. Across political parties, caste, religion, region, and language all represent cleavages in society that have acquired ideological import over time.[64] In diverse societies, the practice of ethnic politics revolves around concepts like "dignity," "honor," "justice," and "inclusion." Although they do not operate on a conventional left-right spectrum, these notions do contain substantive content.

Using this broad definition, Indian politics possesses a surfeit of ideological competition. According to Ashutosh Varshney, three "master narratives" have formed the ideological core of political parties in India since 1947: secular nationalism, Hindu nationalism, and caste-based justice. Secular nationalism has historically been associated with the Congress while its chief national rival, the BJP, is the most prominent representative of Hindu nationalism. Caste justice has been most fervently championed by a host of smaller, regional parties with relatively narrow core constituencies but is regularly exploited across the political spectrum.[65]

But even if we are to expand the definition of ideology in this way, the boundaries between parties still appear to be "highly flexible and permeable."[66] In order to enlarge their appeal by engaging new demographics, parties regularly recruit candidates from a diverse array of backgrounds. So a party like the Bahujan Samaj Party (BSP), which was founded as a vehicle for promoting Dalit interests, has recast itself as a party that seeks to cater to Muslim, Dalit, and Brahmin voters.[67] Even the BJP, an avowedly Hindu nationalist entity, has gone to great lengths to recruit Muslim and other minority members, including setting up a "minority *morcha,*" or outreach wing.[68] And while the caste justice and Hindu nationalist narratives are often portrayed as diametrically opposed, the Hindu nationalist BJP has had great success touting the caste credentials of its candidates to win votes of sought-after communities.

In sum, even though parties espouse differing ideologies (defined in identity terms), with a few exceptions (namely, the extreme Left and Right) they are more or less recruiting candidates from the same talent pool.

THE MERITS OF MONEY

Given the rising costs of elections, the limited funds parties have at their disposal, their organizational infirmities, and ineffectual election finance regulations, it comes as little surprise that parties rely on unreported ("black") sources of campaign funds. For instance, an independent analysis of the disclosed income of the six national parties between 2004–5 and 2011–12 indicates that 75 percent of parties' income comes from unidentified sources. Around half of these funds came in a period of four months around elections, largely in cash (for the Congress Party, this figure stood around 90 percent).[69]

The sources of black money are numerous and diverse, but two are especially important. First, parties solicit businesses for financial contributions to party coffers. These donations can be voluntary, typically made in exchange for a favor to be paid down the road, or can be achieved through more coercive means. Although companies can legally make tax-deductible contributions to political parties and candidates (with some limitations), most continue to give under the table rather than report their giving. This is an outgrowth of the continued regulatory intensity of the state, whereby politicians and bureaucrats can use their discretionary authority to punish firms who do not do their bidding by denying licenses, cancelling permits, or giving contracts to competitors. The nexus between builders and politicians cited in Chapter 2 is a good example of this.

Recruiting self-financed candidates is a second source of raising private, often unaccounted funds. Increasingly in India, personal wealth is widely considered to be a prerequisite for seeking (and winning) higher office. Indeed, a 1996 survey of sitting MLAs revealed that personal funds were an important source of campaign finance for a majority of legislators. While a large percentage also benefited from party funds, the author of the survey clarifies that each respondent "added that this was extremely small" and usually came not in cash but in publicity support. The author concludes that, with the exception of the Left parties, "all candidates must generate personal resources if they hope to contest an election . . . without which they believe they do not have any chance of getting elected."[70]

If the costs of elections have risen and parties, as a consequence, are under intense pressure to raise funds, what exactly are these funds used for? Money greases the wheels at all stages of the electoral process, beginning with obtaining a party nomination. The process of prospective candidates paying for party tickets is known as "ticket buying," whereby potential candidates pay parties to contest elections under their banner. If party leaders can sell party tickets to the highest bidder, they can create new sources of revenue for themselves and the party.

Ticket buying is a common practice carried out by most parties, with the exception of the Left; what differs is the extent to which parties acknowledge its use. For example, Mayawati, the former chief minister of Uttar Pradesh and president of the BSP, is quite open about her expectation that prospective candidates should make a hefty contribution to the party in exchange for a nomination.[71] As described by Farooqui and Sridharan, potential candidates must first make a payment to district-level party functionaries in order to have their names sent up the chain to Mayawati and her inner circle. Then, in order to be seriously considered for the nomination, they must make direct payments to Mayawati for the honor. The authors estimate that the total cost could be upwards of 5 million rupees ($76,000).[72] Other parties follow similar procedures although in a much more clandestine fashion. For instance, the Congress Party in the 2002 state election reportedly demanded a mandatory 5,000 rupees ($76) "application fee" from prospective ticket-seekers. In order to obtain an audience with the party's central election committee, aspirants had to cough up another 25,000 to 75,000 rupees, or between $380 and $1140 (without any guarantee of a party ticket).[73]

Assuming a candidate is lucky enough to get a party nomination, he or she then has to distribute funds for party maintenance and support. Often, this takes the form of regular cash payments to "social workers," who are the candidate's "captains" in the constituency. These workers are often only loosely connected to the party, but because they often function as the candidate's eyes and ears, they must be adequately compensated lest they switch allegiances. The fascinating ethnographic work of Lisa Bjorkman from a Mumbai slum reveals that, contrary to popular opinion, the money distributed by candidates around elections is not principally about buying votes but rather about spreading enough cash to stay in the game. Instead of explicitly buying votes, "cash works to produce and shore up relations of trust, facilitate flows of information and reduce the incentives for a social worker to 'flip.'"[74]

Of course, money is also necessary to cover the practical aspects of campaigning: advertising, rallies and meetings, care of party workers, and so on. In the municipal election Bjorkman observed, the local candidate she followed paid between 15 to 1,000 people 200 rupees ($3) per day to attend rallies and accompany the candidate on the campaign trail.[75] Election campaigns in India are typically very short—officially they last no longer than two to three weeks—but the frenzied pace and sheer number of activities involved is bewildering. A partial list of expenses includes posters, billboards, vehicles for transport, polling agents, booth managers, workers to distribute publicity materials, and food and shelter for campaign workers. This list, of course, reflects only the legal expenses that are openly acknowledged. The vast majority of election spending takes place in cash, which further complicates the regulator's monitoring efforts. As one former chief election commissioner estimated (in 2011), "For every 100 rupees spent on elections, 90 rupees is spent in cash."[76]

The list of illicit expenditures ranges from the obvious to the surreal. As Sanjay's example demonstrated, candidates routinely engage in the provision of material inducements to voters. This practice is, of course, explicitly forbidden, yet it is routinely pursued. Gifts typically include cash, jewelry, liquor or other consumables—ranging from opium paste to bricks for home construction. In the run-up to Gujarat's 2012 state election, candidates competed with one another to provide free mobile phone minutes to voters. In one neighborhood of metropolitan Ahmedabad that I visited, the ruling MLA had instructed local owners of mobile kiosks to provide free 200-rupee ($3) "re-charges" to customers courtesy of the candidate. A candidate from a rival party, catching wind of the scheme, instructed kiosks to provide 300-rupee ($4.5) charges on the candidate's dime in an effort at one-upmanship. On the eve of the election, liquor flowed uninhibited despite the fact that Gujarat is a "dry" state; the Election Commission reported seizures of 550,000 liters of country liquor during the campaign.[77]

In recent years, parties have had be more innovative in their vote-buying practices thanks to more aggressive enforcement action by the ECI. A former chief election commissioner once told me that a popular form of vote buying candidates often pursue is to sponsor a "wedding," in which thousands of locals would be invited to drink, eat, and engage in general merrymaking (and leave with a shiny parting gift) when in actuality there was no bride and groom. The entire evening is a ruse to woo voters. A U.S. diplomatic cable on elections in south India, made public by Wikileaks, serves as an engaging ethnography of the current state of pre-election handouts. The cable details the exploits of M. K. Azhagiri, a powerful MP of the ruling DMK Party in Tamil Nadu, who allegedly spared no expense to win a crucial 2009 by-election.[78] A local mayor and confidant of Azhagiri's claimed the latter paid 5,000 rupees ($76) per voter ahead of the election by distributing the cash in envelopes which were delivered to houses tucked inside their morning newspaper, along with the DMK's voting slip.[79]

As Bjorkman points out, with the advent of the secret ballot and the increased range of candidates voters typically can choose from, the actual purchase of an individual's vote is near impossible. But candidates are trapped in an impossible situation. If they provide cash or gifts to voters, there is no guarantee those voters will ultimately vote for them. If they do not provide such payments, however, there is a decent chance the voters will *not* support them. Hence, the logical course for candidates to follow is to continue paying off voters.[80]

The extent of trickery does not stop there. Another common practice is the financing of "dummy candidates," meant to confuse voters or cut into your opponent's vote share.[81] In one constituency election I observed in Bihar, the incumbent candidate hired a dummy candidate to contest the election in order to steal urban votes in the constituency away from his main rival. The dummy candidate, a friend and sympathizer of the incumbent legislator, had no interest in holding office; he was merely acting as an instrument to peel off votes from an opponent. Arun Kumar, in his study on India's black economy, documented one MP who paid for eight dummy candidates in 1998 to contest elections at a cost of 7.5 million rupees ($114,000).[82] When the Congress Party ended its relationship with Jagan Reddy in Andhra Pradesh, it allegedly tried to sabotage his election campaign by fielding eleven candidates named "Jagan Reddy" in an effort to trick voters into wasting their votes on his similarly named opponents. The party directed a similar effort at Reddy's mother, Vijayalakshmi, in a neighboring constituency, where they backed six "false" Vijayalakshmis.[83]

Last but not least is the publicity budget. In addition to the traditional practice of advertisements and flyers, in today's environment, candidates and parties must also budget for activities such as social media.[84] According to official disclosures (which are almost certainly an underestimate), the BJP spent nearly 7.15 billion rupees (or $108 million) on the 2014 parliamentary election. More than 40 percent (roughly $43 million) was spent on media advertisements.[85]

On the more sordid side, many candidates engage in a practice known in India as "paid news," or campaign advertising masquerading as legitimate reporting. Typically, news organizations and politicians will strike a deal whereby the latter can buy a "package" of media coverage from the former for a fixed cost. The packages, also called "rate cards," read like restaurant take-out menus, with more expansive coverage fetching accordingly higher prices.[86] According to a 2009 investigation by the newsmagazine *Outlook,* one rate card involving a Hindi newspaper charged candidates 14,000 rupees ($210) for three election stories with black-and-white photographs. Color photos required an additional 4,000 rupees ($60). A "soft focus" interview—running 84 column centimeters—with a color photo of the candidate sold for around 9,000 rupees ($135).[87] What makes the practice especially pernicious is the inherent difficulty of establishing a quid pro quo between the reporter or media company and the politician in question. Unless there is documentary evidence, both sides can easily plead ignorance.[88]

WHERE MONEY MEETS MUSCLE

The coexistence of costly elections and inadequate in-house funding has resulted in a serious financial dilemma for parties, prompting them to respond by devising new ways of covering the costs of campaigns— such as recruiting self-financing candidates. Thanks to the weak pull of ideological considerations and the oligarchic organization of parties, this strategy opens the door to financially secure candidates who might also be associated with criminal activity. The coming together of parties and politicians associated with criminal behavior is a product of parties' financial stress as well as suspected criminals' desire to avail themselves of the perks to office. Although the disclosed income of parties has consistently gone up, it is still inadequate relative to even more conservative estimates of true cost of elections. As one observer once told me, in India "parties claim to be dirt poor but politicians are filthy rich."

The political and regulatory environment in India provides an opportunity for those with criminal links to enter the electoral marketplace. Their financial capacity represents a crucial incentive for resource-strapped parties. Money and muscle are not independent forces shaping India's electoral politics but are deeply intertwined.[89]

Comparative Advantage

There are several reasons why candidates associated with crime are likely to both have a financial advantage and be willing to deploy these resources in politics. First, candidates with criminal records may be involved in illegal activity that provides them with ample liquid financial resources. Candidates with hardened reputations can also play this perception to their advantage. The use, or even the threat, of force, can be advantageous in obtaining government contracts or extorting money.

Second, existing research shows that candidates with criminal reputations tend to be strongly embedded in the villages and towns that make up their constituency.[90] They tend to be "native sons," clearly identified with a local base that is territorially rooted, and are usually people of prominence in the local community, who maintain significant kinship and patronage networks. Such candidates can accumulate resources through local networks and leverage their power within network structures to obtain political support from other members. In turn, these networks help to form the candidate's base of support come election time.

Third and related, given the short (but intense) time frame and the nature of retail politics in India, campaigns rely on manual labor to organize rallies, operate vehicles, and recruit volunteers. Candidates tied to criminality, to the extent they are embedded within larger social networks (often dominated by underemployed males), are connected to labor resources that help them run campaigns. Although these social bonds may have been developed for nonpolitical reasons, they can easily be redirected toward campaign activities.

Finally, if an individual is implicated in ongoing criminal proceedings (especially those of a serious nature), one can plausibly assume that he might be willing to cut legal corners from time to time. This potential ethical deficit means that criminally suspect candidates may be able to raise significant funds through illicit means (or may already possess considerable ill-gotten gains) and will be inclined to condone rent-seeking activities by the party.

Campaign Finance as Investment

Of course, the financial advantage criminal candidates possess is complemented by the fact that they also have deep-seated incentives for joining the political arena. In the previous chapter, I discussed the baseline motives of self-preservation and protection. But there is another reason criminals may want to try their hand as politicians: the sizeable financial rewards associated with holding office. Because politics can be a highly lucrative proposition, the money candidates spend on securing a party ticket and—if they are fortunate—an election victory can be thought of as a promising investment.

Once in power, legislators have significant discretion and influence in the awarding of government contracts and licenses, especially in sectors where the regulatory footprint of the state is high. This sets the stage for bribe taking and regular conflicts of interest. As the government's allegations against Jagan Reddy indicate, the progeny of an incumbent politician can set up, say, a construction firm and receive favorable dispensation from regulatory agencies (with a behind-the-scenes assist from a close relative), which gives them an advantage over their competitors. The profits can then be shared within the family.

In an attempt to quantify just how lucrative a career in politics can be, a 2013 study analyzed the financial disclosures of state and national incumbent legislators who won elections and then stood for reelection several years later. The average wealth of sitting legislators increased by 222 percent during one term in office (from an average of 18 million rupees, or $270,000, in the first election to 58 million rupees, or $880,000, at the time of reelection).[91] Of course, the 2000s were a period of rapid economic growth for India, so one would expect assets to grow at an exceptional rate, especially for the politically connected. Indeed, when one considers a broader pool of candidates who re-contested elections (and thus had to disclose their wealth at two points in time), it appears that the assets of all candidates, current incumbents and previous runners-up, grew quite impressively. The average declared wealth of re-contesting candidates (to include losers and winners both) was 17.4 million rupees ($264,000) in 2004 and 40.8 million rupees ($618,000) in 2013, an increase of 134 percent.[92] Thus, while re-contesting candidates all saw an increase, there was a distinct winner's advantage.[93] Moreover, legislators with criminal records fared even better than comparable "clean" candidates. This latter finding is not unexpected given the fact that politicians engaged in illegal activity might be more inclined toward misusing their office to extract greater financial rewards.[94]

More statistically rigorous explorations of the financial rewards of office suggest more modest, though still significant, returns. For instance, economists Ray Fisman, Florian Schulz, and Vikrant Vig studied a subset of razor-thin election contests where the same two candidates ran against each other in two consecutive elections. By virtue of the close electoral margin, the identity of the winner is effectively decided by a coin toss, which makes it easier to isolate the true impact of holding office. When it comes to changes in financial assets, the winners of the first election (the incumbent officeholders) enjoy an average annual "winner's premium" of 4.5 percent compared to those who lost the first election and were shut out of office. The additional returns to ministers and to incumbents who face off against freshmen legislators are even higher: 10 and 12 percent per annum, respectively.[95] One should be careful in interpreting these results as the authors look only at reported income (not black money) and restrict their attention to close elections. Moreover, since both candidates finished either first or second in an election, the sample is biased in favor of the politically connected.[96]

But joining politics and winning office is associated not just with financial benefits; there are also psychological benefits related to social status and prestige. One survey of MLAs shows that an overwhelming majority of respondents report an increase in their social status since entering politics. Similarly, large majorities viewed their future social position with great optimism.[97] The financial and intangible gains associated with holding office support Sumanta Banerjee's conclusion regarding the quality of Indian politicians: "Politics as a career is indeed more remunerative and power-enhancing in India than any other profession."[98]

Initially, the presence of criminally suspect candidates contesting elections could be limited to a few "bad apples," yet over time their entry could create long-run path dependency.[99] Irrespective of why candidates implicated in wrongdoing contest elections—whether for status reasons or due to material interest—they can generate negative externalities for politicians who do not have criminal records. Rising numbers of criminal candidates could sour electoral politics more generally, thereby making it less enticing for clean politicians to run for office. Over time, polities can get stuck in a bad equilibrium trap whereby bad politicians are attracted to office while the so-called good ones are filtered out. India clearly exhibits worrying signs of succumbing to this trap.

Crores and Criminals

The financial and psychological rewards of office, not to mention the protection politics offers, applies to legislators of all types, but the lucrative nature of politics in India has been particularly important in

explaining the entry of individuals tied to crime. Although not all legislators are necessarily criminals, the system in India "tacitly permits an
increasing number of opportunists who use politics to further their own
personal interests" to seek office.[100] As one observer asks rhetorically
of "unscrupulous" politicians, "Where else can they get ever-increasing
income, the unrestricted privileges, and absolute immunity"?[101]

Although the link between money and "muscle" has not been systematically scrutinized, several analysts have previously linked the two.
For instance, James Manor has argued that parties in India recruit
criminals because "criminals bring with them money and the capacity
to raise it."[102] According to him, legislators have gotten mixed up with
criminal elements because such individuals "can assist in generating
funds to meet the soaring costs of elections."[103] This mode of recruitment may have started with the Congress Party's embrace of "a very
large number of extortionists and racketeers" in order to enlarge party
coffers, but it was soon copied by all political parties.[104]

An ethnographic account of politicians associated with criminality in the western state of Gujarat highlights the fact that for parties,
"goondas are indispensable for the money they bring in."[105] Describing
the prevailing conditions in a poor, urban constituency, anthropologist
Ward Berenschot states that the election budget of the local MLA—a
dada who had deep ties to criminal elements—came largely from hafta,
the payments owners of illegal businesses (such as liquor bootleggers
and gambling dens) make to politicians for protection. In this way, politicians who rely heavily on goondas are able to marshal both "muscle
power" and "money power" for political ends.

The political scientist Francesca Jensenius reports speaking with a
senior MLA in western Uttar Pradesh who claimed that the price for
tickets was one of the main reasons for the criminalization of politics
in the politically critical state, because only criminals could afford to
cover the price of admission.[106]

The financial incentive for parties to recruit criminal candidates is
also borne out by my own interviews with MPs, MLAs, and leaders of
state and national parties over the last several years. In 2009, I paid a
visit to a Congress MP from Andhra Pradesh in his official residence
in New Delhi. As is the case across India at all hours of the day and
night, the politician had a long line of people eager to see him, their
wait slightly eased by the repeated cups of homemade chai on offer.

The man was a longtime Congress stalwart, having commenced his association with the party years earlier when he was a university student. His residence was sparsely furnished, a contrast to the gaudy opulence of the homes of many of his parliamentary colleagues. Perhaps it was his decades in politics or the fact that I had come to see him at the end of a long day when Parliament was in session, but the MP was jaded about the state of politics in the country when we sat and talked in his drawing room. When I first asked whether parties recruit criminals because of their money, he interrupted, snorting, "What do you think?" Realizing perhaps the condescension in his voice, he went on: "Look, if you put a few big-time criminals in a room and you have a few *crores* [an Indian unit of wealth equal to 10 million rupees, or $150,000], you can call yourself a party. *Crores* and criminals are the essential ingredients."[107]

I heard the same story in Bihar around the state's 2010 election. As the campaign was getting under way, I spent a morning in the party office of one of the national parties in the center of Patna, the capital. I had come to meet the state party vice president, but when my interlocutor spotted the party treasurer and knowing my interests, he immediately introduced me. After all, the party treasurer of all people should know where the money comes from. After some initial small talk, the man candidly fessed up that his party made the money-muscle calculation when determining the distribution of party tickets. At first I was taken aback by his candor, but he went on to say that all parties selected candidates facing criminal cases, at least in part, because of their deep pockets. There was hardly any shame in it, the treasurer assured me. "All parties claim to shun criminality," he said, "but the reality is different. As they say, 'All is fair in love and war.' Parties select people who can win by *saam daam dhand bhed* [by hook or by crook], and the most important criterion is financial assets."[108]

When I interacted with Sanjay, the aspiring candidate in Andhra Pradesh, on the campaign trail in 2014 I asked him about the link between money and muscle. As far as I could tell, he had no direct involvement with any criminal elements and he himself had a clean record. He had family in politics and none of them had been implicated in any wrongdoing either. But he told me he could see the attraction parties would have. "Parties have a pretty good sense of what elections cost now and what they're likely to cost in the future," he said. "They know

that they have to find well-off candidates to fight elections for them."
What costs 100 million rupees today will cost 200 million rupees five
years from now when the next election comes around, he said. But, I
interjected, not all were criminals—HE did not have a criminal record,
for instance. "But there are not enough of us," he replied. "Without
money, you cannot do anything. You will be wiped out. You first have
to make money, and then you can do good after you're entrenched and
secure." Sanjay related to me the example of one of his party's senior
leaders, who had amassed a large fortune through a series of questionable business dealings that traded heavily on his political connections.
He is a good man, Sanjay assured me (in what sounded like a blatant
rationalization), but he needed to build a big enough war chest that
would allow him to do good in the future. For those in a rush to make
money, there were lots of shortcuts available, and parties are always
willing to look the other way. "Political parties are full of excuses," he
said with a smile.

NEW DATA SOURCES

Scrutinizing the link between money and muscle more closely requires
fine-grain data on the personal attributes of candidates. Typically, such
information is lacking, particularly in developing countries. Even when
researchers can construct credible data, the latter are often restricted
to election winners rather than all candidates standing for office. But a
major breakthrough for political data in developing countries occurred
in 2003. A wellspring of information about India's political class was
tapped for the first time, introducing a new level of transparency about
India's electoral aspirants and elected officials.

Window into a Private World

As part of its effort to address the criminalization of politics, the
ECI had long agitated for candidates to make public disclosures about
their criminal antecedents. The first breakthrough came in 2002 when
the Supreme Court ruled in a public interest litigation (PIL) suit filed
by ADR requiring that each candidate standing for election at the state
and national levels submit at the time of nomination a judicial affidavit
detailing their educational qualifications, financial assets and liabilities,
and information about pending criminal cases.[109]

Politicians and political parties strongly opposed the move, but soon after the government promulgated an executive ordinance severely watering down the new transparency regime.[110] A coalition of civil society groups once again appealed to the judiciary, which invalidated the ordinance. With the court's backing, the ECI framed new guidelines for disclosure, which have increased the level of political transparency and the ability of ordinary citizens to access information about competing candidates.[111]

Building on the work of some pioneering civil society groups, I set out to build a dataset that contains information on virtually the entire universe of candidates standing for state and national election in India between 2003 and 2009. This database includes details on 46,739 candidates who contested 35 state assembly elections and 21,697 candidates who contested national elections in 2004, 2009, and 2014.[112] Details of the dataset, its creation, and caveats can be found in Appendix A.

A few salient points about the data are worth mentioning. First, the affidavit data are self-reported, immediately raising concerns about their veracity. It is less of a concern for criminal cases, given that these are a matter of public record, but it is likely to affect the data on financial assets and liabilities. It is best to treat the financial data as an underestimate given that candidates face incentives to underreport their wealth in order to obscure financial assets from prying eyes. Nevertheless, the assets candidates do report are very high relative to the average Indian, as are the monetary gains over time.

The bigger concern with the criminality data is not underreporting but rather the scope for politically motivated cases. The good news is that candidates have to disclose only those cases a judge has taken cognizance of or in which charges have been framed, rather than the existence of a police report, known as a first information report (FIR). This (and the fact that candidates are only required to disclose cases initiated at least six months before the election) helps to protect against political vendettas—but only partially.

A second safeguard is to distinguish between "minor" and "serious" cases. Any coding of charges is clearly subjective, but following convention I code charges as "minor" if they might, arguably, be related to assembly, campaigning, or speech—or acts that lend themselves most easily to political retribution. I consider the remainder to be "serious" charges. The definition is admittedly minimalist, and it differs slightly from other available definitions, including the one favored by ADR, which is detailed in Appendix A. The differences are not substantively important, however; the two measures are highly correlated (the correlation coefficient is .78 in the dataset of state elections and .79 in the national elections dataset). Throughout the book, I restrict my attention to serious cases. In the few instances where I use a narrower definition of "serious" cases for descriptive purposes (typically, ADR's definition), I clearly note that fact.

Crunching the Numbers

Although one should be cautious about using data that are self-disclosed and unverified by a third party, the affidavit data—taken as a whole, warts and all—present a reasonable snapshot of the biographical profiles of India's most influential lawmakers. The picture isn't pretty.

My analysis of data from parliamentary candidates contesting elections in 2004, 2009, and 2014 reveals a strong correlation between a parliamentary candidate's personal assets—again, serving as a proxy for financial capacity—and the likelihood of election (figure 4.7). Consider the following statistic: the poorest 20 percent of candidates, in terms of personal financial assets, had a 1 percent chance of winning parliamentary elections. The richest quintile, in contrast, had a greater than 23 percent likelihood.

If quintiles are confusing, consider the following thought exercise. The poorest candidates, say those with less than 100,000 rupees ($1,500) to their name, have a less than 1 percent chance of winning a seat in Parliament. For those who are slightly richer, who possess between 100,000 ($1,500) and 1 million rupees ($15,000), the odds of winning are slightly better: 1 percent. The odds are significantly better for those in the next wealth bracket, those whose assets range between 1 and 10 million rupees (or $15,000 and $150,000). These candidates have a 9 percent chance of gaining entry into Parliament. Not surprisingly, the odds of winning are greatest for those in the richest wealth category— those candidates who are known as *crorepatis* in the Indian parlance (or whose wealth is greater than one crore, or 10 million rupees). Of the 4,857 candidates who found themselves in this bracket, 18 percent were electorally successful.

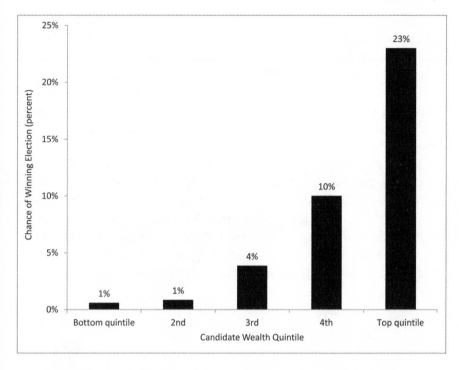

Figure 4.7. Candidate wealth and electoral success in Lok Sabha elections, 2004–14. (Author's calculations based on affidavits submitted to the Election Commission of India by candidates contesting the 2004, 2009, and 2014 parliamentary elections)

Not only does wealth provide an electoral advantage, there is evidence that the magnitude of that advantage may be growing. In 2004, of the 543 elected members of the Lok Sabha, 156 (or 29 percent) were worth at least one crore. By 2009, 315 (or 58 percent) of MPs belonged to this wealthy tier. That share grew to 82 percent in 2014.[113]

When it comes to campaign cash, candidates accused of serious violations of the law have a distinct advantage. In 2004, Samuel Paul and M. Vivekananda conducted one of the first analyses of elected officials using newly public affidavit data. The authors found a strong correlation between a candidate's criminal record and his financial assets; in fact, the overall asset base of members increased with the severity of the charges filed. "It is almost as if with larger assets one can graduate to a higher level on the crime ladder," the authors remark.[114]

Based on my own analysis of data from the last three parliamentary elections, roughly 4 percent of candidates in the lowest quintile of candidate wealth (or poorest one-fifth) faced serious criminal cases compared to nearly 15 percent of candidates in the top quintile (figure 4.8). Put slightly differently, the median "clean" candidate has a personal wealth of just above 900,000 rupees ($13,500), compared to roughly 4.1 million rupees ($62,000) for the median candidate with a serious criminal case.

To test the money-muscle link more formally, I analyzed an identical dataset to the one on MP aspirants but this one gathered from nearly all state legislative candidates seeking office between 2003 and 2009. The results again provide strong support for the hypothesis that money and muscle do in fact go hand in hand: the size of a candidate's personal financial assets is strongly and positively associated with his criminal status (figure 4.9). Controlling for a range of factors, the probability

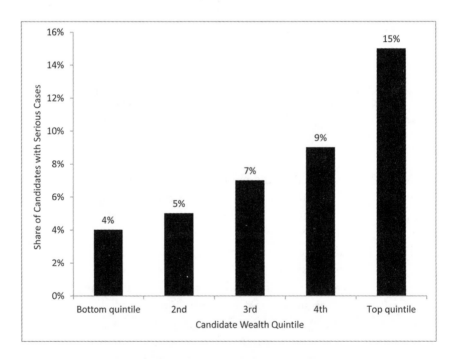

Figure 4.8. Candidate wealth and share of candidates with pending serious criminal cases in Lok Sabha elections, 2004–2014. (Author's calculations based on affidavits submitted to the Election Commission of India by candidates contesting the 2004, 2009, and 2014 parliamentary elections)

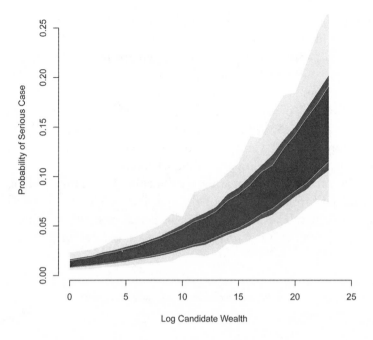

Figure 4.9. Positive association between personal wealth and probability state assembly candidates have at least one serious criminal case, 2003–9. Dark, medium, and light gray shading represent 90, 95, and 99 percent confidence intervals, respectively. Candidate wealth is measured using a log scale. (Author's calculations based on affidavits submitted to the Election Commission of India by candidates contesting state assembly elections between 2003 and 2009)

of facing a serious criminal case increases by 12 percent as an average candidate's wealth moves from the mean to maximum value in the sample. The relationship between wealth and criminal status is non-linear; the positive association between the two is more pronounced for very large levels of candidate wealth.[115] This association also holds when one uses data from national parliamentary candidates.

When it comes to a candidate's electoral prospects, possessing a serious criminal record seems to pay significant dividends, even after controlling for a candidate's wealth. Previous analyses demonstrated that (1) wealth reaps electoral dividends, and that (2) suspected criminal candidates are more likely to be wealthy. Yet even beyond the impact of money, alleged criminality seems to provide an added bonus to candidates' electoral fortunes. Comparing candidates who did not face serious cases and those who did at every level of candidate wealth, from the poorest to the richest quintile, candidates facing serious cases were more likely to win election (figure 4.10).

We can confirm this result more systematically by looking at the much larger dataset of candidates in state elections. Wealth and criminality have an interactive effect: wealth significantly magnifies the electoral success of criminal candidates. The effects are heterogeneous, such that at very low values of wealth criminality has a negligible impact (figure 4.11).[116] Conversely, the interaction between wealth and criminality is more meaningful at higher levels of wealth.

Yet the data indicate that while wealth enhances criminal candidates' electoral performance, it is not the sole factor. The gap between the two shaded bands (candidates who have serious cases and those who do not) suggests that criminality provides candidates with advantages

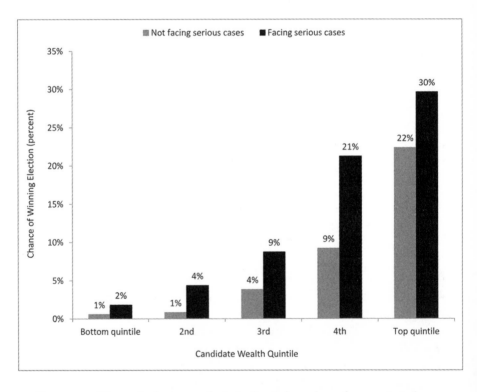

Figure 4.10. Electoral advantage of criminality independent of money in Lok Sabha elections, 2004–14. (Author's calculations based on affidavits submitted to the Election Commission of India by candidates contesting the 2004, 2009, and 2014 parliamentary elections)

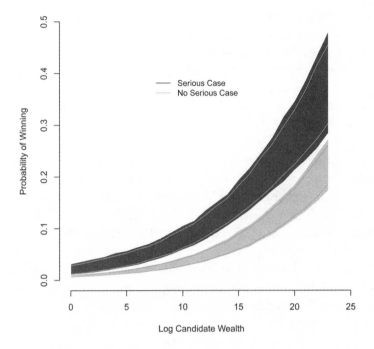

Figure 4.11. Interactive effect of wealth and criminal case status on electoral success in state elections, 2003–9. The thin lines and shading represent 90 and 95 percent confidence intervals, respectively. Criminal case status is defined as having at least one serious criminal case. Candidate wealth is measured using a log scale. (Author's calculations based on affidavits submitted to the Election Commission of India by candidates contesting state elections between 2003 and 2009)

above and beyond their access to money alone. At nearly every level of wealth, candidates with serious cases outperform their "clean" counterparts, suggesting that one has to dig deeper to find other sources of this "criminality premium."

MOVING BEYOND MONEY

A criminally suspect candidate's ability to self-finance elections and subsidize party activities tells us something important about why parties are attracted to candidates with criminal records. As Yogendra Yadav has stated, with the partial exception of Left parties, "Anyone who does not have access to vast, unaccountable and disposable wealth has little chance of getting a 'ticket.'"[117] Yet the fact that criminality has an effect on electoral success independent of wealth suggests that money is a partial explanation of a party's embrace of muscle.

While money helps explain the supply of tainted politicians into the electoral marketplace—namely, why parties might value their candidacy—the puzzle of India's criminal politicians does not end there. After all, a model of political selection built on money alone is an incomplete explanation of the selection of criminal candidates, since parties also might conceivably recruit other wealthy, *noncriminal* candidates (such as businessmen, celebrities, or other notables).

Indeed, a cursory glance at the financial disclosures of India's elected MPs confirms this: of those MPs elected in 2014, the five richest MPs were all wealthy industrialists—Jayadev Galla (6.83 billion rupees, or $103 million) and Gokaraju Ganga Raju (2.88 billion rupees, or $44 million) run large conglomerates with interests ranging from packaged foods and sheet metal to ayurvedic products; Konda Vishweshwar Reddy (5.28 billion rupees, or $800 million) is an entrepreneur who has successfully launched numerous tech companies; Butta Renuka (2.42 billion rupees), whose husband is a successful industrialist, runs a chain of clothing and jewelry outlets; and Kamal Nath (2.06 billion rupees, or $37 million) gets most of his wealth from a vast network of companies, primarily in the real estate sector, controlled by his wife and two sons.[118] Together, they were worth more than 19.5 billion rupees (or $295 million). Beyond industrialists, rich celebrities are represented in Parliament—from Kirron Kher, the film and television actress and talk show host, to actress-dancer-producer Hema Malini, to onetime film celebrity Shatrugan "Shotgun" Sinha. Even cricket icon Sachin Tendulkar, one of the most revered figures in Indian sports history, was inaugurated into the upper house of Parliament, in 2013.[119]

These facts suggest that parties have access to candidates who are wealthy but are not known for their criminal connections, raising obvious questions about why they persist in selecting candidates with serious criminal records. To gain a more comprehensive picture of how these candidates add electoral value, the demand-side imperatives of the electoral marketplace, which bring voters squarely to the fore, merit close examination.

5 Doing Good by Doing Bad
The Demand for Criminality

"ANANT SINGH IS not a murderer. He merely manages murder," the man said flatly and without a trace of irony. The person who spoke these words was a well-educated engineer, a friend of an acquaintance of mine, and we were sitting in the living room of his stately ancestral home on the banks of the Ganges River in central Bihar, sipping our third cup of sickly sweet homemade chai while discussing the local political scene. I had sought out the engineer to chat about a local politician, Anant Singh, a three-time MLA from Mokama, a surprisingly lush constituency in the poverty-stricken easternmost reaches of Patna district. Singh was one of the area's most well-known politicians, not least because of the length of his rap sheet.

The engineer's family had long known Anant Singh and was connected to the political party he was affiliated with, the ruling Janata Dal (United) or JD(U). The engineer's remark about Singh lingered in the air, much like a word cloud from a newspaper cartoon. I paused for a second, not knowing whether the man was joking or serious. It was clear from the expression on his face it was the latter.

Anant Singh is an unlikely poster child for electoral success in a flourishing democracy like India. He is fond of wearing dark sunglasses, a cigarette perched on his lips, his body adorned in all white, occasionally gussied up with a dark leather jacket. If he were not in politics,

Singh could have had an alternate career as a cinematic villain—his practiced bad boy look was straight out of central casting.

In addition to his official designation as an elected representative of this poor, rural constituency, Singh doubles as something of a local godfather, or *dada*. Singh rose to political prominence on the back of his other brother, Dilip, who emerged as a Bhumihar (upper caste) gang leader in the region in the mid-1980s. Dilip parlayed his muscle power into political power, eventually entering state politics and winning the Mokama seat in 1990 (a feat he repeated in 1995). Anant, who allegedly began his criminal career as Dilip's enforcer, ultimately took over the political reins of the family—first winning election to the Bihar assembly in a 2004 by-election in Mokama. He was reelected in February 2005 and again in October 2005, when a fresh state election was called after the previous one furnished a hung assembly. When I arrived at the engineer's house in the fall of 2010 to discuss Anant Singh, he was days away from winning his fourth consecutive election.

Over the years, Singh has been implicated in dozens of criminal cases, and many of his alleged criminal acts, widely reported in the press, have been carried out in a brazenly public manner. There was the killing of a contractor, a cousin of Singh's, in the streets of Bihar's capital, Patna, in broad daylight. The victim was waiting in line at a government office when he supposedly took four bullets at close range from a group of six assailants.[1] There was the beating of two television journalists who showed up at Singh's house to inquire about his alleged involvement in the rape and murder of a young woman. When a cameraman subsequently arrived at Singh's compound to inquire about his colleagues, he too was reportedly assaulted.[2]

The circumstances surrounding Anant Singh's first (alleged) murder are something of a local legend. Anant's older brother, Birachi, was a *mukhia* (village headman) and a prominent landlord in the area. Several villagers told me that a sympathizer of Naxalite rebels, who were carrying out targeted assassinations of upper-caste landlords throughout the region, shot and killed Birachi before taking refuge on a boat in the middle of the Ganges River. Anant, seeking to avenge Birachi's death, supposedly tracked his brother's killer for months. When he eventually learned of the killer's location, Anant swam across the river and murdered the man. When asked about the crime, Anant coolly responded that "justice needed to be done."[3]

With such a history of high-profile transgressions, videos circulating on the Internet of Singh drunkenly dancing while brandishing an AK-47 seem downright tame in comparison. Indeed, newspaper stories openly speak of Singh's unique penchant for "guns and goons."[4] Anant Singh himself has bragged of being shot at least twenty times but claims he does not live in fear: "They tell me there is an emotion like fear. What does it feel like?" Singh once asked a reporter. "I don't lose courage in life's battle."[5]

Constituents in Mokama rarely call Singh by his given name, instead referring to him as *chhote sarkar* (little lord) for his dominance over the constituency. A reporter who traveled to interview him in 2014 was warned against traveling to Mokama by a senior police official, who claimed that he and his officers could not guarantee her safety on Singh's turf.[6] Though dozens of cases have been lodged against Anant, local police and prosecutors have yet to obtain a single conviction. Cases against Anant have languished for years, during which time judges have passed away, law enforcement officials have been transferred, witnesses have developed cold feet, and evidence has suddenly gone missing.[7]

Singh's alleged criminal acts are not his only attributes that have gained notoriety; the lawmaker's idiosyncrasies and penchant for extravagance are also widely discussed. In the thick of the Hindi heartland, Singh speaks little Hindi, preferring instead the local Magahi dialect; he keeps a python as a house pet as well as an elephant who is trained to shake hands; and he raises expensive horses who are tasked with pulling an antique buggy in which Singh often rides around Mokama.[8]

But perhaps the most perplexing fact about Anant Singh is that his political patron is a man who burnishes a reputation as one of the cleanest politicians in India: the reformist chief minister of Bihar, Nitish Kumar.[9] Kumar swept into office in 2005 with promises of cleaning up one of the poorest, most corrupt, and socially fractured states in India. Between 2005 and 2010, when Kumar's ruling alliance won a resounding reelection, Kumar made great strides, against all odds, in doing exactly that. So why would Kumar risk his reputation by giving Anant Singh, a man who has seemingly profited by consistently running afoul of the law, a party ticket to contest elections and then campaign tirelessly on his behalf?

FROM SUPPLY TO DEMAND

With ample resources in hand, politicians with criminal reputations gain traction with political parties. In the language of the electoral marketplace, money helps explain the supply of tainted politicians joining mainstream politics. Yet while candidates linked to crime do appear, on average, to have more wealth than the average "clean" candidate, it also appears that their criminality gives them an edge in elections extending above and beyond their financial prowess.

What explains this additional and perhaps less tangible electoral advantage is something of a mystery. After all, the notion that voters might reward rather than reject candidates with criminal connections challenges some fundamental tenets of democratic theory, even calling into question widely accepted notions of accountability and representation. Indeed, theory dating back centuries tells us that a key distinction between democratic and nondemocratic systems is the fact that in democracies, voters can utilize elections to "throw the rascals out," if they so choose.[10] Indeed, the ability to sanction bad politicians and to reward good ones is one of the defining touchstones of representative democracy.[11]

Over the years, however, social scientists have recognized that voters are perfectly capable of voting *in*, rather than kicking *out*, candidates with less-than-angelic bio-sheets. The alleged reason for this state of affairs is entirely intuitive: voters might support bad politicians because they simply do not know any better. If voters are not able to identify criminal or corrupt candidates during election campaigns, they may become unwitting pawns in a game rigged by political elites. I refer to this proposition as the "ignorant voter" hypothesis. Restated simply, voters in democratic systems must have information on the quality of candidates if they are to hold their representatives accountable to a certain standard. If voters do not have reliable information on the backgrounds of politicians, democratic representation may not necessarily lead to political accountability. So perhaps the puzzle of support for criminality in politics is not such a puzzle after all?

In this chapter I hope to make two points. First, under certain conditions it can be rational even for well-informed voters to support politicians associated with illegal behavior. Second, electoral support for politicians with criminal records is not necessarily symptomatic of a breakdown in democratic accountability. Although the ignorant voter hypothesis provides a compelling explanation for why so-called bad politicians thrive, it leaves no room for the possibility that there can be an affirmative case for the selection of tainted politicians by voters.

Yet in contexts where the rule of law is weakly enforced and social divisions are rampant, a candidate's criminal reputation could be perceived as an asset. In the rough-and-tumble of electoral politics, where there is a dynamic pattern of competition between rival social groups, voters just might value politicians who are willing to engage in extralegal tactics to protect the status of their community. If politics is viewed as a zero-sum game, a candidate's criminality can provide an added advantage in two respects: it can mobilize support by both pledging to deliver benefits to a defined group of supporters while simultaneously weakening opposition from rival groups.

The popular embrace of candidates with criminal reputations at the ballot box doesn't necessarily mean that wily politicians and party bosses are duping India's voters or that elections are a sham. To the contrary, it is quite possible that many citizens are making a self-interested calculation by lending their support to such politicians.

This argument has far-reaching implications because it suggests that information about a candidate's criminality is not only *available* to voters, but that it is *central* to understanding the viability of their candidacy. Voters aren't ignorant or uninformed; they are simply looking for candidates who can best fill a perceived vacuum of representation. Viewed in this light, the electoral success of politicians associated with illegal activity might in fact be compatible with democratic accountability, albeit of a partial nature. Bad politicians can simultaneously engage in "bad" behavior and "good" politics, at least for some segment of the electorate. Ironically, the conventional hypothesis about information breeding accountability is correct—just not in the ways that proponents of this argument had foreseen.

INFORMATION, DEMOCRACY, AND ACCOUNTABILITY

Political scientists have long recognized that one of the principal advantages of democracy over alternative forms of governance is that democracy empowers a country's citizens to hold their elected representatives accountable. Unlike authoritarian systems in which leaders can rule by fiat, diktat, or whim, democracies are marked by the rule by, for, and of the people. If citizens living in democratic systems no longer approve of the job their representatives are doing, they have a safety valve. Voters may not be able to exert total control over their representatives after they have been elected, but they can always withdraw their acceptance by refusing to reelect them when the time comes.[12]

Over time and based on a wide variety of country experiences, scholars have acknowledged that accountability is not an automatic feature of democratic politics. In the real world, the connection between democracy and accountability is often partial, imperfect, or completely broken.[13] Instead, the link between democracy and accountability is contingent on the effective functioning of democratic institutions.

In the search for identifying the culprit to blame for breakdowns in accountability, there are many places one can point fingers. But in recent years, a consensus seems to have formed that for democracy to engender accountability, the average voter must have access to a free flow of information about the quality of candidates standing for elections.[14]

Armed with information, the logic goes, voters can collect information about the broader candidate pool and make informed voting decisions about who is best fit to represent their interests.[15] "The degree of information citizens have, either through news media, personal networks, or their own direct experiences, curbs the opportunities politicians may have to engage in political corruption or mismanagement," reports one oft-cited cross-country study.[16]

The idea that information about the behavior of public officials produces greater accountability is not a new one. In the late 1700s, the British philosopher Jeremy Bentham wrote of the necessity of "publicity" in politics, referring to a situation in which information is both made available to, and used by, the public in electing their representatives. He writes: "The greater the number of temptations to which the exercise of political power is exposed, the more necessary is it to give those who possess it, the most powerful reasons for resisting them. But there is no reason more constant and more universal than the superintendence of the public. The public compose a tribunal, which is more powerful than all the other tribunals together."[17] Bentham argued that the public evaluation of politicians acts as a deterrent to behavior that the public would consider unacceptable: namely, any behavior that is contrary to the public interest. Where voters have perfect information, rent-seeking should disappear.

Ignorant Voters and Bad Politicians

The hypothesized link between access to information and better governance is not simply a theoretical one dreamed up by philosophers and democratic idealists. In recent years, a growing body of research provides empirical support for the idea that voters who are armed with more information can induce better government.

Bentham's insights were brought back into the limelight more recently by the economist and Nobel laureate Amartya Sen, who famously argued that the free flow of information is the essential variable that explains why democracies (such as India) do not experience famine, yet nondemocracies often do. Sen's argument is twofold: thanks to the ballot box, democratic governments are already incentivized to prevent catastrophes, but it is a free flow of information in this democratic context (manifest by a free press) which gives citizens both the necessary information and the medium with which they can hold their leaders accountable.[18]

Economists Timothy Besley and Robin Burgess set out to validate Sen's theoretical arguments.[19] By looking at state-level data from India over a period of three decades, the researchers found that state governments are more responsive to shortfalls in food production (often caused by natural disasters) in places where newspaper circulation is higher. The intuition tracks Sen's argument well: greater information flows about public policy create an incentive for governments to respond to the needs of voters because—if they fail to respond adequately—informed voters will express their displeasure at the ballot box by voting them out. This finding is not unique to India. For instance, scholars have discerned a similar pattern using historical data from the United States. In the wake of the Great Depression, U.S. counties with a greater share of radio listeners—a reasonable proxy for access to information—received more New Deal welfare funds, even after one adjusts for the severity of unemployment in those localities.[20]

These and other studies link information provision to better, more responsive government. But there is also emerging evidence that directly evaluates the importance of information when it comes to the fate of individual politicians. In 2003, Brazil's federal government randomly selected municipalities to receive a thorough audit of their expenditures, including funds that had been granted to them by the central government. Local governments in Brazil are notoriously corrupt and the audits were designed to make their dirty laundry public in the hope that voters would act on the new information. While all of these local audits were made public and widely disseminated through the media, by pure luck some of the audit disclosures were made before municipal elections held in 2004 and some after.

An ingenious study exploited this unintended feature of the program to explore whether audits released before elections had any impact on political outcomes, compared to municipalities whose audits had not yet been released (but which experienced similar levels of reported corruption).[21] It turns out that incumbent politicians from towns where pre-election audits had uncovered acts of corruption fared significantly worse than their counterparts who had not *yet* been exposed. In line with the research cited above, this effect was more pronounced where local radio stations were more prevalent (which presumably could relay news of the audit findings).

Similar findings have also emerged from the other side of the Atlantic. Voters in postwar Italy had long elected (and reelected) deputies in parliament whom their own government suspected of engaging in all manner of malfeasance. However, things began to change in the 1990s. From then on out, voters began punishing allegedly corrupt deputies by voting them out of office. The authors of one widely cited study believe that voters changed their tune thanks to increased media scrutiny and the resulting widespread availability of information about deputies' corrupt dealings following a sweeping series of nationwide anticorruption investigations. Their story, like the others' above, fits nicely with the ignorant voter hypothesis.[22]

The Ignorant Voter Hypothesis in India

Based on this influential body of work, scholars who have studied the sources of electoral support for tainted politicians typically make two assumptions. The first is that if voters possess information about the quality of candidates, this information will influence their voting behavior and reduce support for corrupt or criminal candidates. If voters lack information about candidate quality, they cannot punish wayward officials at the ballot box. The second assumption is that the election of a significant number of tainted politicians represents a breakdown in the democracy-accountability link.

There is no reason to doubt the studies on Italian deputies, Brazilian local councilors, or related research that have found merit in the idea that once ignorant voters are no longer uninformed, the quality of politicians takes a turn for the better. The real question is whether this claim is generalizable and, hence, applicable to the case of India.

On first glance, the ignorant voter hypothesis would seem to travel to the Indian context quite seamlessly. For starters, according to the 2011 census, one-quarter of India's population above the age of six is illiterate, which suggests that there is a significant pool of voters vulnerable to making uniformed voting decisions.

Second, although India is home to a vibrant independent media, the lack of access many individuals have to mainstream media resources severely limits its influence. According to the 2014 National Election Study conducted by CSDS, 40 percent of respondents report never reading the newspaper. Of those polled, 59 percent and 15 percent, respectively, report never listening to the news on the radio or watching the news on television, and 72 percent claimed they never even once consulted the Internet to access election-related information.[23]

Third, although credible information on candidates' criminal records does exist in India, these disclosures have only been available publicly since 2003. Since then, groups affiliated with India's RTI movement have regularly urged voters to punish tainted candidates by publicizing personal information extracted from their electoral affidavits. Even so, the availability of this information is questionable, given the above constraints and the uneven attempts by the government and civil society organizations to disseminate it widely. The ECI, for its part, merely scans and posts images of candidates' affidavits on their homepage.[24]

Are Voters in India Truly Ignorant?

Notwithstanding the intuitive appeal of applying the ignorant voter hypothesis to India, closer inspection suggests there are several reasons to be skeptical. First, an existing body of research—discussed in greater detail below—highlights the fact that candidates with criminal records often openly embrace their outlaw reputations. Candidates who have been charged with perpetrating serious criminal acts often do not hide their supposed transgressions; they do the opposite: they actually burnish them.

This leads to a second important point: voters in poor democracies can be quite well informed about the nature of local leadership and governance despite their illiteracy, lack of education, and irregular access to news media.[25] Community life, especially in predominantly rural, agrarian societies, can actually be a conducive environment for informal information flows. Interpersonal communication, contact with one's neighbors, and the pace of village life all facilitate the spread of information about local-level politics.[26]

Third, if a lack of information explained the appeal of candidates facing criminal cases, one might expect the success rate of such candidates to decline over time as the level of political awareness increases and voters correspondingly adjust their behavior. In fact, the opposite appears to be true: there has been no clear decrease in the share of elected legislators who face serious criminal cases. As I pointed out in Chapter 1, the percentage of elected MPs with criminal cases has actually increased with every successful election since 2004. Insofar as state elections are concerned, 17 states have seen rates of suspected criminality increase over the prior election, 4 states have seen no change, and 9 states have seen at least some decline (figure 5.1).

Finally, the only study to have rigorously evaluated the impact of informing voters of their candidates' criminal records found that such information had no impact on voter behavior at the ballot box. Researchers from the Massachusetts Institute of Technology's Poverty Action Lab created "report cards" on the performance of municipal councilors in New Delhi and distributed them to a random set of slum households just before local elections. When the researchers interviewed these households after the election, they found those that received information on candidate criminality did not modify their voting behavior in any statistically discernible way from those who had not gotten this information. This is in contrast to other performance measures the researchers disseminated to households (such as attendance in the legislature), which did incentivize voters to change their behavior.[27] One possible conclusion emerged: by informing households about candidates' alleged criminality, researchers were not telling voters anything they did not already know.

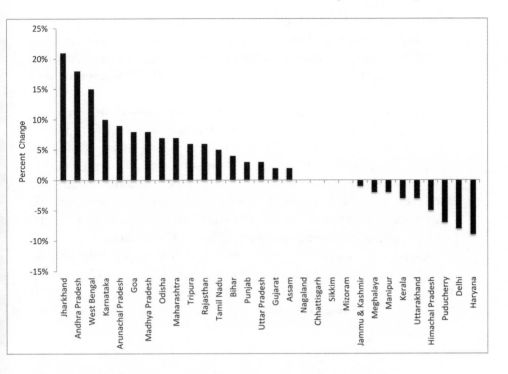

Figure 5.1. Trends in share of MLAs with pending serious criminal cases, as of December 2015. Each bar represents the change in the share of MLAs with at least one serious case over the two most recent state assembly elections. (Author's calculations based on data from the Association for Democratic Reforms)

AN AFFIRMATIVE LOGIC

If voter ignorance does not provide a compelling explanation for why voters in India support politicians with criminal records, what *is* motivating Indian voters to behave in such seemingly strange ways? It seems odd that voters would knowingly support candidates with dubious credentials.

Although it may seem counterintuitive, well-informed voters can have an underlying strategic logic for supporting criminal candidates when two conditions are present. First, social divisions, typically (though not exclusively) manifest by ethnic differences, must be politically salient. The very fact of ethnic differences does not necessarily mean that these cleavages are politically activated; politicians "turn them on" when they are perceived to have electoral benefits. One instance in which they might be deemed beneficial is when there is an intense contest over local dominance. Second, the rule of law must be weakly or inconsistently applied. This both creates a vacuum for a savvy political entrepreneur to present himself as a "savior" and increases the probability that he can manipulate the allocation or distribution of state resources.

In settings where both conditions are operative—salient social divisions and weak rule of law—voters often have an incentive to reward politicians whose criminal bona fides serves as a signal of their enhanced capacity and willingness to do whatever it takes to protect their supporters' interests (figure 5.2). These interests are often cast in terms of preserving the status of the ethnic community (or communities) in question, which further allows a candidate to spin his criminal reputation as doing whatever is necessary to "defend" his followers. However, such politicians have an incentive to ensure that the solutions they invest in are not systematic, lest they put themselves out of business as fixers. Thus, their enforcement of the rule of law is likely to be highly selective. According to this logic, information about a candidate's crim-

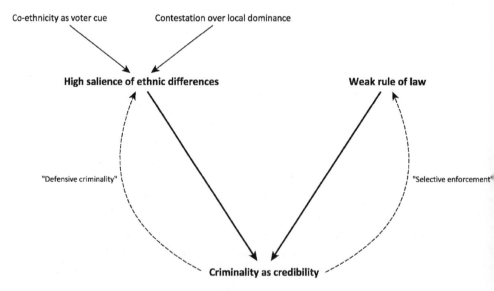

Figure 5.2. From social divisions and weak rule of law to criminality in politics.

inality is not only well known to many voters, but it is *intrinsic* to their voting behavior.

The Ethnic Cue

There is a vast literature that suggests that ethnic identity is the most important axis around which politics in India—and in a range of other democracies around the world—revolves. By "ethnicity" I refer to identities based on ascriptive categories, such as language, caste, and religion. These categories are not necessarily interchangeable, but for simplicity's sake, I group them together.[28]

In her seminal book *Why Ethnic Parties Succeed,* Kanchan Chandra argues that in multiethnic "patronage democracies" like India, a reliance on a series of cognitive shortcuts leads voters and politicians to favor co-ethnics in the reciprocal exchange of votes and benefits.[29] By mobilizing on ethnic lines, political elites can take advantage of deep, preexisting social networks, organizations, and focal points that allow them to efficiently communicate with voters.[30] Ethnic identity serves as a kind of commitment device—voters are more likely to deem promises made by co-ethnic politicians as credible, and politicians can rely on norms of reciprocity and social sanctioning within the group to ensure voters uphold their end of the bargain.[31] Ethnicity, then, functions as a clear signal of a politician's credibility among those who share his or her ethnic identity—"co-ethnics" for shorthand. Whether politicians actually deliver on their promises of favoring co-ethnics once in office (or curbing the advantages previously granted to non-co-ethnics) is less relevant than the perception that they will act in this way if elected.

While Chandra's theory is primarily focused on the ethnic makeup of political parties and party brands, ethnic considerations also extend to the identities of individual candidates as well. This is especially true where party labels have little salience or where parties must rest on diverse coalitions to win election. One would also expect the identity of candidates to matter in countries where the state plays a crucial role dispensing benefits and services because elected representatives will play an outsized role in directing those items to maximize electoral returns.[32]

Although in India—and many other low-income democracies—it has been well documented that ethnic identity is the most relevant social cleavage in society, there might be social cleavages other than ethnic-ity that politicians can exploit for political purposes. It may well be the case; the central assumption is merely that social cleavages exist and that they provide a reasonable shortcut for politicians to identify, target, and mobilize voters. The proclivity toward mobilizing on such social cleavages is greatly enhanced when parties are pragmatic, rather than ideological, in a programmatic sense.[33]

The Salience of Ethnic Differences

Within multiethnic democracies, the import of ethnic cleavages is not felt the same in all places at all times. The relevance of social divisions is likely to vary across time and space, according to local conditions—ranging from the actions of political elites, to demographic characteris-tics, or to the strategic behavior of voters.[34] In other words, the salience of ethnic identity is socially constructed; it is important insofar as it serves a purpose—at a given time and place—for individuals or politi-cians looking to mobilize groups of people.[35] For instance, one study found that survey respondents in Africa tend to identify "ethnically" the closer the survey is to elections and where elections are highly com-petitive.[36] Why? The authors conclude that this could be due either to wily politicians "playing the ethnic card" or to forward-looking voters seeking to maximize post-election benefits from co-ethnics. Another study by political scientist Daniel Posner found that the salience of ethnic identity often varies according to the size of ethnic groups and whether they are large enough, relative to the electorate, to serve as vi-able blocs for coalition building.[37] Where ethnic groups are too small to be politically consequential, politicians do not waste their time "ac-tivating" social divisions in society.

Whatever the precise reason, the importance of ethnicity in politics works like a volume dial on your stereo: it is not stuck permanently in any one place, but can be turned up or turned down at will.

Contestation over Local Dominance

One instance in which ethnic differences are particularly salient is when there is a contest over local dominance; that is, when mul-tiple competing (and sizeable) social groups are at odds over which group exerts primary control over the levers of political and economic power in an area.[38] A contestation over dominance is more than just politics-as-usual; it is fundamentally about reordering social hierarchies. In India, this has traditionally meant a clash over who is able to set new ground rules over social status, labor relations, and access to state patronage.[39]

Contests over dominance are likely in one of two cases: when a community is trying to protect, or prevent the erosion of, traditional patterns of dominance; or from the opposite end of the spectrum, when a community is trying to consolidate newfound political and economic gains.[40] For instance, imagine a scenario in which lower-caste residents are seeking to upend centuries-old practices of labor subordination by upper castes or eliminate discriminatory behaviors in everyday social relations. For their part, traditionally dominant upper-caste communities will be reluctant to alter the status quo and will instead try and preserve their entrenched position. In such a scenario, where rivalries between multiple groups run high and local dominance is contested, social cleavages are salient and identity-based voting takes on greater importance.

Under these conditions, politics becomes a zero-sum game: any gains made by one community are perceived to come at the expense of the other's overall standing in society. As political scientist Steven Wilkinson points out, whether the probability of the threat posed by the "other," rival community is high is irrelevant—what matters is that the people believe that the stakes are high.[41]

Weak Rule of Law and the Abuse of Discretion

In settings where the rule of law is weak, once politicians are ensconced in office they can use (and abuse) their powers of discretion to serve the interests of their constituents. This is what allows "patronage democracies" to function as such; voters cannot rely on the impartial delivery of key state-provided goods and services.[42] When politicians can manipulate their discretionary authority over goods and services the state provides, they often choose to do so along ethnically motivated lines. "Patronage" here refers not simply to jobs, handouts, or other transfers and permissions but to privileged access to state power more generally.

Here, three dimensions of a weak rule-of-law environment are important. First, in weak rule-of-law settings the state is unable to adequately enforce its writ. When it comes to dispensing justice, basic public goods, and security, the state's performance is hamstrung. Second, where the rule of law is weak, politicians can exercise considerable discretion over state resources once in office. The ability to direct (or misdirect, as the case may be) public resources to favored constituencies on the basis of political criteria, as opposed to objective need, increases the value of holding office. This inflates what would-be officeholders are willing to do—and crucially, what they are willing to pay—to get elected. There is undoubtedly a positive relationship between the ability to direct state resources and the cost of elections, thereby limiting the talent pool for public office. A third aspect of weak rule-of-law societies is that politicians can engage in extralegal activity with a reasonably strong assurance that they will face only weak legal consequences for those actions. This "culture of impunity" lowers the costs of engaging in illegal acts because the credibility of punitive action is limited.

In a political context characterized by divisive politics and discretionary authority, the incentives to appeal to co-ethnic sentiment are high. Thus, in addition to salient social divisions, weak rule of law contributes the second factor necessary for criminality to emerge as an integral sign of credibility (see figure 5.2). Given the void that exists where state authority might ordinarily function, politicians can find adequate space to entrench themselves as an institution that supplants the state's role, replacing rule of law with identity-based group politics.

Criminality as Credibility

When there is a sharpening of ethnic differences in weak rule-of-law settings, there are payoffs for candidates who can exploit this friction by providing an additional signal of their credibility.[43] This creates space for a candidate to use his criminality to signal his ability to protect the interests of his community. This signal can be sent using at least four distinct channels: redistribution, coercion, social insurance, and dispute resolution.

First, a candidate's criminal reputation can serve as a clear indication of his willingness and ability to bend the rules to suit his group's own interests. For instance, candidates can use extralegal means (or the threat of resorting to such means) to safeguard a community's economic interests or to influence the distribution of public sector benefits. This is especially relevant in those democracies where access to the state's resources is a vital lifeline for a large swath of citizens.

Second, a candidate's criminality can also help to weaken or counterbalance political opposition from rival groups through coercion and intimidation. This can work in a variety of ways. In a context of competition among rival social groups, a candidate's willingness to "flex his muscles"—or the perception that he is capable of doing so—allows him to enhance his credibility to "get things done."[44] At the same time, a criminal reputation can simultaneously help keep rivals at bay insofar as coercion is used to provide physical security for in-groups or intimidate and pressure rival out-groups. Another possibility is that some elements of a voter's core base might receive some psychic or expressive benefits from a politician's calculated use of force.[45]

A third way criminality can serve as a cue of credibility is through its potential to act as a de facto social safety net. After all, criminality (and serious criminality in particular) often requires an organizational platform, and this platform can serve multiple purposes: it is useful both for engaging in criminal acts as well as for carrying out constituency service. Because candidates with criminal reputations portray themselves as credible fixers who can effectively interface with the state (or, in some cases, substitute for it), voters often turn to them as a last resort if they experience some kind of economic or personal shock, such as shouldering the burden of covering costs for a sick relative, helping an unemployed family member get a job, or making payments for a daughter's wedding.

Importantly, an organizational platform requires financial resources. Money helps explain why political parties might find muscle attractive, but the resource advantage suspected criminal candidates might possess also has an impact—both direct and indirect—on voters' bottom lines. These candidates can provide resources out of their own pocket to help constituents experiencing difficulties. But money also has an indirect impact on voters, in the sense that it can enable politicians to set up effective organizational platforms for dealing with voters' everyday problems.

Finally, in weak rule-of-law settings, ordinary citizens often do not have faith that the official mechanisms for resolving social disputes will operate in an impartial manner. The inability, or unwillingness, of the state to adjudicate disputes in a transparent, fair, and timely fashion creates the space for a strongman who can use his position of strength to serve as local arbiter. Although such informal justice is often a poor substitute for the effective functioning of formal adjudication mechanisms, an imperfect settlement that offers certainty may be preferable to a formal resolution that might never come (or might not be properly enforced were it to come to pass). Indeed, the state's failure to provide adequate justice and channels of resolving disputes has been one of the factors driving the proliferation of criminal organizations in many parts of the world such as Italy, Japan, and Russia.[46]

Although criminality signals credibility primarily among co-ethnics, in many cases it may not be possible for candidates to win election solely on the backs of their kinsmen. In highly fractured environs, candidates may need to construct a minimum winning coalition formed of multiple social groups to get elected. Here, candidates associated with wrongdoing can add to their core voter base by relying on their comparative advantage in deploying redistribution, coercion, or social insurance to voters outside of their bailiwick, especially those groups occupying weaker positions in society. These voters might lend their support, either out of fear or because they perceive that a politician attached to crime will be more likely to deliver on his promises.

Politics of Dignity

The interests suspected criminal candidates claim to protect are often grounded in the politics of dignity and self-respect.[47] The provision of redistribution, physical protection, social insurance, and justice are tangible benefits that voters desire and candidates seek to deliver, but they are inextricably linked with larger issues of a community's status or honor (in Hindi, *sammaan*).

Material benefits are important insofar as they represent tangible manifestations of an improvement in the level of respect, equality of status, and associated symbolic gains that accrue to a given community.[48] We know from scholars of social identity theory that an individual's evaluation of his or her self-worth is often a product of how others recognize the status of the group to which he or she belongs.[49] The political scientist Donald Horowitz explains: "If the need to feel worthy is a fundamental human requirement, it is satisfied in considerable measure by belonging to groups that are in turn regarded as worthy. Like individual self-esteem, collective self-esteem is achieved largely by social recognition."[50]

Indeed, a candidate's criminality is often cast in defensive terms—a politician who runs afoul of the law can frame such activity as being intrinsic to defending the dignity or status of the in-group. This does not imply, of course, that an individual's criminality was actually defensive in nature. Rather, the point is that there are incentives for both a politician and his supporters to characterize the criminality in such terms. A similar argument has been made by Steven Wilkinson to explain why democratic politicians often stand to gain from sponsoring ethnic violence: because most voters did not witness the original illegal act, they will rely on accounts provided by fellow co-ethnic kinsmen and factor in stereotypes about out-groups.[51]

Creating a Feedback Loop

The modus operandi of candidates linked with crime requires that they act to reinforce the very conditions that give them relevance in the first place. Without them, they risk becoming dispensable. This is why candidates with criminal reputations cast their behavior within the framing of "defensive criminality" and consistently embrace the "politics of dignity" rhetoric. The preferred discourse is typically about protecting "our community" in the context of a troublesome, untrustworthy, and—crucially—aggressive "other." This thinking, in turn, further deepens social divisions, creating a positive feedback loop. For instance, it is possible that politicians calculate that it is in their narrow self-interest to engage in criminal acts in order to polarize the vote along ethnic or sectarian lines, thereby rendering the protection or other services they can provide even more relevant.[52] This is not to suggest that criminal politicians engage in identity-based rhetoric purely out of cynical motivation. They might well be true believers who are articulating very real social grievances; the limited point is that they are deriving political benefit from doing so and perpetuating their own "heroic" status.

Furthermore, the "defensive criminality" justification and the constant references to the "politics of dignity" are what provide political parties who embrace criminal politicians an easy out when pressed as to why they choose to give tickets to tainted candidates. I once spoke with a leader of one national party's state unit in Bihar, who confidently asserted that his party had not fielded even one tainted candidate in the coming election. When I pressed him about one well-known candidate who had recently been released from jail just in advance of the election, he replied: "Oh, yes, but he is one exception. He was in prison until recently but he is a respected leader in the [upper caste] Bhumihar community. They are feeling insecure and he will help address that. He looks after their interests and makes sure they are well protected."[53]

A similar dynamic is at work when it comes to the rule of law. Weak or patchy enforcement of the rule of law is what gives criminal candidates the space to swoop in as saviors while reassuring them of the low probability of being held to account by the state. The appeal of criminality in this context is to fill in a governance vacuum that is being ceded by the public sector. It is accomplished often by serving as judge, jury, and executioner—not to mention police officer as well. But this enforcement of the rule of law must, by definition, be highly personal. If the rule of law vacuum were solved by investing in state capacity to provide basic public goods, criminal candidates would lose their luster. Thus, the enforcement of the rule of law must be selective, giving the candidate a highly personalized role.

The Centrality of Information

If criminality signals enhanced credibility, it implies that there are incentives for politicians with criminal records to make their reputations widely known. After all, if a strongman politician cultivates a reputation as someone who is willing to run afoul of the law, he needs to occasionally publicly engage in activities befitting such a figure and ensure that his constituent voters are aware of his credibility. This flips on its head the argument that voters support candidates with criminal records because they *lack* information about candidate characteristics:

rather, voters support such candidates *because* they have information about their reputations. Information about candidates' alleged criminality is central—indeed, essential—to understanding their appeal.

THE BIHAR CASE

To understand how this alternative logic works on the ground, and why the ignorant voter hypothesis cannot explain the puzzle of India's criminal politicians, there is no better place to start than in Anant Singh's Bihar. Virtually every discussion on the criminalization of politics in India begins and ends with Bihar, which for decades has been synonymous with "dirty politics." On a percentage basis, Bihar has regularly elected to its state assembly a large share of politicians facing serious criminal cases (figure 5.3). In terms of its share of criminally

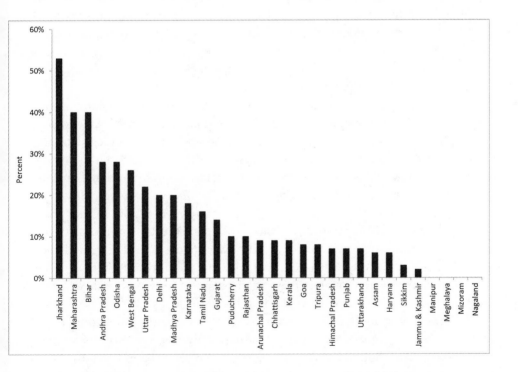

Figure 5.3. State-wise distribution of MLAs with pending serious criminal cases, as of December 2015. (Author's calculations based on data from the Association for Democratic Reforms from each state's most recent state assembly election)

suspect legislators, it is tied with the state of Maharashtra and lags behind only the state of Jharkhand, which was a part of Bihar prior to the latter's bifurcation in 2000.

The political economy of current-day Bihar has its roots in the colonial power structure, the foundation of which had two pillars: land and caste. In Bihar, the British colonial authorities implemented a system of land revenue—known as the "Permanent Settlement"—that entrusted a powerful class of feudal landlords (*zamindars*) with the legal responsibility for collecting revenue as well as overseeing most aspects of local governance.[54] With few exceptions, the *zamindars* belonged to the upper castes. In many instances, the *zamindari* elite abused their powerful position by presiding over an agrarian economic system that systematically exploited the lower castes. This structure of economic relations stood in contrast with the overall demographics of Bihar: according to estimates from the 1931 census (the last census which collected detailed caste data), the upper/forward castes made up around 15 percent of Bihar's population, whereas OBCs made up 50 percent.[55] The 2011 census, which does have data on the population of SCs (Dalits) and Muslims, finds that those two groups currently account for roughly 33 percent of the total population.

After independence, the ruling Congress Party inherited and perpetuated the local dominance of the landed upper-caste elites.[56] Due to popular pressure, however, Congress was compelled to enact legislation to formally abolish the *zamindari* system. Although the resulting legislation was riddled with loopholes, land reforms did succeed in damaging the upper castes' social prestige.[57] The newly empowered cultivators-turned-landowners came largely from the upper sections of the OBCs. Initially, the newfound economic power of the OBCs stood in stark contrast to their lack of political power (figure 5.4). The period from 1967 until 1989 was one of conflict and political instability in Bihar, marked by a gradual increase in the share of legislative seats occupied by OBCs.[58] Among the OBCs in Bihar, the Yadavs emerged as the most politically dominant subgroup. Notwithstanding the tremendous social churning underway, the upper-caste-heavy Congress Party maintained a tenuous hold on power during this tumultuous period, in part due to the strength of its patron-client networks.[59]

In the late 1980s, the politics of backward caste empowerment was given a huge shot in the arm by the government-sponsored Mandal

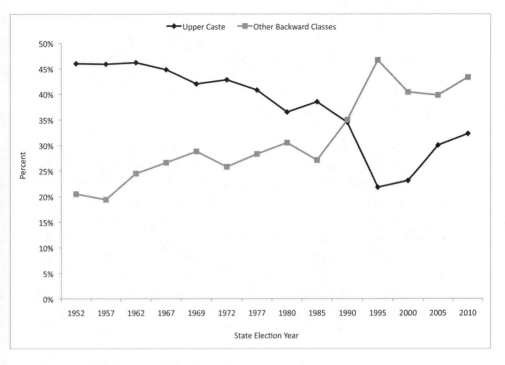

Figure 5.4. Caste identity of Bihar MLAs, 1952–2010. (Data from Christophe Jaffrelot and Sanjay Kumar, eds., *Rise of the Plebeians? The Changing Face of Indian Legislative Assemblies* [New Delhi: Routledge, 2009]; Manish K. Jha and Pushpendra, "Governing Caste and Managing Conflicts in Bihar, 1990–2011," Policies and Practice No. 48 [March 2012], Mahanirban Calcutta Research Group, http://www.mcrg.ac.in/PP48.pdf)

Commission, which advocated quotas for OBCs in public sector employment and education. Agitation in favor of these quotas, as well as fierce opposition by those who stood to lose out, ultimately led to the defeat of Congress in 1990 and the rise to power of the Janata Dal, led by Lalu Prasad Yadav, who would dominate the Bihar political scene for the next fifteen years.[60] Lalu served as chief minister for ten years, until he was forced to resign after being named in a massive corruption scandal involving the embezzlement of funds earmarked to purchase livestock feed (known as the "Fodder Scam").

While nominally stepping aside, Lalu managed to install his wife, Rabri Devi, as chief minister. Lalu Yadav's rise to power represented a critical juncture in Bihar's politics. Although caste had been a factor in Bihar's politics for centuries, Lalu's reign was associated with the entrenchment of identity politics. He skillfully combined language, symbols, and a gift for retail politics to build and maintain a coalition strong enough to usher in a reconfiguration of patterns of caste dominance in Bihar.[61] In addition, Lalu expressed deep distrust for an upper-caste dominated bureaucracy. Rather than investing in reshaping formal institutions, Lalu encouraged the creation of informal networks of power that sought to circumvent the state and mediate social demands directly. This strategy created a vacuum through which many criminals gained a foothold in politics, using their resources and local networks to promote themselves as local strongmen.[62]

The proliferation of criminals in politics during the Lalu era was a culmination of factors, including many that had been under way for some time.[63] Lalu accelerated, but did not initiate, many of these ongoing trends. Politicians and criminals had long worked hand in glove in Bihar; what Lalu did was make the connection almost "respectable."[64] To that end, his reign came to be termed "Jungle Raj," to signify the marked deterioration in state institutions and breakdown of law and order.[65]

In 2005, the Lalu era gave way to a period of reform under Chief Minister Nitish Kumar. Once an ally of Lalu's, Kumar eventually struck out on his own and formed a new party, JD(U). After years toiling in the opposition, the Kumar-led National Democratic Alliance (a coalition of the JD[U] and the BJP) won election and took over the reins to the state in 2005. Kumar dedicated himself to pursuing a development and good governance agenda in Bihar.

Between 2005 and 2010, Kumar made significant strides in strengthening state institutions to combat Bihar's lawlessness and reinvesting in pro-poor development. Yet for all of his accomplishments, Kumar also skillfully manipulated social divisions to build and maintain political support; he was hardly above engaging in the art of "social engineering" that Lalu and others had perfected. Whereas Lalu explicitly prioritized backward caste empowerment over development (*vikaas nahin, sammaan chahiye*—we need dignity, not development—was his defining motif), Nitish Kumar's innovation was marrying social justice concerns with a development plank.[66] As two close observers of Bihar's politics quipped, Kumar's rhetoric was infused "with the subtext of caste and religious identities. For his rival, Lalu Prasad, caste was the only text and the subtext as well."[67]

Although he may have improved law and order in Bihar, Kumar recognized that he could not win elections by completely ostracizing the state's powerful criminally linked politicians.[68] Because these politicians doubled as influential caste leaders, repudiating them would have had catastrophic consequences for Kumar's political standing, especially for a man who came from a relatively small and politically insignificant backward caste. Indeed, Kumar's willingness to embrace politicians with questionable pasts is evident when one looks at the candidates he has supported within his party.[69] In the October 2005 election, according to my analysis of the affidavit data, 22 percent of MLA candidates from Nitish Kumar's JD(U) faced serious criminal cases; in 2010, when Kumar's alliance won reelection, that proportion grew to 35 percent. One of those JD(U) contesting elections while under serious criminal suspicion was none other than Anant Singh.

Anant Singh's Mokama

On the morning I set out to meet *chhote sarkar,* the *Times of India* published a prominent story on page two of its Patna edition titled, "Anant's Sarkar [*government*] in Mokama." The profile described Anant Singh as a *dada* who—true to his moniker—wielded more influence in his constituency than the actual government. The reporter who penned the piece mixed in anecdotes about Singh's feared personality with talk of improved safety and better access to services in the constituency in recent years under his watch.

Located along the southern bank of the Ganges River in the eastern reaches of Patna district, Mokama is situated in what locals call the *taal* area—where low-lying, fertile farmland is submerged by the Ganges during monsoon rains for nearly half the year. This annual submersion makes it difficult to demarcate land boundaries, rendering property rights more of an aspiration than a reality. The resulting tensions over land, coupled with a nonexistent state and simmering resentment over the long-standing dominance exercised by upper-caste Bhumihars, has made Mokama a haven for gangsterism. Here the transition from lawbreaker to lawmaker is considered an established career trajectory.

"We take our inspiration from our seniors," one small-time criminal operating in Mokama confessed to a visiting journalist. "One of our former leaders has even become an MP and I also wish to follow that path and reach the same pinnacle as him."[70]

Bhumihars, in addition to controlling most of Mokama's economic and political power, are also numerically dominant in the constituency: according to local estimates, 90,000 of Mokama's 220,000 voters are Bhumihars.[71] Yadavs, who primarily work as cultivators, tillers, and small-hold farmers and are thought to be the main rivals to Bhumihar dominance, bitterly complain of upper-caste oppression.[72] At least as far back as 1977, Mokama's representative in the state assembly has hailed from the Bhumihar caste. Although Bhumihars remain dominant in Mokama even today, internal factions have emerged due to issues of family, turf, and local contract (*thekadari*) business. When I set out to visit the constituency, Anant Singh was without question the dominant Bhumihar political player in the area.[73]

The *Dabangg* Mystique

Several hours after departing the capital, having suffered through the rocky ride from downtown Patna and a breakdown of our vehicle along the way (in hindsight, the two were likely connected), I found myself face-to-face with Singh in the dusty village of Punarakh, which Singh was gracing with his presence as part of his pre-election campaign rounds. When I reached the village, local elders had gathered in the market area sitting on plastic chairs and drinking chai while they waited for *chhote sarkar* to arrive, busying themselves with idle election handicapping. Our quiet gossiping was abruptly interrupted by the sound of car engines approaching. Soon a convoy of ten or so high-end SUVs roared into the village, and Singh hopped out of one of the cars, sauntering over to the group accompanied by several burly-looking men and a well-armed bodyguard.

As I caught my first glimpse of him, Singh appeared exactly as had been advertised—wearing all white, donning stylish black sunglasses, and sporting a handlebar moustache. Without skipping a beat, one of Singh's aides quickly lit a fresh cigarette and slipped it to his boss, completing the image I had etched into my mind. Another associate of Singh's, with whom I had been in contact, brought me over to the candidate and we exchanged pleasantries; before I knew it, I was seated on a plastic chair as a guest of honor at Singh's village meeting, bottled mango juice thrust into my hand. The actual "meeting" lasted just a few minutes before Singh and his entourage stood up and commenced their walking tour of the village.

Several houses in the village displayed Singh's campaign poster near their front entrance (figure 5.5). The poster featured a picture of Singh

Figure 5.5. Election poster of JD(U) candidate in the Mokama constituency of Bihar, Anant Singh. (Author's photograph, 2010)

with his trademark sunglasses looking quite imposing—a stark contrast to the campaign posters typical in many Western democracies, where the candidate is made to look like the neighbor next door, surrounded by his spouse, kids, and the family dog.

At that moment, it dawned on me that Singh's appearance was entirely calculated—he held the reputation of being a strongman and carefully styled himself to reinforce this image. I couldn't help think of the uncanny similarities between Singh's election poster and those heralding the Bollywood blockbuster sweeping across India at the time, *Dabangg*. In the movie, superstar Salman Khan plays the role of police officer Chulbul Pandey (nicknamed "Robin Hood Pandey"), a wayward cop with a sympathetic streak. Singh's resemblance to the Salman Khan character (himself a play on a perennial good guy/bad guy character found in so many Indian movies) in the film was hardly coincidental.

Indeed, the Hindi word *dabangg* is one I heard repeatedly used to describe Singh and his fellow strongmen politicians in Bihar. *Dabangg* is a word that lacks a hard-and-fast definition but typically connotes a powerful leader who is both feared as well as fearless. Individuals described as *dabangg* are those who tout their rough edges—either their direct involvement or simply the veneer of criminal association—as a badge of honor. One voter in the nearby constituency of Bakhtiarpur explained the *dabangg* concept to me succinctly. He said: "Someone who is *dabangg* is like a paperweight. He makes his presence felt." Like Salman Khan's character, such individuals are self-styled Robin Hoods, who can use their reputation of doing bad to do good for their supporters.

Although Mokama is a poor, rural constituency with a low literacy rate (even for India), voter ignorance does not appear to be a convincing explanation of Singh's popular support.[74] To the contrary, Singh's prior brushes with the law are common knowledge among voters. Judging by his appearance that day (and by his campaign materials and media coverage), Singh is hardly bashful about coming across as a tough guy.

This anecdotal impression is backed up by hard data. Survey evidence I collected (in collaboration with CSDS) from more than 2,000 voters across Bihar following the election also suggests that a lack of access to information is not the primary motivation for supporting candidates with criminal cases (see Appendix B).

Consider, for example, the relationship between the educational qualifications of Bihari voters and the frequency with which they vote for candidates with serious criminal cases (figure 5.6). Although education level is not the same as access to information, the two are likely to be highly correlated; one would expect better-educated voters to have better access to information (and to be more able to process that information in a useful manner). As such, if the ignorant voter hypothesis were correct, one would also expect better-educated voters to be less likely to vote for criminal candidates facing serious cases. However, there is no clear relationship between a voter's education level and his or her propensity to vote for a candidate facing serious criminal charges. In fact, if anything, it appears as if more educated voters (those

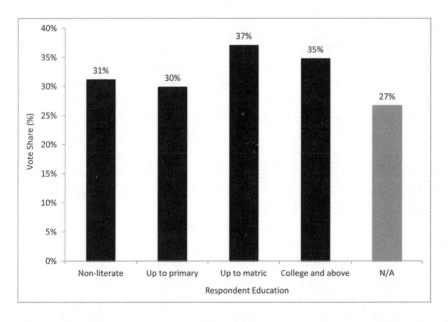

Figure 5.6. Level of education and support for candidates with serious criminal cases in Bihar, 2010. N/A indicates responses of "don't know," "can't say," or "refused." (Data from a 2010 post-election survey conducted in Bihar. See Milan Vaishnav, "Ethnic Identifiability: Evidence from a Survey of Indian Voters," unpublished paper, Carnegie Endowment for International Peace, 2015)

who have completed matric/high school or college) are slightly *more likely* to vote for such candidates than their lesser-educated peers.

When I asked local residents in dusty Punarakh about the *Times of India* story I had read that morning about Singh, many nodded their heads and shrugged. One upper-caste villager and Singh supporter reacted by saying: "Every election, reporters will write such stories. Do you think we need a reporter from Patna to tell us what is happening in Mokama? There is nothing in this we do not already know." Indeed, virtually every voter I interviewed in Mokama was aware of Singh's pending criminal cases, and many of them could recite specific alleged criminal acts in great detail.[75] Voters were familiar with at least two incidents in particular. Although Anant Singh had not yet been convicted of any crime at the time of the election, voters in Mokama widely believed the allegations to be true.

The first incident was a 2004 shoot-out between Anant Singh's men and special police commandos that broke out when the police attempted to raid Singh's compound. According to interviews with several local residents who were Anant Singh supporters (and later confirmed by news accounts), the commandos were repelled by gunfire emanating from Singh's compound, the walls of which were fitted with specially constructed holes through which guns could conveniently fit. The police were eventually forced to abort their operation.[76]

A second well-known incident occurred in 2007 when news reporters visited the same compound to question Singh about his alleged involvement in the rape and murder of a young woman found dead in Patna. Incensed at their probing questions, Singh and his men allegedly held the reporters captive for several hours in his house, assaulting them as well as a cameraman who came to investigate the reporters' detention.[77]

The fact that voters were keenly aware of Singh's alleged connection to illegal behavior reinforces the point Thomas Hansen made in his study of the Shiv Sena: under certain conditions, candidates who are accused of crimes go to great lengths to ensure that information—or at least rumors—about their alleged criminality is known to voters. A candidate's criminal reputation must be well known to the public if he is to use it to either attract political patronage or build a support base of constituents.[78]

The Utility of Criminality

Anant Singh's core support comes largely from fellow Bhumihars who think of him as a bold leader who can credibly protect their interests. Indeed, one local resident plainly remarked to a visiting reporter that the Bhumihar "dons" active in politics thrive because they effectively represent the interests of the upper castes.[79] As the theory suggests, Singh's criminal reputation signals his credibility to be an effective representative through each of the four channels previously identified: redistribution, coercion, social insurance, and dispute resolution.

Redistribution

For starters, many Bhumihars favored Anant Singh because they perceived that he was the only Bhumihar candidate (in a field with at least two other prominent caste-mates) with the ability to protect the economic interests of Mokama's upper castes. In Mokama, land is the most highly prized economic asset, and Bhumihars as a group make up the bulk of the landed gentry, the most powerful of whom are former *zamindars*. In Mokama, backward-caste Yadavs traditionally worked as laborers on farms owned by Bhumihar landlords. As Yadavs gradually became empowered, they began to resist the traditional modes of landlord control and demonstrated their resentment over the Bhumihars' monopoly on land.

For their part, many Bhumihars felt that only a *dabangg* MLA would be able to either slow down or reverse their declining dominance. "Those [castes] which have risen up now think they can be the landowners and make decisions in Mokama," one upper-caste landowner who pledged his vote for Anant Singh lamented to me. "We used to tell them what to do, how to act. Now we are worried they will think for themselves."[80]

To the extent voters connected Anant Singh with a specific policy stance in the run-up to the election, it was on the issue of land reform. During Nitish Kumar's first term, a government-sponsored commission recommended the implementation of a new round of land reforms, including granting legal rights to *bataidars* (sharecroppers), which could further erode the Bhumihars' status. Kumar never implemented the recommendations, but many of Mokama's landed elites were nervous that he might revisit the issue if granted a second term.

Although Anant Singh is an MLA from Kumar's party, most Bhumihars that I spoke with in Mokama believed that Anant would never allow the reform to be implemented in the area, given the negative ramifications for landed Bhumihars as well as the potential positive benefits for lower-caste sharecroppers.[81] "Anant is with Nitish [Kumar] and his party. But on the [land] issue, he stands with the Bhumihars. . . . He is one of them," an unemployed Dalit agrarian laborer explained to me.

Indeed, Anant's status as a local strongman was thought to enhance his profile with Nitish Kumar and other state leaders. Interviews with JD(U) party officials, Nitish Kumar's associates, and several local residents indicate that Anant Singh was simply too powerful for the chief minister to deny him a party ticket. When Kumar had previously contested parliamentary elections from the region, Anant Singh was the dominant local strongman and an inevitable force for any party to contend with.[82] Kumar became Singh's patron because he believed that any candidate who allied with Anant would have a strong advantage in the region, especially among the upper castes, a constituency not intrinsically supportive of Nitish Kumar or his party.[83] Thus, Kumar brought Singh within the JD(U) fold and gave him a party ticket in 2005. And when Anant won that election, rumor has it that he brought Nitish Kumar to his constituency and weighed him in gold.[84] Once asked why he had embraced known criminals like Anant, Kumar bluntly retorted, "There are certain compulsions of politics."[85] Anant Singh's status (and the respect it earned him from powerful state leaders) further reinforced the perception that he wielded enormous influence over day-to-day matters in Mokama.

"You may think of Anant Singh as evil," one supporter stated, "but you could also call him necessary. Real evil is what the Yadavs would do to us if they had their way." When probed further on what "damage" Yadavs could realistically inflict on Bhumihars, one local Bhumihar resident with landholdings in the *taal* area worried aloud about the lack of property rights protection and the possibility that, without a local strongman keeping watch, Yadavs could encroach on his land and the state would be unable (or unwilling) to adjudicate the dispute.

Yadav residents, for their part, decried Anant Singh for running Mokama as his own personal fiefdom. As one Yadav villager said, "Anant is a *bahubali* [strongman] and he can squeeze the system so that it gives him what the upper castes want. I say this is my land and he says it belongs to his friends. . . . I cannot win." When asked whether the Yadavs could field their own strongman candidate, the villager waved the suggestion off: "Although upper castes fear us now, we are not in a strong enough position to counter their [Bhumihar] dominance. This place has only known one way."

Coercion

In addition to redistribution, criminally linked politicians also wield coercion as a political tool. The introduction of electronic voting machines, the deployment of central paramilitary forces, and the expanded reach of the ECI have largely tamed the most egregious behaviors (i.e., booth capturing) come election time. By 2010 Anant Singh and his ilk were no longer able to resort to such overt forms of coercion.[86] But Anant had not relinquished the use of coercive measures as an electoral tool—both to keep his supporters in line and to intimidate unsympathetic voters. Fear and coercion remained important elements of his campaign strategy, although their manifestations have become subtler in nature.

Thanks to ECI regulations and a beefed-up police presence, candidates in India can no longer openly brandish weapons while on the campaign trail. Yet strongman candidates have found new ways of projecting power, as was amply demonstrated by my interaction with Singh during his village "meeting" in Punarakh. The meeting in which I had inadvertently been made guest of honor was held the week before the election, ostensibly in order for the candidate to meet with local residents and hear their grievances.

However, it soon became clear that this meeting was more performance than substance. The village was home to a mix of castes, including many who did not belong to Singh's traditional support base: they included Dalits, members of the Koeri and Yadav backward castes, and Muslims. The "meeting" itself lasted but a few minutes before Singh started a walking tour through the village. The tour was perfunctory: Singh raced from house to house in the village, often stopping for just a few seconds to greet residents before moving on. His interaction with villagers was kept to a minimum on issues of substance. As one reporter once wrote, "There are no nuanced conversations with Anant Singh."[87] To me, it appeared there were no conversations at all.

What soon became clear was that the purpose of Anant Singh's visit was not to meet villagers or to discuss issues they were facing in their daily lives; rather, it was a display of force and virility. The procession of Singh and his young, male followers throughout the village was designed to send a message to villagers that Singh was the person they were to vote for if they did not want to be punished after the election. A member of Anant Singh's campaign told me in the middle of this village walkabout that they worried this village would vote against them, which helps explain the gruff demeanor. As Singh went from house to house, several villagers shouted after him with their complaints about basic services (such as a lack of water hand pumps or shortages of electricity). But neither Anant Singh nor his minions stopped to take note of their grievances; he had already moved on to the next house. When I asked a bystander what the point of the exercise was, he replied: "He showed his face, and the message to villagers is clear: 'You better vote for *chhote sarkar.*' This message does not need words."

The role coercion plays does raise the concern that perhaps voters do not willingly vote for candidates implicated in criminal activity, but do so out of fear of retribution. Obviously, one cannot dismiss coercion as a contributing factor; indeed, it is a tool often wielded by *dabangg* candidates—especially with regard to voters who are not hardcore backers—to win support.

Yet the logic of coercion is just one element of the overall phenomenon of support for candidates linked to crime. One piece of evidence in this respect is the large proportion of voters who believe in the sanctity of the secret ballot. Using data from the survey I conducted of voters in Bihar, I charted voter responses to a question about their views about whether politicians or candidates can find out how people voted in their locality (figure 5.7). More than 75 percent of respondents stated that politicians could rarely or never learn how they voted.[88] The introduction of a highly secure system of electronic voting has undoubtedly reduced suspicion of ballot tampering or fraud and violations of ballot secrecy to a great extent. Furthermore, given the high degree of electoral volatility and anti-incumbency present in Indian elections, there is a substantial degree of turnover in public office, which suggests that achieving a lock on power through coercive means is extremely dif-

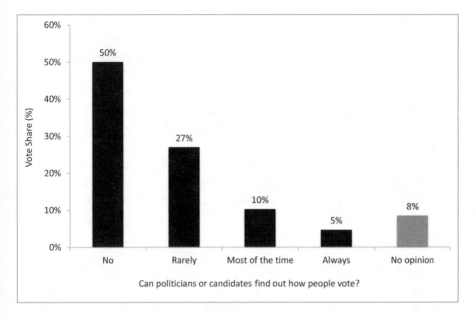

Figure 5.7. Perceptions of effectiveness of the secret ballot in Bihar, 2010. (Data from a 2010 post-election survey conducted in Bihar. See Milan Vaishnav, "Ethnic Identifiability: Evidence from a Survey of Indian Voters," unpublished paper, Carnegie Endowment for International Peace, 2015)

ficult. If this is truly the case, coercion in and of itself is an inadequate explanation for the electoral success of politicians like Anant Singh.

Social Insurance

A third way suspected criminal politicians signal credibility is their ability to cushion economic shocks by doling out handouts from their own coffers and providing patronage and employment to those who seek it. Indeed, the provision of social insurance appears to be a key way in which Anant Singh builds bridges with voters from other castes, particularly those who are at the bottom of the pyramid. One Kurmi (backward caste) resident sitting at a local chai stall claimed that local residents regularly gather outside Anant's compound with their pleas for help (usually financial assistance). "You will see people from all backgrounds there: backward, forward, and even sideways castes," he joked. "These people know Anant can help them—they do not need any official papers—and it will be done on the spot. They will owe him something, but it gets them through whatever difficulties they are facing." In 2012 Anant himself boasted that over the years he had arranged for more than 10,000 weddings in Mokama for those less fortunate.[89]

This aspect of Singh's reputation also appears to be why he is respected by many younger voters, who seemed to connect with his persona. High levels of unemployment in Bihar, and in Mokama specifically, mean that there is a vast pool of young men with an abundance of free time. These youths receive jobs working with the candidate as local fixers, often joining one of his various business interests, and provide the manual labor candidates need to contest elections.

Dispute Resolution

The final channel through which criminality signals credibility is dispute resolution. One of the greatest casualties of a weak rule-of-law system is a functioning system of peacefully resolving differences between citizens. According to data compiled by the Indian government, as of April 2016 there were as many as 1.4 million pending cases winding their way though Bihar's courts. Nearly 17 percent of these cases had been pending for a decade or longer. The pendency of criminal cases was especially egregious: there were five times as many criminal cases awaiting resolution as there were civil matters.[90] It became clear in Mokama that the absence of an effective justice system greatly enhanced Anant Singh's position because it allowed him to use his stature to fill this legal vacuum. As one local reminded me during my time in Mokama, "Oftentimes, speedy justice is better than no justice." Holding court at his *durbar,* Singh would take a call on everyday disputes that arose between citizens, hear complaints about the police, or initiate action against "miscreants."

One popular story among locals involved a local businessman who was kidnapped by Rajput *goondas.* According to the story making the rounds, Singh demanded that the kidnappers release the man, and when they refused, he initiated a shoot-out and freed the man on his own. This resort to vigilante justice may have been illegal (it may even have been apocryphal), but it earned him popularity as a man who could solve problems. The relevance of a *dada* is somewhat heightened in Mokama given the way in which geography makes the demarcation of property rights problematic. The annual submerging of parts of the constituency when the Ganges overflows its banks creates a steady stream of complaints from locals about land grabbing or boundary disputes. Without effective courts or police in whom the citizenry reposes trust, strongman justice was at least a timely alternative solution.

Dignity and Defensive Criminality

The notion of "defensive criminality" turns out to be a critical one. By and large, supporters of Anant Singh did not view him as a "criminal" because his alleged criminal acts are either far removed from their daily lives and/or because he regularly burnishes his credentials as a protector of Bhumihar interests. Many of his closest supporters vociferously argued that the criminal label was misplaced. This echoes a sentiment I heard from supporters of several candidates facing criminal prosecution; they regularly claimed that a candidate's alleged criminality had no negative impact on constituent interests because the notion of breaking the law does not per se conflict with the needs of ordinary citizens. Moreover, a candidate's suspected crimes often take place outside of the constituency.[91]

The engineer who educated me on the difference between "murder" and "murder management" was one such voice. Of all the locals I spoke with, it was this man who launched the most vigorous defense of Anant Singh. In response to the distinction the man sought to draw about Anant Singh's alleged activities, I pointed out that ordering a murder and carrying out a murder are both heinous criminal acts under Indian law. The engineer cut me off, waving his hands as if I did not understand; Singh, he said, was not a criminal but a "defensive" criminal. Anant does not commit offensive acts of violence against anyone, he reasoned. "He is known for being ruthless with his rivals in a kind of reaction/counterreaction way—but not in a brazen, terrorizing way." Although this distinction has no legal basis, it is central to understanding the calculations of those who support Anant Singh. To them, Anant is not a violent outlaw but a CEO of a protection racket; his alleged involvement in the occasional murder is but one aspect of his administrative responsibilities.

To the extent Singh engages in criminality, the engineer continued, it is only "to counter other criminals." When I pushed the man further on who exactly these "other criminals" were, it became clear that he was referring to Anant's political rivals. These crimes—even if Anant were responsible for them—have little bearing or effect on an average villager's daily life, said the man. In other instances, Anant's defensive criminality is seen as upholding order in Mokama.

In my interviews, the characterization of Anant Singh as a "criminal" or not largely depends on caste affiliation. Across Bihar, candidates who engage in extralegal activities—and the voters who support them—rarely characterize those activities as "criminal" or even "illegal." This would involve making a normative judgment.[92] When I asked Anant's supporters—from the Bhumihar community or an allied caste group—whether he was a criminal (*apradhi*), the overwhelming response was "No, but he is *dabangg*." When I asked Mokama voters who were not core supporters of Anant's of their opinion, they readily referred to the candidate as an *apradhi* and adamantly refuse to call him *dabangg*. The term *dabangg* carries with it a recognition of power, which nonsupporters are reluctant to acknowledge. Voters' perceptions of who is *dabangg* versus who is criminal is clearly in the eye—or in the *jati* (caste)—of the beholder.

There is a third category of voters—those that labeled Anant a "criminal" yet still expressed support for him. These voters, who were largely from marginal communities or from lower segments of society, lack the numbers or the economic power to acquire a position of dominance themselves, but they still have a stake in which group ultimately calls the shots. Interestingly, a great many non-Bhumihar, non-Yadav voters I interviewed expressed a preference for Anant Singh in part because, in their eyes, Yadav dominance has far less legitimacy than upper-caste dominance. Although the decline in upper-caste dominance meant that old forms of feudal bondage slowly weakened, these were often replaced by new forms of oppression perpetuated by the big landowners among the upper OBCs.[93] As the scholar Atul Kohli has written, the newly empowered backward castes have had a difficult time legitimizing their access to new positions of domination in the eyes of the weaker sections of society.[94] The old upper-caste-dominated order had more legitimacy because of religious-cultural traditions (the upper castes were revered as "twice born," after all) and because of routinized, well-established mechanisms of reciprocity between lower-caste subjects and upper-caste rulers.

Thus Kohli writes, "Although the scheduled castes may have been habitually subservient in the old elaborate system of traditional caste domination, they fail to see any legitimacy in this new domination."[95] Anant Singh, in this context, is seen as the lesser of two evils. "If not Anant, then who? Them [over there]?" one Dalit street vendor asked, pointing to the section of the village where backward-caste villagers resided. "I am not a friend to Bhumihars. They do not respect me. But I do not want them [the backward castes] to run this place."

This highlights the (often underplayed) relevance of negative voting, wherein voters do not so much choose whom they support as whom they are *against*. It is an issue that often crops up where voters do not have the option of voting for a fellow co-ethnic and so must make electoral decisions on some other basis.[96] As such, some voters who choose to vote for candidates with criminal cases do so not because they are co-ethnic supporters but because they are choosing in their mind between the lesser of two evils.

BIHAR BEYOND ANANT SINGH

It is not difficult to paint a portrait of Anant Singh as a quintessential strongman politician who "does bad in order to do good." By aesthetics alone, Singh does an admirable job of playing the part. The real question, however, is whether Anant Singh is representative of a larger phenomenon.

The first thing to note is that the narrative presented here jibes well with that described by others who have closely examined the crime-politics nexus in Bihar. The scholar who has done some of the best work on this subject—and to whom my own research is highly indebted—is Jeffrey Witsoe. Based on years of fieldwork, Witsoe has ably documented the social bases of support for criminal politicians that exist in Bihar.

In one revealing passage, Witsoe recounts asking villagers from an upper-caste Rajput community how they felt about the presence of a local *goonda* named Shiv, the local proxy of a powerful "mafia don" state politician from the area: "I [Witsoe] asked an older Rajput farmer why villagers tolerated the presence of goondas like Shiv. He pointed to the distance and explained, 'The Bhumihars [a rival upper caste] reside just over there.' He said that without people like Shiv, 'Bhumihar goondas would prey on the village. He [Shiv] protects the village, protects the Rajputs, that's why we tolerate him.'"[97]

As Witsoe explains, locals' reliance on criminally connected politicians is useful for keeping rivals at bay as well as for exercising local dominance. One Rajput villager, commenting on relations with the Chamar [a Dalit caste] population, stated: "We (Rajputs) dominate them. . . . They are also scared of Shiv."[98] Locals Witsoe spoke with viewed Shiv and, by extension, the criminal *dada* he served as a "necessary protector of Rajput interests, a guard against the territorial intrusion of other castes. People considered the presence of goondas like Shiv to be a necessary evil, 'our goonda.'"[99]

Second, the aggregate data confirm that alleged criminality among Bihar's political class is quite widespread. According to my data from 2010, 27 percent of candidates in the 2010 Bihar election declared pending criminal cases, and 20 percent of candidates faced charges of a serious nature. There are a staggering number of politicians suspected of criminal activity across the state (figure 5.8). Of the 242 (of 243) constituencies for which I have data, a mere 14 percent did not feature a single candidate facing a serious criminal case. On the opposite end of the spectrum, in at least one constituency, there were as many as nine such candidates facing off.

Criminality cuts across parties, including the "reformist" ruling BJP-JD(U) alliance: in 2010, 39 percent of BJP candidates boasted serious pending criminal cases against them compared to 35 percent of JD(U) candidates. Interestingly, these numbers were on par with the supposed brazenly corrupt party-mates of Lalu Prasad's RJD, of whom 29 percent faced serious pending cases. The numbers were even larger for the candidates who were actually elected; 50 percent of MLAs were named in at least one declared criminal case, and 35 percent of legislators faced cases of a serious nature. Attempted murder charges were the largest category of pending cases, comprising one-quarter of all pending cases against Bihar's illustrious politicians.

Beyond the aggregate figures, research in Bihar led me to several other politicians with criminal reputations who—though they come from a variety of backgrounds—corroborate Anant Singh's Mokama narrative. The day before I ended up in Mokama, I visited the town of Fatuha, which sits just 25 kilometers outside of Patna along National Highway 30. There, Ramanand Yadav of Lalu Prasad's RJD

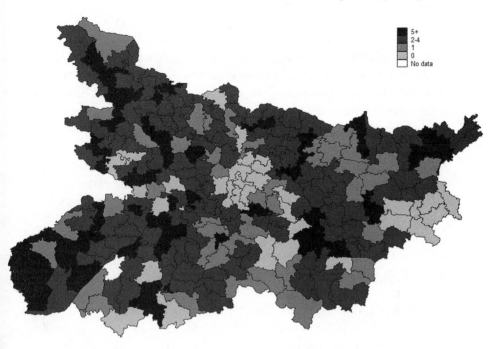

Figure 5.8. Distribution of Bihar state assembly candidates with pending serious criminal cases, 2010. (Author's calculations based on affidavits submitted to the Election Commission of India by candidates contesting the 2010 state assembly election in Bihar)

was contesting elections in an area regarded as a Yadav stronghold. Ramanand was a longtime fixture in the Patna-area political scene; supporters and detractors alike testified to his solid grassroots base. Local media reports published before the election described Yadav as a "feared" local leader unafraid to "flex his muscle" and as a man who could "guarantee" security.[100]

The stories I heard in Fatuha, and in follow-up conversations with individuals in Patna who knew Ramanand Yadav, bore an uncanny resemblance to my conversations in Anant Singh's Mokama. For starters, Yadav's "strongman" reputation was well known to nearly everyone I spoke with. Indeed, this was a primary motivation for why his party had embraced him. An official from the RJD explained his party's support of Ramanand by noting how the candidate was able to marshal considerable muscle power from his Patna base. "In five minutes,

Ramanand could arrange for 500 young men to show up here," he boasted. Another local supporter boasted that even RJD chief Lalu Yadav was "afraid of" crossing Ramanand because of his influence.[101]

As in Mokama, supporters of Ramanand's decried the notion that he is a serious criminal despite the fact that he stands accused of several criminal violations, including attempted murder.[102] Unlike Anant Singh, Yadav was not described as a "don." Most noticeably, and in contrast to Anant, he did not adopt the aesthetics of one either. While he might not be a "don," backers readily acknowledged Ramanand was not afraid to use force to get his way. One Yadav resident remarked that whatever illegal activity Ramanand might have allegedly been involved in, it was always in the service of constituents.

To that end, one analyst claimed that Ramanand has earned a reputation as a tireless "fixer" in Patna for many years, a perception supported by interviews conducted in Patna and corroborated by news reports. In an informal capacity, Ramanand is said to have helped poor residents of Patna deal with threats to their safety or difficulties in accessing public benefits. Several residents of Patna and Fatuha recalled that during the days of Lalu's reign, when Patna was ground zero for criminal activity in Bihar, Ramanand held regular office hours, at which residents came to him for help with their assorted day-to-day problems.

I heard the same story on the other side of the capital, in the heart of Bhojpur district, where Sunil Pandey was seeking his fourth election win in a row on a JD(U) ticket—another supposed "hardened" criminal-turned-politician selected by Nitish Kumar's party.[103] Pandey holds a special place in Bihar's troubles of the 1990s; he was once a leader of Ranvir Sena, the notorious Bhumihar militia that did battle against the Naxalite rebels and other low-caste *senas* (armies) during the era of Jungle Raj.[104] A local JD(U) party official described Pandey as a "godfather for Bhumihars" because of his prior connections to the militia group. Thanks to his involvement with the Sena, Pandey gained statewide notoriety for his conduct and even did jail time for a kidnapping conviction. According to prosecutors, Pandey orchestrated the kidnapping of a prominent Patna doctor in exchange for a ransom payment. He was convicted and given a life sentence, though he was later acquitted due to a lack of evidence.[105]

When I asked the local party worker whether Pandey still profited from his reputation, he candidly replied that Pandey's criminal days were "mostly" over, but that he "has not left bad elements completely behind." One of those supposed "bad elements" was his own brother, Hulas, himself a reputed gangster who won election to Bihar's upper house in 2009 and was believed to be his brother's "main shooter."[106] The friend was clearly not exaggerating about Sunil Pandey's continuing legal troubles. Just a few years earlier, an inebriated Pandey was caught on camera verbally abusing members of the media who dared to ask why Pandey had failed to pay for a stay at a posh Patna hotel. Pandey, according to one report, threatened to have the reporters killed.[107]

A few days before voting was to take place, I drove out to Pandey's constituency of Tirari to meet him. That afternoon, the JD(U)-BJP alliance was hosting a large campaign rally in an open field, and several senior party leaders were due to helicopter in for the event. When we arrived, the crowd was still gathering and an interminable number of low-level party officials were trying in vain to keep the audience's attention. When Pandey was informed that a researcher had traveled a great distance to see him, he instructed my colleagues and me to join him on the front row of the dais, where we sheepishly appropriated the seats of several visibly annoyed party workers who had to relocate.

After some small talk about the campaign, I asked Pandey directly if he considered himself to be a *dabangg* leader. Stroking his beard and looking up at the sky, he first rejected the notion but then clarified that he is *dabangg* for those who oppress the "weaker sections" of society. If being *dabangg* is like being a Good Samaritan for the oppressed, he continued, then yes, he fits the definition. He then launched into a recitation of a laundry list of development works he claimed to have brought to the area.

Eager to change the subject, I mentioned to Pandey that I had read a newspaper article about him claiming that he had earned a PhD while in jail and had written a dissertation on Mahavir's philosophy of *ahimsa*, or nonviolence. His oral defense before his thesis committee supposedly took place under close police scrutiny.[108] Pandey smiled, clearly pleased, and nodded. I asked whether he found this ironic given his reputation and the time he spent behind bars. Pandey's smile immediately morphed into a frown, and he countered that violence is never the first option. But, he said rather cryptically, "Life is limited and people have unlimited requirements. Thus there can be a need for force in some cases."

I confessed that I didn't fully understand, but Pandey went on to say the media had unfairly targeted him: he claimed he was not a criminal but someone who resorted to using force only if compelled to do so. This time, I understood—it was the same "defensive criminality" trope I had heard in Mokama and Fatuha. Having heard enough, I thanked Pandey for his time and quickly scurried off the stage—the same local party workers still prattling away at the podium and the audience still trickling in.

One of the most captivating figures in the election was a man who would go unseen by voters during election season. His name was Ritlal Yadav, and he hailed from a semi-urban satellite of the capital called Danapur. In contrast to rural, poor Mokama, Danapur is a suburb of Patna and has a markedly higher literacy rate and a demography that favors the backward-caste Yadavs, as opposed to the upper-caste supporters of Anant Singh.

Ritlal went unseen because he was being held in jail without bail, his requests to campaign denied, even though his name was on the ballot. As a younger man, Yadav was known as a classic small-time thug, a *chhota mota goonda* in local parlance. As he gained notoriety and took on the role of a classic *dada*, Ritlal's ambitions grew and he allegedly turned his eyes toward extortion and contract work associated with the local railways. During Lalu's reign as chief minister, Ritlal became an active member of the RJD and won election as a *mukhia* (village headman). Ritlal's suspected criminal exploits were the stuff of local legend. In 2003, he and his associates allegedly carried out a stunning murder of two small-time contractors who were fast asleep aboard a moving train. Apparently the hit was revenge for their securing a railway tender Ritlal coveted.[109]

But Ritlal is perhaps best known for his alleged involvement in the 2004 murder of rival BJP leader Satya Narain Sinha. Ritlal is said to have had a long-running feud with Sinha and allegedly carried out his murder as an act of revenge hours after gunmen tied to Sinha shot and killed a fellow RJD leader.[110] Sinha's widow, Asha Devi, went on to win election to her slain husband's assembly seat in 2005. The 2010 election contest was pitched as a battle between Asha Devi and Ritlal.

Three days before voters of Patna district went to the polls, one of Bihar's most popular Hindi newspapers published a startling advertisement. The ad featured the faces of three young children above the words *Papa, ghar kab ayenge?* (Papa, when are you coming home?). The children in the ad were Ritlal's.[111] Several weeks earlier, Ritlal surrendered to the police after absconding from the authorities for nearly seven years. At the time of the election, Yadav was wanted in over twenty criminal cases, some involving murder, extortion, and other serious crimes.[112] The ad, attributed to Ritlal's wife, intended to cast the candidate as a martyr—a revolutionary leader jailed by the oppressive government authorities (indeed, another campaign advertisement explicitly compared Ritlal to other leading revolutionaries from India's independence movement, such as Mahatma Gandhi, Subhash Chandra Bose, and Sardar Patel).[113] The ad, it seemed, was also designed to send a message that Ritlal (despite his arrest) remained a force to be reckoned with. Publicizing his incarceration had the dual aim of evoking sympathy from constituents while simultaneously brandishing his credentials.

For some residents of Danapur whom I spoke with, Ritlal's alleged criminality was perceived to be an asset because it enhanced his ability to both extract benefits from the state and substitute for the state's shortcomings in other areas. As a well-known "muscle man," many voters believed Ritlal was a leader who was willing to take on the local authorities to "get things done," primarily in service of his ethnic base. Even Ritlal's critics could understand his appeal among his caste-mates, the Yadavs. One Dalit shopkeeper expressed it like this: "I do not support him. He wants to take us back to the dark days of Lalu. . . . I cannot allow it. But he is a ray of hope for the Yadavs. If you were at the top once [during the Lalu era], would you not want to return there?"

To his supporters, Ritlal's alleged criminality is cast as part of their ongoing struggle for lower-caste empowerment. Despite being in the majority in Danapur, many Yadav residents expressed uncertainty about their community's future status. In fact, they argue that Ritlal is a "bold leader who is with the masses" (the way many of his supporters chose to define the term *dabangg*, when asked to clarify what the term meant to them). According to a group of villagers I spoke to outside the home village of Asha Devi, even the 2004 murder of the BJP party leader Sinha (Asha's husband) was a "defensive" act allegedly committed by Ritlal to avenge the murder of an RJD party official by Sinha's associates.[114]

CURRENCY WITH THE MASSES

The stories of Anant Singh, Ramanand Yadav, Sunil Pandey, and Ritlal Yadav help to clarify the precise ways in which the criminality-credibility link operates in India today. But the framework used to understand the "demand" for politicians with serious criminal records in the electoral marketplace also gains strength from the extant ethnographic literature on criminality in Indian politics.[115] In fact, a number of scholars in recent years have found that there are legitimate reasons voters often willingly endorse candidates tied to criminal activity. These studies have considerable geographic range.

For instance, Ward Berenschot has documented the extensive nexus between politicians and *goondas* in the prosperous and industrialized western state of Gujarat. Even in this economically successful state, the voters Berenschot studied find favor in a candidate's personal (or proximate) association with criminality due to his or her ability to use (or threaten) extralegal measures to "get things done." According to Berenschot, a politician's willingness to break the law is useful from a voter's perspective because it enhances his or her ability to intervene successfully in the administration and implementation of policy.[116]

Thus a reputation as a *matabhare* (literally, "heavy-headed") person is considered to be an asset in solving local problems, arbitrating disputes, and extracting benefits and services from the state apparatus. As he writes, "Although goondas are often referred to as 'anti-social elements,' the people of the area where they live often consider them to be very social: they help solve basic problems, offer opportunities to earn money, and arrange improvements of basic facilities."[117]

Echoes of this logic can also be found in research undertaken by Lucia Michelutti on Uttar Pradesh, where members of the Yadav caste have elected many of their fellow caste-mates considered to be *goondas* to powerful positions in local, state, and national politics. Yadav voters unabashedly refer to many of their elected politicians as *goondas,* but as Michelutti explains, it does not imply any moral judgment. In fact, she writes that "'force' is seen as a legitimate way of getting 'respect' and an integral part of the Yadav public image, and most local Yadavs think it is precisely through politics and 'goondaism' that they obtained dignity, power and importantly wealth."[118] Yadav voters support *goondas* because they believe such candidates have the credibility (and the ability) to guarantee the social status of, and direct benefits to, their fellow Yadavs.[119]

The ability to act as an effective fixer, essentially delivering constituency service, does have a coercive element; there is no reason to gloss over this fact. In fact, politicians themselves have an incentive to make this attribute widely known. This point is well illustrated by Thomas Blom Hansen's research on the Shiv Sena.[120] Hansen shows that the illegal activities that party politicians engage in can best be thought of as part of a spectacle or performance: it is how party members develop reputations for ruthlessness and as protectors of the common man.[121] He argues that the Shiv Sena has no firm ideology or policy platform but only the capacity to generate "moods"; in his words, party men practice the "politics of presence."[122]

Perception is almost as important as reality. What matters most is that voters believe Shiv Sena politicians are willing and able to use violence to assert the rights of the common man vis-à-vis the state or other potential threats. As political scientist Steven Wilkinson has argued about ethnic riots, riot participation (like criminality) is a cost-effective means of attracting support from voters because it is cheap in terms of the "resources expended compared to the number of voters 'contacted.'"[123] Thus, once a reputation for criminality is developed it can be self-sustaining. The criminality perpetrated by thuggish players in politics is instrumental rather than a sign of "pathologically deviant behavior."[124]

Parties are fully aware of this dynamic and stand ready to pounce where and when the opportunity strikes. One MP affiliated with the BJP explained the process to me in simple terms: "Our party does informal surveys of every constituency in which elections are to be held. Where voters can be mobilized on identity grounds, there can be a payoff to fielding a candidate, who may be a criminal, but also a local 'folk hero' to his community."[125] Another top official from a national party summed up the logic pithily: "Parties support criminals because they have 'currency' with the masses." This "currency" is both literal as well as figurative in terms of the candidates' ability to mobilize popular, caste-based support.[126]

Thus, a characteristic often portrayed as a liability for politicians in democracies with free and fair elections—connections to illegal behavior—can sometimes be an asset. The fact that voters often perceive candidates associated with breaking the law to be more credible than their counterparts suggests that the emergence of tainted politicians in democracies is not necessarily symptomatic of a breakdown in political and electoral accountability.

6 The Salience of Social Divisions
How Context Shapes Criminality

ON JANUARY 14, 2009, the chief minister of Uttar Pradesh, Mayawati, celebrated her fifty-second birthday in lavish style with a giant party in the state capital of Lucknow. Each year, Mayawati—the first Dalit and the first female chief executive of India's most populous state—would direct leaders of her Bahujan Samaj Party (BSP) to commemorate her birthday by raising funds for the party's war chest. This year's celebrations were no different: supporters draped the capital in blue cloth (the party's official color), plastered city walls with signs emblazoned with pictures of Mayawati beneath slogans like *tum jiyo hazaron saal, saal ke din ho pachas hazaar* (May you live a thousand years with 50,000 days in each year), and even baked a birthday cake weighing 52 kilograms—one for each year.[1]

Mayawati, it turns out, knew a thing or two about raising funds. From 2003 to 2007, her self-reported financial wealth grew fiftyfold.[2] The meteoric growth of the BSP leader's pocketbook triggered a federal investigation into her "disproportionate assets," to which Mayawati responded by declaring that her newfound largesse was the result of small donations from party workers.[3] While such an accumulation of wealth in the form of five and ten rupee notes seems fantastical, Mayawati's supporters are known to—literally—adorn her with cash. At one highly publicized rally, supporters greeted her with a garland made entirely out of thousand-rupee notes; the "cash garland" was estimated to be worth tens of millions of rupees.[4] By 2012, Mayawati's assets totaled a whopping 1.1 billion rupees ($17 million)—the vast majority of which consisted of real estate holdings in posh sections of Delhi and Lucknow.[5] The leader's extravagant wealth led some detractors to joke: *Mayawati Dalit ki beti nahin balki daulat ki beti hain* (Mayawati is not the daughter of a Dalit but of wealth).[6]

The birthday festivities in Lucknow took place with national elections mere months away and Mayawati's legislators were under intense pressure not to disappoint in their fundraising efforts, lest they fall out of favor with their beloved leader. Mayawati is widely known to hold her party colleagues to account should they shirk on their responsibilities of bringing funds into the party.[7] In a 2003 speech, Mayawati is reported to have chastised her party's lawmakers for siphoning off funds intended for the party: *Bhai saara mat khao. BSP ne MLA, MP banaya, ek lakh lao* (Brothers, don't eat it all yourselves. The BSP has made you an MLA or MP, so bring the party one lakh [one lakh is equivalent to 100,000 rupees, or $1,500]).[8]

In another fiery speech to key party functionaries, Mayawati refused to mince words about the necessity of refreshing the party's coffers, including by redirecting funds from legislators' constituency development funds: "Now I'll tell you my method of depositing money. It will be applicable from the coming year. In Uttar Pradesh, every MLA gets 75 lakh [$114,000] a year to fund projects. Even an honest MLA gets a kickback of Rs 5 lakh [$7,500] from those he funds. Keep 4 lakh [$6,000] but deposit 1 lakh with the party. Similarly, MPs get 2 crore [20 million rupees, or $300,000] a year and they will have to give 2 lakh [200,000 rupees, or $3,000]."[9]

Unlike many Indian politicians, Mayawati is refreshingly honest when it comes to discussing her "innovative" fundraising techniques. "We make no bones about observing my birthday as a day for seeking donations from our party supporters who shell out their savings, with which we sustain our party," the former chief minister explained.[10] Once, in response to accusations that she took money from aspiring candidates in exchange for party tickets, Mayawati readily admitted to the practice: "Since many rich persons were keen to contest on our party ticket, I see nothing wrong in taking some contribution from them; after all, I use the money to enable poor and economically weak

Dalit candidates to contest. . . . Remember, unlike the Samajwadi Party, Congress or the Bharatiya Janata Party, the BSP does not comprise affluent industrialists, businessmen or traders; we run the party solely with the help of contributions received from party supporters and through membership drives."[11]

According to a classified U.S. diplomatic cable released by Wikileaks, the going rate to "acquire" a BSP party ticket for the 2009 parliamentary elections was in the neighborhood of $250,000.[12] The same cable also insinuated that perhaps not all of the funds raised were for strictly "electoral" purposes, disclosing that when Mayawati was in need of new sandals, she dispatched her (empty) private plane to Mumbai to procure her favorite brand and ferry them back to her.[13] Mayawati, for her part, called the allegations brought to light by Wikileaks "baseless," suggesting that Julian Assange, the organization's founder, be "sent to a mental asylum."[14]

In the lead-up to the 2009 national polls, one supporter who did not want to disappoint his revered party president was Shekhar Tiwari, a powerful MLA. Tiwari was a noted BSP leader with a reputation as a no-nonsense local strongman. Tiwari's criminal past was well known when Mayawati lured him into the BSP fold; when he won election to the Uttar Pradesh state legislature in 2007, he was reportedly implicated in no fewer than 14 ongoing criminal cases.[15]

A few weeks before Mayawati's birthday celebration, Tiwari paid a visit to Manoj Gupta, a mid-level engineer in the state public works department, to solicit a donation for his party. Tiwari's methods of using his position to influence government employees were well known. According to one local bureaucrat, Tiwari "always tried to pressurise engineers to award contracts to his chosen men and he was given his cut in every contract."[16] Gupta, an honest public servant, was not willing to give in so easily and reportedly refused Tiwari's entreaties. To add insult to injury, Gupta allegedly slow-walked approving payments demanded by several local contractors who regularly shared their proceeds with Tiwari.[17]

Days later, an infuriated and drunken Tiwari rounded up his associates, drove to Gupta's home, and subjected the bureaucrat to electric shocks and a merciless beating with a wooden baton.[18] The engineer died later that night of a brain hemorrhage, and Tiwari conspired to cover up the killing. A court later found Tiwari guilty and sentenced him to life in prison. Mayawati, for her part, expressed outrage and declared that from then on she would have only "low-key" birthday celebrations.[19] Although the following year's festivities were certainly more subdued, the fundraising did not stop. Even though her official "birthday party" was canceled, Mayawati silently collected millions of dollars.[20]

In a party founded expressly to serve as a political vehicle for advocating the interests of India's historically disadvantaged Dalit community, what is striking about Tiwari is that he is not a Dalit. In fact, Tiwari is a prominent upper-caste leader, touted as one of Mayawati's "Brahmin mascots"—someone she relied on to organize *sammelans* (caste meetings) to mobilize support from upper-caste Brahmins on the BSP's behalf in an effort to diversify her party's appeal. Incorporating key upper-caste leaders like Tiwari was an integral part of Mayawati's political strategy, intended to soften (if not eliminate) the upper castes' traditional aversion for the BSP.[21]

As gruesome as Tiwari's acts were, he was far from the only one of Mayawati's party-mates situated on the wrong side of the law. And like Tiwari, most of the BSP's criminally suspect candidates hailed from non-Dalit communities. In the 2007 Uttar Pradesh state elections, the BSP ran candidates in all 403 of the state's assembly constituencies —15 percent of whom were under serious criminal scrutiny.[22] But in constituencies constitutionally reserved for Scheduled Castes, where only candidates from this group could stand for election, fewer than 7 percent of candidates faced serious criminal cases.[23] In other words, the same pro-Dalit party in the same state adopted different political recruitment strategies depending on whether or not the candidate would contest an election in an area where Dalit quotas were operative.[24]

It turns out that the BSP experience in the 2007 Uttar Pradesh elections was no anomaly; the party's dual-track strategy extends far beyond that one election. Across all states in which the BSP was active between the years 2003 and 2009, 7.1 percent of its 3,656 candidates in general constituencies faced serious criminal cases compared to 3.7 and 1.7 percent in constituencies reserved for Scheduled Castes and Scheduled Tribes, respectively (figure 6.1).

By now, it is pretty clear what factors grease the wheels of India's electoral marketplace for criminality. But what explains the discrep-

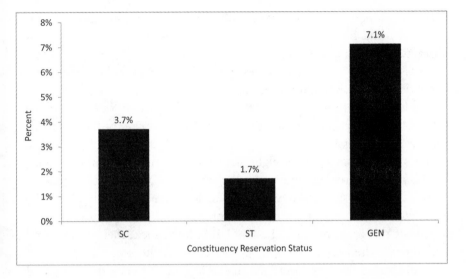

Figure 6.1. Share of BSP candidates with pending serious criminal cases contesting state assembly elections, by constituency reservation status, 2003–9. Legislative seats are reserved for Scheduled Tribes (ST) and Scheduled Castes (SC); all other seats are unreserved or general (GEN) seats. (Author's calculations based on affidavits submitted to the Election Commission of India by candidates contesting state assembly elections between 2003 and 2009)

ancy between reserved constituencies, where candidates must hail from the community the seat is set aside for, and unreserved constituencies, where anyone can stand for election? And what does this disjuncture tell us, if anything, about the conditions under which the "credibility" of suspected criminal politicians holds sway?

AN EMPIRICAL DILEMMA

Contrary to the expectations of the ignorant voter hypothesis, there can be a demand for alleged criminal politicians in a robust democratic marketplace. As the evidence from Bihar demonstrated, informed voters often rally behind candidates who not only possess serious criminal records but regularly (and publicly) tout them. To study this relationship further, one would ideally like to move beyond case studies and identify a more systematic method of ascertaining the reasons voters provide support for politicians with criminal backgrounds. Unfortunately, using hard data to study this relationship presents numerous practical challenges.

For starters, any systematic review of the connection between social divisions and criminality in India is hampered by the fact that the last detailed enumeration of caste identities took place in 1931 under the British Raj. As this book goes to press, the government of India is finalizing the results of a new caste census it carried out in 2012–13, the first such enumeration in eight decades. Unfortunately, it will likely take years before these granular data are widely disseminated and analyzed.[25] As a result, today we know far less than we should about the caste demographics of populations across India.

As if this were not enough of a stumbling block, there is a second challenge: the lack of comprehensive data on the social identities of candidates contesting elections. In the absence of such disaggregated data, it is very difficult to identify the influence social divisions might have on popular support for suspected criminal candidates.

The scarcity of data renders the prospect of more fine-grained analysis difficult, although not impossible. If the logic explaining the popular appeal of politicians linked to crime detailed in the previous chapter conforms to reality, there are a few ways of validating this argument. Two indirect methods exploit constitutional features of India's electoral design that (unintentionally) introduce variation in the salience of social cleavages and thus can be employed.

The first method exploits a distinct attribute of India's electoral order: ethnic quotas for historically disadvantaged minorities. One of the principal ways through which India's founders sought to redress historical discrimination was to "reserve" legislative seats for two historically disadvantaged groups: Scheduled Castes and Scheduled Tribes. Given the way these quotas are designed, there are good reasons to expect lower levels of criminality among politicians in reserved constituencies. The logic is simple: in reserved constituencies, candidates must hail from the community for which the seat is being reserved. In a constituency reserved for SCs, by law only SC candidates can stand for elections (the same is true for STs in constituencies reserved for that community). Although the candidate pool for these specially designated seats is restricted to the minority community, the entire electorate is eligible to vote—and therein lies the rub.

Because the ethnic identity of the winner is preordained, quotas serve to diminish the salience of social cleavages in reserved constituencies, and so parties have a much weaker incentive to engage in ethnic jockeying for votes. To the extent that parties are constrained from mobilizing along ethnic lines, candidates with criminal reputations will have much less resonance; after all, their popularity often rests precisely on their comparative advantage in activating identity-based divisions. This reality, in turn, accords with the common sentiment that candidates contesting elections in reserved areas are often more interested in wooing voters from other blocs than catering to their own ethnic community.

A second quirk in India's electoral design is the simultaneous existence of direct and indirect elections. At the national level, India has a bicameral legislature consisting of a lower house (Lok Sabha), directly elected by the voters, and an indirectly elected upper house (Rajya Sabha), whose members are chosen by the elected members of the various state assemblies. Several states in India have bicameral legislatures with similar features.

What impact might this have on criminality in politics? If the theory about why criminal politicians are popular is on the mark, one implication is that there should be lower levels of criminality in India's indirectly elected bodies. Because indirectly elected legislators do not have to contest popular elections, those legislators who are electing them are less concerned with how well they might connect with the electorate. The ethnic bona fides of candidates, which are crucial for mobilizing sought-after vote banks, are less relevant when voters are not part of the picture. Thus, if identity politics is an important motivation for why voters support suspected criminal candidates (and, hence, why parties select them), this incentive would likely be muted for indirect elections.

Data exploiting both of these electoral quirks reveal differences in the presence of politicians with criminal records that are consistent with the voter demand logic. However, these methods are still fairly indirect. A more direct strategy is to simply ask voters whether they support politicians with serious criminal reputations. One could then correlate these responses with attitudes on caste or ethnicity to gauge whether attitudes toward criminality in politics and social divisions proceed hand in hand. Thanks to a new survey of Indian voters, I do exactly that in this chapter.

EXPLOITING ETHNIC QUOTAS

The Constitution of India is arguably one of the world's most aggressive in its commitment to using state power to counter ethnic discrimination.[26] Although the constitution and subsequent law established a wide array of affirmative action policies for disenfranchised minorities, one of the principal ways through which policymakers sought to redress discrimination was through the reservation of legislative seats for Scheduled Castes and Scheduled Tribes. India is not entirely unique in this regard; nearly 40 countries around the world employ quotas to manage ethnic tensions.[27]

In order to protect the rights of these minorities, the constitution stipulates that seats in the state assemblies and the Lok Sabha be reserved for SCs and STs in proportion to their population in the state. Under the constitution, each state was required to construct lists ("schedules") of groups that would qualify as belonging to either category. Reservations were introduced as a short-term remedy, but Parliament has consistently renewed them. Although ending the practice of legislative reservation has often been mooted, most politicians are happy to maintain the status quo; the political risks of halting reservations are perceived to be too high to bear.[28] Today, roughly one-quarter of state assembly and national parliamentary seats are reserved for one or the other of these two communities (figure 6.2).[29] Within states, specific constituencies are reserved on the basis of where the share of residents from the respective minority community is largest in number.

Implications for Criminality

It is not immediately obvious what influence reservations, or ethnic quotas, might have on crime in politics. The historical record offers no explicit articulations or even remote suggestions by scholars or statesmen about the connection between quotas and criminality. Yet this is precisely why their introduction provides a unique natural experiment; no one would argue that quotas were legislated to influence criminality in politics. Any impact, therefore, is purely unintentional and allows for a clean comparison of reserved and unreserved areas.

There are good reasons to expect that politics might function differently in general ("unreserved" or "open"), as opposed to reserved,

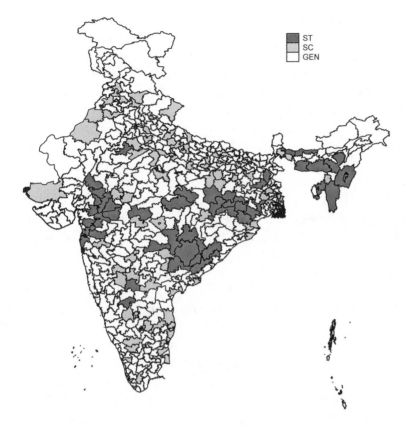

Figure 6.2. Distribution of Lok Sabha constituencies based on reservation status, 2014. Legislative seats are reserved for Scheduled Tribes (ST) and Scheduled Castes (SC); all other seats are unreserved or general (GEN) seats. (Author's calculations based on data from the Election Commission of India)

constituencies. Recall that in general electoral constituencies, there are no restrictions on who can contest elections or who can vote in them. Unlike reserved constituencies, which artificially constrain who can stand for elections, general constituencies have no such limitations. Thus, there is significant potential for parties and candidates to engage in spirited multiethnic competition over votes.

As a result, in general constituencies where quotas play no role, the election stakes are high since the ethnic identity of the winner is not known in advance. In such places, contests over local dominance, which in India typically operate along ethnic lines, will be more prevalent.

Accordingly, social divisions are more likely to be brought to the fore during the course of the campaign; the increased relevance of ethnic voting means there are greater incentives for parties to select candidates whose sweet spot is using their criminal reputations to exploit social divisions while promoting an aura of "protection" for members of their own communities (figure 6.3).

In reserved constituencies, where quotas are in effect, things work somewhat differently (figure 6.4). In reserved constituencies all candidates contesting elections are, by definition, members of the same ethnic group (that is, either SC or ST). Guaranteeing representation for these groups, of course, is the very point of reservations. But the electorate, in contrast, is made up of all eligible, voting-age citizens. While the voters may be a diverse lot, they are compelled to choose from candidates from only one caste or community.

Fixing the ethnic identity of the candidates in this way has a peculiar effect; because all candidates share a common ethnic identity, SC or ST candidates often depend on voters who are *not* like them (that is, who do not share an ethnic affiliation) in order to win elections. Because all candidates for election are from the reserved group, the voters from these reserved communities are likely to be fragmented—rendering everybody else's vote both influential and highly sought after. On the flip side, non-SC/ST voters do not have the option of voting for a co-ethnic ("one of their own"), so they must screen and select candidates on some criterion other than ethnicity.

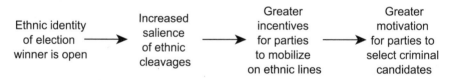

Figure 6.3. Politics, social divisions, and criminality in general constituencies.

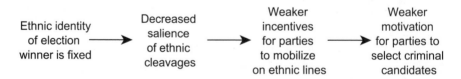

Figure 6.4. Politics, social divisions, and criminality in reserved constituencies.

Compared to seats where quotas are not in play, the electoral stakes are lower in reserved constituencies because the ethnic identity of the winner is known ahead of time; no matter what happens, at the end of the day the winner of the election will be someone from the reserved minority group. For all of these reasons, one would expect the salience of social divisions to be weaker in reserved constituencies.

The diminished relevance of social divisions and the preordained identity of the winner weaken incentives for parties to mobilize strictly along ethnic lines; in reserved constituencies, ethnicity is of limited value as a voting cue. As a result, candidates known for their alleged criminal proclivities and whose popularity rests on their comparative advantage in mobilizing on identity lines will have less traction in reserved seats. Anticipating that this is the case, parties are not likely to select such candidates in reserved areas. If a party were to field a criminally suspect candidate who gains strength from his unabashed willingness to cater to the interests of the reserved community, voters from all the other communities might be more inclined to join forces to defeat such a candidate.

Possible Objections

Before proceeding, it is worth considering several possible objections one could raise with this logic. One potential critique is that this argument disregards the multiplicity of discrete caste or tribal (*jati*) identities that exist within the larger SC/ST headings. "Scheduled Caste" and "Scheduled Tribe" are umbrella groups consisting of many individual *jatis*, or subgroups. As with most caste groupings, such as "upper caste" or OBC, SCs and STs are internally quite diverse. While this is certainly a valid critique, there is some debate about how salient specific *jatis* within the larger SC category are in the political realm, given Dalits' common historical struggle.[30]

Even if it is the case that *jati*-based competition is in play, incorporating *jatis* does not substantively change the analysis for at least three reasons. For starters, emphasizing divisions among SCs/STs is a questionable political strategy for politicians to adopt in reserved constituencies because it only further subdivides the minority vote. A criminal candidate who mobilizes voters from only his own SC/ST *jati* limits his appeal; the incentives are to cater to the median voter.

Second, a candidate in a reserved constituency could mobilize along *jati* lines, but he or she is unlikely to be able to have access to the tools necessary to build a minimum winning coalition given the realities of the caste hierarchy. In many instances, candidates have to construct a coalition in order to win an election, which forces them to attract support beyond their own community. Here too there are divergent incentives in open versus reserved seats. In open seats, suspected criminal candidates from the dominant group(s) can use coercion and/or redistribution to add to their core ethnic voter base. Social groups on the bottom rungs of the caste hierarchy will be more vulnerable to such tactics. The situation is likely to be different in reserved seats, where criminally suspect candidates from reserved minority communities will be less able to wield coercion and/or redistribution to win support from dominant groups. Groups higher up on the caste hierarchy, due to their relative wealth and their superior social status, are likely to resist such tactics and be generally unwilling to support candidates who are harder to control or bend to their will.

Finally, it is true that candidates linked to criminality can sometimes gain support from voters who are not co-ethnics due to negative voting. For instance, a low-caste Dalit may vote for an upper-caste Brahmin strongman because he thinks electing a Brahmin is a better outcome than electing a Yadav. In reserved constituencies, negative voting is less relevant because all the candidates are from the same community.[31] In a reserved constituency, a Brahmin voter does not have to make the trade-off of supporting a criminal ST candidate to ensure another group he dislikes (or another group he dislikes even more) comes to power because reservation disqualifies anyone else from contesting elections.

Stooges and Sycophants

The notion that reserved constituencies are marked by a unique brand of politics is further bolstered by the common sentiment that candidates in reserved constituencies are often perceived to be "dummy candidates" who appear more interested in currying favor with, and appearing palatable to, the median voter than catering to the interests of their own community.

Kanshi Ram, Mayawati's mentor and the founder of the pro-Dalit BSP, famously argued that electoral reservation is counterproductive because it allows more advanced castes to coopt Dalit politicians, who in turn become *chamchas* (sycophants) of dominant groups. By design, he argued, SC candidates contesting reserved seats are forced to cater to the interests of groups other than their own in order to win election. In his words, "a tool, an agent, a stooge or a Chamcha is created to oppose the real, the genuine fighter."[32] Because candidates in reserved constituencies must have broad-based appeal, they are constrained from forcefully representing the group the seat is reserved for.

As the father of India's constitution and its most famous Dalit leader, B. R. Ambedkar, often reminded people, reservations make the minority a slave to the majority. In a joint electorate, Ambedkar wrote, "The representative of the Untouchables [Dalits] would only be a nominal representative . . . for no Untouchable who did not agree to be a nominee of the Hindus and a tool in their hands could be elected."[33] Indeed, it was for this reason that Ambedkar lobbied vociferously in favor of separate electorates for SCs, in which only SC candidates could stand for office and only SC voters could vote. On this score, Ambedkar eventually lost out to Mahatma Gandhi, who feared separate electorates would damage Indian unity.[34]

Ram Vilas Paswan, one of India's most prominent currently serving Dalit MPs, makes a similar distinction between elected officials who act as "representatives of Dalits" and those that are "Dalit Representatives." For Paswan, the tragedy of reserved constituencies is that Dalit voters are more likely to get the latter: "Thus, elected would be Dalits, but they need not be Dalit Representatives, and have to be the Dalits elected by the dominant caste general voters. Hence, the namesake Dalit Representatives, unless they are basically tall within, and morally strong, had to look for approval of the dominant castes, before they speak or do anything."[35]

This sentiment about quotas was corroborated by a conversation I had with a senior official from a major national political party in Bihar in 2010. When I asked the man how his party selected its candidates in reserved constituencies, he laughed and replied, "We pray to God we can find someone who appeals to all segments."[36] Low-caste voters in one assembly constituency in Bihar bound for election complained that all parties had given tickets to relatively unobjectionable Dalit candidates so that they would not alienate other communities. As one voter put it, "Non-Dalit sections [communities] want someone who can be influenced and shaped; they will prefer someone who bends rather than a person who stands up straight."

The experience of reservation for SCs, in particular, stands in contrast to the experience of the OBCs, the segment located immediately above SCs on the traditional caste hierarchy. Unlike SCs, OBCs have not benefited from ethnic quotas for legislative representation. Some have argued that the political mobilization of certain segments of the OBCs—the Yadavs come to mind—has been affected by this struggle for representation, in a way that has fostered greater acceptance of extralegal methods of political practice.[37]

Many scholars agree with the sentiment that the system of reservation has hindered the ability of SC and ST politicians to aggressively fight for their respective community's interests. As Ambedkar and others had pointed out, a system of separate electorates, in contrast, would have been less likely to produce moderate candidates because politicians need only to win the votes of their own communities to succeed electorally.[38]

The political scientist Christophe Jaffrelot writes that Dalit politicians representing reserved constituencies have historically achieved little on behalf of their Dalit constituents because "the reservation system provided hardly any incentive for Scheduled Caste MPs or MLAs to foster the political consciousness of their caste fellows since they depended upon other voters to sustain their careers."[39] Two decades earlier, legal scholar Marc Galanter commented that the system of legislative reservations and the need to appeal to constituencies made up "overwhelmingly of others" tended to produce "compliant and accommodating leaders rather than forceful articulators of the interests of these groups."[40] One scholar interviewed a Scheduled Caste politician from Uttar Pradesh who bemoaned the moderating pressures of the reservation system, stating, "I have to work for all, for the majority of the voters, how would I otherwise win the election?"[41]

This insight perhaps provides an explanation for why many recent empirical analyses have detected no significant impacts of Dalit reservation on various measures of socioeconomic development or redistribution favoring Dalits. For instance, an exhaustive study by the political scientist Francesca Jensenius found that three decades of Dalit reservations had no discernible impact on economic development outcomes of Dalits residing in constituencies reserved for them.[42] A few earlier studies had detected positive gains from reservation, but these focused primarily on spending priorities or indicators measured at the village level rather than at the level of state or national electoral constituencies.[43] Of course, this is not to say that reservation has not produced *any* tangible improvements for reserved groups. An important new study, for instance, has found that reservations have subtly changed Dalits' views of themselves as well as popular perceptions of Dalits writ large.[44]

However, the primary take-away, as far as crime in politics is concerned, is that to the extent candidates under criminal scrutiny win support by advocating forcefully—even ruthlessly—for their narrow sectarian interests, one should see less criminality in reserved constituencies due to the need to appeal to a broader swath of voters.

EVIDENCE FROM QUOTAS

A more systematic review of available data, which goes beyond the example of the BSP described at the start of this chapter, reveals a similar pattern of criminality in reserved versus open seats. Here I focus on state elections for a few reasons, not least of which is the fact that it vastly enlarges the number of observations to study given that there are 30 elected state assemblies in India.[45]

Across all state assembly constituencies for which I have data between 2003 and 2009, 35 percent contain at least one candidate facing at least one serious criminal case. But there is a considerable amount of variation across constituency types. Among unreserved constituencies, 40 percent feature candidates who face serious criminal cases, yet only 27 percent of SC constituencies and 18 percent of ST constituencies claim this distinction (see figure 6.5). On average, if one uses more sophisticated multiple regression techniques and controls for many other possible confounding factors, it appears that reservation is associated with a 14 to 15 percent decrease in the likelihood a candidate facing at least one serious case stands for election.[46] The decrease is marginally greater for SC, as compared to ST, reserved seats.

Although these differences are significant, it is possible that criminality is lower in reserved areas not because of political incentives—

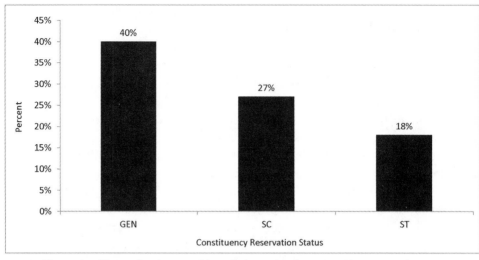

Figure 6.5. Share of state assembly constituencies, by reservation status, featuring candidates with pending serious criminal cases, 2003–9. Legislative seats are reserved for Scheduled Tribes (ST) and Scheduled Castes (SC); all other seats are unreserved or general (GEN) seats. (Author's calculations based on affidavits submitted to the Election Commission of India)

as I have argued—but due to other factors. For instance, one could argue that SCs or STs might be less prone to engage in criminal conduct for cultural, sociological, socioeconomic, or other reasons. If that were the case, then the idea that politicians from reserved communities are less likely to be associated with criminality may not be entirely surprising.

Data from India's Home Ministry, however, suggest that there is no evidence that SCs and STs are underrepresented among the criminal population at large. If one looks at the caste breakdown of convicts and those who are in jail while under trial, SCs/STs are proportionally represented among India's criminal population in the vast majority of states.[47]

A second possibility is that parties have different propensities for fielding SC/ST candidates, in which case partisan preferences for certain types of candidates could be the ultimate source of the variation. Parties that field candidates in reserved constituencies, for various reasons, may not be predisposed to running individuals with criminal backgrounds. This does not turn out to be the case. The top six parties that field the largest number of candidates in unreserved constituencies are largely the same as those that field the most candidates in reserved constituencies. Although the same parties are among the most active in each constituency category, they are clearly pursuing different strategies in reserved (versus open) constituencies—in line with the example of the BSP mentioned at the start of this chapter (figure 6.6). All parties are less likely to field candidates facing serious cases in reserved constituencies.

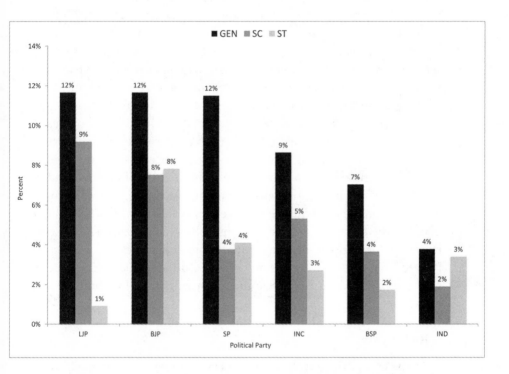

Figure 6.6. Party nomination of state assembly candidates with pending serious criminal cases, by reservation status, 2003–9. Parties graphed are: Lok Jan Shakti Party (LJP), Bharatiya Janata Party (BJP), Samajwadi Party (SP), Indian National Congress (INC), Bahujan Samaj Party (BSP), and Independents (IND). Legislative seats are reserved for Scheduled Tribes (ST) and Scheduled Castes (SC); all other seats are unreserved or general (GEN) seats. (Author's calculations based on affidavits submitted to the Election Commission of India)

Spurious or Significant?

Although differential propensities for criminality or partisan preferences do not explain the differences in reserved constituencies when it
comes to criminality, it is possible that there are still other factors that
explain the divergence. One concern about the analysis thus far is that
it might be difficult to compare areas that are reserved to those that are
not. Reservations are allocated to electoral districts with relatively large
shares of SC or ST populations, and a large literature has documented
the myriad ways in which these communities have lagged behind the
majority of the Indian population on key socioeconomic indicators.[48]
In social science parlance, reservations are endogenous, or determined
by internal characteristics, rather than chosen at random.

Because reservation is not chosen by lottery, there are a host of reasons why reserved constituencies might systematically differ from unreserved constituencies on socioeconomic indicators or along other
important dimensions. These factors, in turn, could influence the composition of the political class. For instance, if the overall level of wealth
is lower in reserved areas, candidates who wish to engage in rent-
seeking once in office might be less motivated to contest elections there.
Candidates interesting in looting the state might be more inclined to
contest elections in constituencies where the financial rewards of office
are more significant. If this were the case, it would be hard to determine
whether the lower levels of criminality observed in reserved constituencies are due to the way in which quotas impact ethnic politics or
the fact that reserved areas simply have a different socioeconomic or
cultural makeup that makes candidates with criminal reputations less
attractive.

Redistricting

At the end of the day, however, reservation per se is not really what
is important; it is what reservation *does* to the practice of identity politics that matters for criminality. Do reservations reduce the salience of
ethnically motivated political divisions, thereby weakening the appeal
of candidates with criminal records? Or is there some other variable,
unique to reserved constituencies, that is driving the differences in electoral outcomes. Fortunately, there are ways of resolving this dispute

that will help remove doubts about the logic sketched out here. The process of determining which seats are reserved (and which are not) has a few idiosyncrasies researchers can exploit to better isolate the links between criminality and politics.

The Indian Constitution stipulates that upon the completion of each census (conducted once every decade), a competent authority determined by Parliament should readjust electoral boundaries and the allocation and reservation of seats. Since independence, Parliament has authorized the convening of an independent "Delimitation Commission" four times in its history: 1952, 1963, 1973, and 2002. The most recent Delimitation Commission was finally constituted in 2002 after a gap of many years, a product of legislative wrangling over the politically sensitive act of redrawing of electoral boundaries. In 2007, the commission completed its work of redrawing India's legislative constituencies to take into account demographic changes emerging from the 2001 census; its orders came into force in May 2008.

The independence of the commission's work means that political tampering (i.e., gerrymandering) of districts is less of a concern than in other democracies, such as the United States.[49] The Delimitation Commission is an independent statutory body created by Parliament, though institutionally separate from it, whose orders have the force of law and cannot be called into question by the judiciary. These protections give it a fair amount of political independence. Indeed, researchers who studied the latest round of delimitation found no evidence of political manipulation in the redistricting process.[50]

While the commission could not alter the overall number of seats in either the state assemblies or national parliament, it was charged with rationalizing the structure and composition of electoral constituencies. This involved two steps. The first was to restructure constituencies to reduce inequalities in their population size, thereby addressing the issue of malapportionment. The second step was to reallocate seats reserved for SCs and STs on the basis of updated population figures from the 2001 census. According to the commission's authorizing legislation, seats for STs were to be reserved in those constituencies in which the share of their population was the largest. The same rule applies to SC seats, with one notable exception: the commission was required to ensure an even geographic distribution of SC seats within a state.

Reallocating Reservations

The redistricting process provides two opportunities to test whether lower levels of suspected criminality in reserved areas are driven by simple demographic differences or, rather, the diminished salience of social cleavages. First, one can compare outcomes in electoral constituencies that changed reservation status in the process of delimitation in order to separate out the effects of reservation from other background characteristics. If demographic characteristics account for the lower levels of criminality, when a reserved constituency loses its reservation one should not observe a corresponding increase in criminality. Conversely, when an unreserved constituency gains reservation, criminality should not decrease. In contrast, if reservation really does affect the salience of social divisions (as I have argued), gaining reservation should have a negative impact on criminality (and vice versa when a constituency loses reservation).

Using data from 14 assembly elections in seven states (one election prior to delimitation and one following), testing this proposition is not hard. Across these seven states, the vast majority of constituency designations did not change, but there were 150 constituencies that either gained or lost reservation status in the 2007 delimitation (table 6.1).[51]

Table 6.1. Changing Reservation Status in Seven States, 2007

Reservation status	Legislative seats
GEN ↔ GEN	515
GEN → SC	**62**
GEN → ST	**23**
SC ↔ SC	66
SC → GEN	**50**
SC → ST	**7**
ST ↔ ST	92
ST → SC	**2**
ST → GEN	**15**

Note: Numbers in **bold** indicate constituencies that changed reservation status and thus are included in the statistical analysis. Legislative seats are reserved for Scheduled Tribes (ST) and Scheduled Castes (SC); all other seats are unreserved or general (GEN) seats.
Source: Author's calculations based on data from the Election Commission of India and the Delimitation Commission.

The change in reservation status is linked to a discernible change in the share of candidates under serious criminal scrutiny in a given constituency (figure 6.7). Constituencies that were reserved in 2003 but lost their reservation in 2008 saw the average share of criminally suspect candidates nearly double. Conversely, constituencies that were unreserved in 2003 but gained reservation during the delimitation process experienced a significant decline in criminality. These differences are statistically significant and are borne out by more systematic analyses.[52] On average, 4.3 percent of candidates in "switching" constituencies (those 150 seats changed status one way or another) are under serious criminal scrutiny. Reservation is associated with a 2.3 percentage point decrease in the criminal share, which represents a more than 50 percent decline—a sizable effect.

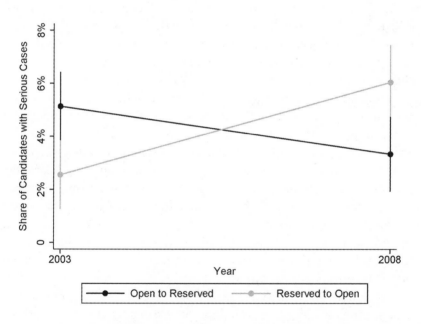

Figure 6.7. Changing reservation status and the share of state assembly candidates with pending serious criminal cases, 2003–9. Data is from seven states that had two elections between 2003–4 and 2008–9. The vertical bars represent 95 percent confidence intervals. (Author's calculations based on affidavits submitted to the Election Commission of India by candidates contesting state assembly elections between 2003 and 2009 and data from the Delimitation Commission)

A Useful Quirk

This result provides greater confidence that reservation is affecting levels of criminality in the way I have hypothesized, but it still leaves some room for doubt. If a constituency gained (or lost) reservation because of a movement in the underlying population share of SCs and STs (say, due to migration), it leaves open the possibility that demographics are driving criminality outcomes.

To check if this is the case, one can run a second test, exploiting Parliament's mandate that the Delimitation Commission ensure adequate geographic distribution of SC seats within a state when allocating reservations. In order to avoid a situation in which all reserved constituencies were clustered in one corner of a state, Parliament instructed the Delimitation Commission to ensure geographic diversity in the allocation of seats reserved for SCs. Excessive clustering of reserved constituencies, it was argued, might lead to the "ghettoization" of minorities. This mandate was specific to reservation of SC seats and had no bearing on ST reservation, perhaps because Dalits are distributed more evenly throughout the population while tribal settlements are naturally clustered into select pockets.

In practice, this legislative requirement introduces a bit of randomness into the reservation allocation process. For instance, imagine a scenario in which there are two constituencies in a state that have very similar SC populations but differ in their reservation status for purely geographic reasons. In other words, one constituency was granted reservation not because it had a higher share of SCs living there but because the commission had to ensure that reserved seats were not spatially clustered. Statistically, one can compare constituencies that earned reservation to those that did not, but otherwise have nearly identical SC population shares. This strategy allows one to tease out the subtle effects of reservation.

An example helps clarify things. Consider the state of Andhra Pradesh, a large state of more than 70 million people. Under law, each state assembly is given a quota of SC seats in proportion to the share of SCs living in the state. Because roughly 16 percent of Andhra's population consists of SCs, 16 percent of the state's 294 assembly seats (48 seats) are reserved for them.

The next step is to allocate seats across the state's administrative districts according to the district population shares of Scheduled Castes. Again, the decision of the Delimitation Commission to allocate seats to districts is designed to ensure adequate geographic spread of reserved seats. In Andhra Pradesh, the Adilabad district received an allocation of two SC seats while Nizamabad and Karimnagar districts received allocations of one and three SC seats, respectively. Within districts, constituencies are then rank-ordered according to their SC populations so that those with the largest percentage of SCs are reserved. Hence, if Karimnagar district has a quota of three SC seats, the three constituencies in the district with the highest SC share of the population are deemed reserved (table 6.2).

Now, if reservation were granted to constituencies solely on the basis of their SC population, as is done with ST seats, Manthani constituency would be granted reservation. Indeed, it has a higher SC share than

Table 6.2. Allocation of Scheduled Caste Reservations for State Assembly Constituencies in Andhra Pradesh, 2007

Examples of district-wise allocation of SC seats in Andhra Pradesh

District no.	District	District population	SC population	SC seat— allocation	SC seat— actual
1	Adilabad	2,488,003	461,214	1.79	2
2	Nizamabad	2,345,685	348,158	1.35	1
3	Karimnagar	3,491,822	650,246	2.53	3

Assembly constituency-wise allocation of SC seats in Karimnagar district

Constituency	Constituency population	SC population	SC population share	SC reserved?
Manakondur	258,789	57,792	22.33%	YES
Choppadandi	268,346	59,843	22.30%	YES
Dharmapuri	256,622	56,628	22.07%	YES
Manthani	267,261	56,764	21.24%	NO
Huzurabad	271,248	55,675	20.53%	NO
Husnabad	294,066	60,115	20.44%	NO

Source: Data from Delimitation Commission.

several constituencies in neighboring districts. As it turns out, Manthani was not reserved because of the need to ensure geographic diversity—a fact that allows for comparing constituencies that are above and below this somewhat artificial cutoff. Using this workaround, statistical analyses indicate that reservation is linked to lower levels of suspected serious criminality in areas that were reserved compared to those which had very similar SC populations but lost out solely for reasons of geography.[53] On average, reservation is linked to a 12 percent decline in the probability that a constituency has at least one candidate facing a serious criminal case.

Taken as a whole, the tests in this section build greater confidence in two facts: first, that reservation is associated with lower levels of criminality, insofar as state elections in India are concerned; and second, that the connection between reservation and criminality works through the identity politics channel, as opposed to some other mechanism such as partisan differences, demographics, or culture.

EXPLOITING INDIRECT ELECTIONS

A second method for testing the identity politics narrative around criminal politicians is to exploit another feature of India's constitutional design: the method of indirect elections. These differences in electoral design, much like electoral quotas, also have unanticipated consequences for political selection.

Bicameralism

The 543 members of the Lok Sabha, or "House of the People," are directly elected through popular franchise to serve five-year terms.[54] Seats are divided up among India's states in proportion to their population so that more populated areas have a greater number of MPs. Elections to the lower house are governed by identical "single-member, first-past-the-post" electoral rules; in plain English, each constituency sends one person who obtains the largest number of votes in the district to the Lok Sabha. This is the same process followed in U.S. congressional elections.

The Rajya Sabha, or "Council of States," is the upper house of Parliament. Like the U.S. Senate, it was created to represent the interests of India's federal states. As with the Lok Sabha, seats are divided up among the states in proportion to their population. The members of the Rajya Sabha, whose size is capped at 250 members, are elected to six-year terms, and they are chosen, not by voters, but by the respective state legislative assemblies.[55] Elections are held biennially, with one-third of the seats up for election every two years.

In terms of standing, the two houses generally share equal legislative powers, except in a few key areas. First, money bills must be introduced in the Lok Sabha and the Rajya Sabha can only suggest (nonbinding) amendments on such bills.[56] Second, only the Lok Sabha can introduce and pass motions of no confidence. Third, if there is a deadlock on a bill between the two houses, the government can call a joint session of Parliament and pass a bill with a simple majority of the combined house. Given the Lok Sabha's significantly greater number of seats, the lower house has an advantage over the upper house when a joint session is called.[57]

The "Rajya Sabha Route"

There are at least two reasons why the share of politicians facing serious criminal cases should be lower in the indirectly elected upper house. First, members of the respective state assemblies, rather than the electorate at large, elect members of the Rajya Sabha. Because indirectly elected legislators do not have to contest elections that are decided by a popular electorate, those legislators who are electing them are less concerned about the ethnic allegiance of candidates. Winning over crucial "vote banks" is far less of a concern when voters are subtracted from the equation, as they are in Rajya Sabha elections.

This is not to say identity considerations are entirely absent when it comes to candidate selection; what is different is that parties are not motivated to search for the most "credible" candidate who can appeal to a particular community or vote bank. Indeed, it is this imperative that drives parties—and voters—toward suspected criminal candidates in direct elections. With identity considerations taking a backseat, this incentive becomes weaker for indirect elections; party leaders are likely to be concerned with candidates' resources and elite connections, but they will be less inclined to prioritize who is most electable. A more likely outcome is that wealthy individuals find their way into the Rajya

Sabha, but not necessarily large numbers of candidates with serious criminal records.

For upper house elections, party leaders typically nominate candidates with minimal consultation with ordinary party rank and file. To call the selection process an "election" slightly overstates the democratic significance of the process. Because power within parties is highly centralized and voters are not a consideration, party bosses—both from the nominating party as well as the other parties in the legislature—are highly empowered to engage in horse trading to come to a pre-election deal on the slate of candidates. This often results in the number of candidates being exactly equal to the number of open seats; in fact, uncontested elections for upper house seats are a common occurrence.[58]

Thus, it perhaps comes as little surprise that the Rajya Sabha is often derisively called a "house of patronage," where party bosses, moneyed interests, and lobbyists wield considerable influence on nominations.[59] The chief minister of the state of Madhya Pradesh, Shivraj Singh Chouhan, raised a stir in 2010 when he suggested abolishing the Rajya Sabha altogether. "Nominations to the Rajya Sabha are sold in an open market, like a commodity in a *mandi* (wholesale market). It resembles an auction for MPs," Chouhan remarked. "If you don't have a Rajya Sabha, how would you hold elections for the upper house of Parliament? And without the Rajya Sabha elections, how would money flow in?"[60] Others too have commented on the patronage-based process for determining Rajya Sabha members. One journalist likened elections for a Rajya Sabha seat from Rajasthan in the early 1990s to "camel-trading." Writing about the candidates on offer, he commented: "The only common link among all these aspiring politicians was their money power. They were not only loaded with the stuff but also willing to loosen their purse strings for the honour of getting into the Rajya Sabha. Fantastic sums are being quoted in the context of the not-too-concealed horse-trading that took place on the eve of the elections in an effort to persuade the MLAs to vote for these men."[61]

In 2012, the ECI countermanded a Rajya Sabha poll for a vacant seat in Jharkhand because of the abuse of "money power," the first time it actually halted an upper house poll midway through the actual vote. In the wake of credible allegations that MLAs were being bribed to vote a certain way, the ECI ruled that the electoral process "has been seriously vitiated" thanks to a grave case of "money power, horse trading and influence" among members of the lower house to shape the election outcome.[62] In fact, on the day of voting itself, the ECI seized more than 20 million rupees ($300,000) from a car belonging to the brother of one candidate contesting the election. It alleged that the seized cash was being ferried to the state capital in order to purchase the votes of MLAs.[63]

There is also a growing consensus among observers of Indian politics that parties have aggressively used the Rajya Sabha as a way of deepening links with corporate interests and attracting greater resources (although accurate data on the occupations of parliamentarians are hard to locate).[64] As businessman-turned-Rajya Sabha MP Rajkumar Dhoot proclaimed in 2002, "Corporate leaders have money power and Rajya Sabha membership gives them political authority which is necessary to solve problems of the country."[65]

Furthermore, there is likely to be a degree of self-selection when it comes to the type of person who puts himself forward as a candidate for the Rajya Sabha. Many individuals who seek berths in the Rajya Sabha do so in part because it is a backdoor to Parliament. Given the perception (and reality) of the role of criminality and corruption in electoral politics, aspirants to the upper house may not want to contest elections because they are concerned with the reputational risk involved. In addition, the Rajya Sabha maintains an institutional perception of a body of individuals who are "above the fray" of the "dirty business of politics." Like the House of Lords in the British system, the Rajya Sabha has cultivated an ethos of a "House of Elders" whose "members are mature and knowledgeable persons with considerable experiences in public life."[66] Hence, the "Rajya Sabha route" is likely to appeal to individuals who value the status of being an influential parliamentarian without the baggage of being labeled a retail politician.[67]

On the flipside, many of India's politicians who wear their criminal reputation as a badge of honor often take great pride in contesting elections. Indeed, such candidates thrive via the direct electoral connection. Perhaps it is not a coincidence that in India, most people speak in terms of "fighting" elections rather than merely "contesting" or "participating in" them. As one political commentator explained: "Most people still go into politics to feel the pulse of the masses and energise themselves by connecting directly with the crowds. This is possible if they fight a Lok Sabha election. The Rajya Sabha is more genteel."[68]

Comparing Houses

The data on the makeup of the two houses of Parliament, as of 2010, support this notion of a more "genteel" Rajya Sabha—although not one that is completely devoid of suspected criminality (perhaps a sign of just how entrenched crime and politics are). Rajya Sabha members are slightly older and more educated, as would be expected given the cultural and institutional characteristics of a "House of Elders." Crucially, Lok Sabha members are significantly more likely than their Rajya Sabha counterparts to face criminal cases (30 percent versus 18 percent, respectively) as well as cases of a serious nature (19 percent to 7 percent) (figure 6.8). On average, Lok Sabha MPs have a greater number of pending cases, IPC violations, and charges warranting stiffer jail sentences (if convicted) than their upper house counterparts.

This difference is statistically significant and is reinforced by more systematic statistical analyses. Controlling for a range of individual

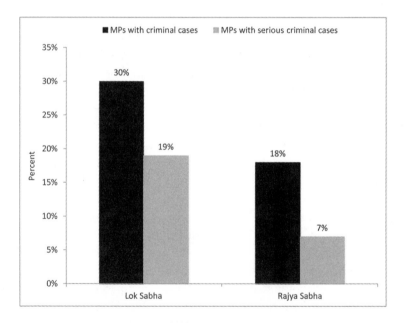

Figure 6.8. Share of Lok Sabha and Rajya Sabha MPs with pending criminal cases, 2010. (Author's calculations based on affidavits submitted to the Election Commission of India by Lok Sabha MPs elected in 2009 and affidavits of Rajya Sabha MPs compiled by the Association for Democratic Reforms in 2010)

factors, if one were to pick an average member of the Lok Sabha and move him or her from the lower to upper house, that move alone decreases the likelihood of possessing a serious criminal case by roughly 9 percent.[69]

GETTING DOWN TO THE VOTER

The data employed thus far provide further validation of the connection between the appeal of candidates with criminal reputations and the salience of social cleavages. Politicians with criminal records play less of a role in reserved constituencies as well as in indirectly elected bodies because in both instances the salience of identity politics stands diminished. These tests bolster confidence in the broader validity of the logic of demand for criminality. Be that as it may, these validation methods are still somewhat removed from the observable actions of voters themselves. While they tell us about where criminal politicians might hold the most appeal, they leave one question unanswered: do voters knowingly support politicians with criminal records because they can act as effective representatives?

Survey Evidence

The most direct way of resolving this lingering question is to ask Indian voters whether or not they support candidates with criminal records who can "get things done." A group of researchers, including myself, had the chance to do exactly this in late 2013, in advance of the 2014 Indian general election.[70] The survey, sponsored by the Lok Foundation, sought to measure the social and political attitudes of more than 68,000 randomly selected respondents across the country (see Appendix C).

To survey respondents, we posed the question, "Would you vote for a candidate who delivers benefits to you even if s/he faces serious criminal cases?" Twenty-six percent of respondents openly admitted that they would vote for a candidate who gets things done but also faces pending criminal cases of a serious nature. In other words, one out of four Indians in the Lok sample was willing to openly admit he/she would sacrifice probity for credibility. This is a sizeable percentage given the potential for social response bias (i.e., respondents might be inclined to say that they would *not* vote for candidates with criminal records—even if they truly believed otherwise—out of fear that the survey enumerator might morally judge their response).

To place this number in context, in the 2004 and 2009 parliamentary elections, the average parliamentary candidate with at least one criminal case of a serious nature earned roughly 17 percent of the vote in his/her constituency (compared to 7.5 percent for candidates not facing any cases of a serious nature).

Social Biases

The survey data support the proposition that a sizeable proportion of Indian voters reward politicians with reputations for engaging in criminal activity *and* for getting things done. The next piece of the puzzle is tying this finding back to the issue of identity politics. The credibility of criminality, as I have argued throughout, is inexorably tied to issues of ethnic politics and their salience: candidates with criminal reputations tend to have the greatest resonance in contexts where the salience of identity politics is greatest. That is, in areas where social divisions are most pronounced, the benefits criminals can provide are most desired.

As part of the same Lok survey, we asked two questions to gauge the degree of social biases among respondents. These questions were meant to pick up how "salient" social cleavages along caste lines actually are on the ground. The first question was designed to detect the degree of "negative" social bias present among respondents. Specifically, we asked respondents, "Would you be troubled if an [upper caste/OBC/SC/other community] candidate wins the election in your constituency?"

Because the survey recorded information on the backgrounds of each of the survey respondents, survey enumerators knew to which caste grouping each person belonged. With this information in hand, the enumerators asked respondents' views on a candidate from *another* caste community. For instance, if the respondent belonged to an upper-caste family, he or she would be randomly shown either a prompt relating to an SC or OBC candidate. All respondents were given an option of a candidate winning the election who was *not* from their own community but hailed from another caste. We found that 36 percent of respondents indicated that they would, indeed, be bothered if a candidate from another community won the election. This provides a reasonable baseline estimate of negative social bias among survey respondents.

To detect "positive" ethnic bias, or the favoritism for one's own group, we asked a second (slightly different) question modeled along the same lines as the previous query: "Is it important to you that [upper caste/OBC/SC/Your community] candidate wins the election in your constituency?" In this variant of the question, the prompt respondents saw corresponded to one's own community rather than to an "out group's." Forty-six percent of respondents answered that it was important for them that someone from their own community should win the election in their constituency.

To sum up, almost half of all respondents declared that having a caste ally represent them in Parliament was a priority, and nearly two in five respondents demonstrated unease at the prospect of an MP from a different caste community winning the election.

Integrating Social Biases and Criminality

Thus far the survey evidence reveals that criminal candidates who demonstrate competence elicit significant levels of approval and that voters harbor strong ethnic biases—in favor of their own as well as against members of other communities. Our next step was to integrate these two insights by taking individual responses to three questions—one on criminality and two on social biases—to see how much overlap there is. Although not all respondents who harbor social biases are willing to support candidates with serious criminal cases, those that do are significantly more likely to exhibit such biases (figure 6.9). The effects are larger for individuals espousing a positive co-ethnic bias.

Another way of visualizing this relationship is to aggregate these results up to the state level and then plot them against one another. When this is done, one sees a striking correlation, for instance, between the positive bias and criminality responses (figure 6.10). States in which a larger percentage of respondents are willing to electorally support candidates with serious criminal cases also tend to boast a greater share of respondents who harbor positive ethnic biases, a finding that is exactly in line with an identity-based explanation for criminality in politics.

Disaggregating the same relationship by a respondent's urban-rural status indicates that while the relationship is strong in both settings, it is stronger for rural respondents—as demonstrated by the steeper slope (figure 6.11). These differences are perhaps an artifact of the diminished presence of civil administration in rural India, which allows

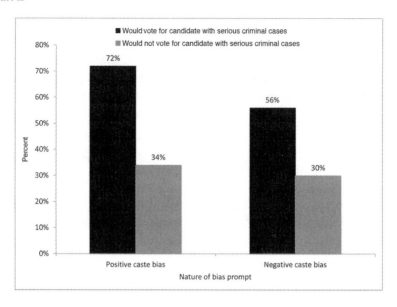

Figure 6.9. Social biases and popular support for criminality, 2013. (Neelanjan Sircar and Milan Vaishnav, "Ignorant Voters of Credible Representatives? Why Voters Support Criminal Politicians in India," unpublished paper, Carnegie Endowment for International Peace, 2015)

for strongmen who fill in the gap in government capacity to win much greater popular support. Obviously, this is speculative; further research is needed to parse the exact driver of the variation. Yet in broad terms, the survey results provide broad support for the demand-side logic of the market for politicians tied to crime.

THINKING ABOUT EQUILIBRIUM

The empirical support for the "demand" hypothesis suggests there are genuine reasons why candidates with serious criminal backgrounds gain traction in the electoral marketplace. Nevertheless, it is important not to push the argument too far. After all, while there is considerable electoral backing for such candidates—recall that 34 percent of MPs and roughly 31 percent of MLAs face ongoing criminal cases (21 and 15 percent with serious cases, respectively)—they have not entirely saturated the political system.

The market, in other words, seems to be situated in a kind of equilibrium where candidates with criminal reputations are a serious factor

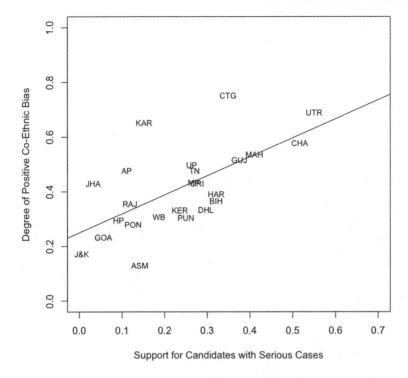

Figure 6.10. Patterns in social biases and support for criminality by state, 2013. The label markers represent individual states. (Neelanjan Sircar and Milan Vaishnav, "Ignorant Voters of Credible Representatives? Why Voters Support Criminal Politicians in India," unpublished paper, Carnegie Endowment for International Peace, 2015)

in politics but have not entirely swallowed up the system whole. This raises an obvious question: why do more candidates tied to criminality not win elections?

The first and most obvious response is to point out the conditional nature of the marketplace. It is best to think of the marketplace for criminality not as a giant wholesale market for the country but as a series of hundreds—even thousands—of local markets. As such, the marketplace is far from monolithic, working in the same manner in all areas of the country. Rather, in any given marketplace support for candidates linked to criminal activity is contextual, varying according to local incentives and circumstances. For instance, my analyses in this chapter have taken advantage of quirks in India's electoral design that—inadvertently—create variation in the importance of social

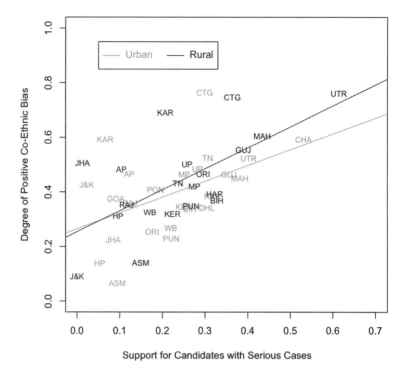

Figure 6.11. Urban/rural patterns in social biases and support for criminality by state, 2013. The label markers represent individual states. (Neelanjan Sircar and Milan Vaishnav, "Ignorant Voters of Credible Representatives? Why Voters Support Criminal Politicians in India," unpublished paper, Carnegie Endowment for International Peace, 2015)

divisions to demonstrate that criminality in politics is *more* prevalent in places where there are incentives for politicians (and parties) to mobilize along ethnic lines.

One data point that gives credence to this notion of "equilibrium" is the relative stickiness, or path dependency, in criminality within states over time. Data from ADR taken from the two most recent state assembly elections (as of August 2015) reveal that the share of MLAs with serious cases that won the previous election is a fantastic predictor of what that share will look like in the future (figure 6.12).

Second, it is also possible that the desire for self-financing politicians, which is one reason parties give tickets to candidates linked to crime, may vary across space. While I have assumed that this desire is relatively constant, one could relax that assumption, thus opening up the possibility than in certain areas, due to socioeconomic, geographic, cultural, or demographic reasons, elections might simply be less costly than in other locales. Where the cost of elections is relatively lower, parties might not weigh a candidate's "money power" as heavily when determining ticket selection. If such were the case, the attractiveness of candidates with criminal cases would stand diminished.

Third, some voters might refrain from supporting candidates with criminal reputations on moral grounds even if doing so hurts their personal or their community's perceived self-interest. For this class of voters, there might be a stigma associated with voting for candidates accused of breaking the law.[71] Recall that the Lok survey data discussed above found that 26 percent of respondents would be willing to vote for a candidate who faced serious cases if he or she were capable of

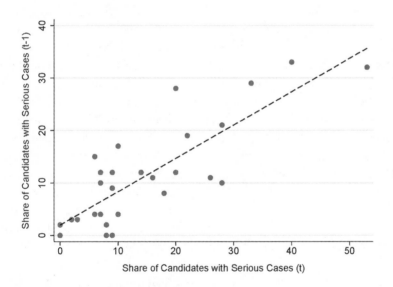

Figure 6.12. Path dependency in the share of state assembly candidates with pending serious criminal cases. The x-axis represents the share of state assembly candidates in the most recent election (as of August 2015) with at least one serious criminal case. The y-axis represents the share of state assembly candidates in the previous election with at least one serious criminal case. Each dot represents a state. (Author's calculations based on data from the Association for Democratic Reforms)

"getting things done." Presumably this also means that the vast majority of respondents were not willing to make that trade-off. It is impossible to know how these voters would act in an actual electoral setting, but even if a sizable percentage voted their conscience, they could possibly prevent a large number of candidates tied to criminality from triumphing at the polls.

On occasion, there is also a point when a politician's criminal linkages become a liability. When voters in India perceive that candidates are no longer delivering on their promises, they have a track record of throwing such nonperformers out of office. While candidates with criminal cases have a statistically significant electoral advantage, they do not possess an indefinite hold on power. The competitive nature of Indian elections denies them such a luxury.

Furthermore, there are times when parties are forced to part ways with candidates if their alleged criminality attracts excessive attention beyond their local constituencies. Criminality in politics is largely salient at the local level when it is clearly rooted in the social context of a given constituency. Once a politician's criminality turns into a larger state or national issue, parties often get nervous because they fear such attention might draw investigative scrutiny and/or because it could create a backlash among voters in constituencies (or among demographics) where criminality holds little (or less) appeal.

There are many instances of parties dropping politicians once their alleged criminal exploits get too "hot."[72] For instance, a senior BSP leader and onetime health minister in the Mayawati cabinet, Babu Singh Kushwaha, was forced to resign in 2011 when authorities uncovered a significant scam in his ministry. Auditors claimed that a network of politicians, led by Kushwaha, engineered a massive fraud in which they embezzled billions of rupees from public health funds and later conspired to cover it up. The alleged conspiracy involved the murders of several top health officials with knowledge of the corrupt activities.[73]

At a time when Uttar Pradesh was gearing up for elections, Mayawati did not want to risk the possibility that Kushwaha might damage her party's fortunes, and he was soon forced out of the BSP. His departure was hailed as a big loss for the party given his status as a leading backward-caste leader. Interestingly, the very moment the BSP ousted the tainted minister, he became the subject of an intense bidding war among the BSP's main competitors in the forthcoming 2012 elections.

The BJP quickly moved to induct him into the party, citing his caste appeal: "Kushwaha represents a very backward class community. He has come into the party and we have welcomed him. . . . SP, BSP and Congress are not serving the Most Backward Castes. . . . OBCs feel their rights are being taken away."[74] The party was forced to suspend his membership once it too came under national media fire for embracing him.[75]

PAINTING WITH A NARROW BRUSH

The dynamics of support for criminally suspect candidates are not limited to Bihar or any one state in India. The data presented in this chapter demonstrate that the marriage of crime and politics is a much broader phenomenon. The identity-based logic suggests that criminality will be lower in reserved constituencies and among indirectly elected legislators, and, indeed, the evidence is consistent with these hypotheses. These findings point to two paradoxes. It appears that while voters regularly elect legislators allegedly engaged in illegal activity, when legislators themselves are given the opportunity to select their peers, they are *less likely* to embrace such candidates. This is not because politicians are more virtuous than voters, but rather because the two actors face different incentives.

Second, although the elite discourse in India often points to the mobilization of lower castes as contributing to a coarsening of Indian politics, politicians affiliated with the lowest groups in the social hierarchy are significantly less likely to be under criminal scrutiny than their peers higher up the ladder.[76] This is not due to inherent differences in criminal propensities, or socioeconomic or cultural factors per se, but rather the way electoral politics is structured in reserved versus open constituencies.

Writing for the *New York Times*, one commentator noted in 2012, "Criminals and strongmen have long been a feature of Indian politics. Their ill-gotten wealth provides easy campaign cash, and they often control constituencies with strong caste or religious loyalties."[77] It is as concise an explanation as can be given for the supply and demand of suspected criminals in contemporary Indian politics.

III

7   Crime without Punishment
From Deep Roots to Proximate Causes

AT FIRST GLANCE, Arvind Kejriwal cuts an unlikely figure as a rabble-rouser. As an interviewer once noted, the middle-aged, bespectacled Kejriwal "comes across as a simple, but stubborn man, with no material taste. He wears trousers that seem a size too big, his shirts are what government clerks in small towns wear."[1] The only thing remarkable about his appearance is the cap he is fond of sporting: a white hat inscribed with the words *Main Aam Aadmi Hoon* (I am a common man).

Before 2011, few in India had any clue who Arvind Kejriwal was. Like many other bright young men and women who enjoyed solid middle-class upbringings, Kejriwal studied engineering at one of the prestigious Indian Institutes of Technology. After graduating, he worked for a leading business house before gaining entry into the Indian Revenue Service, one of the many branches of the Indian civil service. Frustrated by the confines of the Indian bureaucracy and the sclerotic pace of government decision making, Kejriwal eventually quit the service and devoted his full attention to social activism, immediately making waves by stridently advocating for the enactment and full implementation of the Right to Information (RTI) Act, a landmark government transparency initiative passed by Parliament in 2005.

Yet it was not for another six years that Kejriwal's likeness would be beamed into the living rooms of millions of Indian households around the country. The issue the former *babu* (bureaucrat) rode to stardom was a proposed piece of legislation to set up a federal anticorruption ombudsman known as a *Lokpal*. An entire book could be written about the tortuous history of the *Lokpal* bill, but in a word it can best be described as "fraught." Parliament first considered the bill in 1968, although it failed to win approval. Futile attempts at passage were mounted in 1971, 1977, 1985, 1989, 1996, 1998, 2001, and 2008. Each time the bill failed to make it through both houses.[2] Politicians typically enjoy espousing anticorruption rhetoric, but they prefer to leave the implementation to the next guy.

In 2010, in the wake of a crippling series of big-ticket corruption scandals, the UPA government was compelled to try once more. One high-profile scam after another, from "Coal-gate" to the Commonwealth Games scandal, had sapped the energy of the government, forcing it to find ways of saving face. Kejriwal was convinced that establishing a *Lokpal* was a game changer as far as India's governance was concerned. He felt passionately that existing anticorruption agencies, such as the CBI, were all compromised, due to either incapacity or outright government sabotage. Kejriwal, unsurprisingly, reserved his greatest ire for the country's crooked politicians. "There are honest and efficient officers in the CBI," Kejriwal told a reporter, "but their political bosses do not allow them to work freely."[3]

Parliament, he insisted, was full of "rapists, murderers and looters."[4] According to him, given the endemic corruption generations of Indians have suffered, only an independent and autonomous *Lokpal* would "set this country in the right direction."[5] "If the *Lokpal* bill was passed," he once remarked, "half of the MPs would go to jail."[6]

There was one catch, however: Kejriwal greatly disliked the government's proposed bill, which he felt lacked the teeth necessary to make much of a dent in the country's corruption scourge. Furthermore, he was deeply anxious that the government would pass a feckless bill yet receive political credit for "doing something." Under the aegis of a new social movement called India Against Corruption (IAC), Kejriwal launched a campaign to replace the government's bill with what came to be known as the *Jan Lokpal* bill, literally the "citizen's ombudsman" bill. The bill proposed by IAC had much stronger provisions than the one the government proposed and would apply to politicians operating at the highest level of the government, including the prime minister.

But Kejriwal and his colleagues lacked a compelling face, someone who could raise the movement's profile in the mass media as well as with ordinary citizens. The answer to Kejriwal's dilemma came in the form of Anna Hazare, an octogenarian social reformer and noted devotee of Gandhian methods of civil disobedience. For decades, Hazare had toiled in relative obscurity in the state of Maharashtra working on issues of social reform, government transparency, and local governance, but he had a solid reputation as a selfless social crusader. The very sight of the slight Hazare taking on the mighty government of India made him an overnight celebrity.

Once united, Kejriwal and Hazare succeeded beyond their wildest dreams in getting the corruption issue on the national agenda. One crude, back-of-the-envelope method of quantifying this is by tracking the relative number of times Indians ran Google searches for "corruption" over the past decade (figure 7.1). A large spike in 2011, at the height of IAC's agitations, is clearly discernible.

After joining forces with IAC, Hazare's opening salvo was to announce that he would fast until his group's demands for a *Jan Lokpal* bill were met. After almost 100 hours, during which sizeable crowds gathered at Delhi's Jantar Mantar to cheer Hazare, Kejriwal, and colleagues on, the government capitulated, announcing the creation of a joint drafting committee consisting of government and civil society representatives. Together, the government proclaimed, ministers and activists would work to forge a compromise solution.

The negotiations and the polarized debate were tumultuous, to say the least. A key government representative on the drafting committee called the *Jan Lokpal* bill a "Frankenstein Monster without accountability" and an "oppressive institution" operating outside the bounds of the state.[7] Even respected independent voices, broadly sympathetic with IAC's larger objectives, did not withhold their fire. In a stinging op-ed piece, one scholar accused the IAC bill of "crossing the lines of reasonableness . . . premised on an institutional imagination that is at best naïve, at worst subversive of representative democracy."[8] One of the critics' biggest issues had to do with the moral certitude of the bill's backers. Calling the *Jan Lokpal* neither the best nor the only solution to India's corruption malaise, political scientist Pratap Bhanu Mehta

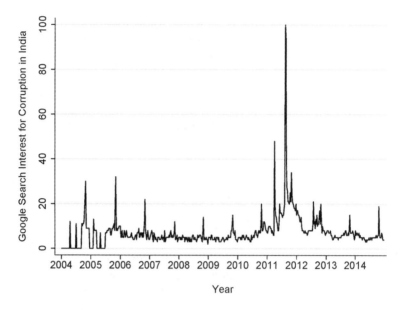

Figure 7.1. Weekly Google search interest in India for "corruption," 2004–14. The total volume of Google searches is divided by the total searches of the geography in a given time range. The resulting numbers are then scaled to a number between 0 and 100, as represented on the y-axis. (Author's calculations based on data from Google Trends)

dismissed as a "dangerous illusion" the idea that any one institution could be a "magic wand" to tackle corruption.[9]

Kejriwal, Hazare, and their colleagues were undeterred, calling their fight India's "second struggle for independence."[10] In response to the claim that his agitational style was antidemocratic, Kejriwal turned the criticism around: "We want real democracy. Not going out and voting once in five years democracy. That is pretense democracy."[11]

The negotiations, however, failed to reach a compromise, at which point Hazare once again announced his intention to go on a hunger strike. This time he endured nearly 300 hours without food and drew criticism from many of his IAC colleagues for blackmailing the government into submission. Aruna Roy, one of India's leading advocates for greater government transparency and a onetime IAC ally, blasted Hazare and Kejriwal's "my-way-or-the-highway" approach: "A Lokpal Bill is not a hereditary right of a group of people anywhere in this country."[12]

The government introduced a revised version of its own bill in late 2011, but it was not until 2013 that both houses managed to provide their assent and the bill became a law. Kejriwal, far from celebrating this victory, was irate. The government, he boomed, had turned the *Lokpal* bill into a "Jokepal."[13]

After the *tamasha* (spectacle) of hunger strikes, protests, and failed negotiations, Hazare chose to return to his village home in rural Maharashtra. Kejriwal, who had once proclaimed that "all the politicians are thieves—throw them to the vultures," opted for politics, announcing his decision to create a new anticorruption political party, the Aam Aadmi (Common Man) Party, or AAP.[14] The party's first test was the upcoming Delhi state elections, and its number one objective was to pass a *Jan Lokpal* bill for the city-state. In the Delhi elections, AAP surprised political pundits by performing extremely well, capturing 28 of Delhi's 70 seats, enough to form a government with the outside support of the Congress Party and to make Arvind Kejriwal, once described as "the man the government loves to hate," the chief minister of Delhi.[15]

Even after the AAP formed its inaugural government in Delhi, Kejriwal maintained his activist style, eschewing the comforts and, some argued, the responsibilities, of public office. In one of his first actions as chief minister, Kejriwal led a *dharna* (sit-in) at one of Delhi's main roundabouts, referring to himself as an "anarchist" and noting that "there are some things that cannot be done from air-conditioned offices."[16]

As it turns out, Kejriwal's *Jan Lokpal* bill for Delhi faced enormous hurdles; when the opposition signaled its resistance, Kejriwal resigned and pulled the plug on his ill-fated 49-day government, claiming it was "more important to fight corruption than to run a government."[17] Initially, Kejriwal appeared confident in the rightness of his resignation, saying, "We have come here to save the country. If we have to give up the chief minister's post for the sake of the country, we will do it not a hundred times but a thousand times."[18] However, he would later come to regret his decision: *Bharat ki politics mein jo bhi ho jaye, kabhi isteefa nahin dena chahiye!* (Whatever happens in Indian politics, one should never give their resignation!), he admitted months later.[19] Yet the damage was done. Soon after his resignation, AAP announced its intention to take its fight across the country. In the 2014 national elections, it contested 432 seats but won just 4 (all in the state of Punjab).

In Delhi, to add insult to injury, it was shut out entirely. Kejriwal had moved too far too fast, forsaking local power for a place on the national stage. In January 2015, having profusely apologized to the Delhi electorate and recommitted himself to local matters, Kejriwal pulled a rabbit out of a hat—again surprising political handicappers by leading the AAP to a sweep in fresh elections in Delhi.

The political upstart partially redeemed himself after badly misjudging the national political mood in 2014. But perhaps an even more grave miscalculation was focusing excessively on *Lokpal* to the detriment of broader institutional reform. Kejriwal and IAC had a unique moment, coming on the heels of revelations detailing spectacular corruption, to construct a broad governance reform agenda and rally support for it. Although they may not have intended it, IAC and Kejriwal portrayed *Lokpal* as a panacea for India's corruption woes, which it most certainly was not. This, of course, leads to the question: what steps are needed to weed criminals and corrupt individuals out of India's politics?

DRIVING AT TWO SPEEDS

In Part II, I examined the marketplace that exists in India today, and in the recent past, for politicians who possess serious criminal records. In Part III, I begin with a focus on the menu of policy actions that should be considered to curb their popularity. However, any discussion of policy reform prompts an obvious response: if there is a demand (and supply) for allegedly criminal lawmakers, must any action be taken at all to remove them from politics? At the end of the day, such politicians emerge victorious in some of the world's most competitive elections where voters often have a choice between candidates with criminal records and those without. If voters choose the former, should that be grounds for policy intervention?

Notwithstanding the existence of a competitive electoral marketplace, there are several reasons why cleansing Indian politics of politicians with serious criminal records, many of whom exploit those very reputations for political gain, makes good public policy sense. If one is convinced that making a concerted effort to shape public policy in ways that might minimize, if not totally eliminate, the nexus between crime and politics is worthwhile, the next step is to identify the universe of potential reform solutions. Previous chapters have established fairly conclusively that a lack of information on the part of parties or voters is not the binding constraint. If the constraint were principally oriented around information asymmetries, one could imagine relatively straight-forward remedial policies, such as campaigns to raise voter awareness, bolster media scrutiny, or improve the quality of civic education. But the story is *not* one primarily about information failures; rather, it is about the failure of the state to produce effective governance in a complex, multiethnic democracy. This reality makes the menu of possible actions much more difficult—but not impossible—to pin down.

If criminality in politics is truly a product of widespread governance failures, any single institutional fix—such as setting up a *Lokpal*—will be insufficient. The underlying cause of the problem is far too deep and too complex to lend itself to silver bullet policy prescriptions. In order to achieve sustainable solutions, reformers must instead operate at two distinct levels: they must systematically address the deep roots of these failures, which represents a long-run objective, while simultaneously addressing proximate factors in the short term.

On the former, there is no getting around the fact that the capacity of the Indian state to perform even its most basic tasks of governance and service delivery is wholly inadequate (a syndrome discussed at some length in Chapter 2). These critical failures have, in turn, created space for political entrepreneurs to leverage their criminality into sizeable political support. By strengthening the state's capacity to project its authority, the governance vacuum that criminal politicians seek to fill will gradually contract.

Ironically, much of the policy debate in Delhi or in other world capitals when India is discussed is focused on how to get the Indian state out of the way. This is not without cause. Even as many have pronounced the License Raj era dead and gone, the Indian state continues to frustrate and confound with the unending red tape its bureaucracy generates and the innumerable ways in which it acts as an oppressive force. From the mundane—getting an Indian passport or obtaining a driver's license—to the major—filing a police complaint or seeking damages from a court of law—a large percentage of those who interact with most public sector agencies comes away with a feeling of dissatisfaction if not outright frustration. A 2014 Pew survey found that 83 percent of Indians believe that corrupt public officials are a "very big" problem for the country.[20] Surveys of citizen satisfaction with many basic public services, such as water or healthcare, also demonstrate tremendous popular disenchantment.[21]

This red tape then becomes the lifeblood for self-interested politicians to manipulate the state's discretionary levers in ways that contravene the public interest once they are in office. In reorienting the state, reformers must proceed thoughtfully. In some areas, India has to massively cut down on the procedural burdens its bureaucracy imposes, but in other areas—many of which touch upon core activities of sovereign nations—the state must be built from the ground up. "Downsizing the state" or "enlarging the state" are imperfect catch phrases; what is needed, in a nutshell, is for the Indian state to be "right-sized." A priority area of action in tackling the challenge posed by criminal politicians is in the rule of law domain, whose weaknesses both give rise to criminal politicians and help perpetuate their relevance. This is an area marked by oppressive legal and regulatory frameworks *and* serious capacity constraints that render the state far too weak to effectively enforce its writ.

Building state capacity, however, is not something that can be accomplished overnight. As Max Weber famously wrote, politics is a long, hard slog—akin to watching the "strong and slow boring of hard boards."[22] Refashioning the state represents, at every step of the way, the quintessential political challenge. Thus, resizing India's state, as it were, is—at best—a generational task. Hence, while pushing for systemic long-term reforms, those seeking to reduce the relevance of criminality in politics must work on parallel tracks. While reformers continue to push for major governance upgrades, they must simultaneously grapple with the proximate causes of the criminal-politician nexus. This means engaging in a variety of near-term steps, such as fixing India's broken system of regulating political finance, reforming political parties' internal functioning, restricting the most egregious suspected lawbreakers from holding office, and curbing the most overt campaigning on sectarian lines.

WHY REFORM?

Politicians with serious criminal records do not appear out of thin air; to the contrary, individuals who face serious criminal scrutiny have their own self-interested motivations for joining the democratic process. And, of course, there are animating factors that make them attractive to both political parties and voters.

This reality should inform any conversation about freeing, or cleansing, the political sphere of candidates linked to wrongdoing. A cynic might reasonably ask: if politicians with criminal records succeed in highly competitive elections where voters willingly elect—indeed, often reelect—them, where is the harm? This skeptical line of questioning, though natural, glosses over the corrosive effects the fusion of crime and politics can have in democratic systems.

For starters, the fact that many of India's leading lawmakers, across all tiers of governance, are also among its foremost (alleged) lawbreakers has serious implications for the sanctity of the rule of law. The presence of so many legislators who possess serious criminal records can have a subtle but pervasive negative impact on popular perceptions of the rule of law. If citizens believe that the rule of law can be openly flouted without repercussion, given that so many individuals who actually write the country's laws may be doing the same, these perceptions can create a self-fulfilling reality, thereby encouraging widespread disrespect for the law.

Second, one new study shows that constituencies with an elected representative who has an ongoing criminal case experience significantly lower rates of economic growth. This negative effect is even larger when the incumbent faces serious cases or cases involving financial crimes or hails from states with endemic corruption and weak institutions. The authors of the study surmise that this is a by-product of lower investment in public goods provision.[23]

When it comes to social welfare, it is true that there is some segment of the electorate that stands to gain from the presence of criminal politicians. If politicians linked to crime are able to successfully deliver on their promises to "get things done" for their constituents, it could generate real welfare gains for society. Yet these improvements are not likely to be evenly distributed; there may be gains for certain segments of society, but politicians who tout their criminal reputations thrive by exploiting—not resolving—social divisions. Their modus operandi, as repeatedly shown in Part II, relies principally on catering to narrow segments of the electorate rather than the population at large. Given India's first-past-the-post electoral system, in which elections at the constituency level are regularly won with substantially less than a majority of votes, winning coalitions can be quite narrow.[24] Although members of the winning coalition might be better off with an allied criminal politician ensconced in power, those outside this coalition could remain unaffected or perhaps even worse off.

One researcher, Matthieu Chemin, has tried to quantify the welfare effects of India's suspected criminal politicians. Chemin looks at extremely close contests from India's 2004 general election, or those places where an allegedly criminal candidate narrowly won (or narrowly lost) by just a few percentage points. By looking at such close elections, Chemin takes advantage of an established statistical trick—in places where the margins of victory are razor thin, one can argue that the difference between a candidate winning or losing is essentially as random as a coin flip. Using this clever design, which focuses on this subset of extremely competitive races, Chemin finds that electing a candidate under criminal scrutiny severely reduces the everyday consumption of the most vulnerable groups in society. This means that the presence of a criminally suspect MP actually *increases* poverty for those segments of society that are worst off.

These findings are interesting but hardly conclusive. For instance, if criminals themselves hail from lower segments of society (Chemin places SCs, STs, and OBCs into this category), it is not clear why individuals from these communities should necessarily end up worse off. The implicit assumption is that criminal candidates hail exclusively from upper-caste communities, a fact at odds with reality.

Nevertheless, it at least seems plausible that politicians associated with crime have a mixed effect on the social welfare of constituents, depending on whether a given individual is in their electoral coalition or not. This ambiguous outcome reflects a more general uncertainty about the broader effect of criminally linked politicians on governance. In terms of the overall performance of the public sector machinery, these politicians do often bolster their standing by appearing to fill a vacuum of authority. Candidates with criminal records regularly campaign on pledges of delivering benefits of various sorts to their adherents (see Chapter 5). While these can be material in nature, they also involve things like physical protection or dispute resolution and justice.

Yet while politicians suspected of wrongdoing appear to plug a governance vacuum, they also benefit from the persistence of broken public sector machinery. If the state were able to adequately dispense benefits and services, justice, or protection, these candidates would certainly lose much of their relevance. For instance, a reform commission set up by the government of India in 2005 wrote that criminals in politics thrive in a setting in which the state cannot adequately implement the rule of law. In such settings, according to the report, it is the "criminal who, paradoxically, is able to ensure speedy justice and in some cases becomes almost a 'welcome character'!"[25]

An analogy worth considering here is the role and functioning of mafia groups. In his landmark work on the Sicilian Mafia, sociologist Diego Gambetta argues that a lack of social trust in Italy first gave rise to the Mafia, which could offer citizens protection—especially over property rights—in an environment where ordinary people lacked trust in the sanctity of even basic interpersonal transactions. What the *mafioso* could offer—to all parties involved—was the credibility that a transaction would be honored, thus overcoming the social trust deficit. But, as Gambetta explains, the "Mafioso himself has an interest in making regulated injections of distrust into the market to increase the demand" for the very protection he offers.[26] After all, if business agents were able to organically develop bonds of trust among themselves, the Mafia would be out of business. Similarly, politicians tied to crime may be able to solve various governance dilemmas, but the emphasis will be on short-term solutions rather than sustainable ones that might render them irrelevant in the long run.

Finally, while one can debate the welfare or governance impacts of politicians with criminal records, government statements, numerous official documents, and various committees and commissions reveal that the government of India itself is very concerned by the interaction of crime and politics. Indeed, the government has repeatedly identified the need to rid politics of criminals as a key public policy objective. Perhaps most famously, the Vohra Committee sounded alarm bells in 1993 by noting that a politically connected mafia was "virtually running a parallel Government."[27] And a commission charged with reviewing the workings of India's constitution stated in 2002: "The visible presence of many criminals is in fact a very large factor in the loss of legitimacy for politicians as a whole. This is also extremely dangerous for the country because apart from distorting the political culture of the country, criminal elements progressively get to influence leadership and governance. The spectacular success of some criminals in politics invites emulation."[28] Five years later, a government report stated that the "increasing criminalisation of politics and persistent interference in the due process of law" was a root cause of public disorder in various parts of the country.[29]

Thus, even though the marketplace for criminal politics chugs along, there are many good reasons why democratic citizens should be uncomfortable. But if ridding politics of such elements is deemed to be an important objective of public policy, what is to be done?

THE LOPSIDED INDIAN STATE

Devising a reform agenda to mitigate the role criminality plays in everyday politics is a complex undertaking.[30] For starters, and this is the harsh reality, it is difficult to get people excited about an intellectual debate on "how best to fix civil administration." Second, "governance" is such an all-encompassing catchphrase that pleas for investing in "good governance" can often obscure more than they illuminate. Finally, building state capacity involves time horizons that extend far beyond the sorts of timelines that politicians, many of whom are looking only as far as the next election, are able to mentally grapple with. Most politicians in India—indeed, in most developing countries—do not perceive fixing basic services as a readymade path to electoral success. Furthermore, many politicians might also view systemic governance reform to be at odds with their short-term political objectives, especially if reforms loosen their party's grip on power.

As a result, governance has been allowed to stagnate. Popular disenchantment with this state of affairs, further fueled by repeated instances of large-scale government corruption, has made the Indian state an easy target. But despite a reflexive inclination to harp upon the failings of the Indian state and to devise ways of curbing its power in order to minimize the frequency and intensity of abuses, the Indian state is the problem as well as a principal element of the solution. This is not a popular stance, but it is an incredibly important one to grapple with.

Smarter Regulation

The overbureaucratization of the Indian state in procedural terms has had many pernicious effects. It has led to poor developmental performance, bred corruption and collusion, and created space for political entrepreneurs to circumvent or cut through regulations using dubious means. Despite the problems of hyper-regulation, wanton deregulation is also not the solution. Reformers must make efforts to reduce red tape and excessive discretionary powers belonging to the state, but the need for regulation will not disappear. What is needed is smarter regulation—and, fortunately, there are recent examples to draw from.

In 2011, a group of scholars and experts were commissioned by the Ministry of Finance to reimagine the laws and regulations governing India's financial system. This effort, known as the Financial Sector Legislative Reforms Commission (FSLRC), spent two years evaluating and modernizing the sector's regulatory framework, identifying overlaps and inconsistencies, and drafting a lasting unified financial code. Divided into multidisciplinary groups, the commission developed objectives for each area of the financial market, identified the sources of market failures, critically assessed the role of government, and evaluated the costs and benefits of redrafting legislation.[31] The work of the FSLRC has not been free of controversy; some critics have derided it for its purist adherence to economic first principles, and others have quibbled with specific institutional reforms it has proposed. Any ambitious reimagination of legal and regulatory frameworks will be faulted on such grounds, but—substance aside—there is no reason why the commission's methodology cannot be replicated across multiple sectors beyond finance. Similarly, in early 2016, the BJP government of Narendra Modi was hard at work consolidating and rationalizing India's innumerable labor laws into a streamlined set of four labor codes. The legal patchwork governing labor has grown immensely since independence, providing huge rent-seeking opportunities for corrupt bureaucrats while simultaneously hampering business activities and, rather ironically, failing to protect workers' rights.[32]

Separating Fat from Muscle

The underlying infirmities of the state frequently get lost in the clamor to ratchet back the most burdensome manifestations of the Indian bureaucracy. Nearly everyone realizes that state capacity is a crucial determinant of development outcomes, yet it remains a slippery, amorphous concept that is frustratingly difficult to pin down. At its core, state capacity refers to the ability of the state to effectively design and implement public policies.

Disaggregated further, the concept can be broken down into two constituent parts: incentives and competence. In considering questions of state capacity, economists have traditionally prioritized incentives, arguing that public officials must face the right set of incentives if they are to behave in a manner that benefits the general public they are charged with serving. All too often, bureaucrats in India do not face such incentives, thereby opening the door to a slew of self-serving behavior ranging from brazen venality to simple absenteeism. For instance, the egregious level of absenteeism by public school teachers in India (estimated in 2014 to be around 25 percent) undoubtedly has grave consequences for the quality of education imparted to India's youth, but it also has enormous financial costs. One study estimated that the fiscal cost of teacher absence in India is around $1.5 billion *per year.*[33]

Another study, examining operations at over 1,400 public health centers across the country, found that nearly 40 percent of doctors and medical service providers were absent from work on a typical day.[34] One experimental study from Delhi revealed that despite higher salaries, greater training and qualifications, and medical knowledge, public doctors provided worse care than their private sector peers.[35] Researchers examining public health facilities in rural India found that in 63 percent of recorded doctor-patient interactions, the "doctor" who met with the patient was not a provider with recognized medical training, even though possessing such credentials is standard government policy.[36] The uneven quality of public service delivery is certainly not unique to India. But even when compared to other low-income developing countries, India performs poorly in terms of ensuring that public sector employees show up to work during normal office hours.[37]

Designing incentives for bureaucrats and public employees to perform their duties in a more efficient and less venal manner is a puzzle that has occupied the brains of some of the world's best and brightest researchers, practitioners, and management gurus for years. There is still a lot to learn, but there is a growing body of evidence, much of it from India itself, on the effectiveness of a range of potential strategies— from the creative use of technology to incentive compensation and legal reform.[38] In some cases, the solution rests with bypassing the bureaucracy entirely. For instance, India has enjoyed great success with "smart card" programs that allow citizens to access benefits via bank accounts rather than middlemen.[39] Furthermore, the introduction of the potentially path-breaking *Aadhaar* scheme, which offers all Indians the possibility of obtaining a unique biometric identity, has the potential to shift a great many transfers, subsidies, and benefits to direct cash transfers, which can be accessed without delay or hassle. Interventions such as these, which transfer significant bargaining power into the hands of ordinary citizens while circumventing the often-dysfunctional local machinery, hold considerable promise.[40] Of course, efforts to bypass the state must proceed hand in hand with, rather than substitute for, genuine efforts to fix the heart of the bureaucratic problem.

In this regard, one popular remedy often pursued is to pass laws guaranteeing citizens a "right" to a specified set of basic services. If citizens are denied access to any of these services within a limited, preset time frame, bureaucrats would incur monetary penalties until the issue is resolved. This follows the model engrained in the RTI Act, which imposes fines on empowered government officials who do not promptly respond to freedom of information requests. Many states have already passed "Right to Services" laws, but the jury is out on how effectively they are working. One concern with this rights-based framework is that the public sector lacks the manpower to process inquiries in a timely fashion and the government is often reluctant to impose financial penalties on officers, citing lack of experience or systemic failures as the real reason for delay. A legislated "Right to Services" will engender favorable delivery outcomes only if the state is properly equipped to carry out its various provisions.[41]

Clearly, generating the right incentives for public sector officials to faithfully execute their official duties is a major constraint when it comes to building a more efficacious state. But even if India's political leaders are able to set the right incentives for government rank and file, there remains the question of competence, such as ensuring that officials possess the right skills and training. But before matters of skills and training, there is an even more basic challenge that needs to be overcome: across almost all dimensions, India's public sector institutions are grossly undermanned. In many parts of the country, the state simply lacks presence.

Heated debates over the size of government are not unique, especially among large democracies. In the United States, Republicans and Democrats regularly wage pitched battles over the size of the federal workforce. In much of southern Europe, in the wake of the financial crises of 2007–8 and the ongoing Eurozone debt crisis, governments and citizens similarly debated the merits of downsizing the state to reduce the state's fiscal burden. While debates over the optimal size of the state are quite common, there is one key difference in the Indian context: the task is not simply about modifying the state but—in many corners of the country—building it from the ground up for the very first time.

Therefore, investing in competence requires first and foremost staffing up government agencies, beginning by filling vacancies where posts have been officially sanctioned. There can no longer be any excuses made for the fact that huge chunks of the bureaucracy simply do not exist due to positions going unfilled, particularly in a country with a giant labor surplus. Unlike the aging societies of the West, India is poised to reap a "demographic dividend," with 300 million working-age adults joining the labor force between now and 2040. The vast majority of these jobs will have to come from the private sector, but surely in such an environment, the public sector should not be perennially understaffed.

In some cases, the government can rely on private contractors rather than hiring full-time government staff. Indeed, public sector reliance on contractors has grown substantially in recent years.[42] Contractors have to be part of the solution, but there is a danger of excessively relying on contract labor in areas where the government ought to be a central actor, such as in the provision of public goods. For instance, while India's police force has languished, hamstrung by personnel shortfalls, poor pay, low morale, and endemic political interference, there has been a massive growth in the private security industry. One of India's leading business federations estimates that private security is roughly a 400 billion rupee ($6 billion) industry, estimated to grow at an impressive rate of 20 to 25 percent over the next several years and currently employing more than 6 million guards.[43] This growth in private sector guards is natural given the swelling of the middle classes, the rise of gated communities, and the growth of commercial establishments, but it cannot substitute for the basic provisioning of law, which is inherently a government function.

Beyond quantity, quality too is an important element in building up competence, and the fact of the matter is that India faces a skill shortage across the board. This is due, in no small measure, to persistent shortcomings in higher education and vocational training.[44] However, there are a significant number of talented people with specialized skills who have found work in the private sector and for whom public service remains an aspiration. When the UPA government wanted to create a unique biometric identification scheme for India's citizenry, it successfully lured Nandan Nilekani, the founder of the tech giant Infosys, to lead the effort. Similarly, the government successfully recruited Subramanian Ramadorai, the former CEO of Tata Consulting Services, to serve as an adviser to the prime minister and to take charge of a national council on skill development. Facilitating the "lateral entry" of such talent is a no-brainer, although it remains politically sensitive given the influence many public sector unions continue to wield. This battle has to be waged politically, but it is one worth fighting.

THE RULE OF LAW SUPPLY CHAIN

Talk of "rightsizing" the state can get pretty abstract pretty quickly in the absence of concrete examples. The rule of law, a core function of any democratic sovereign, is as good an example as any to help place things in proper focus. This domain merits deeper exploration given its intimate connection to the nexus of crime and politics. Furthermore, it is another area where the state has exhibited legal and regulatory excesses as well as endemic weakness in human capital terms.[45]

India is a young nation, in terms of both its population (it boasts a median age of 27 years old) and its status as an independent nation (less than seven decades old), but it is subject to exceptionally old laws. The most important piece of legislation governing India's police force, for instance, is the Police Act of 1861, written by a British administrator nearly a century before independence.

On paper, India's commitment to the rule of law distinguishes it from many of its peers and neighbors, which have had a decidedly mixed record in this regard. According to 2015 data collected by the World Justice Project, India scores well on open government and democratic controls (table 7.1). In the category "constraints on government powers," which evaluates checks on government power, India ranks thirty-eighth of the 102 countries surveyed around the world, is second among 6 in its region, and fifth out of 25 middle-income countries.

Table 7.1. India's Ranking on Select Rule of Law Indicators

	Global rank	Regional rank	Income group rank
"Rule of law on paper"			
Constraints on government powers	38/102	2/6	5/25
Open government	37/102	1/6	3/25
"Rule of law in practice"			
Absence of corruption	68/102	2/6	11/25
Order and security	90/102	4/6	20/25

Note: India is classified as belonging to the South Asia region and lower middle-income group of countries.
Source: Data from World Justice Project, *World Justice Project: Rule of Law Index 2015* (Washington, D.C.: World Justice Project, 2015).

On "open government," India ranks thirty-seventh of 102 worldwide and does well compared to its peers.[46] Yet the rule of law that exists on paper does not always exist in practice. As a nation, India has not fully come to grips with the vast gulf between the laws on its books and their often dysfunctional, partial, and corrupt application. On metrics related to procedural effectiveness, India fares poorly. In the categories of "absence of corruption" and "order and security," India ranks sixty-eighth and ninetieth globally.[47]

"Rule of law" is a rather abstract concept; it is not a single entity but rather a spectrum of activities or a supply chain. The first link in the chain is the structure of the laws and statutes (not to mention the lawmakers who write them), since nearly everything else flows from what is codified in law. The next links involve the investigative arms of the state, followed by the prosecutorial agencies; the judiciary and penal system constitute the final components. Nearly every element of India's rule of law supply chain is problematic—threatening not only the rule of law but a *belief* in the value of law itself.

Laws

For India the trouble begins with the first step of the chain: the archaic laws on the books, such as the colonial-era Police Act, many of which were written by India's former imperial rulers. India, unlike many other democracies, does not employ sunset clauses that require the expiration of certain laws after a fixed period of time. To make matters worse, rather than pursuing a coherent and focused process of cleaning up the statutes on the books, politicians—urged on by a zealous civil society—have typically rushed to enact new laws without repealing existing ones.

Because many laws at the central level have been poorly drafted—and are now riddled with ambiguities, amendments, clarifications, and exemptions—they have inevitably led to conflicting interpretations, spawning endless litigation. In 1998, a government commission reviewed existing laws and sought the repeal of more than 1,300 central laws out of the 2,500 it reviewed.[48] There is an entire agency of the government—the Law Commission—whose mandate is to identify laws worthy of repeal. Still, the country has made very little progress in clearing out the cobwebs.[49] The resulting legal thicket has created considerable confusion about what the law actually says, hampering effective enforcement and encouraging noncompliance.

The only solution to this morass is to revise, repeal, and update old laws and to insist on greater precision in the drafting of replacement language. Despite the apparent enormity of the task, legislative consolidation and simplification is not as hard as it seems at first blush. A recent civil society collective dubbed the "100 Laws Project" identified 100 laws the government could scrap tomorrow if it could muster the effort. The laws targeted for outright repeal range from obsolete Partition-era legislation like the Imperial Library (Change of Name) Act of 1948 to vestiges of misplaced nationalism like the Swadeshi Cotton Mills Company Limited Act of 1986 to the downright oppressive Newspaper (Price and Page) Act of 1956.[50] If civil society, working with the commission, can succeed in getting these 100 laws repealed, they could easily come up with another 100, and then some. In its first year in office, the Narendra Modi government did make some headway on this issue. Although Prime Minister Modi did not quite live up to his statement "if I end one law a day, I will be the happiest," Parliament did pass two bills repealing 126 redundant laws. The elimination of hundreds of other obsolete laws awaits Parliamentary action.[51]

Police and Prosecutors

The next link in the chain—not counting India's lawmakers, of course —is the police. In keeping with their anachronistic legal underpinnings, the primary objective of the police in India is maintaining law and order, not preventing crime, a holdover from the days before Independence when ensuring crowd control was vital for British authorities. Colonial-era laws, deep politicization, and an overcentralized hierarchy have severely burdened the police.[52] With the passage of time, policing became a deeply political enterprise. One scholar writes that policing has been "transformed from the professional imposition of a coherent moral consensus to an intensely political activity."[53]

Over the years, several attempts have been made to reform India's police; nearly all have failed.[54] Caught in a vicious cycle of demoralization, low popular support, and scarce resources, the police remain understaffed and undertrained.[55] This understaffing, of course, is further compounded by widespread vacancies. Although the government has occasionally raised the idea of enabling lateral entry into the police, both to enhance quality as well as quantity, entrenched interests have revolted, calling such an effort a move to "dilute the quality of the elite police."[56] In addition, India's police lack many of the technological capabilities necessary to perform quality investigations. For instance, Delhi's sole government-run forensics lab reported a backlog of nearly 10,000 cases in late 2013, resulting in three-year delays for forensics reports.[57]

All of these factors, in turn, contribute to the low conviction rate that discredits both the police and the courts. Unfortunately, things do not get much better the higher up the food chain one goes. India's premier investigative agency, the Central Bureau of Investigation (CBI), is widely perceived to be the handmaiden of the sitting government, to be unleashed or reined in on its whims (AAP leader Arvind Kejriwal was not off the mark in his assessment of the problem).[58] In the words of former bureaucrat S. K. Das, the CBI has become an "instrument of control" used to protect public functionaries from embarrassing investigations or "to settle political scores."[59] Indeed, many CBI corruption investigations of leading politicians seem to ebb and flow in accordance with that individual's relationship with the party in power in Delhi.[60] The CBI's lack of independence from the executive and its reliance on approvals from state governments to open investigations into their affairs seriously constrains its autonomy. Even when government interference is minimal, public prosecutors are still stymied by a lack of human and financial capital.[61]

Those urging reforms of India's police have not failed for lack of trying; numerous police commissions over the past several decades have articulated both the need for and underlying content of sweeping changes in the way India conducts policing. Nearly all experts agree that police reforms must include more autonomy as well as greater accountability, personnel, and material resources. Yet India's political class has repeatedly balked at moving this agenda; the political impasse is fueled not only by politicians' preferences for maintaining the status quo (which provides them with obvious benefits) but also the fact that law and order is under the purview of India's states under the constitution, making the reform process infinitely more complex.

But when leaders have mustered the political will to initiate reform, the payoffs can be significant, even from relatively low-cost tweaks. For instance, one police reform experiment in Rajasthan found that simple fixes such as freezing the transfers of officers and professional training had positive effects both on public satisfaction of police forces and the quality of actual police work. Though some experiments by the Rajasthan government did not succeed, the ones that worked could be instituted from the top down and would not require much local implementation.[62] The judiciary has tried to circumvent politics by directing all states to set up technocratic bodies such as "police establishment boards" to determine transfers and promotions and "police complaint authorities" to resolve citizen disputes, but the court has failed to ensure adequate compliance.[63]

Courts

The courts in India suffer from a peculiar paradox. On one hand, in the face of a weakened executive and gridlocked legislature, the courts (particularly the Supreme Court) have attempted to fill a vacuum of authority and policymaking. Yet on the other hand, the institutional underpinnings of the judiciary are growing weaker over time.[64]

Perhaps the single biggest affliction of the justice system is the snail's pace at which it proceeds. As a recent government inquiry put it, "Denial of 'timely justice' amounts to denial of 'justice' itself."[65] Each year, the courts take on more cases than they are able to process—a function of personnel shortfalls as well as interminable judicial formalities. Underlying these weaknesses is a lack of financing. The courts are, unfortunately, caught in a chicken-and-egg scenario. The judiciary regularly appeals to politicians to provide them with more resources while politicians point to the inefficiencies in the justice system and demand that judges first get their own house in order. Yet without additional resources, reducing inefficiencies in the justice sector is a monumental task.

But a shortage of qualified personnel is not the only constraint; timely justice is also stymied by the inordinate delays in the justice system.[66] The ease with which parties to a legal dispute can receive a seemingly infinite number of adjournments means that those seeking to avoid justice have plentiful opportunities to throw sand into the gears of the justice system. There are few penalties, for instance, for a party's failure to comply with judges' timelines and directives. Furthermore, without a functioning electronic case-monitoring system, judges themselves face difficulties in tracking the status of ongoing cases.

The shortfalls facing law enforcement and the judicial logjam ultimately mean those who have matters pending before the judiciary or are in prison awaiting trial are kept in limbo for longer periods of time. As of 2011, approximately 24 percent of court cases had been pending for at least five years; 9 percent had been pending for more than ten years.[67] Data from 2013 show that while the number of convicts only grew by 1.4 percent over the previous year, the number of those "under trial" increased by more than 9 percent. All told, in 2013 there were 280,000 individuals awaiting the resolution of a trial before the courts—two-thirds of all those residing in Indian jails—and 3,000 of those had been languishing behind bars for at least five years or more.[68]

Fortunately, the government has begun to articulate solutions to this blot on India's democracy. For starters, the Supreme Court established a National Court Management System to assist in the tracking and monitoring of cases. This is a good first step, but it must proceed hand in hand with stiffer penalties for parties who defy predetermined deadlines. To staff the courts with judges who both are competent and have integrity, one solution worth pursuing, recommended by the Law Commission and endorsed by several advisory bodies, is to create an all-India judicial service (along the lines of the Indian Administrative Service or the Indian Police Service).[69]

A common measure successive governments have pursued is setting up fast-track courts or special tribunals in order to alleviate the burden of the mainline judiciary. These courts are promising in theory but regularly struggle in practice—often because, sooner or later, they too succumb to the pathologies of the broader justice system.[70] A case in point is the network of fast-track courts established in the wake of the 2012 Delhi gang rape. In response to widespread public outcry over the number of sexual assault cases languishing in the courts, the chief justice of India ordered the creation of fast-track courts to consider these cases on an expedited basis. Sadly, within one year, the disposal rate of some of these courts was even worse than the regular courts.[71] Unless the broader impediments to obtaining speedy justice are directly addressed, workarounds are not likely to work all that well.

Resizing the Indian state and reforming its rule of law apparatus is undoubtedly a long-term enterprise. There are several steps the government can adopt now to begin the process of reimagining India's governance institutions, but the process of building up capacity and streamlining regulation requires a sustained investment over the course of many years, if not decades. While political leaders move forward on this front—and even if their progress is stymied along the way—there is a complementary agenda for the short run, which can ameliorate some of the proximate drivers of criminality in politics. Fortunately, there is no need to reinvent the wheel; over the years, there have been multiple electoral reform commissions that have helped generate a consensus around certain commonsense reform steps.[72] These measures fall into four categories: political finance, political party reform, restrictions on candidate entry, and the management of ethnic tensions.

POLITICAL FINANCE

The political thinker Pratap Bhanu Mehta once wrote that the "reform and regulation of the ways in which elections are financed remains the single most difficult challenge for Indian democracy."[73] Any serious discussion of reducing the role criminals play in politics must, therefore, grapple with India's political finance morass. If India can clean up its system of funding elections, it can possibly contain—if not totally eliminate—the allure of criminal politicians.

Candidate Assets

During the 2000s, reformers made considerable headway in improving the level of transparency about the backgrounds of candidates running for elected office. The affidavit disclosures candidates must now make regarding their criminal records and financial assets have, to some degree, made public details about the roles money and criminality—and the interaction between them—are playing in politics.

Yet as enlightening as these affidavits are, the new disclosure regime does not go nearly far enough. For starters, there are serious concerns about the veracity of candidates' financial declarations.[74] Independent investigations conducted by the media have typically found that candidates routinely understate their true wealth. The data provide a useful ballpark estimate, but there is no independent check of any information that appears on candidate affidavits. Furthermore, the disclosures do not pick up "black money" or *benami* assets that are owned by the candidate but placed under the name of a family member or friend in order to evade detection. Instituting a system of random audits on even a small sample of candidates would bolster incentives for more truthful reporting. Without an audit capacity, it is nearly impossible to discern what constitutes "false" or "misleading" information (which is the standard that must be met for prosecution).

Strictly speaking, candidates who file false information or conceal information can be subject to prosecution, resulting in imprisonment of up to six months if convicted. Unfortunately, this provision is rarely enforced in practice. To strengthen the ECI's hand, Parliament should amend the Representation of the People Act to explicitly make false or misleading disclosures the basis for electoral disqualification.[75] When it comes to disclosing the most basic information about their personal backgrounds, candidates found trying to game the system should face harsh penalties. As it is now, they receive merely a slap on the wrist.

In addition, the ECI requires candidates to disclose their income tax details, yet more than 50 percent of parliamentary candidates in the 2014 elections failed to do so; this group includes 293 "high asset" candidates (accounting for 3.5 percent of the total candidate pool).[76] The requirement that candidates disclose tax information allows for a natural collaboration between India's election and tax authorities, both of which have a vested interest in cross checking the authenticity of candidate disclosures. At present, no system of corroboration exists between the two branches.

Candidate Expenditure

Just as candidates are required to file disclosures in advance of elections, they are similarly required to submit detailed statements of expenditure within thirty days of an election's completion. Ostensibly the purpose of these statements is to assess whether candidates have remained within the strict election expenditure guidelines set out by the ECI. Politicians and political parties have regularly lambasted these requirements for being grotesquely low, a charge not without merit considering the elevated costs of campaigning. As one politician jokingly remarked, a candidate contesting state elections could easily surpass his or her spending limit simply by sending a one-rupee postcard to every voter in the constituency.[77] In response to this recurring complaint, the ECI has thrice revised candidate expenditure ceilings since 2003 to bring these limits into greater alignment with reality.[78] That candidates routinely report spending *just over half* what they are legally entitled to confirms the suspicion that candidates are vastly underreporting their election expenditures.[79]

On campaign spending, the ECI has made strides in cracking down on illegal expenditures by introducing real-time expenditure tracking, which includes random audits by commission officials during the course of campaigning. Armed with shadow ledgers and videographers, expenditure observers working for election authorities have tried to ensure that what candidates report is actually what was spent on the ground. All of this activity will change reporting incentives only if there are strict penalties attached to filing false or misleading disclosures. By law, candidates who file false expenditure statements or who conceal information can face punishment of imprisonment for a term up to six months, a fine, or both. In practice, however, there is a great deal of legal ambiguity around the exercise of this punishment.

For instance, the ECI had for years been pursuing a case against former Maharashtra chief minister Ashok Chavan for filing false election expenditure paperwork. According to the ECI's allegations, Chavan's disclosures omitted the fact that he paid journalists to write positive news articles about him during his 2009 election campaign. Rallying behind one of its own, the Congress Party government openly challenged the commission's power to disqualify a candidate for falsifying election finance filings.[80] The government instead contended that the

ECI can disqualify candidates only for a failure to file their expenses but that it has no legal basis upon which to sanction candidates on the "correctness" of election accounts.[81] In July 2014, the ECI ruled against Chavan, recommending that he forfeit his seat in Parliament and face judicial prosecution, but the Delhi High Court later exonerated Chavan.[82] In its ruling, the court stated that the advertisements taken out were not reported to Chavan, and thus he had no knowledge of them when filing his election expenditure statement.[83] The court's ruling in this high-profile case was widely interpreted as a setback for the ECI's enforcement powers.[84]

Beyond expenditures made by the candidates themselves, for many years candidates did not have to declare any spending carried out by their party or by third-party supporters on behalf of their campaigns. A 2003 amendment to the law changed this, compelling candidates to report these expenditures as well. Although a step in the right direction, the legal changes were shot through with loopholes, limiting their effectiveness. For instance, a new amendment exempted all party and supporter expenditure meant for propagating the general "party program," as opposed to highlighting the candidate him- or herself, from reporting requirements. Drawing a fine distinction between the two is difficult, and so this major loophole renders the entire disclosure regime futile.[85]

Party Finances

Beyond the personal finances of candidates, the finances of political parties themselves require greater scrutiny. Under the RTI Act, all citizens have the right to petition any "public authority" and request information about the operations undertaken by those public authorities if it is deemed to be in the public interest. The relevant authorities must consequently respond within thirty days to a citizen's request or risk incurring financial penalties for the failure to respond expeditiously.

Citizen groups have successfully used this provision to gain some visibility into party finances. In 2008, ADR successfully petitioned the Central Information Commission (CIC), the agency that regulates the RTI Act, to publicly release the income tax returns of parties dating back to 2004. Unfortunately, few parties regularly file their tax returns each year, even though their tax-exempt status is supposedly conditional on compliance with these requirements.[86]

More recently, the CIC ruled that parties should be considered "public authorities" for the purposes of the RTI Act. This ruling was highly controversial because, if implemented, it could crack open the opaque functioning of parties. But not all opponents of the present system support this change; indeed, many critics of the status quo have objected to the notion that parties are public, rather than private, entities.[87] Lawmakers seem to agree with them. Before departing office, the Congress-led UPA government introduced a bill that would amend the original RTI Act to explicitly stipulate that parties are private entities, thus freeing them from complying with information requests.

The BJP, which came to power in May 2014, has also dismissed the CIC's ruling. Indeed, all six major national parties steadfastly refused to even meet with the CIC in the wake of its order.[88] Unable to compel the parties to comply with its ruling, the CIC eventually gave up, stating that "in cases such as this, the Commission is bereft of the tools to get its orders complied with."[89] On the heels of this unprecedented act of noncompliance, the Supreme Court stepped in, asking the ECI, the central government, and the six parties to make their case as to why parties should or should not be exempt from RTI.[90]

The issue has yet to be resolved, but assuming the government and the major parties reverse course, there are reasons to be skeptical that the ground realities will change as significantly as some RTI proponents suggest. The primary reason for skepticism is that party financial statements are not independently audited by a third party, much less one selected by a neutral authority. They are instead blessed by an internal auditor who has been carefully handpicked and, hence, widely perceived by outsiders to be quite unreliable. There are all sorts of ways in which party accounts could be doctored or fabricated.

Going forward, there are several options for resolving this impasse. For starters, the ECI mandates that parties file election expenditure statements within a prescribed window of time, yet many parties regularly ignore this requirement. Indeed, as of January 2015 many political parties had not submitted expenditure statements for the 2014 Lok Sabha election even though the deadline was late August 2014. The ECI must be empowered to sanction parties that fail to comply.

Furthermore, in 2014 the ECI drew up guidelines for how parties should maintain and report their accounts, soliciting technical inputs from the Institute of Chartered Accountants of India.[91] Parties have argued against these new guidelines on legal and technical grounds. Enforcing these requirements and making them mandatory would greatly assist in establishing a common reporting format and in ensuring that parties do not omit key financial details. But the commission should take further steps and seek authorization from Parliament to demand that parties be subject to third-party audits by a private firm or public agency, such as the CAG (or by a firm the CAG verifies to be credible). Given the opacity of political finance flows and the repeated opportunities parties have been given to reform themselves, not to mention the fact that political parties avail themselves of considerable tax benefits given by the state, demanding that parties submit to independent audits of their books is hardly a draconian measure. Those parties that refuse to comply with ECI orders should be scrutinized by income tax authorities.

Political Contributions

One area of particular concern is political contributions. Recall that between 1969 and 1985, corporate funding of politics was banned, effectively pushing political finance underground. When the ban was lifted, firms had become inured to the prevailing system, which allowed them to give in excess of legislated limits while protecting their anonymity. This anonymity was—and is—prized in a highly regulated economy where the state retained the discretionary power to punish firms that fell out of favor with the ruling dispensation.

The rules governing contributions slowly evolved in the 1990s and 2000s, but in 2003 two legislative changes were enacted. First, donations to political parties were made tax deductible, and, second, parties (as receiver) and businesses (as sender) were required to declare all contributions in excess of 20,000 rupees (now, $300). While both tweaks incentivized public disclosure, the latter stipulation still proved problematic. Savvy contributors who wanted to shield their identity could simply make an unlimited number of payments below the threshold without having to declare their giving.

As it stands, the sources of the vast majority of funds collected by parties remain highly opaque. One analysis of the income and expenditure statements of India's six national parties between 2004–5 (the first year they were made available) and 2012–13 demonstrates that roughly 75 percent of party income arrives in increments below 20,000 rupees. As a consequence, the sources of these contributions are unknown.[92]

To address this loophole, Parliament should amend the law to strip the 20,000-rupee threshold and make all donations (of any size) subject to public disclosure.[93] The fixed-rupee threshold serves as a fig leaf for illicit fundraising; politicians and parties can always claim that they raised massive amounts of money through small donations from well-wishers. Under the current regime, there is no way for any authority to call their bluff. Indeed, Mayawati's BSP has claimed to have raised the overwhelming majority of its funds in such small, opaque increments; therefore, it has not had to disclose the name of even a single contributor in eight years.[94]

Is Public Funding the Answer?

One perennial reform proposal discussed at policy roundtables is public funding of elections. Many advanced democracies implemented some form of public sector funding of elections in the late 1950s and 1960s. Many pro-reform voices have suggested that India do the same in order to move beyond the corrupt and inefficient status quo.

Unfortunately, there are two problems with creating a system of public financing. On the one hand, parties in India already receive various forms of direct and indirect funding from the state; indeed, this was a central part of the argument watchdog groups made when petitioning the CIC to recognize parties as public authorities under the RTI law. For instance, parties can access land for party offices at concessional rates, are exempt from paying income tax, and receive free airtime on public television and radio.

On the other hand, it is not clear that providing parties with additional funds—to subsidize campaign costs, for example—would address the issue of corruption, criminality, or illicit finance. After all, there is nothing to stop parties from taking funds from the exchequer while continuing to reach under the table for funds. Without fundamentally reforming the present system, introducing public funds would not address the underlying problem. Until candidates and parties subject themselves to much greater scrutiny, election authorities receive greater authority to punish wrongdoers, and legal loopholes are closed, introducing state funding of elections would allow the political class to have their cake and eat it too.

CLEANING UP POLITICAL PARTIES

Reforming political party finances is a critical step toward cleansing politics, but reform of political parties should not be reduced to their financial accounts alone. Across virtually all parties, the complete absence of internal party democracy has concentrated power in the hands of a formidable clique. It has had a pernicious effect on two important aspects of party operations: information transmission and political selection. Oligarchic leadership has limited the ability of parties to transmit information about policy positions and principles downward and has simultaneously guaranteed that very little information about party member preferences percolates upwards through the ranks. Similarly, when it comes to political selection, elite control has both stymied the upward mobility rank-and-file members can experience within the party hierarchy and facilitated the influx of opportunistic candidates who have questionable allegiance to the party but the money, reputation, or connections to win party tickets.

To reverse this trend, one possible solution is to grant the ECI expanded authority to regulate the activities of political parties. However, here reformers must tread carefully. There is an ongoing debate about whether political parties can be considered "public authorities" for the purposes of the RTI Act, but even if one believes that they qualify, parties must be given sufficient space to operate outside of the ambit of state control. For instance, the ECI and some civil society activists have suggested that the commission be entrusted with ensuring that parties adhere to a modicum of intraparty democracy. Proponents would like to see election authorities given the power to disqualify parties that do not hold internal party elections or fail to conduct their internal deliberations transparently.

While such regulations have their appeal, they also risk perpetuating the worst tendencies of the *mai-baap sarkar* (nanny state) in India.

One could easily imagine such powers being abused for purposes of political vendetta in the hands of the wrong leaders. The truth is that there is relatively little outsiders can do to reform the inner workings of political parties. But there are at least two basic proposals reformers could coalesce around.

First, while the ECI has the potential to register political parties, it has no power to *de-register* them. Giving election authorities carefully delimited powers here could have several benefits. If new rules are imposed to compel parties to disclose their finances, the threat of deregistration could give such rules credible teeth. In addition, there is evidence that many registered parties are "parties" in name only. Of the 1,600 parties registered with the ECI as of 2014, only 464 fielded at least one candidate in the 2014 national election. Top election officials have openly voiced their concern that many of these dormant parties exist solely to serve as tax havens (since parties' income is tax deductible).[95] Given the serious political fragmentation in India, parties could be required to meet some minimal threshold of support (a fixed number of validated signatures, for instance) or risk deregistration. Any new powers in this regard must be highly circumscribed because, if construed broadly, they could be ripe for abuse.

A second proposal is to insist parties respect some basic principles of democracy and transparency. For instance, parties could be required to make public their list of key officeholders, their party constitution, or their by-laws. Forcing parties to adhere to such limited requirements may not have much impact on the quality of party democracy in the short run, but they would represent a small shift in that direction. Pushing for more sweeping restrictions risks overreach, which could be counterproductive.

WEEDING OUT THE RASCALS

Reforming political finance and the internal functioning of political parties are two indirect ways of reducing the role of criminality in politics. But there are also more direct measures that reformers could consider to more frontally address the issue, such as placing restrictions on the candidate pool eligible for elected office. These restrictions could be imposed in advance on all candidates or, in the aftermath of elections, only on the victors. Regulating who can and cannot contest elections or ultimately hold office is an area fraught with controversy since there are many ways in which well-intentioned rules can be manipulated for political effect.

Pre-Election Remedies

The most direct way of reducing the number of criminal politicians in India is to prohibit candidates with criminal credentials from contesting elections. There are a host of potential objections to this idea, not least of which is the contention that banning candidates with criminal *cases*, as opposed to *convictions*, violates one's "presumption of innocence" (or the legal notion that the accused is innocent until proven guilty).

The difficulty inherent in the Indian system is that, since the judicial system operates at a snail's pace, it can take decades for a criminal case to reach its logical conclusion. This process can take even longer when one of the parties involved is a politician with considerable political and financial resources at his disposal. As of 2009, according to one civil society analysis of MPs with declared cases, the average case against a suspected politician had been pending for seven years. Of this group, 50 MPs had a total of 136 criminal cases pending against them for at least a decade.[96] In at least one case, an MP from West Bengal faced a case involving rioting and theft that was first filed 28 years prior.[97]

These statistics demonstrate just how thorny the issue of keeping criminals out of politics truly is. The solution is, in a fundamental way, internal to the problem: enacting measures to keep candidates associated with criminality out of politics is potentially problematic if such individuals have not been pronounced guilty by a court of law. At the same time, individuals named in serious criminal cases only rarely face the long arm of the law due to the grave weaknesses of the justice system. From a narrow legal perspective, candidates charged with crimes are legally innocent until proven guilty. Indeed, an analysis by ADR found that, of the more than 47,000 candidates who contested state and national elections between 2009 and 2013, only 0.3 percent had ever been convicted by a court of law,[98] a remarkable finding given that 17 percent of these candidates faced criminal cases at the time of their nomination, with 8 percent facing serious cases.[99]

In 2013, the Supreme Court ruled that any individual who was in jail or in police custody at the time of elections could be barred from contesting elections, even if that person had not been formally charged. The court's reasoning was that a jailed person is prohibited from voting, so allowing a jailed person to contest elections would be treating politicians differently from the common man. Although the court's ruling may have been well intentioned, it was deeply problematic because it created strong incentives for politically motivated arrest and detention. Given the temptation of Indian politicians to misuse the police to punish political rivals, without clear safeguards, the ruling could easily be misused. Parliament moved quickly, amending the law to negate the court's ruling.

This example illustrates the moral and practical issues that prevent strong action to restrict candidate entry. One compromise solution that has been mooted is to narrow the scope of potential candidates who would be subject to disqualification on the basis of their criminal record. For instance, a recent ECI proposal stipulates that only candidates who face criminal charges of a *serious* nature would be disqualified from contesting office. To guard against politically motivated charges, the commission has suggested a number of additional safeguards: charges must be framed by a judge (that is, charges must meet a certain threshold of prima facie credibility); they must carry a potential sentence, upon conviction, of at least five years in prison; and they must be brought at least one year prior to elections.[100]

One could go even further by amending electoral laws so that any candidates whose cases satisfy all three criteria would be automatically eligible for an expedited judicial process. The problem with this last fix, as discussed above, is that fast-track courts are akin to a Band-Aid when what is needed is a lasting solution. Indians must have this important policy debate, but there is at least a good case to be made that, at the very least, there should be timely justice for those who are in charge of making the laws.

Post-Election Remedies

If restricting the entry of candidates into the electoral marketplace is too controversial, an alternative solution would be to focus on those candidates who are actually elected as legislators in India's state and national assemblies. Both on the campaign trail and later during his initial months in office, Prime Minister Narendra Modi hinted at exactly such a compromise, a position later endorsed by the Supreme

Court, which separately ruled that cases pending against sitting MPs and MLAs should be concluded no more than one year after charges have been framed.[101]

The Supreme Court has recently put into place a process of disqualification for those *convicted* of crimes specifically enumerated in the Representation of the People Act.[102] In an important 2013 judgment, the court found that any MLA or MP currently holding office, once convicted by a court for a class of serious crimes enumerated in the law, would be immediately disqualified from the date of conviction (unless he or she obtained an immediate stay on that conviction).[103] Prior to this ruling, convicted lawmakers could retain their seats as long as outstanding appeals were still pending before the courts. Although the government first contemplated an executive ordinance to supersede the court's ruling, and later introduced a bill to the same effect, it backed down in the face of widespread criticism. One of the first MPs to lose his seat on account of the court's ruling was none other than Lalu Prasad Yadav of Bihar. Soon afterward the chief minister of Tamil Nadu, Jayalalithaa, who was found guilty on graft charges, became the first sitting chief minister of India ever to be convicted and forced to leave office (although her conviction was later overturned by the Karnataka High Court). According to one analysis, of the 543 MPs elected in 2014, 53 face charges that could trigger immediate disqualification if they were eventually convicted by a court of law.[104]

MANAGING ETHNIC TENSIONS

A final area where smarter public policy could play a role in reducing the appeal of criminality relates to the management of ethnic tensions. The ability of politicians with criminal reputations to connect with voters is mediated by the prism of identity politics. This reality both perpetuates the exploitation of identity politics in political campaigns and shapes the way politicians rule once in office.

To tackle this issue, there are a few policy options worth considering. The first would be to institute a zero-tolerance policy for candidates who openly campaign or seek support on the basis of inciting ethnic or communal enmity. During the course of the heated 2014 election campaigns, BJP general secretary Amit Shah (who later became party president) made highly inflammatory statements (captured on video) in a communally sensitive electoral district of Uttar Pradesh that had just experienced gruesome ethnic riots. Although the ECI swiftly banned Shah from campaigning in the state, within a few days it withdrew its ban, stating that Shah had expressed remorse.[105] Needless to say, handing out mere slaps on the wrist is not a credible deterrent to politicians intent on stoking ethnic tensions.

The second option is to invest in public service campaigns meant to deter voters from lending support to politicians who mobilize largely on sectarian grounds. Here one needs to make a distinction between information provision and persuasion. As demonstrated in Part II of this book, pure information campaigns in which civil society or the media provide factual information on the criminal antecedents of politicians will have only limited success in contexts where voters are already aware of politicians' criminal reputations. This is likely why some experimental studies from India have found that informing voters of the criminal profiles of their candidates is not sufficient to move the needle on voter behavior.

But pure information campaigns are distinct from hortatory campaigns that seek to persuade voters to change their behavior through implicit or explicit social pressure. In this area there has been some limited success in India. Scholars working in Uttar Pradesh designed an experiment in which an NGO conducted meetings and puppet shows to urge villagers to vote in the coming election and to do so by "voting on issues, not on caste" lines.[106] The experiment succeeded both in raising voter turnout and in reducing the extent of caste-based voting in the election. Interestingly, the decline in caste-based voting was highly correlated with a measurable decline in voter support for candidates charged with serious crimes.

One conclusion of this experiment was that voters who are urged not to vote on the basis of caste might, in the face of implicit social pressure, consider alterative evaluative criteria that could detract from criminals' support. This is consistent with an argument that popular support for criminal candidates is, in part, a by-product of identity-based voting. It also suggests that the salience of identity is malleable; while politicians may ratchet it up, there are also ways of dialing it down.

CHIPPING AWAY

Freeing Indian politics from the grip of politicians with serious criminal records is not a job for the faint of heart. The entrenched nature of the electoral marketplace virtually eliminates any possibility of swift, transformative progress. The deep causes that give rise to criminality in politics emerge, at the end of the day, from weaknesses having to do with the sovereign state's most essential functions. Generating the right sorts of capacity to fulfill these essential mandates requires time, patience, and a grand vision—three factors that are often anathema to politicians looking only to win the next election.

As Raghuram Rajan has argued, reducing the functions and activities of the government is worthwhile, but getting the government of India to perform its essential functions better is harder—and arguably more important. "Much of what needs to be done," he has postulated, "requires better, cleverer, focused government rather than less government."[107]

The good news is that India's federal system has become a hotbed of experimentation; in recent years, civil society, the private sector, and public agencies have worked together in various permutations to figure out what works when it comes to public sector reform. Under the constitution, India's federal states have primacy over a great many subjects related to day-to-day governance; this decentralized framework, if harnessed properly, can aid the diffusion of good ideas and squelch bad ones as well. This spirit underlies the Modi government's stated desire to kick-start a process of "competitive federalism" in which "leading" states making sound policy choices would govern by example, eventually compelling "laggard" states to mimic what works.

A second piece of good news is that there are many actions political leaders can take in the interim to ameliorate the situation in the short run. Cleaning up political finance or strengthening norms surrounding intraparty democracy are within the realm of the possible, although the past tells us that gains are likely to be incremental rather than sweeping. Many politicians have fought, and will continue to fight, tooth and nail against any restrictions that hamper their ability to maneuver freely when it comes to conducting their political business. Fortunately, a combination of civil society activism and the courts have—especially in the last decade—kept up the pressure. Let's hope they continue.

8 An Entrenched Marketplace
Rethinking Democratic Accountability

AS THE SWELTERING sun set on the banks of the Godavari River in Andhra Pradesh, evening traffic along a two-lane highway abutting the river ground to a halt as our car approached a police checkpoint. With state and national elections only days away, the ECI had set up a series of checkpoints to clamp down on the movement of illicit campaign cash. As traffic backed up and the incessant honking of cars grew intolerable, I exited the car and found my way to a roadside stall serving soft drinks, where a group of college-age boys were chatting. I asked one of them how he felt about the coming May 2014 general election.

"Modi is going to win. It is not even a contest," he replied confidently.

Taken aback by his certitude, I felt that it was my duty to point out that neither Modi's name nor his party's symbol was actually on the ballot in this area. Voters had to pick a parliamentary candidate and, in this particular constituency in Andhra Pradesh, the BJP had given the seat to its local alliance partner, the TDP. For years, this part of the state had been a TDP bastion.

"I will vote for the TDP candidate because the TDP has an arrangement with the BJP," the boy explained. "With the votes the alliance gets in Andhra, the BJP will form the government in Delhi and Modi will become prime minster."

When I asked the boy why he wanted so badly for Modi to win, he responded: "Because he has done good work in Gujarat. And because he will tackle corruption." When I probed further about the nature of Modi's good work as Gujarat chief minister, the boy demurred. He gestured in the direction of the checkpoint and suggested that such things would no longer be necessary if Modi won and could enforce his will.

This idea—that one man would be able to make a serious dent in the problems that plagued India's politics—seemed fantastical, but I could not fault the boy for thinking that it was possible. For the previous several months, Modi had traversed the Indian heartland pledging to root out corruption and, specifically, to end Indian democracy's dalliance with politicians linked to criminality.

One day before I arrived in Andhra Pradesh, Modi campaigned in the state of Rajasthan, touting his commitment to tackling the underbelly of Indian democracy. "There is a lot of discussion these days on how to stop criminals from entering politics. I have a cure and I have vowed to clean Indian politics."[1] His plan, Modi went on to explain, was to set up fast-track tribunals that would hear the cases of sitting politicians accused of wrongdoing. "I am positive after five years of our rule, the system will be absolutely clean and all criminals will be behind bars," he continued. "I promise there will be no discrimination and I won't hesitate to punish culprits from my own party."[2]

A week later, while addressing a series of campaign rallies in the battleground state of Uttar Pradesh, Modi again picked up the thread. "We need to rid Parliament of criminals. . . . I won't let them off the hook if I'm elected to power," Modi told his audience in Hardoi.[3] At a rally later in the day, this time in Etah, Modi reiterated his pledge: "We must do away with [the] criminalisation of politics, and delivering more lectures won't help."[4] In the town of Mathura, the fabled birthplace of the Indian deity Krishna, Modi declared: "No [criminal] accused will dare to fight polls. Who says that this cleansing cannot happen? I have come to cleanse politics."[5]

These frank words, emerging from the mouth of the most popular politician in all of India, came as a breath of fresh air. Politicians in India rarely speak candidly, or self-critically, about the challenge criminality poses to Indian democracy. The idea of setting up tribunals to dispose of high-profile criminal cases involving politicians, a proposal discussed in Chapter 7, has been floating around for several years.

But Modi was perhaps the first major politician to provide such full-throated support for the move.

Offsetting these strong words, however, was the simple fact that the prime minister's own party had embraced dozens of candidates who had serious criminal cases winding their way through the creaky Indian justice system. Indeed, 33 percent of BJP candidates contesting the 2014 Lok Sabha elections declared at least one pending criminal case, while 21 percent possessed cases of a serious nature.[6] In response, the BJP leadership argued that the cases against their party men were politically motivated and lacking any legal basis, a standard first line of defense.

When the final votes were tallied on May 16, 2014, the share of elected lawmakers implicated in criminal proceedings climbed to new heights despite Modi's fiery campaign speeches and the unprecedented level of attention showered on the election proceedings. The 2014 race marked the first time social media was intensively deployed in the service of an Indian election; as a result, details about candidates, campaign rallies, and public statements gained more airtime than ever before. Even for those hundreds of millions of Indians unable (or uninterested) to feverishly check their Twitter, Facebook, or WhatsApp feeds, it was difficult to escape the heightened levels of civil society activism and wall-to-wall media coverage.[7]

On Election Day, the BJP claimed victory in 282 races—an outright majority in the Lok Sabha. Of its record number of MPs, 35 percent faced ongoing criminal cases, and 22 percent had serious cases pending.[8] In one of his maiden speeches in Parliament, Modi reprised his verbal assault on the criminalization of politics, comparing the entry of bad governance into administration to diabetes infiltrating a person's body.[9] Notwithstanding these harsh words, 13 of the BJP's suspected MPs would eventually find their way into Modi's first cabinet, including 8 legislators with serious cases.[10]

In fact, within the BJP, allegations of serious criminal transgressions began near the very top. Around the globe, the election was rightly celebrated as a triumph for Narendra Modi, but never far behind the BJP prime ministerial candidate stood his longtime associate Amit Shah, who oversaw the party's campaign in the crucial battleground state of Uttar Pradesh. Described as "the one man who holds the key to the mysteries of Modi's mind," Shah had been Modi's right hand for

decades, previously serving as a minister overseeing several key portfo-
lios in the Gujarat government, including those involving internal security.[11] For the entirety of Modi's tenure in Gujarat, Shah was widely
seen as Modi's sole trusted election organizer and all-around Mr. Fix-It.
To be fair, Shah was a dominant politician in his own right, winning
four consecutive elections to the Gujarat state assembly, some by margins larger than what his boss had been able to secure. Before the 2014
general election, Shah had had a hand in as many as thirty elections—
with nary a loss, earning him the title "master strategist."[12]

Notoriously media-shy, Shah had long been trailed by a cloud of
controversy stemming from his time as Gujarat's home minister. In
that capacity, Shah was connected to three cases of extortion and conspiracy, including a famous 2010 case in which he was accused of authorizing the encounter killing of a known extortion artist, his wife,
and a witness to the extrajudicial murder.[13] An "encounter killing" is
essentially a premeditated act of murder, whereby police officials cook
up a scenario under which they kill a suspected criminal by alleging
that he or she put the policemen's lives at risk, typically by brandishing
a weapon or threatening force. Human rights organizations claim the
phenomenon is commonplace in India.[14] Shah's influence in Gujarat
was so widespread that upon his arrest the Supreme Court of India
forcibly exiled him from his home state for fear that he would exert
undue influence over the state's law enforcement apparatus.[15]

When I visited Ahmedabad, Gujarat's most important metropolitan
hub, in 2012 to observe state elections, I asked several longtime political watchers about Shah's role in the Modi regime. "He is Modi's bag
man," one local journalist told me. "What is in those bags—one does
not know . . . or care to ask!" Another individual I spoke with, a longtime resident of the city who had observed Shah's rise to prominence,
told me that the top aide was nothing short of indispensable to Modi
during his tenure. Indeed, Shah was openly referred to as the "second
most important man in Gujarat."[16]

Shah masterfully managed the BJP's 2014 campaign in India's most
populous state, Uttar Pradesh; his fastidious ground game led the party
to victory in 71 of the 80 seats on offer, a rout few had thought possible
and made even more impressive by the fact that the BJP's 2009 tally
was a paltry 10 seats. Although typically most comfortable functioning
out of the limelight, Shah earned headlines for a fiery speech he made
during a campaign stop in Muzaffarnagar, a communally tense con-

stituency where fierce religious riots had broken out in the preceding months. At the rally, Shah told a gathering of Hindus, the BJP's main votaries, to reject parties with Muslim candidates as Muslims in the area were responsible for raping and killing Hindus. Shah thundered that the coming election was about extracting *badla* (revenge) and protecting the Hindu community's *izzat* (honor).[17]

Shah's inflammatory remarks immediately went viral, earning him a rap on the knuckles from the ECI, which briefly banned him from addressing rallies in the state due to his "objectionable" comments.[18] These assorted blemishes, real or alleged, were not enough to damage Shah's meteoric political career. After the 2014 general election rout, Modi used his newfound stature to appoint Shah national president of the BJP. Rising from the second most important man in Gujarat, Shah became the second most powerful man in the BJP—and some would argue in the entire country.[19] A week before the election results were announced, the CBI cleared Shah in one of the fake encounter cases for lack of evidence.[20] Sixth months after assuming the powerful post, a special court dismissed the charges against Shah stemming from the remaining two cases linked to the alleged encounter killings, saying that it found fault with the CBI's evidence.[21] Although the CBI could have appealed the decision, it decided against it, a move some argued was politically motivated.[22]

Although Shah rose to a position of nearly unmatched prominence, he formally remains a state legislator in Gujarat, never making the jump to parliamentary politics in Delhi. But dozens of other men and women also allegedly involved in serious criminal acts did follow this well-trodden path. One member of the sixteenth Lok Sabha elected to office in May 2014 was Sanjeev Baliyan, a man allegedly connected to the tense ethnic situation in Muzaffarnagar. Baliyan won the constituency's seat in Parliament in spite—indeed, perhaps *because*—of his having been charged with inciting the violent riots that led to the death of more than 50 people and the displacement of more than 50,000.[23]

A report in the *New York Times* describes Baliyan, a political dilettante who had previously been employed as a veterinarian, as "a first-time officeholder famous for precisely one thing"—his role in the riots.[24] Indeed, Baliyan not only rode that notoriety to Parliament, but also was rewarded with a ministerial berth.[25] In summer 2014 BJP sources told me that Baliyan's inclusion in the cabinet was a fillip to the RSS, the nationalist organization affiliated with the BJP, since he was widely regarded as a strong pro-Hindu, anti-Muslim voice. "Yes, I am a novice in politics," admitted Baliyan, "but I am a fast learner."[26]

Joining Baliyan on a BJP ticket from Uttar Pradesh was a longtime *neta* allegedly mixed up in criminal activities, Brij Bhushan Sharan Singh, ringing in his fourth term as an MP. Sharan Singh had gotten his political start with the BJP but later abandoned the party, only to be lured back in 2014. In a somewhat ironic twist, he rejoined the party to much fanfare at a major event attended by key BJP leaders, at the same time Narendra Modi was barnstorming the state railing against the use of criminal politicians by the state's regional parties.[27]

Sharan Singh had gotten his start in student politics in the 1980s, earning a reputation as a vocal leader of the Thakur community.[28] His political career was given a boost in the early 1990s around the time of the controversial Ram Janmabhoomi movement. During the movement, activists associated with the BJP sought to dismantle a contested Muslim mosque in Uttar Pradesh, which they claimed was located on the birthplace of the Hindu god Ram, in order to construct a temple on the site. Sharan Singh, who had already carved out a role for himself as a strongman in the Gonda region of the state, used his influence to aid the Janmabhoomi *karsevaks* (volunteers) and later get himself elected to Parliament.[29] The CBI also accused him of having knowingly harbored associates of noted international terrorist Dawood Ibrahim, booking him under the TADA Act, though he was later acquitted.[30] At one point, he is reported to have racked up as many as 40 criminal cases, involving murder, kidnapping, and aiding terrorism, and other serious infractions.[31]

As an MP, Sharan Singh was not bashful about brandishing his strongman reputation, though he claimed it was for those who were helpless. "I have never troubled the poor and the decent," Sharan Singh once stated. "And I have never shied away from taking on those who oppress others."[32] Once, when launching a protest over the inaction of the local police, Sharan Singh was asked about his tendency to create a ruckus for political gain: "I am a mafia man. How can I be Gandhi? I have forty cases lodged against me," the MP stated. "How can I be any good? I try to do my best. This is the public. I want to be of some help to them."[33] In 2015, Sharan Singh added another title to his CV: he was unanimously reelected president of the Wrestling Federation of India.

The year 2014 also marked the triumphant return of Pappu Yadav to Parliament. Yadav, readers will recall, was one of the six MPs temporarily furloughed from jail to vote in the 2008 no-confidence motion over the proposed US-India civil nuclear deal. After a surprise acquittal in a case involving the murder of a bitter political rival, Yadav seamlessly moved from jail to the hallowed halls of Parliament House. While he was sidelined in jail, Yadav had recruited his wife, Ranjeet Rajan, to act as the family's torchbearer. She campaigned in his name, winning a seat in Parliament. In 2014, they assumed their seats in Parliament next to one another.

The election also served as a political revival of sorts for the Bellary brothers of Karnataka. In the wake of the Karnataka mining scandal, the fall of the state's BJP government, and the sudden death of YSR (their political patron in Andhra Pradesh, on the other side of the border), the brothers had come upon hard times. In spite of these setbacks, there appear to have been limits on how low they could plummet. By 2014, the brothers had put their political stock in their honorary fourth brother, B. Sriramulu, who had previously served as health minister in the BJP government that the brothers had bankrolled. Sriramulu enjoyed his fair share of the Bellary brothers' mining success; in Bellary it was rumored that he was so wealthy that he regularly bathed in Bisleri brand bottled water.[34]

Perhaps as a way of keeping the brothers within the tent, the BJP gave Sriramulu a party ticket to contest the Bellary seat. The honorary brother was more than an empty stand-in; he had represented Bellary in the state assembly on four previous occasions dating back to 2004. A constituent once commented that the constituency used to be "a place you sent people as punishment. Now government officers pay for postings in Bellary. It is because of Sriramulu."[35] A loyal representative of the tribal Valmiki community of north Karnataka, Sriramulu was also a bare-knuckled politician in his own right, with a reputation as an enforcer—confirmed by the fact that he was battling a criminal case involving an allegation of attempted murder.[36] Notwithstanding this fact, Sriramulu defeated his Congress rival by nearly 10,000 votes in the 2014 general election.[37]

The Maharashtra-based Shiv Sena, another entity whose electoral fortunes had waned, found itself ascendant again in 2014. The previous year, the militant Sena suffered a major blow when its founder and chief agitator, Bal Thackeray, unexpectedly passed away. The Sena's standing had taken a hit but its electoral fortunes, and those of its avowedly fearsome legislators, quickly rebounded—thanks in no small measure to its alliance with the BJP.

One of the men who would come to represent the Sena in the newly formed Lok Sabha was Rajan Vichare, who put up a sustained record of electoral success in the Thane constituency of Maharashtra while also being fingered in at least thirteen criminal cases winding their way through the courts.[38] A longtime Shiv Sainik, Vichare openly embraced Bal Thackeray's methods of "direct action." "Shiv Sena is known to be in such a way," explained Vichare to the scholar Thomas Blom Hansen, "that if there is injustice we will fight it in a rather dashing way."[39] Indeed, Vichare claimed his illustrious criminal record was the result of his no-holds-barred brand of constituency service: "The cases against me pertain to issues related to the public for whom I have been fighting all along," he explained to a journalist. "One case is of assaulting an engineer, which was over a delay in flyover work. It was not a personal issue but for the people."[40]

Vichare's work on behalf of "the people" was perhaps less evident in an incident that grabbed headlines after the election, in which the MP was caught on video abusing a cook at a state-run facility for the lousy quality of the food. In recorded images that made prime-time cable news, Vichare was seen stuffing a *chapati* (bread) into the mouth of the cook, a Muslim who was fasting in observance of Ramadan.[41] Despite claims that the tussle was merely about the sad state of the cuisine in the Maharashtra canteen in Delhi, the visual of a powerful member of a pro-Hindu party stuffing food down the throat of a fasting member of the Muslim community likely helped Vichare's grassroots appeal, a man who even close associates say is renowned for his "rude" manner.[42]

The "good governance" election of 2014 ushered in many other members of Parliament associated with criminal wrongdoing. Accompanying Pappu Yadav from the Bihar delegation was Yadav's longtime partymate Taslimuddin, who had previously served five terms as an MLA and four terms as an MP, racking up numerous criminal cases along the way.[43] A political survivor of unique caliber, in 1996 Taslimuddin earned a cabinet berth in the short-lived United Front government, but he was compelled to resign once his criminal record attracted a hailstorm of negative media attention.[44] Adhir Ranjan Chowdhury won election from Baharampur in the state of West Bengal on a Congress Party ticket. Chowdhury, who faced 16 ongoing criminal cases at the time of election and is the president of the Congress unit in the state, once made light of his lengthy criminal rap sheet by asking reporters not "to talk of any charge lower than that of murder against me. If you do so then my status would go down."[45] Known as the "Robin Hood of Baharampur," Chowdhury was arrested on murder charges in 2005, but he has yet to be convicted of any serious criminal violations. During the 2006 West Bengal state assembly elections, a jailed Chowdhury was unable to campaign but asked his supporters to play his prerecorded speeches in lieu of a campaign; he won the race.[46] Vitthalbhai Radadiya was a long-serving politician from Modi's home state of Gujarat, lured to the BJP just before the 2014 election. This courtship occurred despite the fact that Radadiya had no fewer than 10 pending criminal cases against him at the time of the election.[47] In one much-discussed incident, Radadiya was caught on CCTV footage brandishing a gun when a frightened toll plaza operator in his home state dared ask the MP to pay the standard toll fare. What business does "a man who earns 100 rupees" have stopping an MP, Radadiya mused before the press.[48] Radadiya claimed he was acting in self-defense: "They said I was a bogus MP. I am an MP, I deserve respect."[49]

The list goes on and on . . .

GOOD GOVERNANCE?

Judging by the results of India's 2014 election, politicians with serious criminal records are not going away any time soon. Despite recent reform victories, the relevance of individuals with criminal reputations remains deeply entrenched in India's electoral marketplace. That they should fare so well in an election widely believed to be a vote in favor of good governance might appear to be a puzzle at first glance but perhaps is less of one when considered in light of the findings described in previous chapters.

After all, criminally suspect MPs seem to gain strength from the fact that they are perceived to be, rightly or wrongly, delivering governance to their constituencies. Of course, the precise manifestation of "governance" that criminal politicians are able to offer (and its repercussions) may be at odds with prevailing notions of what successful democratic politicians should deliver. But then again, India's suspected criminal politicians must be seen as political creatures embedded in a social context that gives rise to their very existence.

To this end, the vitality of the nexus between crime and politics has larger implications for democracy in India and around the world. It also raises additional questions deserving of much closer scrutiny than they have received to date.

The coexistence of democratic politics and rampant criminality is a puzzle for students of politics and political behavior. Although this cohabitation may seem paradoxical at first, there can be a symbiotic relationship between the two. In this book I have claimed that this coexistence can best be understood if politics is conceptualized as a marketplace. As with any market, there are both supply and demand factors at work that allow the market to survive. The realities, and the diversity, of India make its particular electoral marketplace a case worthy of close study.

In India, the initial supply of criminality into politics resulted from strategic decisions taken by criminal entrepreneurs who had long been active in the political sphere. In the early years of the republic, they operated as free agents, willing to sign up with political parties and incumbent politicians to help them get elected. Many of these criminal elements signed up with the Congress Party, which dominated India's political scene in the immediate post-independence era. In providing assistance to politicians, criminals occasionally engaged in illegal activity, such as booth capturing or voter suppression. But they also used their social capital and local standing to bridge the divide between state and society in ways that political parties increasingly struggled to do, especially as party organizations gradually exhibited signs of decay.

A number of trends pulled criminals into a more direct role in electoral politics. These included the Congress Party's decline, rising social demands often expressed through identity politics, and the deterioration of public sector institutions. An important, previously underemphasized factor contributing to the entry of criminals in politics was the collapse of the prevailing system of financing elections, paving the way for the rise of black money. Criminals were further pushed into politics by their quest for self-preservation. As political competition grew and the party system became increasingly fragmented, criminals allied with the

Congress could no longer take their political protectors' reelection for granted. This uncertainty created huge new risks for criminals: without secure political protection, they would be subject to retribution, either at the hands of the state or from their political rivals.

The obvious solution to this dilemma was for criminals to take matters into their own hands and join electoral politics. Having accumulated considerable local clout upon which they could build, criminals could reduce uncertainty as well as reap serious returns from holding office. This transition played out in the 1970s and 1980s; by the 1990s, the rise of candidates—and elected representatives—facing criminal charges, including those of a serious nature, had been locked in.

The supply of criminally linked politicians, however, cannot be reduced to a story of individual incentives alone. In nearly all democracies, parties are the key gatekeepers that decide which politicians eventually get a spot on the ballot. Candidates always have the option of running as independents without a party affiliation, but the success of those choosing this option is rather limited, in India and elsewhere. Why parties recruit candidates linked to wrongdoing is not obvious, but parties' underlying quest for resources suggests one possible explanation. In settings where elections are costly yet parties are weakly organized, seeking out self-financing candidates is an attractive option. Candidates with deep pockets can contribute financial rents in numerous ways; in addition to plugging election funding gaps, they can directly provide financial payments to party leaders or engage in other kinds of rent-seeking behavior that could ultimately benefit the party. The vagaries of Indian elections suggest that money is a prime motivation for why parties are willing to embrace muscle, or candidates linked with serious criminal acts. Indeed, that is exactly what the qualitative evidence suggests and quantitative analyses of candidate affidavit data confirm. Candidates with greater financial resources (read: spending capacity) are much more likely to win election. Candidates linked with criminality, in turn, often have better access to accessible financing.

However, the appeal of candidates with criminal reputations transcends matters of a purely financial nature. Money can only partially explain the electoral advantage of candidates with criminal backgrounds. Politicians with criminal reputations possess another form of "currency" that has more to do with their connection to voters. This brings us to the "demand" side of criminal politicians. If individuals associated with crime choose to join active politics and parties choose to nominate them, what is in it for voters? In contexts where the rule of law is weak and identity divisions are especially salient, candidates linked with criminality possess an additional advantage. In these environments, they can use their criminality as a sign of their credibility to protect the interests of voters in their constituencies. When the state is either unable or unwilling to adequately perform its most basic functions in an impartial manner, voters are often willing to turn to someone who can substitute for the state, even if that person is linked to allegations of illegal activity. This inclination is further enhanced when identity-based cleavages render politics a zero-sum game; the fierce contestation over local dominance, which typically occurs when social hierarchies are collapsing but new ones have not yet been forged, gives voters an added incentive to ensure that the representative they choose is best suited to protect and lock in the status of their community and its allies. Politicians with criminal reputations, for their part, have an incentive to perpetuate the underlying drivers propping up their local support.

Taken together, the demand politicians attached to crime are able to engender from the electorate suggests that a lack of information cannot adequately explain why they thrive at the ballot box. In fact, there can be an affirmative case for why voters willingly back candidates suspected of wrongdoing. In many instances, this popular nexus of crime and politics has been portrayed as a primarily north Indian, or Hindi belt, phenomenon. On the contrary, it is far more widespread; there is evidence of criminality in Indian politics in many diverse parts of the country, defying any simple categorization of rich versus poor states, urban versus rural localities, or north versus south.

Testing the underlying logic for why criminal politicians succeed in some areas and fail in others is no easy feat. This is due to the lack of quality data on social divisions and on the varied, contextual nature of the demand. A combination of indirect methods—such as exploiting quirks of electoral politics like ethnic quotas and indirect elections—and more direct survey data can build confidence in the "criminality as credibility" thesis.

Understanding the precise supply and demand motivations, it turns out, is crucial if society's goal is to take steps to curb the entrenched marketplace for crime in electoral politics. For instance, if information truly did act as a binding constraint, it would imply a very different set of policy interventions than if the root cause were poor (or absent) governance. Unfortunately, the latter does appear to be at the heart of the matter, leaving reformers with few short cuts to grasp onto. Hence, fixing what ails the Indian state is essential to reducing the demand for criminal politicians. Unless and until the state is seen as an impartial and credible provider of security, justice, and social and economic benefits, there will always be space for those seeking to fill in the gap between institutions and popular expectations to make a living. But "fixing the state" means more than simply shrinking India's stifling bureaucracy; rather, what is needed is to bring regulatory procedure and human capital into much better alignment. At present, the former is suffocating, and the latter is anemic.

Curbing the demand for politicians mixed up with criminal activity is a long-term proposition since state capacity is, put euphemistically, a slow-moving variable. There are, however, complementary steps that can be pursued to address the supply side. For starters, India's regime for regulating political finance is in dire need of an overhaul. Cleaning up political finance can help to reduce parties' incentives to embrace candidates associated with crime. Tackling the issue of black money in politics is also linked to fixing the infirmities of political parties, whose inner workings are autocratic and highly opaque.

The dilemma criminally suspect politicians pose is somewhat distinctive in that many potential solutions to ridding politics of criminal elements are internal to the precise nature of the dilemma to begin with. Politicians with criminal records are able to persist in everyday politics because, as far as the law is concerned, they are innocent until proven guilty. Furthermore, establishing guilt is difficult for a host of reasons, not least of which is the fact that the justice system in India is so backlogged that it can take decades (if at all) for criminal cases to reach their logical conclusion. This important reality implies that barring such individuals from joining politics risks interfering with basic attributes of the rule of law in democratic settings. While it is worth pursuing reform interventions to address the supply side in the near term, one must proceed with caution since the first rule of reform is always "do no harm."

UNANSWERED QUESTIONS

Any study that attempts to shed light on themes as complex as democracy, governance, or criminality is likely to throw up as many questions as answers. This book is certainly no exception. Going forward, digging deeper in order to decipher answers to these queries will paint a more refined picture of the ins and outs of the electoral marketplace for criminality in India and beyond.

By Hook or by Crook

A key takeaway from this book is that criminal candidates can use their criminality to signal their credibility in at least four ways. As shorthand, I have referred to these mechanisms as: *redistribution, coercion, social insurance,* and *dispute resolution.* As evidence for each of these, I rely on the extant ethnographic literature as well as insights from fieldwork in India. Nevertheless, further research is necessary to understand the relative weights voters place on each of these mechanisms. One could imagine, for instance, that the utility of each of these strategies might vary according to contextual factors as well as the characteristics of the relevant target population. Voters of a certain type might prioritize justice, whereas residents of another area might place a higher value on social insurance. An experimental research design (such as a survey experiment) could shed light on the relative merits of these various mechanisms and possibly uncover others not contemplated here.

Criminality and Policy Outcomes

To date, collective understanding of the impacts of the electoral marketplace for criminality on citizens' daily lives is quite limited. The trick, of course, is to find suitable data on a policy outcome that is measurable *and* that politicians can appreciably impact in the short run.

The few studies that have found innovative ways of measuring impacts thus far have focused largely on welfare or crime measures. What remains unexplored is the effect that criminality in democratic politics is having on people's attitudes. How does the existence of criminal politicians affect how people view the rule of law? How does it shape their perception of politics? And how does it influence the choices of those who are considering a life in active politics?

The Talent Pool for Politics

One shortcoming of this analysis, and of nearly all studies that are interested in the quality of candidates, is that very little is known—typically, nothing at all—about those candidates parties do *not* select to contest elections. No doubt, one can learn a great deal by observing those candidates who contest elections, but this misses out on the broader pool of possible candidates.[50] Only by peering into that typically invisible group can one more conclusively examine how parties decide whom, from within that pool, to select.[51] This is, of course, especially relevant in democratic countries where intraparty democracy is weak, party organization is largely a top-down affair, and primaries are not operative. To properly look into this, researchers need access to the inner workings of the party decision-making process. Doing so could open up a new frontier in the study of candidate selection.[52]

Corruption versus Criminality

Corruption and criminality are not mutually exclusive, but they are distinct analytical concepts. Corrupt activities might be criminal, but not all criminal acts are inherently corrupt (where corruption is defined as the "use of public office for private gain").

When it comes to voter behavior, there is sufficient reason to believe that voters might respond differently to candidates who are known to be "corrupt" as opposed to those who are "criminal." Thinking about, and testing, the differences between the two could help resolve why voters from diverse settings, when exposed to information regarding the corrupt behavior of their politicians, do often appear to punish them for their transgressions. Much of the extant evidence for voters responding to new information about the malfeasance of politicians concerns financial corruption (namely, embezzlement or bribe taking) rather than criminality.

There is one obvious explanation for why information about corruption in a place like India might impact voters in a fundamentally different manner than revelations about criminality. One might expect, for example, that voters would react more negatively to information that reveals their representative is embezzling local funds than to news of him attacking a political rival or beating up a government official in order to extract benefits for the constituency.

Or perhaps, as some recent research has found, voters might be willing to "hold their noses" and vote for corrupt politicians insofar as those same corrupt politicians find ways of directing material benefits to them. For instance, research from Brazil has found that while voters do punish corrupt incumbents, this punishment is contingent on the amount of public expenditure they receive. As public expenditure increases, the negative relationship between corruption and reelection disappears.[53] A similar study from Spain finds that voters ignore corruption allegations against incumbents in circumstances where they derive clear side benefits from those corrupt actions.[54] The extent of this kind of behavior in India remains an open question, but it seems plausible that voters in India might also condition their voting behavior on whether they perceive the corrupt acts in question to materially benefit them or not. Corruption, in and of itself, could be a neutral cue; it is the *nature* of the corruption and, more important, the externalities it produces that matter.

Illicit Financing

Illicit political finance is an issue that touches a great many democracies, especially those in the developing world. Advanced democracies are not immune to malfeasance or scandals associated with election funding, and in countries like the United States, there are concerns that the transparency and accountability that have characterized the operations of these regulatory systems are weakening. But in more established democracies, by and large, there are well-established systems of monitoring and accounting for election finance and for prosecuting those who break the law. While imperfect, the strength of these regulatory systems likely acts as an effective deterrent.[55]

The situation in developing countries and nascent democracies is often worse. In developing countries, illicit campaign finance expenditures are typically orders of magnitude larger than what campaign spending disclosures suggest. As one scholar has noted, this reality is often referred to as the "rule of ten"—the idea that actual election expenditures are ten times the reported amounts.[56] There is a great deal of anecdotal evidence regarding the presence of illicit (or black) money in elections, but there has been little analysis of these flows, and for obvious reasons. After all, flows of black money are opaque: they involve under-the-table transfers that are unobservable and therefore difficult to quantify.

Resorting to candidates associated with criminality is one way money warps politics, but parties typically oversee a more diversified portfolio or "menu" of election finance options. In a developing country context, for instance, one needs to consider that parties might rely on business-men candidates, illicit money from abroad, and/or kickbacks from government contracts. There is very little known about what these options are, their relative merits, and under what conditions parties resort to a given strategy in a given electoral setting.

SCOPE CONDITIONS

One obvious issue any study that draws heavily from one country's experience must confront is the applicability of this single case to the broader world. Any such exercise must first begin with an articulation of the "scope conditions" of the theory, or the conditions under which one would expect to see criminality and politics interact. These conditions can tell us something about the universe of cases this book may hold lessons for.

First and most obviously, the core arguments of this book are restricted to democracies and, specifically, to that subset of democracies where deep social divisions exist, which politicians can exploit for political or electoral purposes. Throughout the text, I have taken as a given that the relevant cleavage in society, insofar as India is concerned, revolves around the question of ethnic identity. This condition is clearly evident in a wide range of democracies, and there is a vast literature that suggests that ethnic identity is the most important axis around which politics revolves in many developing as well as developed societies. The presence of social divisions alone, it is important to point out, does not necessarily mean that these differences will have political salience. But their existence is a necessary condition, creating a permissive environment for identity-based forms of mobilization to occur. Whether they are activated depends on numerous contingent factors, including the incentive calculations of political elites.

A second scope condition is the weak rule of law. When the state cannot adequately enforce its writ, voters will be more inclined to exchange political support to non-state actors who can privately provide these goods. Politicians, in turn, can exercise considerable discretion over state resources once in office, and they can comfortably break or bend the rules with a reasonably low probability that they will face legal consequences for those actions.

When these conditions—democracy, social divisions, and weak rule of law—are operative, space opens up for political entrepreneurs who can take advantage by marketing themselves as self-styled Robin Hoods, willing to act as a surrogate state. Democracy affords opportunities for political entrepreneurship, social divisions provide a platform for opportunistic mobilization, and the weak rule-of-law setting offers a permissive environment to engage in extralegal behavior to obtain political office and to reap the spoils once ensconced there.

It is, of course, possible to relax the assumption that social divisions necessarily manifest themselves through ethnicity alone. Although I assume that ethnicity is the primary relevant cleavage throughout this study, one could imagine other possibilities. The validity of the theory rests on the fact that social cleavages exist and that they provide a sufficient basis for politicians to identify, target, and mobilize voters.

For instance, in Colombia's criminalized politics there was a proliferation of politicians in the 2000s either actively tied to left-wing guerrillas (such as the Fuerzas Armadas Revolucionarias de Colombia, or FARC) or linked with paramilitaries (such as the Autodefensas Unidas de Colombia, or AUC) established to counter the influence of such fringe groups. This collusion between politicians and paramilitary organizations came to be known as "parapolitics," and it helped spawn bottom-up political economy regimes built around crime.[57] Politicians from both camps did not mobilize on ethnic grounds but rather on their ability to use their associations with violent groups to take control of the local state and channel benefits and protection to individuals associated with their respective causes. This cleavage operated on an ideological or class divide rather than one centered on ascriptive identities.[58]

Indeed, one can discern such non-identity-based cleavages even within India itself. For instance, the prevalence of criminal politics in West Bengal ostensibly has little to do with ethnic divides. Rather, the overriding salient social cleavage in Bengali politics is party identification. For decades, politics in that state has revolved around a pro-Left/anti-Left axis, with the Congress Party largely filling the anti-Left space.[59] Today, both the Congress Party in Bengal and the Left Front have been badly degraded; a spin-off of the Congress, the Trinamool Congress, is currently politically dominant. Today Bengali politics is perhaps more accurately described as pro-Trinamool/anti-Trinamool, but the overall dynamic is similar.

Whereas ethnicity might serve as the principal social cleavage and basis upon which criminal politicians mobilize in Bihar or Andhra Pradesh, in West Bengal the "politics of dignity" revolves around partisan attachments. Across all political stages in the state's recent history, the embrace of criminality on the part of politicians representing dueling political fronts has remained constant.[60] "Goondaism is a great political leveller in West Bengal," writes one observer. "One regime changes, another comes but political goondaism goes on forever" in the state.[61]

Partisan affiliation, not ethnic identity, is also the primary axis around which political criminality and violence transpire in parts of Kerala, particularly in the state's northern reaches. There, since at least the 1960s, violence has "become the public face and means of enhancing influence and power" in politics.[62] Some accounts claim that there have been between 150 and 200 deaths due to "political clashes" over the last few decades, most occurring between right-wing Hindu nationalist forces affiliated with the RSS/BJP and members of the CPI(M).[63] Yet the use of criminality in everyday politics functions in remarkably similar ways; in the words of one scholar, politicians in Kerala regularly deploy "illiberal means to achieve ends that are at the heart of liberal electoral democracy."[64] Each of the warring partisan sides, in turn, accuses the other of being the aggressor, choosing to hide behind the cloak of "defensive criminality."

EXTERNAL VALIDITY

With these scope conditions in mind, are there examples of democracies—other than India—in which these conditions pertain and we observe politicians linked with illegal activity thriving in the electoral domain? One example is Nigeria, which (like India) is a populous, multiethnic, federal democracy. Several scholars have pointed out that Nigeria's return to democracy following its landmark 1999 election has been marked by the presence of a pervasive nexus between criminals and politicians.[65] As several scholars of Nigerian politics have noted, a political candidate's strength is measured by his ability to mobilize support and financial resources, including through the use of violence.[66] Because Nigeria's parties are elite-driven entities with little ideological core or organizational foundations, political competition revolves around ethnic identity such that elections are transformed into "highly competitive zero-sum games."[67] "In the absence of other viable social categories for the protection of group interests," writes scholar Daniel Smith, "one ethnic group's apparent political gain is viewed by others as a potential loss."[68] The winner-take-all nature of Nigerian politics helps explain the viability of candidates who can use any means at their disposal (including extralegal means) to maximize their group's social position.[69]

Many politicians in Nigeria gain strength from their connection to "godfathers," who are typically party elites who wield outsized influence in party decision-making processes. Godfathers play a role not only in deploying violence on behalf of their preferred candidates but also in financing elections and organizing fraud.[70] Because the costs of elections are high and rising (the spoils of Nigeria's natural resources have long been shared among the country's politicians, thus making elected office highly lucrative), many aspirants to elected office struggle to raise the funds necessary to be electorally competitive. As a result, electorally successful candidates are often those sponsored by godfathers, who can easily channel funds into campaign coffers in exchange for fealty.[71]

Jamaica is another example of a democracy whose politics is defined by the coexistence of democratic elections and politicians tied to criminality.[72] Historically, politicians used their influence with the police to provide cover for the illegal activities of gangs, including gun running and drug smuggling. In exchange, politicians enlisted gang members to provide the requisite muscle power, especially during elections, and to deliver votes.[73] Many residents viewed the local "dons" who presided over the criminal racket as "protectors," and politicians benefited immensely from brandishing their intimate links with them.

Indeed, research suggests that a core attribute of political life in Jamaica is a phenomenon referred to as "badness-honor," which is not entirely dissimilar from the Indian concept of *dabangg*.[74] "Badness," in Jamaican parlance, is a form of stylized outlawry, scholar Obika Gray has argued, which affirms racially charged defiance as the basis for social respect or honor. In recent decades, political displays of this attribute have become de rigueur in urban Jamaican politics. In elections, politicians campaign by brandishing their badness-honor in an attempt to outdo their opponent's credentials with respect to criminal activity, especially in the urban slums of the Jamaican capital of Kingston.[75] Poor voters, often mobilized around issues of discrimination or other social gripes, value a candidate's degree of badness-honor because they seek ways to redress local grievances, especially those related to individual or group status concerns.[76] At stake are competing claims over dignity and the respect or status afforded a given community.[77]

In ethnically divided Macedonia, research has shown that Albanian politicians have regularly exploited minority nationalist sentiment to gain political support on the basis of their connections to paramilitary groups, bolstered in part by the continuing socioeconomic plight of ethnic Albanians in Macedonia. A deep-seated feeling of exclusion under the prior communist regime further fuels this dynamic. Politicians and criminal organizations have mutually overlapping interests, with the former interested in winning votes and enjoying the spoils of power and the latter concerned with protection.[78] A weak, corrupt state where the rule of law is unevenly enforced provides the underlying foundation for this quid pro quo to take place.[79]

And in India's neighbor and rival to the west, Pakistan, there is evidence of a complex interplay between crime and politics, especially in the southern port city of Karachi, the country's largest metropolis. There, stubborn ethnic cleavages dating back to the partition of the subcontinent have led most major political parties to incorporate criminal elements, who in turn use their criminality to protect the interests of warring ethnic factions.[80] According to a study by journalist Huma Yusuf, the root of the ethnic conflict has to do with growing tensions between Indian migrants (known as *mohajirs*), who settled in Pakistan, and ethnic Pashtuns, who moved to the city from the country's northwest. Political parties representing the two groups, the Muttahida Qaumi Movement and Awami National Party, respectively, sponsored politicians with criminal or extralegal reputations in order to cater to their own constituencies as well as offer a coercive deterrent against the other. The situation became even more complex as the Pakistan People's Party, with a strong base in rural Sindh province, began mobilizing ethnic Sindhis and Balochis in a similar fashion.[81]

Although the two countries' political trajectories could not be more different in many respects, the underlying drivers of criminality in the politics of India and Pakistan appear quite similar. In both South Asian nations, a growing crisis of governance, deteriorating law and order, sharp ethnic tensions linked to changing social hierarchies, and growing public sector–controlled rents have fostered a marriage between crime and politics. In Pakistan's case, terrorism and extremist violence have provided an additional layer to the conflict.[82]

CONTINGENT FACTORS

Of course, the precise balance of forces between crime and politics will range considerably from country to country. Here, political competition—coupled with some degree of historical contingency—can affect the calculus of criminals to directly intervene in day-to-day electoral politics.

Political Competition

Scanning across these examples, there is clearly a difference between criminals who double as politicians and politicians who are associated (in some cases, tangentially) with criminals. While in both cases there is an alleged engagement with illegal activity, the embodiment of both avatars in the same individual is striking. Why this melding together occurs in India but not in several other cases is an interesting question.

Clearly, the extent of electoral competition plays a role in shaping the form criminality takes. Before the seismic shifts in the competitiveness of Indian politics occurred and before the era of Congress hegemony came to an end, there was some degree of separation between the "politician" and the "criminal." That dividing line became blurred with the onslaught of intense political contestation and fragmentation, especially during the 1980s and 1990s. In other settings, in the presence of the weak rule of law and strong social divisions—but absent intense competition—it is possible that criminals could refrain from direct political engagement, as they did in previous eras of Indian politics. In this latter equilibrium one is much more likely to observe some variant of the "godfather" syndrome, whereby powerful and shadowy players tied to illegal activity exert their influence by backing candidates rather than becoming candidates themselves.

In Nigeria, for example, one author writes of the transition some godfathers have undergone from "brokers" to "patrons." As brokers, godfathers were essentially middlemen, mediating relations between political parties/politicians and voters. In places where politics was characterized by high levels of uncertainty, godfathers assumed a more direct role in electoral politics, either standing for election themselves or capturing the party machinery to impose their will.[83] This process appears similar to the "vertical integration" criminals in India underwent, described in Chapter 3.

In Jamaica, although politicians profit from their connections to local dons, there is often a separation between the criminals and the politicians. Here too, competition seems to be a prime reason. Kingston's gangster politics is oriented around a set of "garrison" constituencies, where the entire community votes en bloc for a particular political party. These garrisons are strongholds of local dons, who exert strong hierarchical control over the political allegiance of the community. Although there is robust competition across constituencies, in areas where gangs have established strongholds competition is limited, and, hence, the dons can easily contract with their preferred politician without having to directly engage in electoral politics.[84]

Historical Legacies

Although they are difficult to quantify, a country's unique historical legacies also influence the crime-politics nexus in powerful ways. In India, for instance, the image of a politician courting arrest or even incarceration was an intrinsic part of the country's nationalist struggle and historical self-narrative. Indeed, the political act of courting arrest as a method of civil disobedience even has its own nomenclature: *jail bharo* (fill the jails).[85] Therefore, on one hand, the fusion of politician and so-called criminal is considered culturally acceptable in India. But, on the other hand, it seems excessive to suggest that ordinary voters cannot differentiate between Jawaharlal Nehru and Pappu Yadav, both of whom served jail time but under very different circumstances.

With regard to criminality, perhaps more powerful than the historical legacy of the independence struggle is the legacy of the *zamindar*. During the colonial era, large swathes of India were exposed to local control by *zamindars,* who functioned not only as landlords in the feudal sense but also doubled as the local state in many ways.[86]

This assumption of the state's responsibilities meant that the landlord wielded instruments of violence and coercion in the way police and law enforcement might in a modern state.[87]

Although India abolished the *zamindari* system after independence, it never fully disappeared. Rather, it was displaced for an alternative form of governance: rule of the strongman. This strongman may not have borne any formal relation to land tenure arrangements or agrarian relations, but much like the *zamindar* of yesteryear, he was a socially embedded figure who commanded local authority.[88] The legacy of *zamindari* rule is felt in India even today. An influential study in 2005 found that decades after *zamindari* abolition, districts that were previously under *zamindari* control exhibited worse developmental outcomes than parts of India where land revenue was directly imposed on cultivators, as opposed to through landlords or middlemen (known as the *ryotwari* system).[89]

Historical contingencies have played a role in other contexts where politics and crime go hand in hand. For instance, research on the Philippines has shown that the subordination of the local state to elected leaders in the colonial era in a context of "primitive capitalist accumulation" led to the emergence and persistence of "bossism" in local politics. This unique pattern of state formation a century ago is arguably responsible for the color of electoral politics the island nation enjoys today.[90]

Comparative research has also asked why the rule of law in Jamaica looks so different from the rule of law in Barbados, another Caribbean island nation with similar historical and socioeconomic attributes at the time of independence. This work has shown that variation in the race-class correlation, the role of religion, and notions of cultural autonomy had differential impacts on how citizens viewed the legitimacy of the state. In Jamaica, where these variables combined to produce misgivings about the state's legitimacy, the transition to democracy institutionalized a violent system of patronage politics. In Barbados, the opposite occurred; the move to universal suffrage was accompanied by a less corrupt brand of politics, which helped consolidate the rule of law.[91]

MAJOR IMPLICATIONS

Now it is time to take yet another step back to examine the macro picture and ask: how does the notion of a "market for criminals" shape larger understandings about democracy, accountability, representation, and the role of information? I would stipulate that there are five big-picture lessons one can draw.

Political Finance

A major implication of the book is that private wealth is fast becoming a requirement of gaining entry into electoral politics. The skyrocketing cost of elections is, of course, a phenomenon with relevance far beyond India's borders. It is nearly impossible to read of a truly democratic election occurring anywhere in the world without encountering stories about how expensive the democratic process has become.

There is widespread recognition that democratic politics cannot function without healthy infusions of money to finance campaigns, pay for advertisements, employ party workers, and so on. But what is less understood is the manner in which the imperative to raise money is shaping the talent pool for political office. Most of the existing studies of political finance focus on the developed world and/or examine the impact of money on political or policy outcomes. This has left two major gaps in our knowledge.

The first is that we know very little about the role money is playing in the political systems of the developing world. Clearly, a paucity of data is partially to blame for this; reporting requirements and data transparency are much weaker outside of the advanced industrial democracies. Although detailed data are still hard to come by, at least one recent initiative has created a scorecard for 54 countries around the world using 50 different indicators from public funding to reporting requirements, monitoring, and enforcement.[92]

The second is that a focus on outcomes has inadvertently drawn attention away from how money shapes who gets into politics in the first place. And yet, there is a strong case to be made that *who* gets elected has a strong impact on *what* policies government pursues. In India, the quest for riches has seriously narrowed the talent pool from which parties select candidates. After accounting for businessmen, celebrities, criminals and dynasts, there is very little room for ordinary citizens to get their foot in the door. There is mounting evidence from the developed world, and a handful of studies from the developing world, that show there is a clear "elite bias" among democratically elected representatives.[93] This skewed representation, in turn, is having an impact on the policies representatives pursue once in office. An important study of the United States, for instance, has found that the socioeconomic profiles of elected legislators have a meaningful impact on how these representatives perceive policy issues as well as how they choose to act on them once in office.[94]

Bad Politicians and Accountability

From the standpoint of democracy and its many virtues, the intimacy of crime and democratic politics confounds many commonly accepted notions. After all, many of the leading lights from political science and political philosophy who have written eloquently about democracy over the past several centuries suggest that what distinguishes democracy from nondemocracy is that the former engenders accountability because elections offer citizens the opportunity to sanction their representatives at regular intervals. This mechanism is at the heart of the democratic project and is thought to provide the carrot and the stick by which "bad" politicians can be weeded out and "good" politicians ushered in.

Later scholars came to the realization that democracy did not always work as advertised. On the contrary, they postulated that democracy could facilitate accountability only when voters participating in democratic processes had access to information about the behavior of their representatives. Armed with this information, voters could then make rational decisions on whether to reelect or reject their incumbent politician, thus facilitating true accountability (figure 8.1).

Based on this reasoning, it is no surprise that most studies of wayward lawmakers contain an assumption that the political success of bad politicians in democratic countries is inherently symptomatic of a breakdown in the chain of democratic accountability. This is taken as a given; an alternative scenario in which bad politicians and accountability might coexist is typically not envisioned.

In some instances, some scholars actually begin with this premise and then work in reverse. Once the accountability failure is identified, scholars work backwards to identify the primary cause. In many instances, information is often believed to be at the heart of this breakdown—the missing ingredient which, when absent, creates the space for bad politicians to creep in under the cover of darkness. This process of reverse induction (figure 8.2) is more likely subliminal than intentional.

Whichever causal logic is pursued—that depicted in figure 8.1 or figure 8.2—the ignorant voter thesis is a compelling narrative and has been shown to be true in a great many cases. But it is not a universal truth. Indeed, importing this logic to the puzzle of India's criminal politicians can be deeply problematic. Under certain conditions, malfeasant politicians and accountability can in fact be compatible. Where some scholars go astray is in assuming away the possibility that connections to illegal behavior can sometimes be an asset, rather than a liability, for politicians in consolidated democracies. This turns the standard logic on its head: well-informed voters may, in fact, have good reasons to lend their support to bad politicians, thus creating a victory for democratic accountability (figure 8.3). Granted, of course, the ensuing form

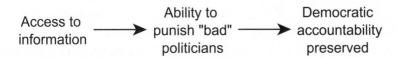

Figure 8.1. Bad politicians and accountability: standard view.

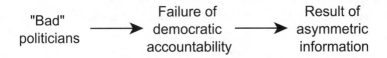

Figure 8.2. Bad politicians and accountability: reverse induction.

Figure 8.3. Bad politicians and accountability: revisionist view.

of democratic accountability is partial, imperfect, and flies against many common normative conceptions. Furthermore, it is not without its adverse side effects. Yet it offers a corrective to the narrative that voters, and parties, are saddled with malfeasant politicians. To the contrary, they might have rational, affirmative reasons to give them support.

Limits to Transparency

A third implication is that there are limits to what greater transparency and openness on their own can deliver in terms of cleaning up politics. Just as many analysts often move too quickly in assuming that the coexistence of criminal lawmakers and democracy is representative of serious accountability failures, they often move too hastily in placing the blame on information asymmetries for those perceived failures.

Over the past decade, a consensus has formed among social scientists and development practitioners postulating that citizens' access to a free flow of information on government performance is vital for improving governance outcomes.[95] This book is a contribution to a growing literature that suggests there are reasons to be skeptical about the "information consensus." For instance, a spate of recent research studies has shown that providing information without making corresponding investments in collective action capacity; offering voters plausible, tangible alternatives; or addressing concerns about the credibility, specificity, and accessibility of the information provided often does little good.[96]

The idea that under certain conditions a candidate's criminality can serve as a positive, informative cue is at odds with the oft-repeated assertion that voters "hold their noses" and vote for crooks or, in other words, trade probity for competence. If criminality is a positive, informative cue, voters are not necessarily trading probity for competence, but they might actually be rewarding a lack of probity because this attribute (to their mind) *connotes* competence. This is a subtle, but important, difference.

Status Concerns

A fourth implication is that identity considerations linked to status matter in politics, both in terms of influencing who gets elected as well as how representatives behave. For many decades, scholars of politics did not take seriously the fact that the identity of politicians played much of a role, either in terms of getting elected or in terms of influencing policy once in office. In the 1950s and 1960s, for instance, the prevailing wisdom espoused a rather mechanistic view of how politics operates. In any given election, there would be multiple candidates in the fray and the candidate who best represented the preferences of the median voter would emerge victorious. This "median voter" model of politics became the standard paradigm for studying how politicians won election, but the identity of the politician (his or her gender, religion, ethnicity, and so on) was largely irrelevant.[97]

Over time, of course, this way of thinking became passé. There was a growing recognition that the identity and policy preferences of politicians were, in fact, intrinsic to establishing their credibility.[98] In this book I incorporate this realization into the exploration of why corrupt and criminal politicians thrive in democratic settings. Whereas previous scholars have made the connection between parochial politics and malfeasance, they have not provided a framework for understanding how that malfeasance is not simply *incidental* to status concerns among voters but is in fact *intrinsic* to them.[99]

To be sure, there is a debate over this issue, with some scholars arguing that voters do not prefer criminal candidates; when suspected criminals win election, it is because voters either place more weight on ethnicity than probity or allow ethnic biases to shape their perceptions of candidate quality.[100] Although not the last word in this debate, the argument presented here provides a compelling logic for why a criminal record might provide an additional boost to candidates, above and beyond their ethnic background. It also helps explain the puzzle of why these candidates often succeed—even in places where the winner shares the same ethnic background as other "clean" candidates in the race.

It bears repeating that the role of status concerns cannot necessarily be reduced to patronage, although the two may be linked. In social settings where there is a great deal of churning taking place and in which it is an open question which group is "on top," respect and dignity can often represent key objectives for voters. These benefits have material manifestations, to be sure, but they also have psychic or expressive ones.

Context Matters

A final implication is that the marketplace for criminality in politics is context-specific, often driven by factors that are highly variable across constituencies. Even in India, no one can legitimately argue that every politician at every level is potentially a criminal. There can be a temptation to paint a monolithic picture of politics in India and the role criminality plays in it. Without writing off the substantial proportion of those who do face cases, it is useful to recall that two-thirds of MPs face no cases of any kind. Within India, as is the case in all democracies, the electoral market often responds to highly contextualized supply and demand factors, which can vary substantially within a single country—especially one as vast and diverse as India.

Therefore, the criminalization of politics clearly does not apply equally to India's political class as a whole. For instance, as discussed in Chapter 6, electoral design can influence the selection of politicians in often unintended ways. Ethnic quotas and indirect elections are two examples of how electoral rules can dampen the incentives for ethnic mobilization, inadvertently shifting the political calculus for criminal politicians—even though the imposition of these legislative rules was driven by altogether unrelated considerations. In this regard, the book's findings build on, and add to, the notion that the salience of ethnic divisions in society is not static but can vary over time and space. When all is said and done, ethnic identities are socially constructed.

PARTING THOUGHTS

The scholar Francis Fukuyama has argued that a political system that is able to effectively balance an effective state apparatus, adherence to the rule of law, and a foundation of democratic accountability "is both a practical and moral necessity for all societies."[101] These three components are the building blocks of modern liberal democracy, yet they are often in tension with one another and do not always advance at the same pace.

On the plus side, India has sustained a nearly uninterrupted commitment to democratic governance for nearly seven decades. Given the odds the fledgling democracy faced at the time of independence, its survival is no minor accomplishment. In terms of longevity, it is one no other developing country can boast, a distinction made even more admirable when India's low level of per capita income is taken into account.

India's constitution, a document "powerful in its vision and intricate in its formulation," provides a modern framework that empowers a sovereign government to carry out its responsibilities but also places constraints on its authority.[102] It enumerates both a detailed set of fundamental rights belonging to the citizens of India and a set of constitutional goals, known as the Directive Principles, which must guide the state's enforcement of its writ.

Alas, Indian's central weakness has been the quality of its state. The mixed capacity of the state to fulfill its most basic functions has meant that the rule of law which exists in practice is at odds with what its constitution aspires to establish. Democratic accountability has survived largely intact but its form has been disfigured by a high degree of administrative ineffectiveness.

India is not alone in experiencing this mismatch; it is a quandary for an increasing number of states. Notwithstanding recent setbacks in many difficult regions of the world, democracy has flourished around the globe over the last quarter century. However, as the ranks of the world's democracies have swelled, their ability to deliver what is expected of them has faltered. Institutional erosion, or in some cases the absence of institutions altogether, has become all too common an affliction. The dalliance between crime and politics is a symptom of this larger malaise. To address it, we first have to ask why it persists. This book, it is hoped, represents a modest effort to provide some initial answers.

Appendix A: Details of the Affidavit Dataset

ELECTIONS IN THE DATABASE

ONE OF THE primary underlying sources of data for this book is a database of affidavits for nearly all candidates who stood for state and national election in India between 2003 and 2009 (a full list of state elections can be found in table A-1). This database includes details on 46,739 candidates who contested 35 state assembly elections and 13,492 candidates who contested two national elections in 2004 and 2009.[1] I also collected limited information on 8,205 candidates who contested the 2014 national election.

CONSTRUCTING THE AFFIDAVIT DATABASE

A ruling of the Supreme Court of India made the public disclosure of candidate affidavits mandatory beginning in 2003. Unfortunately, "publicly available" is not the same thing as "suitable for research." At the time they present their nomination papers, candidates submit sworn judicial affidavits to the ECI in written form, and the ECI in turn posts scanned copies (or images) of these affidavits on its website (figure A-1). Anyone who has tried to jot down information from just a handful of PDFs or images, let alone thousands, can attest that compiling this information is an onerous task.

Table A-1. State Elections in Affidavit Database

State	Election years
Andhra Pradesh	2004, 2009
Arunachal Pradesh	2004
Bihar	2005 (November)
Chhattisgarh	2003, 2008
Delhi	2003, 2008
Goa	2007
Gujarat	2007
Haryana	2005
Himachal Pradesh	2007
Jharkhand	2005
Karnataka	2004, 2008
Kerala	2006
Madhya Pradesh	2003, 2008
Maharashtra	2004
Manipur	2007
Meghalaya	2008
Mizoram	2003, 2008
Nagaland	2008
Odisha	2004, 2009
Puducherry	2006
Punjab	2007
Rajasthan	2008
Sikkim	2004
Tamil Nadu	2006
Tripura	2008
Uttar Pradesh	2007
Uttarakhand	2007
West Bengal	2006

Note: A few state elections held between 2003 and 2009 are excluded from this dataset due to information that is missing either from the ECI or the Empowering India database. The missing state elections are: Assam, 2006; Bihar, February 2005; Jammu and Kashmir, 2008; and Rajasthan, 2003.

राजस्थान   RAJASTHAN

प्ररूप—26
(नियम 4क देखिए)

श्रीगंगानगर (राजस्थान) निर्वाचन क्षेत्र से
(निर्वाचन क्षेत्र का नाम)

लोकसभा (सदन का नाम) के लिए निर्वाचन के लिए रिटर्निंग ऑफिसर के समक्ष अभ्यर्थी द्वारा प्रस्तुत किया जाने वाला शपथ–पत्र

भाग—क

मैं, निहालचन्द पुत्र श्री बेगाराम, आयु 43 वर्ष, जो वार्ड नं. 3, रायसिंहनगर जिला श्रीगंगानगर (राजस्थान) का निवासी हूं, और उपरोक्त निर्वाचन से अभ्यर्थी हूं, सत्यनिष्ठा से प्रतिज्ञा करता हूं, शपथ पर निम्नलिखित कथन करता हूं :–

(1) मैं, भारतीय जनता पार्टी (राजनैतिक दल का नाम) द्वारा खड़ा किया गया अभ्यर्थी हूं ।

(2) मेरा नाम रायसिंहनगर और राजस्थान (निर्वाचन क्षेत्र और राज्य का नाम) में भाग संख्या 65 के क्रम सं. 464 पर प्रविष्ट है ।

(3) मेरा संपर्क टेलीफोन नं. 01507—221317 हैं और मेरा ई—मेल आईडी nihal337@gmail.com है, और मेरा सोशल मीडिया एकाउन्ट शून्य है ।

स्थाई लेखा संख्याक (पैन) के ब्यौरे और आय—कर विवरणी फाईल करने की प्रास्थिति :

ATTESTED
USHA GROVER
NOTARY
GANGANAGAR (RAJ.)

Figure A-1. Example of original candidate affidavit. (Image from Election Commission of India website)

Unfortunately, the ECI does not compile these data in a format that is suitable for systematic analysis, but several India-based civil society organizations have undertaken the task of collecting these affidavits, digitizing and translating them, and placing them online in a standardized format. But because these repositories (such as http://myneta.info or http://empoweringindia.org) hold information about each candidate on a separate webpage, by 2009, information for more than 60,000 candidates was kept on more than 60,000 discrete web pages. Working with a computer scientist, I automated this data collection so that each candidate became a row in a large spreadsheet, with columns of detailed information about his or her personal background. The underlying raw data used were sourced from the Liberty Institute's "Empowering India" initiative (see figure A-2 for a digitized affidavit). The tool succeeded in created a tabular dataset for analysis, but it produced a fair amount of missing or unreadable data. For instance, information

Constituency: **Ganganagar**   District: **GANGANAGAR**   Election Year: **2008**   State: **Rajasthan**

View Original Affidavits(Always verify the information)
Search this Candidate(Compare past affidavits, if any)

Candidate Name	: **Raj Kumar**
Party	: Indian National Congress (INC)
Symbol	: -
Age	: 60
Gender	: Male
Education Status	: Law
Address	: 50, varndavan vihar gaganpath shri ganganagar
District	: GANGANAGAR
Father's Name	: jagdish chandra

Movable Assets	
Cash	17,000
Deposit in Banks, Financial Institutions and Non-Banking Financial Companies	17,000
Other Financial Instruments NSS, Postal Savings, LIC, Policies etc	150,000
Jewellery	Not Specified
	Total : Rs. 184,000

Figure A-2. Example of digitized affidavit. (Image from Liberty Institute "Empowering India" initiative, www.empoweringindia.org)

on the specific criminal charges candidates faced was missing from the Empowering India database for several elections. Wherever possible, I filled in missing data by consulting the candidate's original affidavit on the ECI website.

This solved a major challenge—I now had (nearly) comprehensive data on candidates' criminal and financial behavior—but led to a second impediment: the data on how these candidates actually fared in the elections resided elsewhere in cyberspace, quite apart from the affidavit information. To complicate matters, candidates' names were often spelled differently in the two places: I could be "Milan Vaishnav" on my affidavit but "Milan V." or "Vaishnav Milan" on the official election return. This required an algorithm to match names, but each supposed "match" eventually had to be validated by hand.[2] Many months of work went into compiling, cleaning, and troubleshooting the affidavit data and then carefully matching these data with official returns from the Election Commission. In some cases, I discovered data entry errors in the affidavit dataset. In these instances, I relied on the ECI data as the correct data—updating the affidavit data accordingly.

Using a similar automated data collection technique, I supplemented this core dataset with affidavit data on Rajya Sabha MPs and candidates contesting the 2014 national election. For data on Rajya Sabha MPs, I relied on the online database organized by ADR and made available at http://www.myneta.info. The data on Rajya Sabha MPs include information only on 226 candidates who won election (as of 2010) rather than for the broader pool of candidates and winners. Finally, I collected limited information from ADR on candidates contesting the 2014 national election.

CONCERNS ABOUT THE AFFIDAVIT DATABASE

The candidate affidavit disclosures are not without their shortcomings. Crucially, the information is self-reported, which means that the accuracy of financial affidavits may be questionable. In addition, the data on criminality refer to ongoing cases rather than convictions; due to the vagaries of India's justice system, it can take decades for an ongoing case to produce a conviction, if at all.

Criminal Records

There are potentially two concerns with candidates' self-reported criminal records: false reporting and frivolous or politically motivated charges. Given the fact that criminal proceedings are a matter of public record (not to mention the fact that interested third parties might have an incentive to serve as whistleblowers), the former is not a serious concern.[3]

The issue of frivolous or politically motivated charges is more challenging. Under law, a candidate is precluded from standing for election only if convicted of a crime, not if merely charged with one. Before a 2014 Supreme Court ruling, convictions were not necessarily disqualifying as long as sitting politicians had not exhausted all possibilities of appeal. That loophole closed with the court's 2014 ruling.

However, very few legislators are actually convicted or are likely to be convicted due to the inadequacies of India's justice system. Irrespective of a defendant's guilt or innocence, the wheels of justice move slowly in India. Elected representatives can further delay the already slow crawl of criminal investigations and prosecution by using the power of political office to transfer pesky officials for reasons unrelated to their professional performance.

These caveats notwithstanding, one should also recognize that candidates are required to disclose only cases that a judge has deemed credible and worthy of judicial proceedings and that were pending as of six months prior to the election (to avoid the most blatant electorally motivated cases). This threshold is important as it is the difference between an allegation and what I refer to as an "indictment," to borrow a phrase from the American justice system ("indictment" is not a term commonly used in the Indian system). Typically, the first step in the criminal justice process in India is the filing of a First Information Report (FIR) by the police. Next, police conduct a preliminary investigation to determine if there is sufficient prima facie evidence of wrongdoing. If such evidence exists, they file a "charge sheet." If prosecutors concur with the police, they file charges with the relevant court. Finally, a judge determines whether to "take cognizance" of the case and "frame charges" against the defendant. According to regulations issued by the ECI, and affirmed by the Supreme Court, it is only after a judge takes cognizance that a candidate must disclose on his affidavit that there is a pending case against him. Where appropriate, candidates must also disclose whether a judge has "framed charges" in a given case. The act of "framing charges" requires a judge to apply his or her mind to determine whether there are grounds to pursue the enumerated charges.[4] Unfortunately, the format in which the data are collected makes it impossible to distinguish this subset of cases from the overall pool. However, for all cases included in the database, at the very least a judge has taken cognizance of the matter.

These disclosure rules help to reduce (though not eliminate) the presence of frivolous charges. However, one can go even further. On their affidavits, candidates list each pending criminal case, including, for each case, the section(s) of the Indian Penal Code (IPC) under which they are charged. In order to create a classification of criminal charges, I first obtained an electronic copy of the IPC. The IPC is a document that originates in the British colonial era and first came into force in 1862, though it has been amended repeatedly since its inception.

I then matched each charge with the relevant section of the IPC, in addition to supplementary information provided under the 1973 Code of Criminal Procedure. Using this matching process, one can distinguish between "serious" and "minor" charges. Following a coding strategy pursued by other scholars, I classify minor charges as those that might, arguably, be related to assembly, campaigning, or speech, that is, those that lend themselves most easily to political retribution. Although many of these charges may in fact be legitimate, I classify them as "minor" because they are linked most easily to political retribution. The remainder I consider to be "serious" charges.[5]

There are two advantages to this approach. First, in India, politicians often court arrest and even imprisonment for political purposes. This likely has something to do with the Gandhian roots of India's independence movement and the subsequent value its political class places on civil disobedience. Analyses that do not distinguish between the severity of charges risk conflating different types of cases.[6] Second, while pending cases present a higher hurdle than mere charges, they are not immune from abuse. However, I assume that it is more difficult to engineer a false case involving serious charges than one involving minor ones.[7]

Coding criminal charges is an inherently subjective undertaking. For instance, I deem "criminal intimidation" to be a "minor" charge, as it is often related to verbal rather than physical threats, leaving open the possibility that statements made in a political setting could be taken out of context. The Indian Code of Criminal Procedure offers the following illustration of an act that could be classified as "criminal intimidation," involving persons A and B: If A, for the purpose of inducing B to desist from prosecuting a civil suit, threatens to burn B's house, A is guilty of criminal intimidation. The same principle can be applied for the charge "voluntarily causing hurt," which is also classified as a "minor" charge. Indian law makes a distinction between "voluntarily causing hurt" and "voluntarily causing *grievous* hurt." I code the latter as a "serious" charge.

There are some sections of the IPC that contain multiple subsections, each for a distinct offense and occasionally a unique sentencing guideline. In those instances where the subsection is not clear on the affidavit, I revert to the least stringent sentencing requirement listed in the overall section, so as to give candidates the benefit of the doubt. This produces a more conservative estimate of "serious" criminality.

In addition, some candidates are charged with violating laws other than the IPC. Aside from violations of the Arms Act, I did not code non-IPC charges. Fortunately, non-IPC charges are usually filed in conjunction with IPC charges; ignoring them does not result in a considerable loss of information.

It is important to note that my subjective coding of what constitutes a "serious" charge is different from the standard developed by ADR, arguably India's leading election watchdog, which is commonly used. ADR's revised guidelines stipulate that a charge is considered serious if it meets *any* of the following criteria:

- Maximum punishment for the offence committed is of five years or more
- Offence is non-bailable
- Offences pertaining to an electoral violation (IPC 171E or bribery)
- Offence related to a loss to the exchequer
- Offences related to assault, murder, kidnap, rape
- Offences that are mentioned in Representation of the People Act (Section 8)
- Offences under Prevention of Corruption Act
- Offences related to crimes against women

There are some differences between my minimalist definition and that used by ADR. For starters, I tend to minimize electoral offenses insofar as they might be linked to electioneering, which is a primary part of a politician's vocation and vulnerable to political machinations. It is for this reason that I also do not consider most charges associated with "public tranquility," "public order," or "elections" to be serious in nature.

Despite some differences between my definition and that used by ADR, they are highly correlated. In the dataset of parliamentary candidates, the correlation between the two is .79. In the dataset of state assembly candidates, the correlation is .78.

Because the affidavit database I employ does not fully extend to the present day (and is missing some elections), I often use ADR's data (and classification of "serious" charges) when providing aggregate statistics. For instance, in discussing data from assembly elections after 2009, I must rely on ADR's data since these elections fall outside of my database. However, for nearly all fine-grained, empirical analyses contained here I rely on my own coding. In either case, I always cite which data I am using.

Candidate Assets

According to ECI guidelines, candidates must disclose their movable and immovable assets, which one can aggregate into an overall indicator of wealth. Candidate wealth is a good proxy for a candidate's financial capacity, which can be nebulous and difficult to estimate because it is likely to be correlated with social networks, fundraising ability, and overall spending power. Unlike pending criminal cases, which are a matter of public record, a candidate's financial details are difficult to verify independently. How much money candidates have in family bank accounts or the quantity of gold jewelry in their possession is hard—if not impossible—to discern. To counteract the possibility of false reporting, the ECI stipulates that furnishing false information is grounds for criminal prosecution or disqualification. In practice, however, it is not clear whether the threat of such punishment is sufficient to deter false reporting.

The natural tendency of most skeptics is to assume that candidates regularly underreport the true value of their assets in order to hide any illegal income or ill-gotten gains. Indeed, there are several examples of candidates doing just that. Despite this possible incentive, the reported assets of winning candidates remains startlingly high, as do the increases in assets over time. Despite possible incentives to underreport, there have been many recent investigations of high-profile politicians, including several current and former chief ministers, on suspicion of possessing "disproportionate assets."

Thus, to the extent that candidates provide inaccurate information, the incentives are to underreport.[8] Given the substantial nature of the declarations candidates do make, there is likely a lower bound on this underreporting. If one assumes that candidates with links to illegal activity have more incentive to obscure the true nature of their resources, it is likely to bias the wealth advantage of criminal candidates downwards.

MODAL CRIMINAL CHARGES

The most frequently appearing criminal charges in the state elections dataset, disaggregated by "serious" and "minor" categories, illuminate interesting patterns (table A-2). Of the five most common "minor" charges, three are violations of "public tranquility," commonly associated with civil disturbances. The five most common "serious" charges account for roughly half of all serious infractions. Four of the top five charges are human body offenses, including attempted murder. The average candidate charged with serious violations of the law faces 2.4 pending cases.

Data for the modal criminal charges in the national elections dataset, disaggregated by "serious" and "minor" categories, were drawn from the 2004, 2009, and 2014 parliamentary elections (table A-3). In terms of criminal charges, there is a significant amount of overlap with the MLA candidate dataset. Indeed, with just a few exceptions, the lists are nearly identical. The average candidate charged with serious violations of the law faces 3.7 pending cases.

TESTING FOR POLITICALLY MOTIVATED CASES

A principal concern about the data on criminal cases is that these cases are not a reflection of actual criminal activity but rather stem from political motivation on the part of rivals. To address this concern, beyond adopting the coding strategy described above, I conducted four additional empirical tests.

Table A-2. Modal Criminal Charges in Dataset of State Assembly Candidates

Serious charges

IPC section	Violation	Category	Frequency	Percent
341	Wrongful restraint	Human body	973	16.6
353	Assault or use of criminal force to deter a public servant from discharge of his duty	Human body	868	14.8
307	Attempted murder	Human body	583	10.0
342	Wrongful confinement	Human body	288	4.9
379	Theft	Property	288	4.9

Minor charges

IPC section	Violation	Category	Frequency	Percent
147	Rioting	Public tranquility	1,775	12.1
323	Voluntarily causing hurt	Human body	1,329	9.1
149	Unlawful assembly	Public tranquility	1,150	7.8
148	Rioting armed with a deadly weapon	Public tranquility	1,123	7.7
506	Criminal intimidation	Intimidation	1,007	6.9

Source: Author's calculations based on affidavits submitted to the Election Commission of India by candidates contesting state assembly elections between 2003 and 2009.

Distribution of Candidates with Criminal Cases

If one is concerned that criminal cases against candidates are primarily driven by political motivation, we would expect to observe an "arms race" in the filing of cases. Imagine I want to sully a rival candidate by getting a false case filed against him or her and that I succeed in doing so. The obvious response from my rival would be to do the same against me. If one assumes many, if not all, candidates think this way, one would expect to find a substantial degree of clustering in the distribution of criminal cases across constituencies. Interestingly, there is no evidence of this in the data.

Table A-3. Modal Criminal Charges in Dataset of
Parliamentary Candidates

Serious charges

IPC section	Violation	Category	Frequency	Percent
341	Wrongful restraint	Human body	786	15.6
353	Assault or use of criminal force to deter a public servant from discharge of his duty	Human body	773	15.4
307	Attempted murder	Human body	534	10.6
120B	Criminal conspiracy	Criminal conspiracy	375	7.5
379	Theft	Property	225	4.5

Minor charges

IPC section	Violation	Category	Frequency	Percent
147	Rioting	Public tranquility	1,570	10.0
149	Unlawful assembly (in pursuit of common object)	Public tranquility	1,324	8.4
143	Unlawful assembly	Public tranquility	1,270	8.1
188	Disobedience to order duly promulgated by public servant	Contempt	1,210	7.7
506	Criminal intimidation	Intimidation	1,021	6.5

Source: Author's calculations based on affidavits submitted to the Election Commission of India by candidates contesting the 2004, 2009, and 2014 parliamentary elections.

For state elections, of the 5,001 state assembly constituencies for which I have data, nearly two-thirds (65 percent) do not have a single candidate in the fray who has a serious criminal case. Just over one-fifth (21 percent) have only one candidate with a serious case (figure A-3). This means that an "arms race" mentality, if it exists, is restricted to a small minority of constituencies (the remaining 14 percent). By and large, where criminal candidacy exists, the dominant form seems to be a single candidate with a serious criminal record.

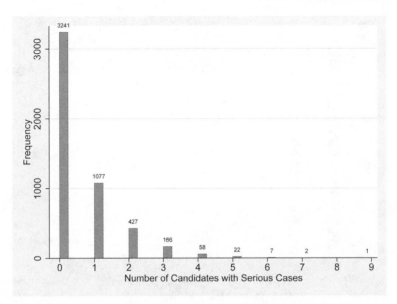

Figure A-3. Frequency distribution of state assembly candidates with pending serious criminal cases, 2003–9. (Author's calculations based on affidavits submitted to the Election Commission of India by candidates contesting state assembly elections between 2003 and 2009)

Data from parliamentary elections paint a very similar picture (figure A-4). Leaving aside the 46 percent of parliamentary constituencies that have no candidate facing serious cases, the next largest category—those with one serious criminal candidate—accounts for 28 percent of all constituencies in the dataset. This means constituencies with two or more seriously charged candidates account for just 26 percent of constituencies in the dataset, again a small minority.

These data, of course, cannot conclusively rule out the political motivation hypothesis, but they do suggest that the dominant model is *not* one of candidates cynically getting cases lodged against one another (or at least cases that result in judicial cognizance being taken).

Political Vendettas

Second, if cases are politically motivated, one observable outcome might be that successful politicians are more likely to be susceptible to

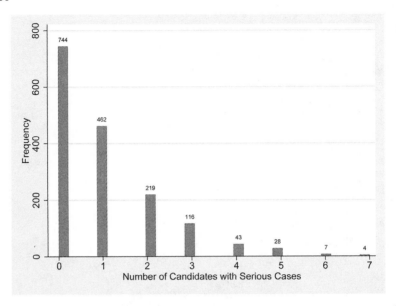

Figure A-4. Frequency distribution of Lok Sabha candidates with pending serious criminal cases, 2004–14. (Author's calculations based on affidavits submitted to the Election Commission of India by candidates contesting the 2004, 2009, and 2014 parliamentary elections)

framing of false charges made by envious rivals. To analyze whether popular politicians disproportionately face criminal cases, I take advantage of the fact that seven states in the dataset (plus the national parliament) have experienced two elections under the affidavit regime (in 2003–4 and 2008–9). Thus, I can examine candidates at two time periods and test whether the presence of a serious case in time t is related to the political success the candidate experienced in the prior election in time t-1. Unfortunately, constructing a dataset of re-contesting candidates presents its own challenges for a host of reasons.[9] After using a name-matching algorithm to identify the potential pool of re-contesting candidates over two election cycles, I used two unique identifying fields—candidates' fathers' names and their home addresses—to identify exact matches.[10]

To test the proposition that politically successful politicians are more likely to face serious cases, I investigated the correlates of having a serious criminal case at the time of the most recent election in time, t. The correlates are prior electoral performance (captured by vote share in the previous election), a binary measure of a candidate's criminal status in the previous election, and a binary measure of candidate incumbency. Whether I use state, national, or combined state and national data, I find no evidence of a relationship between prior electoral performance and a candidate possessing a serious criminal case. In fact, the strongest predictor of a candidate's criminal status is the presence (or absence) of a prior serious case declared before the previous election.

Incumbency Advantage?

A third way of explicitly testing for politically motivated charges is to study differences between incumbent and opposition politicians. If charges are easily manipulated, one would expect that the party in power would manufacture pending cases against its political opposition while simultaneously squeezing the judiciary to drop cases against ruling party politicians. To investigate this claim, I examine data from the north Indian state of Bihar, which is a poor state with a weak bureaucracy that could be vulnerable to political interference. According to data from Bihar's November 2005 and 2010 elections, there does not appear to be any systematic pattern of political targeting: candidates from the incumbent party (marked in bold) are just as likely as opposition candidates to contest elections while facing serious cases (table A-4).

Timing of Criminal Charges

A final method of testing for politically motivated charges is to explore the timing of charges filed against politicians. For instance, if most charges are filed against politicians around election time, it would suggest an underlying political motivation. In their affidavits, candidates are required to disclose the date on which a judicial body has taken cognizance of each pending case. What we would like to know, however, is the date the initial charges were filed (as there is typically a lengthy lag between when charges are filed and when a court takes cognizance of a case). In 2006, the Allahabad High Court (which has jurisdiction over Uttar Pradesh) asked the government to provide information on the criminal records of all sitting politicians in the state.

Table A-4. Share of Bihar State Assembly
Candidates with Pending Serious Criminal
Cases, 2005 and 2010

	2005	2010
BJP	37%	**39%**
JD(U)	23%	**35%**
LJP	25%	**35%**
RJD	**24%**	29%
INC	22%	19%

Note: BJP (Bharatiya Janata Party); JD(U) (Janata Dal [United]);
LJP (Lok Janshakti Party); RJD (Rashtriya Janata Dal); INC (Indian National Congress). Incumbent ruling parties are in **bold**.
Source: Author's calculations based on affidavits submitted to
the Election Commission of India by candidates contesting Bihar state assembly elections in the November 2005 and 2010
elections.

The report, which I obtained from the court, discloses the year in which
charges were filed against Uttar Pradesh politicians with pending cases
(and was current as of 2006).[11]

From these data, it is clear that the majority of charges against incumbent MLAs were not filed in election years: charges filed in an election year account for roughly one-quarter of all charges. While there
is a sharp increase in charges filed in 2002 (the most recent election
year in the data), there are also a substantial number of cases filed in
the years before and after this election.[12] A second interesting finding
from these data concerns the pendency of cases: as of 2006, nearly 50
percent of cases against sitting MLAs were at least ten years old (with
one case dating back as far as 1968). This reinforces the point made
earlier that convictions are few and far between due to inefficiencies in
India's judicial system.

Appendix B: Details of Bihar Voter Survey

THE BIHAR POST-ELECTION survey took place immediately following the conclusion of voting in state assembly elections in October–November 2010. The survey was conducted in collaboration with the Lokniti Programme of the Centre for the Study of Developing Societies (CSDS). Lokniti is the only social science research organization in India that conducts post-poll surveys of voters following each state and national election. The data were collected as part of a special module Lokniti carried out in parallel with their standard post-election survey of voters.

To construct the sample, Lokniti first randomly selected 40 assembly constituencies (out of a total of 243 in the entire state). Assembly constituencies were selected using the probability proportionate to size (PPS) method. Within each of these 40 constituencies, four polling stations were then chosen at random as sites to carry out the survey. Polling stations were again sampled by employing the PPS method. After sampling polling stations, 20 respondents were randomly selected from the electoral rolls provided by the chief electoral officer of Bihar. Respondents were sampled using the systematic random sampling (SRS) method, which is based on a fixed interval ratio between two respondents. A sampled respondent's list for each polling station was prepared, which is a comprehensive list of selected respondents with their complete name, address, age, and gender. Lokniti does not allow substitution in its surveys. Thus, out of a target sample size of 3,200 respondents (40 constituencies x 4 polling stations x 20 respondents), Lokniti successfully interviewed 2,333 respondents (response rate of 73 percent). Survey enumerators, trained by Lokniti and residents of the state, conducted face-to-face interviews at the respondent's place of residence in the respondent's native tongue.

The 2010 elections were held in six phases, with a unique set of constituencies going to the polls in each phase. Lokniti carried out its survey with the target sample within a few days of the end of polling in each phase. In order to obtain information on respondents' vote choice, Lokniti begins its surveys by simulating a mock election. For respondents who affirmed that they were able to vote in the election, enumerators then produced a dummy ballot box and asked voters to cast their vote by marking the symbol of the party they voted for using a dummy ballot paper slip and to deposit the ballot in the ballot box. The dummy ballots are tagged with a unique identifier, which allows for easy merging with the remainder of the respondent's information.

More information about the survey can be found on the author's website, http://www.milanvaishnav.com.

Appendix C: Details of Lok Social Attitudes Survey

IN THE FOURTH quarter of 2013 (September–December), the Lok Foundation carried out a survey of the political attitudes of a broad cross section of Indians in advance of the May 2014 Indian general election. The survey piggybacked on top of a standing quarterly panel consumer survey of more than 150,000 households conducted by the Centre for Monitoring Indian Economy (CMIE).[1] This survey was carried out in collaboration with a team consisting of Devesh Kapur, Megan Reed, and Neelanjan Sircar, based at the Center for the Advanced Study of India (CASI) at the University of Pennsylvania. Collectively, the team assisted Lok and CMIE in the design of the survey instrument on political attitudes.

The survey solicited responses from 68,516 respondents across 24 states and union territories. The sample was drawn as a cluster random sample in the following way. The 24 states and union territories under study were broken into 98 "homogeneous regions." A homogeneous region is a set of contiguous districts (the largest administrative unit inside a state) that satisfy certain similarities in agro-climatic conditions. Within each homogeneous region at least one city (and often multiple cities) were selected. A set of villages was chosen randomly in each homogeneous region. Selecting a random position in the village and selecting every nth household in a randomly chosen direction was used to select households. Cities were broken into wards, which were further subdivided into census enumeration blocks (CEBs). The wards in the city were stratified by average asset wealth (as determined by the 2001 Indian census) and selected randomly. The CEBs (which are of roughly equal population) were selected randomly from each ward. Within each CEB, a randomly selected position and every *n*th household from a randomly selected direction was used to select households. Within each household an individual over the age of 18 was randomly selected.

Although within each locality respondents were randomly selected, the sampling frame itself is not representative of India. The sample includes data from each city that had at least 200,000 inhabitants as of the 2001 census of India as well as a smaller rural sample. As such, the data are skewed toward larger cities in India and the data are biased toward urban respondents. India is 32 percent urban and 68 percent rural according to the 2011 Indian census; using the same classifications, the Lok sample is 62 percent urban and 38 percent rural.[2] For purposes of drawing representative inferences, estimates were reweighted by urban and rural population within each state or union territory.

More information about the survey can be found at: https://casi .sas.upenn.edu/lok-survey-social-attitudes-and-electoral-politics/lok -survey-social-attitudes-and-electoral.

Notes

CHAPTER 1. LAWMAKERS AND LAWBREAKERS

1. While five of the six jailed lawmakers were expected to support the government, the sixth (Umakant Yadav) was expected to vote with the opposition.

2. "A Penchant for Guns, Horses and Cars," *Tehelka,* October 2, 2004.

3. Ibid.

4. According to the affidavit submitted by Ateeq Ahmed to the Election Commission of India, he faced 36 pending criminal cases at the time of his election in 2004.

5. Edward Luce, *In Spite of the Gods: The Rise of Modern India* (New York: Knopf, 2010), 134.

6. Ibid.

7. "A Penchant for Guns, Horses and Cars," *Tehelka.*

8. Venkitesh Ramakrishnan, "Canker of Criminalisation," *Frontline,* February 12–25, 2005.

9. "Former SP MLA in Police Custody for Murder of Raju Pal," *Indian Express,* May 12, 2011.

10. Pappu Yadav declared 27 pending criminal cases in the affidavit he submitted to the Election Commission of India in advance of the 2004 Lok Sabha election.

11. Sankarshan Thakur, *Subaltern Saheb: Bihar and the Making of Laloo Yadav* (New Delhi: Picador, 2006), 153.

12. Ajit Sahi, "The Gangster's Last Gamble," *Tehelka,* May 23, 2009.

13. Ibid.

14. Sankarshan Thakur describes Pappu Yadav as "part gangster, part contractor, part caste-lord, part political profiteer." See Thakur, *Subaltern Saheb,* 153.

15. Nalin Verma, "Importance of Pappu, the Politician," *Telegraph* (Calcutta), September 21, 2014.

16. Kumkum Chadha, "She Married a Don . . . a Criminal," *HT Just People* (blog), March 24, 2009, http://blogs.hindustantimes.com/just-people/2009/03/24/just-people/ (accessed March 19, 2014).

17. "Pappu Yadav in His Book: Cong, BJP Offered Rs 40 Crore," *Outlook*, November 27, 2013.

18. In his affidavit submitted to the Election Commission of India prior to the 2004 Lok Sabha election, Mohammed Shahabuddin disclosed charges in 19 pending criminal cases.

19. Sankarshan Thakur, "Give Me Guns, I Shall Give You Votes," *Tehelka*, April 10, 2004.

20. Ashok K. Mishra, "Shahabuddin Gets Life for Murder of CPI-ML Activist," *Economic Times*, May 9, 2007; "Shahabuddin Is a Habitual Criminal; Says Siwan DM," *Patna Daily* (blog), April 21, 2005, http://web.archive.org/web/20070927230254/http://www.patnadaily.com/news05/april/042105/siwan _dm_justifies_ban.html (accessed November 15, 2016); Rajesh Chakrabarti, *Bihar Breakthrough: The Turnaround of a Beleaguered State* (New Delhi: Rupa, 2013).

21. Saba Naqvi Bhaumik, "The Saheb of Siwan: The Tale of an Indian Godfather," in *First Proof: The Penguin Book of New Writing from India*, vol. 1 (New Delhi: Penguin, 2005).

22. Chakrabarti, *Bihar Breakthrough*, 71.

23. Amarnath Tewary, "From the Barrel of a Gun," *Outlook*, April 2, 2001.

24. Thakur, "Give Me Guns, I Shall Give You Votes."

25. Jyotsna Singh, "Jail No Bar for Bihar Candidates," BBC News, April 21, 2004, http://news.bbc.co.uk/2/hi/south_asia/3645317.stm (accessed December 16, 2008).

26. Vandita Mishra, "As Girls Cycle to School and Shahabuddin Becomes a Fading Memory in Siwan, a State Reimagines Itself," *Indian Express*, June 5, 2010.

27. Sankarshan Thakur, "Lawmaker Lawbreaker," *Tehelka*, September 17, 2005.

28. Aman Sethi, "Rule of the Outlaw," *Frontline*, December 17–30, 2005; Mark Tully, *Non-Stop India* (New Delhi: Penguin, 2011), 69–72; Chakrabarti, *Bihar Breakthrough*, 80; and "Former BJP MP Umakant Yadav Gets Seven-Year Jail Term," *Indian Express*, February 8, 2012.

29. Ashish Khetan, "Cash-for-Votes Scandal: A Trap. And a Cover-Up," *Tehelka*, April 2, 2011.

30. Mian Ridge, "Indian Government Survives No-Confidence Vote," *Christian Science Monitor*, July 23, 2008.

31. "Modi Describes Parliament as 'Temple of Democracy,'" Press Trust of India, May 20, 2014, http://www.business-standard.com/article/politics/modi-describes -parliament-as-temple-of-democracy-114052000994_1.html (accessed May 21, 2014).

32. Data compiled by ADR; for more information, see http://myneta.info.

33. Rajni Kothari, *Politics in India* (Boston: Little, Brown, 1970), 216.

34. Data compiled by ADR; see http://myneta.info.

35. This SMS helpline is an initiative of ADR. For more information, visit http://adrindia.org/media/helpline-sms.

36. Data compiled by ADR; see http://myneta.info.

37. Ashutosh Varshney, "Two Banks of the Same River? Social Order and Entre-preneurialism in India," in Partha Chatterjee and Ira Katznelson, eds., *Anxieties of Democracy: Tocquevillean Reflections on India and the United States* (New York: Oxford University Press, 2012).

38. Based on data from ADR, 17 percent and 21 percent of municipal corpora-tors in Mumbai and Delhi, respectively, declared involvement in criminal cases. Data are available at http://myneta.info.

39. Trilochan Sastry, "Towards Decriminalisation of Elections and Politics," *Economic and Political Weekly* 49, no. 1 (January 4, 2014): 36.

40. Author's calculations based on affidavits submitted to the Election Commis-sion of India by candidates contesting the 2004, 2009, and 2014 national parlia-mentary elections.

41. I first made this point about India's "electoral rhythm" in Milan Vaishnav, "Crime but No Punishment in Indian Elections," Carnegie Endowment for Interna-tional Peace, January 24, 2014, http://carnegieendowment.org/2014/01/24/crime-but-no-punishment-in-indian-elections (accessed January 30, 2014).

42. Joseph A. Schumpeter, *Capitalism, Socialism, and Democracy* (New York: HarperCollins, 1962).

43. Adam Przeworski, Susan C. Stokes, and Bernard Manin, eds., *Democracy, Ac-countability, and Representation* (New York: Cambridge University Press, 1999).

44. Simeon Djankov, Rafael La Porta, Florencio Lopez-de-Silanes, and Andrei Shleifer, "Disclosure by Politicians," *American Economic Journal: Applied Eco-nomics* 2, no. 2 (April 2010): 179–209.

45. For instance, according to the 2011 Indian census, India's most populous state of Uttar Pradesh is home to roughly 200 million people, more than the entire population of Brazil. Maharashtra, with 115 million people, has as many residents as Mexico.

46. Susanne Hoeber Rudolph and Lloyd I. Rudolph, "New Dimensions in In-dian Democracy," *Journal of Democracy* 13, no. 1 (January 2002): 52–66.

47. Matthew S. Winters and Rebecca Weitz-Shapiro, "Lacking Information or Condoning Corruption: When Do Voters Support Corrupt Politicians?" *Compara-tive Politics* 45, no. 4 (July 2013): 418–36.

48. Daron Acemoglu, James A. Robinson, and Rafael J. Santos, "The Monopoly of Violence: Evidence from Colombia," *Journal of the European Economic As-sociation* 11, no. 1 (January 2013): 5–44; International Crisis Group, "Cutting the Links between Crime and Local Politics: Colombia's 2011 Elections," Latin America Report No. 37, July 25, 2011, http://www.crisisgroup.org/en/regions/latin-america-caribbean/andes/colombia/37-cutting-the-links-between-crime-and-local-politics-colombias-2011-elections.aspx (accessed September 1, 2014).

49. James Ockey, "Crime, Society and Politics in Thailand," in Carl A. Trocki, ed., *Gangsters, Democracy and the State in Southeast Asia* (Ithaca: Cornell Univer-sity Press, 1998); John T. Sidel, "Bossism and Democracy in the Philippines, Thai-land, and Indonesia: Towards an Alternative Framework for the Study of 'Local

Strongmen,'" in John Harriss, Kristian Stokke, and Olle Törnquist, eds., *Politicising Democracy: The New Local Politics of Democratisation* (London: Palgrave Macmillan, 2005).

50. Anthony Harriott, *Understanding Crime in Jamaica: New Challenges for Public Policy* (Kingston: University of the West Indies Press, 2003); Omobolaji Ololade Olarinmoye, "Godfathers, Political Parties and Electoral Corruption in Nigeria," *African Journal of Political Science and International Relations* 2, no. 4 (December 2008): 66–73.

51. Charles Onyango-Obbo, "Forget the ICC, Here Are the Real Lawbreakers in Kibaki Succession Race," *East African*, March 3, 2012. In December 2014, prosecutors were forced to withdraw the charges against Kenyatta after the Kenyan government declined to cooperate with their investigation.

52. Campbell Robertson, "Well-Known Felon Still Draws a Crowd, but Louisiana Has Moved On," *New York Times*, October 23, 2011.

53. Edward L. Glaeser and Andrei Shleifer, "The Curley Effect: The Economics of Shaping the Electorate," *Journal of Law, Economics, and Organization* 21, no. 1 (April 2005): 1–19.

54. I readily acknowledge, of course, that the electoral market is shaped by social realities and imperfections that prevent it from consistently operating as a "free market" in the purest sense. I discuss many of these messy realities in the pages that follow.

55. Ashutosh Varshney, *Battles Half Won: India's Improbable Democracy* (New York: Penguin, 2013).

56. Reformers must be mindful of the Latin idiom *Ei incumbit probatio qui dicit, non qui negat* (The burden of proof is on he who declares, not on he who denies).

CHAPTER 2. THE RISE OF THE RENTS RAJ

1. "Over 100 Die after YSR's Death, Son Appeals for Calm," Indo-Asian News Service, September 4, 2009, http://www.hindustantimes.com/india/over-100-die -after-ysr-s-death-son-appeals-for-calm/story-45a9sIfQwFZot7vjFXYAiN.html (accessed October 12, 2014).

2. Saurabh Sinha, "Death Came without Warning for YSR," *Times of India*, November 2, 2009.

3. "Over 100 Die after YSR's Death," Indo-Asian News Service.

4. Shekhar Gupta, "The Tragedy and the Trend," *Indian Express*, September 7, 2011.

5. Yogendra Kalavalapalli, "After 10 Years, What's Going to Be Andhra Pradesh's Capital?" *Mint*, July 31, 2013; Committee for Consultations on the Future of Andhra Pradesh, *Final Report* (New Delhi: Government of India, 2010), http://pib .nic.in/archieve/others/2011/jan/d2011010502.pdf (accessed June 15, 2013).

6. J. S. Sai, "In the Killing Fields of Rayalseema, Fear Dominates the Election Scene," *Rediff*, September 3, 1999, http://www.rediff.com/election/1999/sep/03ap .htm (accessed October 24, 2014). Although hard data are difficult to come by, one account estimates that between 1990 and 2005, 670 members of the Con-

gress Party and 560 from the Telugu Desam Party, the two main parties in the Rayalaseema region, were killed due to factional rivalry. See W. Chandrakanth, "Rayalaseema's Bane," *Frontline,* February 12–25, 2005.

7. K. Balagopal, "Beyond Media Images," *Economic and Political Weekly* 39, no. 24 (June 12–18, 2004): 2425–29.

8. Ibid.

9. Sreenivas Janyala, "Young Guns Revive Rayalaseema Wars," *Indian Express,* January 3, 2013.

10. Praveen Donthi, "The Takeover," *Caravan,* May 1, 2012.

11. A. Srinivasa Rao and Sowmya Rao, "The Making of the Most Powerful Family in Andhra Pradesh," *India Today,* September 4, 2009.

12. Balagopal, "Beyond Media Images," 2428.

13. K. C. Suri, "Politics of Democracy, Development and Welfare," *Seminar* 620 (April 2011), http://www.india-seminar.com/2011/620/620_k_c_suri.htm (accessed January 23, 2012).

14. Balagopal, "Beyond Media Images," 2428.

15. Ibid., 2425.

16. Suri, "Politics of Democracy, Development and Welfare."

17. Swaminathan S. Anklesaria Aiyar, "Famous Populist, Secret Liberaliser," *Economic Times,* March 30, 2011.

18. Suri, "Politics of Democracy, Development and Welfare."

19. Donthi, "Takeover."

20. A. Srinivas Rao, "How Jagan Reddy Became the Richest Lok Sabha MP in India, and What Is His Real Worth?" *India Today,* May 28, 2012.

21. Amarnath K. Menon, "Jagan Mohan Reddy: The Prince of Cash," *India Today,* December 6, 2010.

22. Data from 2009 onwards available at http://myneta.info. The 2004 figures are from Menon, "Jagan Mohan Reddy."

23. Comptroller and Auditor General of India, *Report of the Comptroller and Auditor General of India on Land Allotment: Government of Andhra Pradesh, 2011–12* (New Delhi: Comptroller and Auditor General, 2012), http://gssaap-cag .nic.in/sites/all/themes/marinelli/Reports/2011-12/Land%20Allotment/English/ LandAllotment_Complete_Report_2011-12.pdf (accessed October 21, 2014).

24. "Y S Rajasekhara Reddy's Land Doles Cost Andhra Rs 1 Lakh Crore: CAG," *Times of India,* March 30, 2012.

25. Chinnaiah Jangam, "The Story of a Jailed Prince: Feudal Roots of Democratic Politics in Andhra Pradesh," *Economic and Political Weekly* 48, no. 25 (June 22, 2013): 11–15.

26. A. T. Jayanti and Ch. V. M. Krishna Rao, "Though Distant, My Only Rival Is Chandrababu Naidu, Says Jagan Mohan Reddy," *Deccan Chronicle,* April 11, 2014.

27. S. Nagesh Kumar and N. Rahul, "CBI Arrests Jagan; Call for Bandh Today," *Hindu,* May 27, 2012; "Indian MP Jagan Mohan Reddy Freed from Prison," BBC News, September 24, 2013, http://www.bbc.com/news/world-asia-india-24216527 (accessed November 13, 2015).

28. Donthi, "Takeover."

29. Indeed, India's political, economic, and social transformations have been anything but linear or without reversals. This admission is not meant to minimize the distance India has traveled in a relatively short period of time, but to provide a more accurate portrayal of its nuanced realities.

30. Ramachandra Guha, "Democratic to a Fault?" *Prospect,* February 2012.

31. John Dunn, *Breaking Democracy's Spell* (New Haven: Yale University Press, 2014), 103.

32. Ashutosh Varshney, *Battles Half Won: India's Improbable Democracy* (New York: Penguin, 2013).

33. This tripartite formulation is in line with a typology put forward by economist Pranab Bardhan. In dissecting the tension in modern India between rentier and entrepreneurial capitalism, Bardhan elucidates three sources of rents: traded natural resource-intensive goods, non-traded natural resource-intensive goods and services; and politics. See Pranab Bardhan, "Reflections on Indian Political Economy," *Economic and Political Weekly* 50, no. 18 (May 2, 2015): 14–17.

34. Rajni Kothari, "The Congress 'System' in India," *Asian Survey* 4, no. 12 (December 1964): 1161–73.

35. James Manor, "Indira and After: The Decay of Party Organization in India," *The Round Table: The Commonwealth Journal of International Affairs* 68, no. 272 (1978): 315–24.

36. Yogendra Yadav, "Electoral Politics in the Time of Change: India's Third Electoral System, 1989–99," *Economic and Political Weekly* 34, no. 34/35 (August 21–September 3, 1999): 2393–99.

37. There is a debate, not fully resolved, as to whether the momentous victory of the BJP in India's 2014 general elections heralds the end of the third electoral system and the beginning of a fourth. See, e.g., Milan Vaishnav and Danielle Smogard, "A New Era in Indian Politics?" Carnegie Endowment for International Peace, June 10, 2014, http://carnegieendowment.org/2014/06/10/new-era-in-indian-politics (accessed June 12, 2014).

38. Of course, the British legacy in India was not uniformly negative: a talented, skilled civil service and an extensive railway network were but two of the positive inheritances from which India stood to gain. Yet, independent India was ill served by many other aspects of the British Raj, such as a predatory land revenue system and an economic orientation geared toward natural resource extraction designed to feed colonial manufacturers back home.

39. Devesh Kapur, "India's Economic Development," in Bruce Currie-Alder, Ravi Kanbur, David M. Malone, and Rohinton Medhora, eds., *International Development: Ideas, Experience, and Prospects* (Oxford: Oxford University Press, 2014).

40. Ibid.

41. Jawaharlal Nehru passed away in 1964 and was immediately succeed by Lal Bahadur Shastri. Upon Shastri's death in 1966, Indira Gandhi assumed the prime ministership, an office she would hold until 1977 (and again from 1980 to 1984).

42. Arvind Panagariya, *India: The Emerging Giant* (New York: Oxford University Press, 2008), 6.

43. Montek Singh Ahluwalia, "Economic Reforms for the Nineties," First Raj Krishna Memorial Lecture, University of Rajasthan, 1995, http://planningcommission.gov.in/aboutus/speech/spemsa/msa033.pdf (accessed August 1, 2014).

44. The distinction between "pro-business" and "pro-market" reforms in India was originally made in Dani Rodrik and Arvind Subramanian, "From 'Hindu Growth' to Productivity Surge: The Mystery of the Indian Growth Transition," IMF Working Paper WP/04/77, May 2004.

45. Panagariya, *India: The Emerging Giant,* chap. 5. Although it is not covered here, India also experienced a fourth transformation in the realm of foreign policy. In the initial post-independence period, India was committed to a strategy of "nonalignment." Notwithstanding this doctrinal commitment, over time—and especially after 1971—India enjoyed a warm relationship with the Soviet Union, thanks to the commonalities between the two countries' economic ideologies as well as the vagaries of the Cold War, which saw India's rival Pakistan forge close relations with the United States. With the collapse of the Soviet bloc, India's foreign policy posture also shifted. In recent years, India has developed deep economic and security ties with the West, including a "strategic partnership" with the United States. For more on India's foreign policy transformation, see C. Raja Mohan, *Crossing the Rubicon: The Shaping of India's New Foreign Policy* (New York: Palgrave Macmillan, 2003).

46. Divya Vaid, "Caste in Contemporary India: Flexibility and Persistence," *Annual Review of Sociology* 40 (2014): 391–410.

47. Ibid.

48. Christophe Jaffrelot, *India's Silent Revolution: The Rise of the Lower Castes in North India* (New York: Columbia University Press, 2003).

49. Christophe Jaffrelot and Sanjay Kumar, eds., *Rise of the Plebeians? The Changing Face of Indian Legislative Assemblies* (New Delhi: Routledge, 2009).

50. Christophe Jaffrelot and Gilles Verniers, "The Representation Gap," *Indian Express,* July 24, 2015.

51. Dipankar Gupta, *Interrogating Caste: Understanding Hierarchy and Difference in Indian Society* (Penguin: New Delhi, 2000).

52. Chandra Bhan Prasad, D. Shyam Babu, Devesh Kapur, and Lant Pritchett, "Rethinking Inequality: Dalits in Uttar Pradesh in the Market Reform Era," *Economic and Political Weekly* 45, no. 35 (August 28, 2010): 39–49.

53. Simon Chauchard, *Why Representation Matters: The Meaning of Ethnic Quotas in Rural India* (New York: Cambridge University Press, forthcoming).

54. Yogendra Yadav and Suhas Palshikar, "Ten Theses on State Politics in India," *Seminar* 591 (November 2008), http://www.india-seminar.com/2008/591/591_y _yadav_&_s_palshkar.htm (accessed January 21, 2014).

55. For instance, a novel study by political scientists Amit Ahuja and Susan Ostermann examined the role discrimination plays in India's robust online marriage market. Working with a set of pre-identified prospective grooms, the researchers found that more than two-thirds of Dalits, but only about half of upper castes, demonstrated a willingness to cross caste boundaries for marriage. See Amit Ahuja and Susan Ostermann, "Crossing Caste Boundaries in the Modern Indian Marriage Market," *Studies in Comparative International Development* (forthcoming). Another study by a group of economists employed a similar technique to measure discrimination in employment opportunities. The researchers sent out hundreds of fictitious online job applications to firms, randomly manipulating the caste-based surnames of the "applicants." They found that software employers showed no signs

of discriminating on the basis of caste, but that call center firms regularly discriminated against low-caste job seekers. The reason, the economists surmise, is that call center firms prize "soft skills" for which credentials alone are not enough to go by, which is not the case in the software industry. See Abhijit Banerjee, Marianne Bertrand, Saugato Datta, and Sendhil Mullainathan, "Labor Market Discrimination in Delhi: Evidence from a Field Experiment," *Journal of Comparative Economics* 37, no. 1 (March 2009): 14–27.

56. Ashwini Deshpande and Rajesh Ramachandran, "How Backward Are the Other Backward Classes? Changing Contours of Caste Disadvantage in India," Delhi School of Economics, Centre for Development Economics Working Paper 233, November 2014. Another study found that there was almost no change in the rate of business ownership for Scheduled Castes and Scheduled Tribes relative to the rest of the population between 1990 and 2005. See Lakshmi Iyer, Tarun Khanna, and Ashutosh Varshney, "Caste and Entrepreneurship in India," *Economic and Political Weekly* 48, no. 6 (February 9, 2013): 52–60.

57. Sonalde Desai and Amaresh Dubey, "Caste in 21st Century India: Competing Narratives," *Economic and Political Weekly* 46, no. 11 (March 12, 2012): 40–49.

58. This section draws on material which first appeared in Milan Vaishnav, "Resizing the State," *Caravan*, October 1, 2012.

59. After independence, scholar Selig Harrison famously wrote of India: "The odds are almost wholly against the survival of freedom and . . . the issue is, in fact, whether any Indian state can survive at all." Selig Harrison, *India: The Most Dangerous Decades* (Princeton: Princeton University Press, 1960).

60. Indeed, the only regional peer that comes close to India's level of support for democracy is Sri Lanka. Pakistan, in contrast, enjoys the highest level of support for nondemocrats. See Peter Ronald deSouza, Suhas Palshikar, and Yogendra Yadav, "Surveying South Asia," *Journal of Democracy* 19, no. 1 (January 2008): 84–96.

61. There has been not only an increasing gap between the well-being of rural and urban Indians in terms of income but also a widening inequality among urban residents. S. Subramanian and D. Jayaraj, "Growth and Inequality in the Distribution of India's Consumption Expenditure: 1983 to 2009–10," UNU-WIDER Working Paper WP/2015/025 (February 2015). According to a 2014 report from investment bank Credit Suisse, whereas the richest 1 percent of Indians held just under 37 percent of the country's wealth in 2000, that share grew to 49 percent in 2014. Quoted in Rukmini S., "India's Staggering Wealth Gap in Five Charts," *Hindu*, December 8, 2014.

62. Pew Research Center, *Emerging and Developing Economies Much More Optimistic than Rich Countries about the Future* (Washington, D.C.: Pew Research Center, 2014).

63. Varshney, *Battles Half Won*, 39.

64. Francis Fukuyama, *The Origins of Political Order: From Prehuman Times to the French Revolution* (New York: Farrar, Straus and Giroux, 2011), chap. 12.

65. Lant Pritchett, "A Review of Edward Luce's *In Spite of the Gods: The Strange Rise of Modern India*," *Journal of Economic Literature* 47, no. 3 (September 2009): 771–80.

66. Lloyd I. Rudolph and Susanne Hoeber Rudolph, *In Pursuit of Lakshmi: The Political Economy of the Indian State* (Chicago: University of Chicago Press, 1987).

67. Vaishnav, "Resizing the State."

68. I thank Devesh Kapur for coming up with the distinction between the over-bureaucratization in procedural terms and the undermanning of the Indian state in personnel terms.

69. Surjit Bhalla, "Dismantling the Welfare State," in Bibek Debroy, Ashley Tellis, and Reece Trevor, eds., *Getting India Back on Track: An Action Agenda for Reform* (Washington, D.C.: Carnegie Endowment for International Peace, 2014), 51.

70. Devesh Kapur, "The Political Economy of the State," in Niraja Jayal and Pratap Bhanu Mehta, eds., *The Oxford Companion to Politics in India* (New York: Oxford University Press, 2010).

71. Data on India's performance according to the 2016 edition of the World Bank's "Doing Business" indicators can be found at http://www.doingbusiness.org/data/exploreeconomies/india.

72. Marianne Bertrand, Rema Hanna, Simeon Djankov, and Sendhil Mullainathan, "Obtaining a Driving License in India: An Experimental Approach to Studying Corruption," *Quarterly Journal of Economics* 122, no. 4 (2007): 1639–76.

73. Journalist and former union minister Arun Shourie has compiled a range of such examples in his book, *Governance and the Sclerosis That Has Set In* (New Delhi: Rupa, 2004).

74. Bibek Debroy, *India: Redeeming the Economic Pledge* (New Delhi: Academic Foundation, 2004), 133–34.

75. Milan Vaishnav and Reedy Swanson, "India: State Capacity in Global Context," Carnegie Endowment for International Peace, November 2, 2012, http://carnegieendowment.org/2012/11/02/india-state-capacity-in-global-context (accessed January 1, 2013).

76. Government of India, *Report of the Seventh Central Pay Commission* (New Delhi: Government of India, 2015), http://7cpc.india.gov.in/pdf/sevencpcreport.pdf (accessed April 20, 2016).

77. These data come from India's Ministry of Finance and are from 2011–12. Under Indian law, only individuals who earn more than 200,000 rupees per year are required to pay income tax. Given the paucity of credible income data, it is hard to know how large that potential pool is. One of India's leading tax experts believes that with administrative reforms it is possible to widen the taxpayer base to at least 60 million individuals. See M. Govinda Rao, "Bridging the Tax Gap," *Business Standard,* April 12, 2012.

78. "Income Tax Department Manpower Shortfall at 29.47%," Press Trust of India, December 7, 2012, http://articles.economictimes.indiatimes.com/2012-12-07/news/35670708_1_income-tax-department-shortfall-manpower (accessed August 25, 2012). In 2011, a senior tax official disclosed that tax authorities had to ration their monitoring capacity due to a shortage of officers. As a result of the severe staff crunch, "over 40% of assesses with an annual income above Rs. 10 lakh [1 million rupees]" would likely go unmonitored. See Apurv Gupta, "Income Tax Staff Crunch May Help You Escape Scrutiny," *Economic Times,* July 16, 2011.

79. Krishna D. Rao and Sudha Ramani, "Human Resources for Health in India: Current Challenges and Policy Options," in IDFC Foundation, *India Infrastructure Report, 2013–14: The Road to Universal Health Coverage* (New Delhi: Orient Blackswan, 2014).

80. Praveen Swami, "India's Spy Agencies More Toothless than Ever," *Indian Express,* December 1, 2014.

81. Sarah J. Watson and C. Christine Fair, "India's Stalled Internal Security Reforms," *India Review* 12, no. 4 (November 2013): 284.

82. Andrew MacAskill and Sanjeev Miglani, "India's Intelligence Agency on the Cheap Hampers War on Militants," Reuters, November 7, 2014, http://www.reuters .com/article/us-india-security-intelligence-insight-idUSKBN0IR04420141107 (accessed November 10, 2014). India's ability to project its influence around the world is also badly hamstrung by capacity constraints. For instance, India's diplomatic corps is roughly the size of Singapore's, despite the fact India has a population 200 times larger than that of the island nation and an economy more than six times as large. See Shashi Tharoor, "In the Ministry of Eternal Affairs," *Caravan,* July 1, 2012.

83. Government of India, Ministry of Home Affairs, National Crime Records Bureau, *Prison Statistics India 2012* (New Delhi: Ministry of Home Affairs, 2013), http://ncrb.nic.in/StatPublications/PSI/Prison2012/Full/PSI-2012.pdf (accessed July 13, 2014).

84. Data on personnel vacancies and pendency in the judiciary can be found in the quarterly "Court News" summaries issued by the Supreme Court. These are available at: http://supremecourtofindia.nic.in/courtnews.htm. For an in-depth exploration of the issue of pendency, see Government of India, Law Commission of India, *Arrears and Backlog: Creating Additional Judicial (Wo)manpower,* Report No. 245 (New Delhi: Law Commission of India, July 2014), http://lawcommission ofindia.nic.in/reports/Report245.pdf (accessed October 1, 2014).

85. Kritika Sharma, "Citizens on Their Own as 45,000 Police Protect Delhi VIPs and Office Chores," *Mail Today,* December 24, 2012.

86. Samuel Huntington, *Political Order in Changing Societies* (New Haven: Yale University Press, 1968), 5.

87. Modernization is a fraught term because it often is used as a synonym for "Westernization." In this chapter, I nevertheless use the term to remain consistent with Huntington's terminology. For my purposes, modernization simply refers to a process of rapid social and economic development.

88. Huntington, *Political Order in Changing Societies,* 60.

89. Ibid., 61–62.

90. Ibid., 59–60.

91. Aditi Gandhi and Michael Walton, "Where Do India's Billionaires Get Their Wealth?" *Economic and Political Weekly* 47, no. 40 (October 6, 2012): 10–14.

92. Naazneen Karmali, "For the First Time, India's 100 Richest of 2014 Are All Billionaires," *Forbes India,* September 24, 2014.

93. "An Unloved Billionaire," *Economist,* July 31, 2014; Manu Joseph, "Letter from India: The Image of India's Richest Man Loses Luster," *New York Times,* July 23, 2014.

94. Government of India, Planning Commission, "Press Notes on Poverty Estimates, 2011–12," July 22, 2013, http://planningcommission.nic.in/news/pre _pov2307.pdf (accessed July 23, 2013).

95. Raghuram Rajan, "Is There a Threat of Oligarchy in India?," speech to the Bombay Chamber of Commerce, September 10, 2008, http://faculty.chicagobooth. edu/raghuram.rajan/research/papers/is%20there%20a%20threat%20of%20o ligarchy%20in%20india.pdf (accessed December 1, 2013).

96. This point is also made by Varshney, *Battles Half Won,* 41–42.

97. Milan Vaishnav, "India Needs More Democracy, Not Less," *Foreign Affairs,* April 11, 2013, https://www.foreignaffairs.com/articles/india/2013-04-11/india -needs-more-democracy-not-less (accessed April 12, 2013).

98. Pratap Bhanu Mehta, "A Special Retreat," *Indian Express,* March 19, 2013.

99. Vaishnav, "India Needs More Democracy, Not Less."

100. Vanita Kohli-Khandekar, "The Booming Market for Newspapers," *Business Standard,* June 3, 2013.

101. These data come from an infographic on television news in India produced by the newspaper *Business Standard,* March 25, 2011, http://www.business -standard.com/content/general_pdf/032511_01.pdf (accessed September 13, 2013).

102. World Bank, World Development Indicators database (accessed August 1, 2015); Government of India, Telecom Regulatory Authority of India, "The Indian Telecom Services Performance Indicators, October–December 2014," May 8, 2015, http://www.trai.gov.in/WriteReadData/PIRReport/Documents/Indicator_Reports %20-%20Dec-14=08052015.pdf (accessed August 4, 2015).

103. World Bank, World Development Indicators database (accessed August 1, 2015); Government of India, Telecom Regulatory Authority of India, "Highlights of Telecom Subscription Data as on 31st May, 2015," July 10, 2015, http://www.trai .gov.in/WriteReadData/WhatsNew/Documents/PR-32-TSD-May-15_10072015 .pdf (accessed August 2, 2015).

104. Pratap Bhanu Mehta, *The Burden of Democracy* (New Delhi: Penguin, 2003), 20.

105. R. P. Kangle, *The Kautilīya Arthaśātra,* part 2 (New Delhi: Motilal Banarsidass, 1969), 91.

106. This definition varies slightly from the classic definition of "grand corruption," which refers to corruption occurring at the highest levels of government and involving major government projects and programs. See Susan Rose-Ackerman, *Corruption and Government: Causes, Consequences, and Reform* (New York: Cambridge University Press, 1999).

107. Political scientist Jennifer Bussell argues that a third type of corruption ("mid-level corruption") sits between the two poles of "grand" and "petty" corruption. Whereas grand corruption involves senior politicians receiving bribes to influence policy design and petty corruption refers to small bribe payments to low-level state actors for preferential service delivery, mid-level corruption involves intermediate-level bureaucrats and politicians taking bribes for influencing the implementation of public sector schemes. For illustrative purposes, I focus on the binary classification, but there is surely scope for more disaggregated categorization. See

Jennifer Bussell, "Varieties of Corruption: The Organization of Rent-Seeking in India," paper presented at the "Westminster Model of Democracy in Crisis" conference, Harvard University, May 13–14, 2013, https://gspp.berkeley.edu/assets/uploads/research/pdf/bussell.pdf (accessed April 22, 2015).

108. Sadanand Dhume, "India's Crony Socialism," *Wall Street Journal,* July 6, 2011.

109. Raghuram Rajan, "The Next Generation of Reforms in India," speech at a function to re-release a book of essays in honor of Dr. Manmohan Singh, New Delhi, April 14, 2012, http://blogs.chicagobooth.edu/blog/Fault_Lines_by_Raghuram_Rajan/The_Next_Generation_of_Reforms_in_India/faultlines/49?nav=entry (accessed August 5, 2013).

110. Laura Alfaro and Anusha Chari, "India Transformed: Insights from the Firm Level 1988–2007," *India Policy Forum* 6 (2009): 153–224.

111. "Dancing Elephants," *Economist,* January 27, 2011.

112. Joel S. Hellman, "Winners Take All: The Politics of Partial Reform in Postcommunist Transitions," *World Politics* 50, no. 2 (January 1998): 203–34.

113. Rajan, "The Next Generation of Reforms in India."

114. Laura Alfaro and Anusha Chari, "Deregulation, Misallocation, and Size: Evidence from India," *Journal of Law and Economics* 57, no. 4 (November 2014): 897–936.

115. Anusha Chari and Nandini Gupta, "Incumbents and Protectionism: The Political Economy of Foreign Entry Liberalization," *Journal of Financial Economics* 88, no. 3 (June 2008): 633–56.

116. Sumit Ganguly, "Corruption in India: An Enduring Threat," *Journal of Democracy* 23, no. 1 (January 2012): 138–48.

117. Gandhi and Walton, "Where Do India's Billionaires Get Their Wealth?"

118. KPMG, *Survey on Bribery and Corruption: Impact on Economy and Business Environment* (December 2011), https://www.kpmg.com/Global/en/IssuesAndInsights/ArticlesPublications/Documents/bribery-corruption.pdf (accessed May 16, 2012). A 2009 study by consulting firm Deloitte states, "Corruption in India appears to be more widespread in the construction industry, especially in large infrastructure projects." See Kerry Francis, Walt Brown, and Hema Hattangady, *India and the Foreign Corrupt Practices Act* (Deloitte Forensic Center, 2009), https://www.orrick.com/Events-and-Publications/Documents/2880.pdf (accessed May 10, 2012).

119. Surajit Mazumdar, "Big Business and Economic Nationalism in India," Institute for Studies in Industrial Development Working Paper 2010/09, September 2010. See also Kanchan Chandra, "The New Indian State: The Relocation of Patronage in the Post-Liberalisation Economy," *Economic and Political Weekly* 50, no. 41 (October 10, 2015): 46–58.

120. Simeon Djankov, Rafael La Porta, Florencio Lopez-de-Silanes, and Andrei Shleifer, "The Regulation of Entry," *Quarterly Journal of Economics* 117, no. 1 (2002): 1–37.

121. Sandip Sukhtankar and Milan Vaishnav, "Corruption in India: Bridging Research Evidence and Policy Options," *India Policy Forum* 11 (July 2015): 193–261.

122. Chandra, "New Indian State."

123. Arvind Subramanian, "What Is India's Real Growth Potential?" *Business Standard,* May 23, 2012.

124. Pratap Bhanu Mehta, "It's the Land, Stupid," *Indian Express,* August 19, 2010.

125. One of the best primers on how land markets operate in India is Sanjoy Chakravorty, *The Price of Land: Acquisition, Conflict, Consequence* (New Delhi: Oxford University Press, 2013).

126. Vaibhav Ganjapure, "Maharashtra Govt Spent Rs. 3.71 Crore on Adarsh Probe Panel: RTI Survey," *Times of India,* February 15, 2014.

127. Samyabrata Roy Goswami, "If I Had Sent Them to Jail, Congress Would Have Been Finished: Prithviraj Chavan," *Telegraph* (Calcutta), October 14, 2014.

128. Rajan, "New Generation of Reforms in India."

129. India Brand Equity Foundation, "About Jharkhand: Industries, Mining, Economy, Exports, Tourism, Climate, Geography," February 2016, http://www .ibef.org/states/jharkhand.aspx (accessed April 22, 2016).

130. Shantanu Guha Ray, "The Rise and Fall of King Koda," *Tehelka,* November 14, 2009.

131. Smruti Koppikar and Saikat Datta, "Miner Sins," *Outlook,* November 23, 2009; Manish Tiwari and Madan Kumar, "Koda Empire from Africa to Mumbai," *Hindustan Times,* November 3, 2009.

132. "Madhu Koda Arrested," *Economic Times,* December 1, 2009; "Coal Scam: Court Frames Charges against Madhu Koda, Eight Others," Press Trust of India, July 31, 2015, http://zeenews.india.com/business/news/companies/coal -scam-court-frames-charges-against-madhu-koda-eight-others_132707.html (accessed April 21, 2016).

133. Neeraj Chauhan and Partha Sinha, "CBI Grills Top Tata Steel Officer in Madhu Koda Mining Scam," *Times of India,* March 7, 2013.

134. "Madhu Koda Worked Overtime to Issue Mining Licences," *Economic Times,* November 12, 2009.

135. Koppikar and Datta, "Miner Sins."

136. Ibid.; Shantanu Guha Ray, "Decoding Koda," *Tehelka,* November 21, 2009.

137. DMK leader Karunanidhi once claimed that his relationship with Raja was like that of "a child in the hands of [a] revered and respected leader." See "A Raja Arrives in Chennai to a Hero's Welcome, Karunanidhi Calls Him a Younger Brother," Press Trust of India, June 8, 2012, http://indiatoday.intoday.in/story/ a-raja-tamil-nadu-supporters-dmk/1/199785.html (accessed June 16, 2015).

138. "2G Case: A. Raja Was Main Conspirator, Favoured Firms, Says CBI," Press Trust of India, September 7, 2015, http://www.thehindu.com/news/national/ 2g-case-a-raja-was-main-conspirator-favoured-firms-says-cbi/article7625584.ece (accessed November 8, 2015).

139. Sandip Sukhtankar, "The Impact of Corruption on Consumer Markets: Evidence from the Allocation of 2G Wireless Spectrum in India," *Journal of Law and Economics* 58, no. 1 (February 2015): 75–109.

140. Comptroller and Auditor General of India, *Performance Audit of Issue of Licences and Allocation of 2G Spectrum by the Department of Telecommunications* (New Delhi: Comptroller and Auditor General, 2010), http://www.cag.gov .in/content/report-no-19-2010-performance-audit-issue-licences-and-allocation -2g-spectrum-union (accessed April 21, 2016).

141. See Vinay Kumar, "CBI Arrests Former Telecom Minister A. Raja," *Hindu,* February 2, 2011. In the 2014 Lok Sabha election, Raja narrowly lost the Nilgiris constituency in Tamil Nadu, a seat he won in 2009, despite the fact that he actually polled more votes than he had five years earlier. In his 2014 election affidavit, Raja declared that charges had been framed against him in a pending corruption case in front of a special CBI court. The court granted Raja bail in this case in May 2012.

142. "Kalaignar TV Got Rs. 200 Crores through 2G Scam: ED," Press Trust of India, June 2, 2015, http://www.thehindu.com/news/national/kalaignar-tv-got-rs -200-crores-through-2g-scam-ed/article7271324.ece (accessed November 9, 2015). In October 2014, Raja was formally charged with money laundering in connection with the scam. Final arguments in the case were set for December 2015. See "2G Case: Raja, Kanimozhi Charged with Money Laundering," Press Trust of India, October 31, 2014, http://www.thehindubusinessline.com/info-tech/special-court -frames-charges-against-former-telecom-minister-a-raja-dmk-mp-kanimozhi-and -others-in-2g-scamrelated-money-laundering-case/article6551462.ece (accessed November 7, 2014).

143. In August 2015, the CBI registered a disproportionate assets case against Raja and fifteen others. Prosecutors allege that Raja acquired more 270 million rupees in unexplained cash between 1999 and 2010. See Devesh K. Pandey and S. Vijay Kumar, "CBI Files Assets Case against Raja," *Hindu,* August 19, 2015.

144. It is worth pointing out that politicians need not always make direct regulatory interventions on behalf of firms to make sure the "right" companies get their work done. Quite often, the links between firms and politicians are publicly known, which sends a powerful signal to bureaucrats to approve the favored firms' projects or risk professional sanction. See S. S. Gill, *The Pathology of Corruption* (New Delhi: HarperCollins India, 1999), chap. 12.

145. World Bank data on the ease of doing business in India are available here: http://www.doingbusiness.org/data/exploreeconomies/india. A 2011 survey of Indian firms conducted by international auditor KPMG reported that companies perceive construction/real estate to be the single most corrupt industry in India. See KPMG, *Survey on Bribery and Corruption* (December 2011), https://www .kpmg.com/Global/en/IssuesAndInsights/ArticlesPublications/Documents/bribery -corruption.pdf (accessed May 16, 2012).

146. The savviest politicians encourage their relatives to establish real estate firms so that the favors and monetary benefits can remain within the family. A 2001 media investigation revealed that a quarter of ministers in the Gujarat state cabinet had familial or other close links with builders. See Ranjit Bhushan, "Builders and Friends," *Outlook,* February 19, 2001.

147. Some insiders have speculated that in states headed for polls, there is a spike in the issuance of "change of land use" (or CLU) certificates by the government immediately before elections are held. The clearances are a demonstration of political

commitment by fund-seeking politicians. See Bhavdeep Kang, "Inside Story: How Political Parties Raise Money," *Yahoo! News India,* September 25, 2013, https://in.news.yahoo.com/inside-story—how-political-parties-raise-money-091455119.html (accessed October 1, 2013).

148. The builder-politician nexus is by no means restricted to India. One study of 166 corporate bribery cases worldwide found that construction was the single most bribe-laden industry. See Yan Leung Cheung, P. Raghavendra Rau, and Aris Stouraitis, "How Much Do Firms Pay as Bribes and What Benefits Do They Get? Evidence from Corruption Cases Worldwide," National Bureau of Economic Research Working Paper 17981, April 2012.

149. Devesh Kapur and Milan Vaishnav, "Quid Pro Quo: Builders, Politicians, and Election Finance in India," Center for Global Development Working Paper 276, March 29, 2013, http://www.cgdev.org/sites/default/files/Kapur_Vaishnav_election_finance_India-FINAL-0313.pdf (accessed April 1, 2013).

150. The decline in cement consumption also cannot be simply explained away by the decline in government activity around elections given the lag built into all tenders and contracts.

151. This insight is nicely captured in "Marriage of Money and Politics," *Economic and Political Weekly* 44, no. 45 (November 7, 2009): 5–6.

152. Virendra Nath Bhatt, "Raja Bhaiya: The Godfather IV," *Tehelka,* March 16, 2013. Authors of a book on the 2012 state election in Uttar Pradesh write that Raja Bhaiya has become "a synonym for [the] criminal-political nexus." See Manish Tiwari and Rajan Pandey, *Battleground U.P. Politics in the Land of Ram* (New Delhi: Tranquebar, 2013), 218.

153. Kunal Pradhan, "Raja Bhaiyya and the Badlands of Kunda," *India Today,* March 8, 2013.

154. Yogesh Vajpeyi, "Honour Thy Brother, Flay Thy Foe," *Tehelka,* May 1, 2004.

155. Bhatt, "Raja Bhaiya."

156. Affidavit of Raghuraj Pratap Singh (alias Raja Bhaiya) submitted to the Election Commission of India in advance of the 2012 Uttar Pradesh state assembly election. In 2013, Raja Bhaiya was charged with orchestrating the murder of a deputy superintendent of police. He was forced to resign from the state cabinet, but when the CBI later cleared him of this charge, he was re-inducted. See "Raja Bhaiya's New Portfolio a Comedown?" *Times of India,* November 5, 2015.

157. Of course, not all of this support was entirely voluntary, especially among those who suffered the brunt of the coercive aspects of Raja Bhaiya's repertoire. One village politician remarked of Raja Bhaiya, *Kuch bhay vash karte hain, kuchh prem vash karte hain* (Some support out of fear, some out of affection). See Ramendra Singh, "The Raja's Backyard," *Indian Express,* March 9, 2013.

158. Prem Panicker, "The Secret of Raja Bhaiya's Success," *Rediff,* February 20, 2002, http://www.rediff.com/election/2002/feb/20_upr_prem_spe_1.htm (accessed March 30, 2013).

159. Mehul Srivastava and Andrew MacAskill, "Poor in India Starve as Politicians Steal $14.5 Billion of Food," *Bloomberg Business,* August 28, 2012; Ashish Khetan, "The Raja Who Stole from the Poor," *Tehelka,* April 21, 2012.

160. Srivastava and MacAskill, "Poor in India Starve."

161. Sukhtankar and Vaishnav, "Corruption in India."

162. Paul Niehaus, Antonia Atanassova, Marianne Bertrand, and Sendhil Mullainathan, "Targeting with Agents," *American Economic Journal: Economic Policy* 5, no. 1 (February 2013): 206–38.

163. PricewaterhouseCoopers LLP, *Economic Crime: A Threat to Business Globally*, PwC 2014 Global Economic Crime Survey, 2014, https://www.pwc.ie/media-centre/assets/publications/2014_global_economic_crime_survey.pdf (accessed April 22, 2016).

164. Robert Wade, "The System of Administrative and Political Corruption: Canal Irrigation in South India," *Journal of Development Studies* 18, no. 3 (1982): 287–328; and Robert Wade, "The Market for Public Office: Why the Indian State Is Not Better at Development," *World Development* 13, no. 4 (1985): 467–97.

165. Varinder Bhatia, "Hooda Govt Bent Rules to Favour Robert Vadra Firm: CAG," Press Trust of India, March 26, 2015, http://indianexpress.com/article/india/india-others/cag-raps-haryana-govt-for-showing-undue-favours-to-robert-vadra/ (March 26, 2015).

166. Anand Kumar Patel, "Bureaucrat Ashok Khemka Won't Face Charges in Robert Vadra Case," NDTV, November 4, 2015, http://www.ndtv.com/india-news/haryana-government-drops-charges-against-bureaucrat-ashok-khemka-1239906 (accessed November 13, 2015).

167. Sukhbir Siwach, "Ashok Khemka, Whistleblower IAS Officer, Transferred Again," *Times of India*, April 2, 2015.

168. Lakshmi Iyer and Anandi Mani, "Traveling Agents: Political Change and Bureaucratic Turnover in India," *Review of Economics and Statistics* 94, no. 3 (August 2012): 723–39.

169. Mani Shankar Aiyar, "The Politics of Poverty," *India Today*, August 13, 2009.

170. Nazmul Chaudhury et al., "Missing in Action: Teacher and Health Worker Absence in Developing Countries," *Journal of Economic Perspectives* 20, no. 1 (Winter 2006): 91–116; Karthik Muralidharan, Jishnu Das, Alaka Holla, and Aakash Mohpal, "The Fiscal Cost of Weak Governance: Evidence from Teacher Absenteeism in India," National Bureau of Economic Research Working Paper 20299, July 2014.

171. Rajan, "Is There a Threat of Oligarchy in India?"

172. Comptroller and Auditor General of India, *Report of the Comptroller . . .*, *2011–12*. To date, the CBI has filed at least eleven chargesheets against Jagan Reddy in relation to corruption charges. However, he has not yet been convicted of any criminal wrongdoing. "DA Case: The 10 Chargesheets against Jaganmohan Reddy," Press Trust of India, September 23, 2013, http://www.firstpost.com/india/da-case-the-10-chargesheets-against-jaganmohan-reddy-1128925.html (accessed November 13, 2015); "CBI Files 11th Chargesheet against Jagan Mohan Reddy in Disproportionate Assets Case," Press Trust of India, September 9, 2014, http://www.ndtv.com/south/cbi-files-11th-chargesheet-against-jagan-mohan-reddy-in-disproportionate-assets-case-661542 (accessed November 13, 2015).

173. Sreenivas Janyala, "Reddy-Reddy Link: Mining a Friendship," *Indian Express*, September 7, 2011.

174. Jim Yardley, "Despite Scandals, Indian Mining Bosses Thrive," *New York Times,* August 18, 2010; Vijay Simha, "'Mining Lease Is Used as James Bond's Gun,'" *Tehelka,* April 3, 2010.

175. Sanjana, "The Reddy Flag over Bangalore," *Tehelka,* June 14, 2008; Sugata Srinivasaraju, "Lotus Loofahs," *Outlook,* November 16, 2009; Anil Kumar Sastry, "Ten MLA-Hopefuls Cross 100-Crore Mark," *Hindu,* April 21, 2013.

176. Sanjana, "The Revenge of the Reddy Republic," *Tehelka,* November 14, 2009.

177. Ashok Malik and Imran Khan, "The Baron Might Go: The Robbery Goes On," *Tehelka,* August 6, 2011.

178. Karnataka Lokayukta, *Report on the Reference Made by the Government of Karnataka under Section 7(2-A) of the Karnataka Lokayukta Act, 1984,* Report No. COMPT/LOK/BCD/89/2007, July 27, 2011, http://www.thehindu.com/multimedia/archive/00736/Report_on_the_refer_736286a.pdf (accessed April 22, 2016); Simha, "'Mining Lease Is Used as James Bond's Gun.'"

179. Hari Kumar and Jim Yardley, "India Charges Mining Barons with Fraud," *New York Times,* September 5, 2011.

180. Rama Lakshmi, "In Indian Mining District, the Barons Are Back," *Washington Post,* May 2, 2013.

181. Karnataka Lokayukta, *Report on the Reference Made by the Government of Karnataka;* Sugata Srinivasaraju, "'Bellary Is Mine,'" *Outlook,* August 10, 2009.

182. As Karnataka's anticorruption ombudsman (*Lokayukta*) Santosh Hegde stated, "There was no cross-checking of facts, no counter-checking, and no sending of a team of surveyors and of the mining department to find out if there was a place of such a description." See Simha, "'Mining Lease Is Used as James Bond's Gun.'"

183. T.A. Johnson, "Bellary Brothers Are Back," *Indian Express,* June 24, 2009; "Yeddyurappa Sheds Tears over His Plight," Indo-Asian News Service, November 7, 2009, http://www.hindustantimes.com/india/yeddyurappa-sheds-tears-over-his-plight/story-IdWuV45ToyHHrHpsimFgtI.html (accessed November 13, 2015).

184. Shailendra Pandey, "The Hell Diggers," *Tehelka,* April 3, 2010.

185. Ibid.

186. Sanjana, "The Reddy Flag over Bangalore." According to the affidavit Sriramulu submitted to the Election Commission of India ahead of the 2014 general election, he faced charges in eight separate criminal cases. In the case involving the alleged assault of the Congress worker, where a judge had already framed charges, the lawmaker stood accused of attempted murder.

187. Lakshmi, "In Indian Mining District, the Barons Are Back."

188. Karnataka Lokayukta, *Report on the Reference Made by the Government of Karnataka.*

189. B. Krishna Prasad and Anil Kumar, "Illegal Mining: CBI Arrests Former Karnataka Minister Janardhana Reddy, Cash Seized," *Times of India,* September 5, 2011. Although he still awaits trial, Janardhana was granted bail in January 2014.

190. Lakshmi, "In Indian Mining District, the Barons Are Back"; "Somashekar Reddy Held in Bail Scam," *Hindu,* August 7, 2012.

CHAPTER 3. CRIMINAL ENTERPRISE

1. Syed Firdaus Ashraf, "The Rediff Interview: Arun Gawli," *Rediff*, August 1997, http://m.rediff.com/news/aug/13gawli.htm (accessed July 25, 2013).

2. S. Hussain Zaidi, *Dongri to Dubai: Six Decades of the Mumbai Mafia* (New Delhi: Lotus, 2011), 93–5.

3. Suyash Padate and Sumit Bhattacharya, "Dagdi Chawl's Daddy Cool," *Tehelka*, April 3, 2004.

4. Suhas Palshikar, "Revisiting State Level Parties," *Economic and Political Weekly* 39, no. 14/15 (April 3–16, 2014): 1477–79.

5. Ajith Pillai, "Byculla Bhai," *Outlook*, January 8, 1997.

6. S. Hussain Zaidi, *Byculla to Bangkok* (New Delhi: HarperCollins India, 2014).

7. "The Milkman Who Became a Gangster," *Hindustan Times*, August 25, 2012.

8. Arun Gawli himself has told inquiring journalists that the Shiv Sena abandoned him during his jail stint because it believed he had a hand in the killing of several Sena associates, a charge he denies. See Tony Cross, "Profile of a Gangster Turned Politician," *Radio France Internationale*, April 29, 2009, http://www1.rfi.fr/actuen/articles/112/article_3631.asp (accessed July 15, 2013); Zaidi, *Byculla to Bangkok*.

9. Ashraf, "Rediff Interview: Arun Gawli."

10. Pillai, "Byculla Bhai."

11. Saira Menzies, "Twister in the Tiger's Tale," *Outlook*, August 6, 1997.

12. S. Hussain Zaidi and Jane Borges, *Mafia Queens of Mumbai* (New Delhi: Westland, 2011).

13. Ashraf, "Rediff Interview: Arun Gawli."

14. At the time of writing, a Bollywood film based on Gawli's life, tentatively titled "Daddy," was in production.

15. National Commission to Review the Working of the Constitution, "Review of Election Law, Processes, and Electoral Reforms," Consultation Paper, January 8, 2001, http://lawmin.nic.in/ncrwc/finalreport/v2b1-9.htm (accessed April 22, 2016).

16. An example of this narrative comes from a former senior official in India's Central Bureau of Investigation, N. K. Singh. Singh writes that the immediate post-independence period witnessed the criminalization of politics, whereby politicians took the help of criminals in winning elections. But in due course, he states, "A stage came when criminals felt that rather than helping politicians, why did they not get themselves into the legislatures or Parliament and occupy ministerial positions, and use these to further their criminal activities?" See N. K. Singh, *The Politics of Crime and Corruption: A Former CBI Officer Speaks* (New Delhi: HarperCollins India, 1999), 38.

17. Atul Kohli, *Democracy and Discontent: India's Growing Crisis of Governability* (New York: Cambridge University Press, 1991).

18. As anthropologist Jeffrey Witsoe has argued, "Highly visible instances of 'booth looting' and electoral violence, therefore, were a reaction to the practical absence of the right to vote for many lower-caste people in the past." See Jeffrey

Witsoe, "Caste and Democratization in Postcolonial India: An Ethnographic Examination of Lower Caste Politics in Bihar," *Democratization* 19, no. 2 (August 2012): 13.

19. Yogendra Yadav, "Electoral Politics in the Time of Change: India's Third Electoral System, 1989–99," *Economic and Political Weekly* 34, no. 34/35 (August 21–September 3, 1999): 2393–99.

20. Ibid., 2397.

21. This statement is supported by a February 2014 report by the government of India's Law Commission, which makes reference to fears about a possible nexus between politicians and criminals even during the pre-independence period. See Government of India, Law Commission of India, *Electoral Disqualifications,* Report No. 244 (New Delhi: Law Commission of India, February 2014), http://law commissionofindia.nic.in/reports/report244.pdf (accessed April 22, 2016).

22. E. Sridharan and Milan Vaishnav, "India," in Pippa Norris and Andrea Abel van Es, eds., *Checkbook Elections? Political Finance in Comparative Perspective* (New York: Oxford University Press, 2016).

23. David Gilmartin and Robert Moog, "Introduction to 'Election Law in India,'" *Election Law Journal* 11, no. 2 (June 2012): 140.

24. Election Commission of India, *Report on the First General Elections in India, 1951–52* (New Delhi: Election Commission of India, 1955), http://eci.nic.in/eci_main/eci_publications/books/genr/FirstGenElection-51-52.pdf (accessed July 5, 2013).

25. Vikasa Kumara Jha, *Bihar: Criminalisation of Politics* (Patna: Srishti Prakashan, 1996).

26. Ibid., 134–35.

27. Ibid., 132–33.

28. Although democratic India initially experienced one-party dominance, it was emphatically not a one-party system. In addition to the existence of opposition parties (fractured though they were), Congress itself was the site of tremendous internal political competition and factionalism. See Rajni Kothari, "The Congress 'System' in India," *Asian Survey* 4, no. 12 (December 1964): 1167.

29. Prem Shankar Jha, *In the Eye of the Cyclone: The Crisis in Indian Democracy* (New Delhi: Penguin, 1993), 25.

30. James Manor, "Parties and the Party System," in Atul Kohli, ed., *India's Democracy: An Analysis of Changing State-Society Relations* (Princeton: Princeton University Press, 1988), 65.

31. Historically speaking, the local-level organization and reach of the Congress should not be overestimated. In several parts of the country, the party was either poorly organized or present only in a formal sense. See Pradeep Chhibber, *Democracy without Associations: Transformation of the Party System and Social Cleavages in India* (Ann Arbor: University of Michigan Press, 1999), chap. 3.

32. Steven I. Wilkinson, "Where's the Party? The Decline of Party Institutionalization and What (If Anything) That Means for Democracy," *Government and Opposition* 50, no. 3 (July 2015): 424.

33. Christophe Jaffrelot, "Indian Democracy: The Rule of Law on Trial," *India Review* 1, no. 1 (2002): 98.

34. James Manor, "Party Decay and Political Crisis in India," *Washington Quarterly* 4, no. 3 (Summer 1981): 26.

35. According to criminologist Arvind Verma, politicians would often target booths that were geographically isolated or had a minimal police presence to avoid detection. See Arvind Verma, "Policing Elections in India," *India Review* 4, no. 3/4 (2005): 354–76.

36. S. S. Agarwalla, *Contemporary India and Its Burning Problems* (New Delhi: Mittal Publications, 1994), 31.

37. Pranava K. Chaudhary, "Where Booth Capturing Was Born," *Times of India,* February 14, 2005.

38. Verma, "Policing Elections in India."

39. Jha, *Bihar: Criminalisation of Politics,* 44. When Kamdev Singh was finally killed in a police encounter in 1980, the Bihar chief minister personally paid a visit to his ancestral village to apologize for the police action and to seek his family's forgiveness—a sign of the gangster's considerable political clout. See Sankarshan Thakur, *Subaltern Saheb: Bihar and the Making of Laloo Yadav* (New Delhi: Picador, 2006), 66.

40. Das, "Landowners' Armies Take Over 'Law and Order.'"

41. On Bihar, see Francine R. Frankel, "Caste, Land and Dominance in Bihar," in Francine R. Frankel and M. S. A. Rao, eds., *Dominance and State Power in Modern India: Decline of a Social Order*, vol. 1 (New Delhi: Oxford University Press, 1990), 123. In Andhra Pradesh, K. Balagopal writes that voters either would have to present stamped ballot papers to the landlord's polling agent who was seated inside of the booth before placing it in the ballot box or the landlord's agent would just stamp the ballot paper himself while the voter stayed at home. See K. Balagopal, "Seshan in Kurnool," *Economic and Political Weekly* 29, no. 30 (July 23, 1994): 1903–6.

42. Witsoe, "Caste and Democratization in Postcolonial India," 13.

43. Vikasa Jha writes on the Bihar experience: "Criminal gangs are now given [a] contract by the candidates to capture polling booths. . . . It has become customary for candidates to give their supporting criminal gangs the assurance that after winning the election they would be protected from law and administration and that they would be given contracts for roads, bridges, and buildings [sic] constructions." See Jha, *Bihar: Criminalisation of Politics,* 87.

44. Jha, *In the Eye of the Cyclone.*

45. It suffices to say that the politics of defection was lubricated by a heavy dose of bribe payments and monetary transfers between individuals and parties.

46. Susheela Bhan, *Criminalization of Politics* (New Delhi: Shipra, 1995), 8.

47. Susheela Bhan, quoting Subhas Kashyap, writes that by the end of March 1971 approximately half of India's parliamentarians and 52.5 percent of its state legislators had changed their partisan affiliations at least once. See Bhan, *Criminalization of Politics,* 9.

48. Rajni Kothari, "The Non-Party Political Process," *Economic and Political Weekly* 19, no. 5 (February 4, 1984): 216–24.

49. Paul R. Brass, *Factional Politics in an Indian State: The Congress Party in Uttar Pradesh* (Los Angeles: University of California Press, 1965). James Manor, "Changing State, Changing Society in India," *South Asia: Journal of South Asian Studies* 25, no. 2 (2002): 231–56.

50. Manor, "Parties and the Party System," 66.

51. Gill, *Pathology of Corruption*, 74.

52. Myron Weiner, *Party Building in a New Nation: The Indian National Congress* (Chicago: University of Chicago Press, 1967).

53. Brass, *Factional Politics in an Indian State.*

54. Manor, "Changing State, Changing Society," 239.

55. Ibid.

56. K. C. Suri, "Parties under Pressure: Political Parties in India since Independence," paper prepared for the State of Democracy in South Asia project, 2005, http://www.democracy-asia.org/qa/india/KC%20Suri.pdf (accessed March 10, 2013).

57. Christophe Jaffrelot, *India's Silent Revolution: The Rise of the Lower Castes in North India* (New York: Columbia University Press, 2003).

58. Christophe Jaffrelot and Sanjay Kumar, eds., *Rise of the Plebeians? The Changing Face of Indian Legislative Assemblies* (New Delhi: Routledge, 2009).

59. Pratap Bhanu Mehta, "India's Disordered Democracy," *Pacific Affairs* 64, no. 4 (Winter 1991–92): 541.

60. Jha, *In the Eye of the Cyclone*, 41–42.

61. The frequency of violence grew more intense as the campaign progressed, with the bulk of violent events taking place during the actual polling. The Congress, unsurprisingly, was the most cited aggressor when one could be readily identified. The most frequent type of violence, according to the author, was "stone throwing, brick batting and throwing glass pieces." See D. N. Dhanagare, "Violence in the Fourth General Elections: A Study in Political Conflict," *Economic and Political Weekly* 3, no. 1/2 (January 1968): 151–56.

62. Ibid.

63. Election Commission of India, *Report on the Mid-Term Elections in India, 1968–69* (New Delhi: Election Commission of India, 1970), 78, http://eci.nic.in/eci_main/eci_publications/books/genr/Mid-Term%20Gen%20Election-68-69.pdf (accessed October 3, 2013).

64. Ibid.

65. Quoted in Kohli, *Democracy and Discontent*, 214.

66. Bipin Chandra, Mridula Mukherjee, and Aditya Mukherjee, *India after Independence, 1947–2000* (London: Penguin, 2000), chap. 17.

67. Myron Weiner, "The 1971 Elections and the Indian Party System," *Asian Survey* 11, no. 12 (December 1971): 1156.

68. Sudipta Kaviraj, "Indira Gandhi and Indian Politics," *Economic and Political Weekly* 21, no. 38/39 (September 20–27, 1986): 1697–1708.

69. Jha, *In the Eye of the Cyclone*, 45.

70. Ashutosh Kumar, "Middle Classes, Parties, and Electoral Politics in India," in Arun Mehra, ed., *Party System in India: Emerging Trajectories* (Atlanta: Lancer, 2013).

71. Ironically, the Congress was also guilty of refusing to dissolve its own governments even when it was obvious that they did not enjoy the support of a majority of members in the assembly. The leadership's refusal to allow its chief minister of Madhya Pradesh, D. P. Mishra, to resign in 1967 after thirty-six of his legislators

defected is the most prominent example of this. See Jha, *In the Eye of the Cyclone,* 32–33.

72. Bhagwan D. Dua, "Presidential Rule in India: A Study in Crisis Politics," *Asian Survey* 19, no. 6 (June 1979): 611–26.

73. Anoop Sadanandan, "Bridling Central Tyranny in India," *Asian Survey* 52, no. 2 (March/April 2012): 247–69.

74. Singh, *Politics of Crime and Corruption,* 17; Biplab Dasgupta, "The 1972 Election in West Bengal," *Economic and Political Weekly* 7, no. 16 (April 15, 1972): 804–8.

75. Quoted in N. S. Saksena, *India: Towards Anarchy, 1967–1992* (New Delhi: Abhinav, 1993), 35.

76. Kohli, *Democracy and Discontent,* 16.

77. Mehta, "India's Disordered Democracy," 538.

78. As political scientist Atul Kohli explains: "Personal control over a highly interventionist state has been maintained, but the interventionist arm of that state has gone limp." See Kohli, *Democracy and Discontent,* 16.

79. Lloyd I. Rudolph and Susanne Hoeber Rudolph, *In Pursuit of Lakshmi: The Political Economy of the Indian State* (Chicago: University of Chicago Press, 1987), 7. As the authors artfully wrote, "Jawaharlal Nehru was the schoolmaster of parliamentary government, Indira Gandhi its truant."

80. R. V. R. Chandrasekhara Rao, "Mrs. Indira Gandhi and India's Constitutional Structures: An Era of Erosion," in Yogendra K. Malik and Dhirendra K. Vajpeyi, eds., *India: The Years of Indira Gandhi* (New York: E. J. Brill, 1988), 28.

81. David H. Bayley, "The Police and Political Order in India," *Asian Survey* 23, no. 4 (April 1983): 484.

82. Ibid., 487.

83. Henry C. Hart, "Political Leadership in India: Dimensions and Limits," in Atul Kohli, ed., *India's Democracy: An Analysis of Changing State-Society Relations* (Princeton: Princeton University Press, 1988), 23.

84. Arvind N. Das, "Landowners' Armies Take Over 'Law and Order,'" *Economic and Political Weekly* 21, no. 1 (January 4, 1986): 15–18.

85. Jayant Lele, "Saffronisation of Shiv Sena: Political Economy of City, State and Nation," *Economic and Political Weekly* 30, no. 25 (June 24, 1995): 1520.

86. Thomas Blom Hansen, "Politics as Permanent Performance: The Production of Political Authority in the Locality," in John Zavos, Andrew Wyatt, and Vernon Marston Hewitt, eds., *The Politics of Cultural Mobilization in India* (New Delhi: Oxford University Press, 2004), 26.

87. Ibid., 28–29.

88. Ashwani Kumar, *Community Warriors: State, Peasants and Caste Armies in Bihar* (London: Anthem Press, 2008).

89. Ibid., 131–33.

90. Kohli, *Democracy and Discontent;* Manor, "Changing State, Changing Society."

91. Venu Menon, "The Politics of Blood," *Rediff,* March 21, 1997, http://www.rediff.com/news/mar/21venu.htm (accessed November 17, 2015).

92. In the next chapter, I examine the connections between money and muscle more methodically, using data from the contemporary period to establish precise

linkages. But in this section, I sketch out the evolution of India's system of election finance, its changing nature in the first few decades after independence, and connections with criminality.

93. Chandan Mitra, *The Corrupt Society: The Criminalization of India from Independence to the 1990s* (New Delhi: Viking, 1998), 75.

94. Yogendra K. Malik, "Political Finance in India," *Political Quarterly* 60 no. 1 (January 1989): 75–94.

95. Election Commission of India, *Report on the Second General Elections in India, 1957* (New Delhi: Election Commission of India, 1959), 187, http://eci .nic.in/eci_main/eci_publications/books/genr/Report%20on%20the%202nd%20 Gen%20Election-57.pdf (accessed November 11, 2013).

96. Stanley A. Kochanek, "Briefcase Politics in India: The Congress Party and the Business Elite," *Asian Survey* 27, no. 12 (December 1987): 1278–1301.

97. Ibid.

98. Rahul Mukherji reports that businessmen were an important source of election funding in the immediate post-independence era. Leading businessmen, such as G. D. Birla, helped mobilize Indian industry in support of the Congress during the election years of 1952 and 1957. See Rahul Mukherji, "The State, Economic Growth, and Development in India," *India Review* 8, no. 1 (February 2009): 85.

99. Malik, "Political Finance in India," 77. Of course, even in the early days of the republic not all corporations disclosed their political contributions, considering they often gave in excess of the impossibly low contribution limits permitted by law and feared retribution from parties to which they did not give. Furthermore, due to legislative loopholes, candidates did not have to report expenses incurred by third parties. See Kochanek, "Briefcase Politics in India," 1285–86.

100. Krishna K. Tummala, "Combating Corruption: Lessons Out of India," *International Public Management Review* 10, no. 1 (2009): 41.

101. This feeling of insecurity was further fueled by the Congress's poll debacle in 1967.

102. Gandhi also managed to persuade Parliament to amend the constitution to revoke the right of India's erstwhile princely rulers to their "privy purses," a constitutional compromise that was integral to convincing the rulers of India's princely states to accede to the Union. Gandhi was irate that the former princes were using their influence to prop up the right-of-center opposition Swatantra Party.

103. Jha, *In the Eye of the Cyclone,* 39.

104. The inflow of black money into the electoral domain was discussed by the 1971 report of the government-appointed Wanchoo Direct Taxes Enquiry Committee.

105. Sridharan and Vaishnav, "India."

106. In advance of the 1971 general elections, Congress trade minister L. N. Mishra granted 700 import licenses in just three weeks, presumably in exchange for a timely infusion of election funds. See Suman Sahai, "'Hawala' Politics: A Congress Legacy," *Economic and Political Weekly* 31, no. 5 (February 3, 1996): 253–54.

107. Krishan Bhatia, *Indira: A Biography of Prime Minister Gandhi* (Santa Barbara: Praeger, 1974), 267.

108. Ibid.

109. Manor, "Party Decay and Political Crisis in India," 34.

110. Jha, *In the Eye of the Cyclone,* 38–42.

111. Sahai, "'Hawala' Politics,'" 253.

112. Jha, *In the Eye of the Cyclone,* 40.

113. M. V. Rajeev Gowda and E. Sridharan, "Reforming India's Party Financing and Election Expenditure Laws," *Election Law Journal* 11, no. 2 (June 2012): 226–40.

114. Sridharan and Vaishnav, "India."

115. Inaugural Speech by Congress President Rajiv Gandhi at the Congress Party Centenary Session, Bombay, India, December 27–29, 1985, http://rajivgandhistudycircle.com/rajiv_vision.php (accessed June 10, 2015).

116. Malik, "Political Finance in India," 85.

117. Andrew Sanchez, "Corruption in India," in Nicholas Kitchen, ed., *India: The Next Superpower?* (London: London School of Economics and Political Science, 2012), 51.

118. National Commission to Review the Working of the Constitution, "Review of the Working of Political Parties Specially in Relation to Elections and Reform Options," NCRWC Consultation Paper, January 8, 2011, http://lawmin.nic.in/ncrwc/finalreport/v2b1–8.htm (accessed June 1, 2015).

119. Robert Hardgrave and Stanley Kochanek, *India: Government and Politics in a Developing Nation* (Boston: Thomson, 2007), 342.

120. *Dada* is perhaps the most commonly heard moniker for a criminal who possesses real political power, even in non-Hindi-speaking regions. In Bengal, such figures are often called *mastans*. In Tamil, people often speak of someone who is a *porukki,* literally a "rowdy." But this more closely resembles a *goonda* than a *dada,* who is someone who is higher up the criminal food chain.

121. S. S. Gill, *The Pathology of Corruption* (New Delhi: HarperCollins India, 1999), 192–93.

122. Chandra, Mukherjee, and Mukherjee, *India after Independence,* 311–31.

123. Yogendra K. Malik, "Indira Gandhi: Personality, Political Power and Party Politics," in Yogendra K. Malik and Dhirendra K. Vajpeyi, eds., *India: The Years of Indira Gandhi* (New York: E. J. Brill, 1988), 15.

124. This definition of "Sanjay culture" comes from scholar Atul Kohli. See Kohli, *Democracy and Discontent,* 57.

125. The ECI reported at least 72 cases of booth capturing in the post-Emergency elections of 1977. See Election Commission of India, *Report on the Sixth General Elections to the Lok Sabha and General Elections to the Kerala Legislative Assembly 1977* (New Delhi: Election Commission of India, 1978), http://eci.nic.in/eci_main/eci_publications/books/genr/GenElection-Kerala-Vol-I-77.pdf (accessed March 25, 2013).

126. Oliver E. Williamson, "The Vertical Integration of Production: Market Failure Considerations," *American Economic Review* 61, no. 2 (May 1971): 112–23.

127. Sanjay Kumar, Shreyas Sardesai, and Pranav Gupta, "The Weakening of Electoral Anti-Incumbency," *Economic and Political Weekly* 48, no. 13 (March 2013): 128–31.

128. For instance, when V. P. Singh became chief minister of Uttar Pradesh in 1980 he took strong action against the state's dacoit gangs, despite the fact that

many gang leaders were well connected to Singh's Janata Party. The gang leaders' collective response, Prem Shankar Jha notes, was not to retreat but to join politics to ensure their safety. See Prem Shankar Jha, "How Did India Become a Predatory State," n.d., on file with the author.

129. Robert Wade, "The System of Administrative and Political Corruption: Canal Irrigation in South India," *Journal of Development Studies* 18, no. 3 (1982): 287–328; Frank de Zwart, *The Bureaucratic Merry-Go-Round: Manipulating the Transfer of Indian Civil Servants* (Amsterdam: Amsterdam University Press, 1994); Iyer and Mani, "Traveling Agents."

130. *Shri Ganesh Narayan Hegde vs. Shri S. Bangarappa and Others* (1995) 4 SCC 41.

131. In such instances, politics becomes the arena through which rivalries play themselves out. As a former chief election commissioner of India once remarked, "Whether it is money or criminals, both are competitive phenomena. If a criminal is put up as a candidate by one party the other party feels very disadvantaged. They feel they have no chance until a bigger dada is put up against them." Sreenivasan Jain, "Elections Have Become the Biggest Source of Corruption: SY Qureshi," NDTV, November 14, 2011, http://www.ndtv.com/india-news/elections-have -become-the-biggest-source-of-corruption-sy-qureshi-468841 (accessed November 17, 2011). One voter in the Pratapgarh constituency of Uttar Pradesh, a district known for its warring politically connected gangs, described the scenario aptly: "It is a fight not between candidates and how good they are, or how much development the Congress party or anyone else promises to bring, but between *goonda* and *goonda.*" See Jyoti Malhotra, "Who Will Clean Up Filthy and Feudal Pratapgarh?" *Rediff,* April 23, 2009, http://www.rediff.com/election/2009/apr/23loksabhapolls -who-will-clean-filthy-pratapgarh.htm (accessed May 15, 2009).

132. This is analogous to how unregistered firms operate where informal economies, which operate outside of the ambit of the law, thrive.

133. Quoted in Jose J. Nedumpara, *Political Economy and Class Contradictions: A Study* (New Delhi: Anmol Publications, 2004). Ashok Samrat is commonly referred to as a "dreaded criminal of north Bihar." See, inter alia, Ramashankar, "Flying like a Phoenix," *Telegraph* (Calcutta), November 11, 2010.

134. Of the 1995 party-backed candidates facing criminal charges contesting in the 2004, 2009, and 2014 general elections, 23 percent were ultimately successful. In contrast, only .49 percent of independent candidates with criminal records—or just three candidates—achieved success.

135. S. K. Ghosh, *The Indian Mafia* (New Delhi: Ashish, 1991), vi.

136. Bhan, *Criminalization of Politics,* 25.

137. Indu Bharti, "Usurpation of the State: Coal Mafia in Bihar," *Economic and Political Weekly* 24, no. 42 (October 21, 1989): 2353.

138. Hiranmay Dhar, "Gangsters and Politicians in Dhanbad," *Economic and Political Weekly* 14, no. 15 (April 14, 1979): 690–91.

139. Hardgrave and Kochanek, *India,* 390.

140. Ghosh, *Indian Mafia,* 12.

141. Liza Weinstein, "Mumbai's Development Mafias: Globalization, Organized Crime and Land Development," *International Journal of Urban and Regional Research* 32, no. 1 (March 2008): 22–39.

142. Thomas Blom Hansen, *Wages of Violence: Naming and Identity in Post-colonial Bombay* (Princeton: Princeton University Press, 2001), 54–55.

143. Ibid., 99.

144. Jaffrelot, "Indian Democracy," 100.

145. Ornit Shani, "Bootlegging, Politics and Corruption: State Violence and the Routine Practices of Public Power in Gujarat, 1985–2002," in Nalin Mehta and Mona G. Mehta, eds., *Gujarat beyond Gandhi: Identity, Society and Conflict* (New Delhi: Routledge, 2013), 33.

146. Howard Spodek, "Crisis and Response: Ahmedabad 2000," *Economic and Political Weekly* 36, no. 19 (May 12–18, 2001): 1629.

147. Shani, "Bootlegging, Politics and Corruption," 33.

148. According to K. Balagopal, each faction is organized like a pyramid, with MLAs on top; contractors, smugglers and shady businessmen in the middle; and village landlords at the base. "From the village sarpanch to the MLA, most of the elected representatives today are leaders of gangs armed to the teeth." See Balagopal, "Seshan in Kurnool."

149. Ravi's life was later immortalized in the loosely fictionalized film *Rakhta Charitra,* which chronicled the dramatic evolution of a murderous bandit who decides to become a politician.

150. "A Saga of [a] Chilling Feud between Two Families of Anantapur," Indo-Asian News Service, January 4, 2011, https://in.news.yahoo.com/saga-chilling-feud-between-two-families-anantapur-20110104-042647-540.html (accessed April 20, 2016).

151. Rajeev P.I., "In Andhra's Samurai Country, Ravi Was Always a Cut Above," *Indian Express,* January 31, 2005.

152. K. Balagopal, "A Tough Law for Other People's Crime," *Economic and Political Weekly* 36, no. 16 (April 21–27, 2001): 1285–89.

153. Ibid.

154. Ahead of the 2004 Andhra Pradesh state assembly election, which would be his last electoral contest, Ravi disclosed two ongoing cases in his election affidavit.

155. Gill, *Pathology of Corruption,* 203–4.

156. Rudolph and Rudolph, *In Pursuit of Lakshmi,* 85; William Stevens, "India Politics: The Sun Sets on Old Ways," *New York Times,* November 26, 1984. According to many analysts, Sanjay Gandhi was principally responsible for giving Congress Party tickets to "lumpen elements," though the party did not fully repudiate this tactic after his death nor did other parties desist from engaging in similar activity.

157. Ibid., 141; Sumanta Banerjee, "Serenading the Emergency," *Economic and Political Weekly* 35, no. 26 (June 24–30, 2000): 2205–6.

158. Anil Coomar Maheshwari, "Uttar Pradesh: Rigging in Practice," *Economic and Political Weekly* 15, no. 3 (January 19, 1980): 99.

159. Ibid.

160. Nalini Singh, "Elections as They Really Are," *Economic and Political Weekly* 15, no. 21 (May 24, 1980): 909.

161. Election Commission of India, *Second Annual Report, 1984* (New Delhi: Election Commission of India, 1985), 46, http://eci.nic.in/eci_main/eci_publications/books/genr/ECI-ANNUAL%20REPORT-84.pdf (accessed February 12, 2014).

In the 1983 by-elections, the ECI reported 173 complaints, most having to do with the alleged misuse of official machinery, booth capturing and intimidation, harassment of party workers and voters, and breakdown of law and order. The incidents were spread across a number of states, with Tamil Nadu, Karnataka, Uttar Pradesh, and Bihar topping the list. See Election Commission of India, *First Annual Report, 1983* (New Delhi: Election Commission of India, 1984), 47, http://eci.nic.in/eci_main/eci_publications/books/genr/First%20Annual%20Report-83.pdf (accessed February 12, 2014).

162. Agarwalla, *Contemporary India and Its Burning Problems.* Even the states in India's far-flung northeast were not left untouched by electoral irregularities. See "Parliamentary Elections: Tripura Style," *Economic and Political Weekly* 24, no. 50 (December 16, 1989): 2757–58.

163. Gill, *Pathology of Corruption,* 190.

164. Ibid.

165. Ibid., 192.

166. Subhash Mishra, "A Criminal Record," *India Today,* November 1, 2004.

167. Ministry of Home Affairs, Government of India, *Final Report of the Vohra Committee* (New Delhi: Government of India, 2005), http://adrindia.org/sites/default/files/VOHRA%20COMMITTEE%20REPORT_0.pdf (accessed April 20, 2016).

168. Jaffrelot, "Indian Democracy," 112–13.

169. Ibid.

170. Devesh Kapur, "Explaining Democratic Durability and Economic Performance: The Role of India's Institutions," in Devesh Kapur and Pratap Bhanu Mehta, eds., *Public Institutions in India: Performance and Design* (New Delhi: Oxford University Press, 2005), chap. 1.

171. Sridharan and Vaishnav, "India."

172. For his efforts, Seshan was dubbed a "middle-class hero," although many argued that his draconian measures to clean up politics led to an accumulation of almost "Orwellian power." See David Gilmartin, "One Day's Sultan: T. N. Seshan and Indian Democracy," *Contributions to Indian Sociology* 43, no. 2 (May–August 2009): 247–84; and Ujjwal Kumar Singh, "Between Moral Force and Supplementary Legality: A Model Code of Conduct and the Election Commission of India," *Election Law Journal* 11, no. 2 (June 2012): 165. Seshan's critics argued that he believed (mistakenly, in their view) that he could "hold the election process to a higher morality than existed in 'normal' political life." See Gilmartin, "One Day's Sultan," 271.

173. Specifically, 36 percent of the MLA respondents believed politicians were mainly responsible. This was the modal response. See Vir K. Chopra, *Marginal Players in Marginal Assemblies: The Indian MLA* (New Delhi: Orient Longman, 1996), 269–71.

174. Balagopal, "Seshan in Kurnool," 1904.

175. Manor, "Changing State, Changing Society."

176. Kumar, *Community Warriors,* 174.

177. Aman Sethi, "Rule of the Outlaw," *Frontline,* December 17–30, 2005; Alka Pande, "A Slice of Sicily," *Outlook,* December 19, 2005; Andrew MacAskill and

Kartikay Mehrotra, "Jailed Lawmakers Rule in India as Crime Brings Few Punishments," *Bloomberg Business,* March 5, 2012.

178. "Ansaris Launch Own Political Outfit, Will Contest Polls," *Indian Express,* August 9, 2010; Andrew MacAskill and Kartikay Mehrotra, "Indian Jailbirds Win Election," *Bloomberg Business,* March 8, 2012. At the time of his election in 2012, Mukhtar Ansari had no fewer than 15 cases pending, including at least 8 charges of murder or attempted murder, according to the affidavit he submitted to the Election Commission of India.

179. Patrick French, *India: A Portrait* (New York: Knopf, 2011), 264.

180. MacAskill and Mehrotra, "Jailed Lawmakers Rule in India."

181. An entire book could be written about the cultural iconography of criminal politicians in Indian cinema. In addition to Bollywood films on the subject, such as *Gangs of Wasseypur, Gangaajal,* and *Godmother,* there are a number of films from regional cinema that have focused on the issue of criminality in politics, including *Subramaniapuram* and *Jigarthanda* (Tamil), *MLA Fatakeshto* and the sequel, *Minister Fatakeshto* (Bengali), *Rakhta Charitra* (Telugu/Hindi), and so on.

CHAPTER 4. THE COSTS OF DEMOCRACY

1. Select quotes from this section, drawn from the author's interviews in Andhra Pradesh, previously appeared in Milan Vaishnav, "Votes for Crooks and Cricket Stars," *New York Times,* May 10, 2014.

2. As it turned out, Andhra Pradesh was in the process of breaking up into two states, the newly created Telangana and the rump state of Seemandhra. As a result of the bifurcation, which was bitterly opposed by many residents of Seemandhra, elections had taken on an even more electrifying air than usual.

3. In Tamil Nadu, it is rumored that candidates will sometimes pump bicycle tires with alcohol or stash booze in hidden compartments of milk and water tankers to evade detection during election eve distribution. See Abheek Barman, "How Political Parties Try to Get Past EC Guidelines to Fish for Votes," *Economic Times,* April 3, 2011.

4. A similar strategy was reported in a cable authored by a U.S. diplomat who followed the 2008 elections in Karnataka, and later made public by Wikileaks. See U.S. Consulate Chennai, "A Night on Karnataka's Campaign Trail," diplomatic cable, May 9, 2008, https://wikileaks.org/plusd/cables/08CHENNAI170_a.html (accessed January 10, 2015).

5. Paul R. Brass, *Factional Politics in an Indian State: The Congress Party in Uttar Pradesh* (Los Angeles: University of California Press, 1965), 1.

6. Zoya Hasan, "Political Parties in India," in Niraja Gopal Jayal and Pratap Bhanu Mehta, eds., *The Oxford Companion to Politics in India* (Oxford: Oxford University Press, 2010), 241.

7. Panu Poutvaara and Tuomas Takalo, "Candidate Quality," *International Tax and Public Finance* 14, no. 1 (February 2007): 7–27.

8. Analyses of candidates who contested state elections between 2003 and 2009 also show a striking prevalence of candidates with criminal cases, including those of a serious nature, across leading parties.

9. Author's calculations based on affidavits submitted to the Election Commission of India by candidates contesting state elections between 2003 and 2009.

10. Ibid.

11. "Bad politician" is something of a misnomer; candidates involved in wrongdoing may be badly behaved, but they can actually be "good" politicians in the sense of being successful and even effective representatives.

12. Vincenzo Galasso and Tommaso Nannicini, "Competing on Good Politicians," *American Political Science Review* 105, no. 1 (February 2011): 79–99.

13. Toke Aidt, Miriam Golden, and Devesh Tewari, "Criminal Candidate Selection for the Indian National Legislature," unpublished paper, Department of Political Science, University of California–Los Angeles, March 2015, http://media.wix.com/ugd/o2c1bf_b515ef1dc03b4fooa58a6b4c48043f38.pdf (accessed April 22, 2016).

14. Ibid.; Timothy Besley, *Principled Agents? The Political Economy of Good Government* (Oxford: Oxford University Press, 2006).

15. Timothy Besley, "Political Selection," *Journal of Economic Perspectives* 19, no. 3 (Summer 2005): 43–60.

16. Donald R. Matthews, "Legislative Recruitment and Legislative Careers," *Legislative Studies Quarterly* 9, no. 4 (November 1984): 549.

17. Besley, "Political Selection."

18. Ibid.

19. Adam Ziegfeld, "Coalition Government and Party System Change: Explaining the Rise of Regional Parties in India," *Comparative Politics* 45, no. 1 (October 2012): 69–87.

20. Mark Schneider, "Does Clientelism Work? A Test of Guessability in India," Center for the Advanced Study of India Working Paper 14–01, University of Pennsylvania, September 2014.

21. Lloyd I. Rudolph and Susanne Hoeber Rudolph, *In Pursuit of Lakshmi: The Political Economy of the Indian State* (Chicago: University of Chicago Press, 1987), 135.

22. Liquor is a perennial favorite pre-election inducement because of its great popular demand and the ease of supply. Because government tightly regulates the liquor industry, the latter has notoriously cozy links with the political class. Entrepreneurs in the liquor industry rely on the state for licenses to produce and sell alcoholic products as well as to gain access to needed ingredients (such as molasses). Politicians can regulate the supply of inputs to help favored firms, limit market participants, and falsify excise duty payments in exchange for payments and election-time "donations." For more on the liquor industry's links with the state, see Mehboob Jeelani, "Under the Influence," *Caravan*, November 1, 2013; and Raghu Karnad, "City in a Bottle," *Caravan*, July 1, 2012.

23. Mayank Mishra and Satyavrat Mishra, "The 2015 Money Race: Paying the Price for an Election Bout," *Business Standard*, July 7, 2015.

24. PRS Legislative Research has compiled a useful primer on India's election finance laws and regulations. See Namita Wahi, "Draft Discussion Paper: Regulation of Campaign Finance," Social Science Research Network, August 12, 2008, http://papers.ssrn.com/sol3/papers.cfm?abstract_id=2297767 (accessed April 21, 2016).

25. M. V. Rajeev Gowda and E. Sridharan, "Reforming India's Party Financing and Election Expenditure Laws," *Election Law Journal* 11, no. 2 (June 2012): 231.

26. Also excluded from the ECI's candidate expenditure limits is travel expenditure incurred by party leaders for purposes of propagating the party program.

27. As an example of the brazenness on display, in April 2016 the ruling BJP government planned to introduce a retrospective amendment to the Foreign Contribution (Regulation) Act, 2010 (also known as FCRA). The government proposed the legislation in response to lawsuits brought against the BJP and the Congress, accusing them of accepting foreign funds. The proposed amendment would retroactively alter the definition of a "foreign" company in India. See Anuja, Remya Nair, and Shreeja Sen, "Move to Legalize Donations from Foreign Sources to Benefit Parties," *Mint,* April 9, 2016 (accessed April 20, 2016).

28. Gowda and Sridharan, "Reforming India's Party Financing and Election Expenditure Laws."

29. National Commission to Review the Working of the Constitution, *Final Report: Volume 1* (New Delhi: Ministry of Law and Justice, 2002), chap. 4, http://lawmin.nic.in/ncrwc/finalreport/volume1.htm (accessed June 13, 2013).

30. Election Commission of India, *Report on the Third General Elections in India, 1962* (New Delhi: Election Commission of India, 1965), 93, http://eci.nic.in/eci_main/eci_publications/books/genr/ThirdGenElection-Vol-I-62.pdf (accessed January 22, 2015).

31. U.S. Consulate Chennai, "Cash for Votes in South India," diplomatic cable, May 13, 2009, https://wikileaks.org/plusd/cables/09CHENNAI144_a.html (accessed January 10, 2015).

32. Quoted in Yogendra K. Malik, "Political Finance in India," *Political Quarterly* 60, no. 1 (January 1989): 88.

33. Association for Democratic Reforms, "Analysis of Election Expenditure Statements of MPs 2014 Lok Sabha Elections," August 1, 2014, http://adrindia.org/download/file/fid/4709 (accessed August 7, 2014).

34. Ibid.

35. V. B. Singh, "Grass Roots Political Process: Atraulia Constituency," *Economic and Political Weekly* 31, no. 2/3 (January 13–20, 1996): 125.

36. Vir K. Chopra, *Marginal Players in Marginal Assemblies: The Indian MLA* (New Delhi: Orient Longman, 1996), 176. A 2001 consultation paper written for the National Commission to Review the Working of the Constitution estimated that actual election spending is easily twenty to thirty times the allowable limit. See National Commission to Review the Working of the Constitution, "Review of Election Law, Processes, and Electoral Reforms," Consultation Paper, January 8, 2001, http://lawmin.nic.in/ncrwc/finalreport/v2b1-9.htm (accessed September 15, 2013).

37. E. Sridharan, "Electoral Finance Reform: The Relevance of International Experience," in Vikram Chand, ed., *Reinventing Public Service Delivery in India: Selected Case Studies* (New Delhi: Sage Publications, 2006).

38. Arun Kumar, *The Black Economy in India* (New Delhi: Penguin, 2002).

39. Bhavdeep Kang, "Inside Story: How Political Parties Raise Money," *Yahoo! News India,* September 25, 2013, https://in.news.yahoo.com/inside-story—how-political-parties-raise-money-091455119.html (accessed October 1, 2013).

40. The 2014 study on election spending was carried out by the New Delhi–based Centre for Media Studies. See Sruthi Gottipati and Rajesh Kumar Singh, "India Set to Challenge U.S. for Election-Spending Record," Reuters, March 9, 2014, http://www.reuters.com/article/us-india-election-spending-idUSBREA280AR20140309 (accessed March 10, 2014).

41. Internal surveys of Congress Party elites conducted in 1967 and 1993 demonstrated that very little changed in the intervening two and a half decades. In 1993, party members remained weakly identified with the party and its ideology and rated the organization as ineffective. See Pradeep Chhibber, *Democracy without Associations: Transformation of the Party System and Social Cleavages in India* (Ann Arbor: University of Michigan Press, 1999).

42. Ibid., 77.

43. Ibid.

44. Malik, "Political Finance in India," 83.

45. The source for the information on membership fees comes from the websites of the respective political parties.

46. Ruchika Singh, "Intra-Party Democracy and Indian Political Parties," Hindu Centre for Public Policy Report No. 7, 2015, http://www.thehinducentre.com/publications/policy-report/article6912772.ece (accessed January 2, 2016).

47. Kedar Nath Kumar, *Political Parties in India, Their Ideology and Organisation* (New Delhi: Mittal, 1990), 335.

48. While the lack of internal party democracy within the Congress has been well established, political scientist Zoya Hasan points out that the BJP has not had a contest for the post of party president since its inception in 1980. See Hasan, "Political Parties in India," 249.

49. Singh, "Intra-Party Democracy and Indian Political Parties," 7.

50. Suhas Palshikar, "Revisiting State Level Parties," *Economic and Political Weekly* 39, no. 14/15 (April 3–16, 2014): 1478.

51. Kanchan Chandra and Wamiq Umaira, "India's Democratic Dynasties," *Seminar* 622 (June 2011), http://india-seminar.com/2011/622/622_kanchan_&_wamiq.htm (accessed July 3, 2012).

52. For instance, weeks before critical state elections in 2010, I watched the parliamentary board of a leading opposition party in the state of Bihar (Rashtriya Janata Dal, or RJD) pass a resolution that empowered its party president, former chief minister Lalu Prasad Yadav, to select each of the party's 168 candidates on his own. Indeed, one longtime scholar of Bihar had earlier commented that "no substantial decision-making" took place at the Janata Dal's Patna headquarters (Janata Dal was the predecessor to the RJD). Instead, all major decisions came out of informal sessions with Lalu Prasad Yadav, often at his personal residence. See Jeffrey Witsoe, "Social Justice and Stalled Development: Caste Empowerment and the Breakdown of Governance in Bihar," India in Transition: Economics and Politics of Change series, Center for the Advanced Study of India, University of Pennsylvania, Spring 2006.

53. Adnan Farooqui and E. Sridharan, "Incumbency, Internal Processes and Re-nomination in Indian Parties," *Commonwealth and Comparative Politics* 52, no. 1 (2014): 78–108.

54. Chandra and Umaira, "India's Democratic Dynasties."

55. Kanchan Chandra, "Hardly the End of Dynastic Rule," *Economic and Political Weekly* 49, no. 28 (July 2014): 25–28; Rukmini S., "They Have Politics in Their DNA," *Hindu*, June 9, 2014.

56. Kanchan Chandra, "Hardly the End of Dynastic Rule"; Patrick French, *India: A Portrait* (London: Alfred A. Knopf, 2011).

57. Motilal Nehru, a prominent lawyer involved in the nationalist struggle, was the president of the Congress Party on two occasions prior to India's independence (1919–20, 1928–29). His son, Jawaharlal, was India's first post-independence prince minister, a position he held from 1947 until his death in 1964. Jawaharlal's daughter, Indira Gandhi, served as prime minister from 1966 to 1977, and again from 1980 to 1984. She was succeeded by her son Rajiv, who was prime minister from Indira's death in 1984 until 1989. In 1998, Rajiv's widow, Sonia, assumed the presidency of the Congress, although she turned down the job of the prime minister in 2004. In 2014, Sonia Gandhi remains Congress president, and her son, Rahul, who assumed the party vice presidency in 2013, is widely believed to be her successor.

58. Powerful families like the Abdullahs (National Conference, Jammu and Kashmir); Pawars (Nationalist Congress Party, Maharashtra); Badals (Akali Dal, Punjab); Karunanidhis (Dravida Munnetra Kazhagam, Tamil Nadu); or the Yadavs (Samajwadi Party, Uttar Pradesh) dominate key regional parties. Even parties that are not directly controlled by dynasties exhibit similar tendencies at more local levels.

59. Sumanta Banerjee, "Politics sans Ideology," *Economic and Political Weekly* 39, no. 12 (March 20, 2004): 1204–7.

60. Pratap Bhanu Mehta, "Reform Political Parties First," *Seminar* 497 (January 2001), http://www.india-seminar.com/2001/497/497%20pratap%20bhanu%20 mehta.htm (accessed March 7, 2011).

61. J. V. Deshpande, "Assembly Elections: Winnability Is All," *Economic and Political Weekly* 28, no. 46/47 (November 13–20, 1993): 2505.

62. P. M. Kamath, "Politics of Defection in India in the 1980s," *Asian Survey* 25, no. 10 (October 1985): 1049.

63. One press report discusses the illustrative example of Sukhdarshan Singh Marar, a state politician from Punjab. In 2002, Marar angled for a ticket from the Shiromani Akali Dal (SAD) but was refused by the party high command. He succeeded in winning elections as an independent, rejoined the SAD, but later jumped ship and moved to the Congress midway through his term. Two days after elections were announced in 2007, Marar quit Congress and rejoined the SAD, which rewarded him with a party ticket. In just five years, Marar had changed party affiliations four times. See "Punjab Polls: Turncoats Have a Field Day," Press Trust of India, January 22, 2007, http://timesofindia.indiatimes.com/india/Punjab-polls -Turncoats-have-a-field-day/articleshow/1363650.cms (accessed April 21, 2013).

64. K. C. Suri, "Parties under Pressure: Political Parties in India since Independence," paper prepared for the State of Democracy in South Asia project, 2005, http:// www.democracy-asia.org/qa/india/KC%20Suri.pdf (accessed March 10, 2013).

65. Ashutosh Varshney, *Ethnic Conflict and Civic Life: Hindus and Muslims in India* (New Haven: Yale University Press, 2002).

66. Hasan, "Political Parties in India," 246.

67. Sudha Pai, "From Dalit to *Savarna*: The Search for a New Social Constituency by the Bahujan Samaj Party," in Sudha Pai, ed., *Political Process in Uttar Pradesh: Identity, Economic Reforms, and Governance* (New Delhi: Pearson Education India, 2007).

68. Gyan Varma, "BJP Attempts to Woo Minorities before State Elections," *Mint,* April 27, 2015.

69. Kang, "Inside Story: How Political Parties Raise Money."

70. Chopra, *Marginal Players in Marginal Assemblies,* chap. 9.

71. Sharat Pradhan, "I Take Money for Party Tickets: Mayawati," *Rediff,* June 5, 2006, http://www.rediff.com/news/2006/jun/05maya.htm (accessed June 10, 2012); "Mayawati Admits Taking Money for Tickets," Indo-Asian News Service, October 18, 2006, http://www.india-forums.com/news/politics/6280-mayawati-admits -taking-money-for-tickets.htm (accessed November 14, 2015).

72. Farooqui and Sridharan, "Incumbency, Internal Processes and Renomination in Indian Parties."

73. Lakshmi Iyer and Subash Mishra, "Assembly Elections: Highest Bidders, Criminals, Contractors Get Tickets for Polls," *India Today,* January 21, 2002.

74. Lisa Bjorkman, "'You Can't Buy a Vote': Meanings of Money in a Mumbai Election," *American Ethnologist* 41, no. 4 (November 2014): 617–34.

75. Ibid.

76. Barman, "How Political Parties Try to Get Past EC Guidelines."

77. Bharti Jain, "Dry Gujarat Hit the Bottle Hard during Polls," *Times of India,* December 23, 2012.

78. Gopu Mohan, "On Madurai Poll Trail, Azhagiri's 'Reputation' Does the Talking," *Indian Express,* May 8, 2009.

79. U.S. Consulate Chennai, "Cash for Votes in South India," diplomatic cable, May 13, 2009, https://wikileaks.org/plusd/cables/09CHENNAI144_a.html (accessed January 10, 2015); Abheek Barman, "The Great Indian Election Bait," *Economic Times,* April 3, 2011; P. C. Vijay Kumar, "The Men Who Dare Alagiri," *Open,* April 16, 2011. The extent of the DMK's alleged vote-buying in the 2009 Thirumangalam bypoll led to observers speaking of excessive cash distribution ahead of elections as the "Thirumangalam" model. Even the former chief election commission of India, S. Y. Quraishi, later admitted that the Election Commission was "very worried about the money power [in Tamil Nadu] because during the Thirumangalam by-election, gross violations were reported." See Seema Chisti, "Idea Exchange with S. Y. Quraishi," *Indian Express,* May 29, 2011.

80. According to a leaked U.S. diplomatic cable, Karti Chidambaram, son of then-union minister P. Chidambaram, corroborated this logic. He said that distributing money is useful in buying goodwill, but it does not necessarily win elections. What money does, he claimed, is to help "put you over the top" in a close election. See U.S. Consulate Chennai, "Cash for Votes in South India."

81. Interestingly, this tactic is occasionally employed in advanced democracies such as the United States. See, for instance, David Weigel, "Arizona Congressional Race Devolves into War over Hispanic Surnames," *Slate,* June 12, 2014, http://

www.slate.com/blogs/weigel/2014/06/12/arizona_congressional_race_devolves
_into_war_over_hispanic_surnames.html (accessed May 1, 2015).

82. Kumar, *Black Economy in India,* 295.

83. Madhavi Tata, "Weight Initials," *Outlook,* May 2, 2011; A. Srinivasa Rao, "Congress Fields Namesakes to Queer Poll Pitch for Jaganmohan Reddy," *Mail Today,* April 19, 2011; "11 'Jaganmohans' Enter Kadapa Bypoll Fray," *Times of India,* April 20, 2011. Similarly, in the 2014 elections for the Bilaspur parliamentary seat in Chhattisgarh, there were five candidates in the fray named Lakhan Sahu. The BJP's Sahu was thought to be the "real candidate," whereas the other four stood as independents, allegedly encouraged to stand for election by the opposition party. Rama Lakshmi, "Sahu vs. Sahu vs. Sahu: Indian Politicians Run 'Clone' Candidates to Trick Voters," *Washington Post,* April 23, 2014.

84. Several media reports suggest that printing presses do phenomenal business around election time. For a municipal election in Odisha, local presses previously reported a doubling of demand during the campaign. Binit Jaiswal, "Banners Flex Poll Muscles," *Times of India,* January 13, 2014.

85. Bharatiya Janata Party Statement of Election Expenditure of General Election 2014 (Lok Sabha), January 12, 2015, http://eci.nic.in/eci_main/mis-Political _Parties/ContributionReports/GE_2014/Bhartiya%20Janata%20Party_combined .pdf (accessed May 21, 2015).

86. Press Council of India, "Report on Paid News," July 7, 2010, http://press council.nic.in/oldwebsite/councilreport.pdf (accessed March 15, 2014). According to one account, the report the Press Council eventually issued was heavily watered down. A leaked draft contained far more detail on the controversial practice of "paid news." See Paranjoy Guha Thakurta and K. Sreenivas Reddy, "'Paid News': The Buried Report," *Outlook* (blog), August 6, 2010, http://www.outlookindia. com/website/story/paid-news-the-buried-report/266542 (accessed April 1, 2015).

87. Anuradha Raman, "News You Can Abuse," *Outlook,* March 20, 2009.

88. After the 2014 general election, the Election Commission's media monitoring cell was able to confirm 787 cases of paid news. See Raghvendra Rao, "Paid News: EC Issues 3,100 Notices, Confirms 787 Cases," *Indian Express,* May 24, 2014.

89. In the words of M. R. Madhavan, a scholar of the Indian Parliament, "Who has access to unaccounted funds? Criminal elements. [Money] forces you into bed with criminal elements." See Simon Denyer, "Criminals Flourish in Indian Elections," *Washington Post,* March 5, 2012.

90. Jeffrey Witsoe, *Democracy against Development: Lower-Caste Politics and Political Modernity in Postcolonial India* (Chicago: University of Chicago Press, 2013).

91. Trilochan Sastry, "Towards Decriminalisation of Elections and Politics," *Economic and Political Weekly* 49, no. 1 (January 4, 2014): 38.

92. Ibid.

93. Atul Thakur, "MLA's Fortunes Grow More than All Other Investments," *Times of India,* May 19, 2011,

94. This echoes a point made in Francesco Caselli and Massimo Morelli, "Bad Politicians," *Journal of Public Economics* 88, no. 3–4 (March 2004): 759–82.

95. The winner's premium was also higher (roughly 10 percent per annum) for winners from states in the Hindi belt or that rate poorly according to standard corruption metrics.

96. Furthermore, the study looks at assets net of liabilities, a questionable decision since access to low-interest loans in India is conditioned by political access.

97. Chopra, *Marginal Players in Marginal Assemblies,* chap. 8.

98. Banerjee, "Politics sans Ideology," 1204.

99. Caselli and Morelli, "Bad Politicians."

100. Chopra, *Marginal Players in Marginal Assemblies,* 329.

101. Banerjee, "Politics sans Ideology," 1204.

102. James Manor, "Changing State, Changing Society in India," *South Asia: Journal of South Asian Studies* 25, no. 2 (2002): 231–56.

103. Ibid., 235. Christophe Jaffrelot remarks that, "[with] the growth in the financial outlay of politicians, money has become another major reason for collaborating with the underworld." See Christophe Jaffrelot, "Indian Democracy: The Rule of Law on Trial," *India Review* 1, no. 1 (January 2002): 100.

104. James Manor, "Party Decay and Political Crisis in India," *Washington Quarterly* 4, no. 3 (Summer 1981): 25–40.

105. Ward Berenschot, *Riot Politics: Hindu-Muslim Violence and the Indian State* (New York: Columbia University Press, 2012).

106. Francesca Refsum Jensenius, "Power, Performance and Bias: Evaluating the Electoral Quotas for Scheduled Castes in India" (PhD diss., University of California–Berkeley, 2013).

107. Author's interview with Congress MP from Andhra Pradesh, New Delhi, August 2009.

108. Author's interview with Bihar state treasurer of a major national party, Patna, October 2010.

109. *Association for Democratic Reforms vs. Union of India and Another* (2002), 5 SCC 294.

110. Representation of the People (Amendment) Ordinance, August 24, 2002, http://eci.nic.in/eci_main/ElectoralLaws/OrdersNotifications/Ordinance_Asset_Liabilities.pdf (accessed April 20, 2016).

111. *People's Union for Civil Liberties and Another vs. Union of India and Another, AIR (2003) SC 2363.* For a review, see Ronojoy Sen, "Identifying Criminals and Crorepatis in Indian Politics: An Analysis of Two Supreme Court Rulings," *Election Law Journal* 11, no. 2 (June 2012): 216–25.

112. In addition, the database contains information on 226 members of the Rajya Sabha, as of 2010.

113. Data from http://myneta.info.

114. Samuel Paul and M. Vivekananda, "Holding a Mirror to the New Lok Sabha," *Economic and Political Weekly* 39, no. 45 (November 6–12, 2004): 4927–34.

115. The graph of predicted probabilities was derived from a multilevel logistic regression of a binary measure of a candidate's serious criminality status on candidate wealth, in addition to other candidate and constituency characteristics. The model also included random effects parameters for administrative districts, states

and years. More detail can be found in Milan Vaishnav, "The Market for Criminality: Money, Muscle, and Elections in India" (PhD diss., Columbia University, 2012).

116. The graph depicts predicted probabilities of a multilevel logistic regression of a binary measure of electoral victory as the outcome of interest with wealth, criminality status, and their interaction as the primary independent variables of interest. The regression also controls for various candidate and constituency characteristics and includes random effects parameters for districts, states, and years.

117. Yogendra Yadav, "The Paradox of Political Representation," *Seminar* 586 (June 2008), http://www.india-seminar.com/2008/586/586_yogendra_yadav.htm (accessed July 10, 2012).

118. Aman Malik, "The Business Interests of Kamal Nath," *Mint*, April 15, 2014.

119. Vaishnav, "Votes for Crooks and Cricket Stars."

CHAPTER 5. DOING GOOD BY DOING BAD

1. "Anant Cousin Killed," *Telegraph* (Calcutta), January 9, 2008.

2. Anand S. T. Das, "All Crime and No Punishment," *Tehelka*, December 1, 2007.

3. Chinki Sinha, "The Don of Mokama," *Open,* March 29, 2014.

4. Arun Kumar, "MLA Had a Penchant for Guns and Goons," *Hindustan Times,* November 2, 2007.

5. Sinha, "Don of Mokama."

6. Ibid.

7. Residents of Mokama repeatedly told me that as long as Anant Singh held elected office, few locals would knowingly take the risk of crossing him in open court.

8. Ashish Sinha, "Guns, Dance & Power Play—Cops Recall Brush with Mokama Strongman," *Telegraph* (Calcutta), May 1, 2006; Das, "All Crime and No Punishment."

9. That Nitish Kumar backed Anant Singh was without doubt. As with most political parties in India, the party leader is the one who controls party ticket selection. It strains credulity that Singh would have received a party ticket if Kumar had opposed it. Furthermore, Kumar's reliance on Singh for mobilizing and delivering votes, especially those of upper-caste Bhumihars, in eastern Patna district has been well documented. Amit Rajsingh, "How Changing Equations May Finally Put a Stop to This Criminal Politician's Career," *Wire*, June 28, 2015, http://thewire.in/2015/06/28/how-changing-equations-may-finally-put-a-stop-to-this-criminal-politicians-career-4967/ (accessed November 14, 2015); Arun Sinha, *Nitish Kumar and the Rise of Bihar* (New Delhi: Penguin, 2011), 250; Ashok Kumar Upadhyay, "How Nitish Kumar Plays the Caste Card When It Suits Him," *Daily O,* July 15, 2015, http://www.dailyo.in/politics/nitish-kumar-bihar-assembly-polls-2015-anant-singh-sunil-pandey-jdu-caste-bhumihar-yadav/story/1/5010.html (accessed November 14, 2015).

10. Joseph A. Schumpeter, *Capitalism, Socialism, and Democracy* (New York: HarperCollins, 1962).

11. Adam Przeworski, Susan C. Stokes, and Bernard Manin, eds., *Democracy, Accountability, and Representation* (New York: Cambridge University Press, 1999).

12. Ibid., 272.

13. Torsten Persson and Guido Tabellini, *The Economic Effects of Constitutions: What Do the Data Say?* (Cambridge: MIT Press, 2003); Philip Keefer, "What Does Political Economy Tell Us about Economic Development—and Vice Versa?" *Annual Review of Political Science* 7, no. 1 (2004): 247–72; Philip Keefer and Stuti Khemani, "Democracy, Public Expenditures, and the Poor: Understanding Political Incentives for Providing Public Services," *World Bank Research Observer* 20, no. 1 (March 2005): 1–27; Philip Keefer and Razvan Vlaicu, "Democracy, Credibility, and Clientelism," *Journal of Law, Economics, and Organization* 24, no. 2 (December 2008): 371–406.

14. For a recent review of the literature, see Rohini Pande, "Can Informed Voters Enforce Better Governance? Experiments in Low-Income Democracies," *Annual Review of Economics* 3 (2011): 215–37.

15. Timothy Besley, "Political Selection," *Journal of Economic Perspectives* 19, no. 3 (Summer 2005): 43–60; Timothy Besley, *Principled Agents? The Political Economy of Good Government* (London: Oxford University Press, 2006).

16. Alícia Adserà, Carles Boix, and Mark Payne, "Are You Being Served? Political Accountability and Quality of Government," *Journal of Law, Economics, and Organization* 19, no. 2 (2003): 448.

17. Jeremy Bentham, *The Collected Works of Jeremy Bentham: Political Tactics*, ed. Michael James, Cyprian Blamires, and Catherine Pease-Watkin (Oxford: Clarendon Press, 1999), 29.

18. Amartya Sen, *Development as Freedom* (New York: Oxford University Press, 1999), 180.

19. Timothy Besley and Robin Burgess, "The Political Economy of Government Responsiveness: Theory and Evidence from India," *Quarterly Journal of Economics* 117, no. 4 (2002): 1415–51.

20. David Strömberg, "Radio's Impact on Public Spending," *Quarterly Journal of Economics* 119, no. 1 (2004), 189–221.

21. Claudio Ferraz and Federico Finan, "Exposing Corrupt Politicians: The Effects of Brazil's Publicly Released Audits on Electoral Outcomes," *Quarterly Journal of Economics* 123, no. 2 (2008): 703–45.

22. Eric C. C. Chang, Miriam A. Golden, and Seth J. Hill, "Legislative Malfeasance and Political Accountability," *World Politics* 62, no. 2 (April 2010): 177–220.

23. Center for the Study of Developing Societies, *India National Election Study 2014* (New Delhi: CSDS, 2014).

24. Two leading social activists wrote in 2004 that government authorities were doing a poor job of publicizing the affidavits and had not made them accessible enough to the average voter. See Samuel Paul and M. Vivekananda, "Holding a Mirror to the New Lok Sabha," *Economic and Political Weekly* 39, no. 45 (November 6–12, 2004): 4927.

25. Benjamin A. Olken, "Corruption Perceptions vs. Corruption Reality," *Journal of Public Economics* 93, no. 7–8 (August 2009): 950–64.

26. The information richness of rural life often contrasts with the realities of urban settings, where residents are less likely to know their neighbors or to have time to interact with fellow residents and discuss politics. One piece of suggestive evidence in this regard comes from survey data I collected in Bihar. The survey found that voters who are poorer, less educated, and live in rural areas are significantly more likely to accurately identify the caste of the candidate they supported in state elections. See Milan Vaishnav, "Ethnic Identifiability: Evidence from a Survey of Indian Voters," unpublished paper (on file with author), Carnegie Endowment for International Peace, 2015. For a historical perspective on the pervasiveness of information flows in developing societies, see Christopher A. Bayly, *Empire and Information: Intelligence Gathering and Social Communication in India, 1780–1870* (New York: Cambridge University Press, 2011).

27. Abhijit V. Banerjee, Selvin Kumar, Rohini Pande, and Felix Su, "Do Informed Voters Make Better Choices? Experimental Evidence from Urban India," working paper, Harvard Kennedy School, November 2011, https://www.hks.harvard.edu/fs/rpande/papers/DoInformedVoters_Nov11.pdf (accessed April 20, 2016).

28. Kanchan Chandra, *Why Ethnic Parties Succeed: Patronage and Ethnic Head Counts in India* (New York: Cambridge University Press, 2004).

29. "Patronage democracies," according to Chandra, are those democracies "in which the state has a relative monopoly on jobs and services, and in which elected officials enjoy significant discretion in the implementation of laws allocating the jobs and services at the disposal of the state." See Chandra, *Why Ethnic Parties Succeed.*

30. Steven I. Wilkinson, "A Constructivist Model of Ethnic Riots," in Kanchan Chandra, ed., *Constructivist Theories of Ethnic Politics* (New York: Oxford University Press, 2013), 5.

31. Several scholars have suggested that co-ethnicity induces cooperation among co-ethnics because of norms of reciprocity among group members coupled with a credible fear of sanctioning for would-be defectors. See, for instance, James Habyarimana et al., *Coethnicity: Diversity and the Dilemmas of Collective Action* (New York: Russell Sage Foundation, 2011).

32. The need to focus on candidate identity, as opposed to party brand, is a point made effectively in Simon Chauchard, "Unpacking Ethnic Preferences: Theory and Micro-Level Evidence from North India," *Comparative Political Studies* 49, no. 2 (February 2016): 253–84.

33. Zoya Hasan, "Political Parties in India," in Niraja Gopal Jayal and Pratap Bhanu Mehta, eds., *The Oxford Companion to Politics in India* (Oxford: Oxford University Press, 2010), 247.

34. Robert H. Bates, "Modernization, Ethnic Competition, and the Rationality of Politics in Contemporary Africa," in Donald Rothchild and Victor A. Olorunsola eds., *State versus Ethnic Claims: African Policy Dilemmas* (Boulder: Westview Press, 1983); Donald L. Horowitz, *Ethnic Groups in Conflict* (Berkeley: University of California Press, 1985); Chandra, *Why Ethnic Parties Succeed;* Daniel N. Posner, *Institutions and Ethnic Politics in Africa* (New York: Cambridge University Press, 2005).

35. Chandra, *Constructivist Theories of Ethnic Politics.*

36. Benn Eifert, Edward Miguel, and Daniel N. Posner, "Political Competition and Ethnic Identification in Africa," *American Journal of Political Science* 54, no. 2

(April 2010): 494–510. Other authors have found that the significance of candidates' ethnic identity as a shortcut for voters is mediated by other factors, such as the presence of cross-cutting cleavages, concerns over goods provision, partisanship, or future expectations of patronage. See, inter alia, Karen Ferree, "Explaining South Africa's Racial Census," *Journal of Politics* 68, no. 4 (November 2006): 803–15; Thad Dunning and Lauren Harrison, "Cross-Cutting Cleavages and Ethnic Voting: An Experimental Study of Cousinage in Mali," *American Political Science Review* 104, no. 1 (February 2010): 21–39.

37. Daniel N. Posner, "The Political Salience of Cultural Difference: Why Chewas and Tumbukas Are Allies in Zambia and Adversaries in Malawi," *American Political Science Review* 98, no. 4 (November 2004): 529–45.

38. M. N. Srinivas, *Caste in Modern India and Other Essays* (Mumbai: Asia Publishing House, 1962).

39. Jeffrey Witsoe, "Territorial Democracy: Caste, Dominance and Electoral Practice in Postcolonial India," *PoLAR: Political and Legal Anthropology Review* 32, no. 1 (May 2009): 64–83.

40. Ibid. In Bihar, for example, backward-caste criminal politicians emerged to help assert and protect their newfound dominance in society. Upper-caste communities responded with their own "mafia-politicians" to maintain their traditional dominance. See Jeffrey Witsoe, "Social Justice and Stalled Development: Caste Empowerment and the Breakdown of Governance in Bihar," India in Transition: Economics and Politics of Change series, Center for the Advanced Study of India, University of Pennsylvania, Spring 2006, 32.

41. Wilkinson, "Constructivist Model of Ethnic Riots," 8.

42. Ward Berenschot, "Clientelism, Trust Networks, and India's Identity Politics: Conveying Closeness in Gujarat," *Critical Asian Studies* 47, no. 1 (February 2015): 8.

43. The conventional ethnic voting logic can run into trouble in situations where voters are presented with multiple co-ethnic options. Indeed, it is often the case— in India and elsewhere—that there are multiple candidates who share a common ethnic identity standing for election in the same race. A simple co-ethnic voting logic cannot account for how voters behave under these circumstances because voters are not selecting only on the basis of identity but also on the basis of who among their co-ethnics—in their view—can most effectively serve their interests. If candidates share an ethnic identity, voters have to depend on some other reliable signal in order to determine who is most likely to be the most credible co-ethnic candidate. This is where criminality can offer an advantage.

44. "Ramanand to Fight on RJD Ticket from Danapur," *Times of India,* May 9, 2002.

45. Interestingly, all three of these possibilities are found in the literature on political violence. See, for example, Steven Rosenzweig, "Dangerous Disconnect: How Politicians' Misperceptions about Voters Lead to Violence in Kenya," unpublished paper, Department of Political Science, Yale University, February 2016.

46. Federico Varese, "Protection and Extortion," in Letizia Paoli, ed., *The Oxford Handbook of Organized Crime* (Oxford: Oxford University Press, 2014), 343–58.

47. For discussions of the "politics of dignity," see Myron Weiner, "The Struggle for Equality: Caste in Indian Politics," in Atul Kohli, ed., *The Success of India's Democracy* (New York: Cambridge University Press, 2001); and Vijayendra Rao and Paromita Sanyal, "Dignity through Discourse: Poverty and the Culture of Deliberation in Indian Village Democracies," *Annals of the American Academy of Political and Social Science* 629, no. 1 (2010): 146–72.

48. As Ashutosh Varshney notes, the "politics of dignity" has played a powerful role in ethnic mobilization in post-independence India. Ashutosh Varshney, "Is India Becoming More Democratic?" *Journal of Asian Studies* 59, no. 1 (2000): 3–25.

49. Horowitz, *Ethnic Groups in Conflict.*

50. Ibid., 185.

51. Wilkinson, "Constructivist Model of Ethnic Riots."

52. The strategic use of violence to achieve political ends is nicely summarized in Rosenzweig, "Dangerous Disconnect."

53. Author's interview with deputy president of Bihar unit of a major national party, Patna, October 2010.

54. Francine R. Frankel, "Caste, Land and Dominance in Bihar," in Francine R. Frankel and M. S. A. Rao, eds., *Dominance and State Power in Modern India: Decline of a Social Order*, vol. 1 (New Delhi: Oxford University Press, 1990).

55. Sanjay Kumar, Mohammad Sanjeer Alam, and Dhananjai Joshi, "Caste Dynamics and Political Process in Bihar," *Journal of Indian School of Political Economy* (January–June 2008): 1–32; Harry W. Blair, "Caste and the British Census in Bihar: Using Old Data to Study Contemporary Political Behavior," in Norman Gerald Barrier, ed., *The Census in British India: New Perspectives* (New Delhi: Manohar, 1981); Abhijit Banerjee and Lakshmi Iyer, "History, Institutions, and Economic Performance: The Legacy of Colonial Land Tenure Systems in India," *American Economic Review* 95, no. 4 (September 2005): 1190–1213.

56. As a group, upper castes are—and have always been—heterogeneous; indeed, factionalism has been rife both within and among the ruling castes. Yet pragmatic political considerations as well as the nationalist struggle often united them under the umbrella of the Congress Party.

57. Frankel, "Caste, Land and Dominance in Bihar," 95.

58. Blair, "Caste and the British Census in Bihar."

59. Most upper-caste landowners had long-standing alliances with the Congress Party in which state patronage was exchanged for the votes of villagers beholden to the landlords. Landlords controlled vote banks through mechanisms of self-interest as well as coercion. See Frankel, "Caste, Land and Dominance in Bihar," 123.

60. Janata Dal would later split, with Lalu Prasad Yadav forming a new party known as Rashtriya Janata Dal (RJD), which became his personal fiefdom.

61. It is difficult to overstate the heightened insecurity upper-caste elites began to feel once Lalu Yadav came to power. From their perspective, their once-dominant position in society was in danger of total extinction. Lalu himself used grand rhetoric to deepen these feelings of concern, once confiding to a journalist, "The upper castes want to get rid of me, but I will sit on their chests for another twenty years, . . . I have changed things forever. I have given them [the backward castes] a sense of self-respect. Nobody can stop them." See Sankarshan Thakur, *Subaltern Saheb: Bihar and the Making of Laloo Yadav* (New Delhi: Picador, 2006), 108.

62. Santhosh Mathew and Mick Moore, "State Incapacity by Design: Understanding the Bihar Story," IDS Working Paper 366, May 2011, http://www.ids.ac.uk/files/dmfile/Wp366.pdf (accessed May 4, 2013).

63. As one longtime observer of Bihar noted, the state lacks "an institutional memory of good governance." Vandita Mishra, "The Long Road to Nootan Bihar," *Seminar* 620 (April 2011), http://www.india-seminar.com/2011/620/620_vandita_mishra.htm (accessed October 7, 2012).

64. Thakur, *Subaltern Saheb.*

65. While some refer to Lalu's reign as "Jungle Raj," others have labeled it "Yadav Raj," due to the fact that Lalu's caste-men were seen to have benefited disproportionately from his 15-year reign.

66. Raj Kamal Jha and Farzand Ahmed, "Laloo's Magic," *India Today,* April 30, 1995.

67. Varghese K. George and Mammen Matthew, "Changing the Political Context," *Hindustan Times,* November 25, 2010.

68. Chinki Sinha, "The Battle to Tame Bihar," *Open,* December 22, 2012.

69. Nitish Kumar's willingness to tolerate candidates with criminal reputations is borne out by the quantitative, as well as the qualitative, evidence. See Upadhyay, "How Nitish Plays the Caste Card"; Sinha, "Don of Mokama"; Sinha, *Nitish Kumar and the Rise of Bihar;* and Jeffrey Witsoe, "Bihar," in Atul Kohli and Prerna Singh, eds., *Routledge Handbook of Indian Politics* (New York: Routledge, 2013), 304.

70. Peter Foster, "Burgeoning Lawlessness in India's Wild East," *Telegraph* (United Kingdom), March 19, 2007.

71. An article in the October 31, 2010, Patna edition of the *Times of India* roughly corroborated this estimate, stating that there were 95,000 Bhumihars in Mokama out of an electorate of 215,000.

72. For their part, Mokama's Bhumihars lament that the annual submersion leads to land grabbing by backward communities. Indeed, they remain deeply concerned that their traditional position of superiority is eroding. This sense of insecurity over status stems from the changing patterns of dominance that have swept Bihar—and, indeed, much of north India—over the past two decades. In Mokama, many members of the Bhumihar community resent the 15-year reign of Lalu Prasad Yadav and the social empowerment of the backward castes—empowerment that they perceived came at their expense.

73. In years past, Anant Singh has been locked in a fierce rivalry with fellow Bhumihar strongman, Suraj Bhan Singh. In 2010, Suraj Bhan did not contest elections directly but rather backed his sister-in-law. Suraj Bhan was largely a nonentity in the election campaign.

74. According to approximations based on the 2001 census, the literacy rate in Mokama was around 50 percent. This was roughly on par with the Bihar average but well below the rate for Patna district as a whole (64 percent), which is close to the all-India average.

75. Although Anant Singh did file an affidavit with the Election Commission of India before the 2010 Bihar assembly election, his submission was missing a declaration of pending criminal cases. The affidavit states these cases are listed in an annexure, but that annexure was either omitted or not posted online. Singh's 2015

election affidavit, however, discloses 15 pending cases, with 2 dating back as far as 1979. In total, Singh faced 13 murder-related charges. At least 6 of these cases predated the 2010 election.

76. Sinha, "Guns, Dance & Power Play"; Sinha, "Don of Mokama."

77. Das, "All Crime and No Punishment"; Sinha, "Don of Mokama"; "MLA Arrested after Attack on Journalists," *Hindu,* November 2, 2007.

78. Anant Singh seems to openly embrace his likeness to the stereotypical (and sometimes sympathetic) Bollywood villain. Indeed, the mutual reinforcement between Bollywood and politics helps to explain why Anant Singh's "tough" image might help, rather than harm, him. In fact, there is a well-known tradition in Indian politics of film stars contesting office and politicians imitating the imagery of film stars. See Sara Dickey, "The Politics of Adulation: Cinema and the Production of Politicians in South India," *Journal of Asian Studies* 52, no. 3 (May 1993): 340–72.

79. "Anant or Lalan, Only a Criminal Will Represent Mokameh," *Financial Express,* November 18, 2005.

80. Landlords in many historical and contemporaneous cases have also overseen powerful networks of patronage and control. See, inter alia, James A. Robinson and Jean-Marie Baland, "Land and Power: Theory and Evidence from Chile," *American Economic Review* 98, no. 5 (2008): 1737–65. Landlords in Mokama still claim some influence or control (exactly how much is subject to debate) over the vote of those they employ—typically agrarian laborers who are from the lower and backward castes.

81. Across Bihar the upper-caste blowback to calls for further land reform, such as granting sharecroppers legal rights, was swift. See Rajesh Chakrabarti, *Bihar Breakthrough: The Turnaround of a Beleaguered State* (New Delhi: Rupa, 2013).

82. Indeed, many residents suggested that even Lalu Prasad Yadav had previously courted Anant Singh in order to win elections in eastern Patna district. See Das, "All Crime and No Punishment."

83. Nitish Kumar is said to have believed that rejecting Anant Singh would endanger his prospects in his home turf of Barh (the area that borders Mokama to the west and where Anant Singh's ancestral village is located). See Upadhyay, "How Nitish Plays the Caste Card"; Sinha, "Don of Mokama"; Sinha, *Nitish Kumar and the Rise of Bihar;* and Charu Kartikeya, "Python, Murder & High Drama: Arresting Don Anant Singh Could Harm Nitish," *Catch News,* June 27, 2015, http://www.catchnews.com/india-news/pythons-murders-and-high-drama-how-the-arrest-of-don-anant-singh-could-harm-nitish-kumar-1435332051.html (accessed November 14, 2015).

84. "Both Nitish, Laloo Courted Anant," *Tehelka,* December 1, 2007.

85. Sinha, "Guns, Dance & Power Play."

86. For instance, Anant Singh is believed to have close links with the Ranvir Sena, the leading Bhumihar caste army operating in central Bihar. According to scholar Ashwani Kumar, the Ranvir Sena operates as a surrogate political arm for many politicians in the region affiliated with the ruling JD(U) alliance. Upper-caste candidates with serious criminal records like Anant Singh often cast themselves in the role of "community warriors" who contest elections to protect the interests of their own community. Of course, this appeals to many of the Sena's true believers.

See Ashwani Kumar, *Community Warriors: State, Peasants and Caste Armies in Bihar* (New Delhi: Anthem Press, 2008).

87. Sinha, "Don of Mokama."

88. According to the 2009 National Election Study conducted by CSDS, roughly two-thirds of voters who had an opinion stated that politicians could rarely or never learn how they voted. See Center for the Study of Developing Societies, *India National Election Study 2009* (New Delhi: CSDS, 2009).

89. Sinha, "Don of Mokama."

90. Author's calculations based on data on judicial pendency from the National Judicial Data Grid. Data are available at: ecourts.gov.in/services/njdg/index.php.

91. One journalistic account reaches an identical conclusion in his reporting on the "dons" of Uttar Pradesh. Describing their allure, the reporter Ashish Khetan writes: "His criminal record doesn't matter to the man on the street. Because, one, there is no conflict between his illegal activities and the needs of the poor and the deprived who make up his vote bank. Two, he often carries out his criminal activities outside his constituency. The cases of murder or physical assault that he faces on home turf mostly relate to political or gang rivalry and do not involve the common man." Ashish Khetan, "Lives of the Rich and Infamous," *Tehelka*, October 2, 2004.

92. A similar point is made in Lucia Michelutti, "Wrestling with (Body) Politics: Understanding Muscular Political Styles in North India," in Pamela Price and Arild Ruud, eds., *Power and Influence in South Asia: Bosses, Lords, and Captains* (Delhi: Routledge, 2010).

93. Kumar, *Community Warriors*, 39.

94. Atul Kohli, *Democracy and Discontent: India's Growing Crisis of Governability* (New York: Cambridge University Press, 1991).

95. Ibid., 235.

96. Chauchard, "Unpacking Ethnic Preferences."

97. Witsoe, "Territorial Democracy," 65.

98. Ibid.

99. Ibid. It is no coincidence that criminal politicians are often referred to as "protectors," "guardians," or even "saviors."

100. See, inter alia, "Ramanand to Fight on RJD Ticket from Danapur," *Times of India*, May 9, 2002.

101. In the 2000s, Ramanand Yadav briefly joined the BJP and even contested against Lalu Prasad Yadav in the 2000 Bihar state assembly election, though he lost the Danapur constituency to his onetime political mentor.

102. According to the affidavit Ramanand Yadav submitted to the Election Commission ahead of the 2010 assembly election, he faced three pending criminal cases.

103. At the time of the 2010 Bihar assembly election, Sunil Pandey faced 23 separate criminal cases according to the affidavit he filed before the Election Commission. Both Anant Singh and Sunil Pandey were members of the JD(U), Nitish Kumar's party. According to one account, "As long as the dons did not break party discipline, Nitish allowed them to be in the JD(U)." Indeed, Kumar renominated both of these men in 2010. See Sinha, *Nitish Kumar and the Rise of Bihar*, 254. One journalist was less charitable in his assessment: "Nitish had no qualms in

taking advantage of Sunil Pandey's criminal antecedents to consolidate his own position." See Upadhyay, "How Nitish Kumar Plays the Caste Card."

104. Kumar, *Community Warriors*, 156–58.

105. "Prison Term for Bihar Legislator," BBC News, September 17, 2008, http://news.bbc.co.uk/2/hi/south_asia/7620999.stm (accessed November 17, 2015); "Bihar Legislator Acquitted in Abduction Case," Indo-Asian News Service, December 11, 2010, http://www.sify.com/news/bihar-legislator-acquitted-in-abduction-case-news-national-kh2pOcedcafsi.html (accessed January 12, 2011).

106. Dan Morrison, "The Dark Side of India's 'Mr. Clean,'" *Al-Jazeera*, August 8, 2012, http://www.aljazeera.com/indepth/opinion/2012/08/2012869281872518.html (accessed July 24, 2015); Nalin Verma, "MLC Arrested from House," *Telegraph* (Calcutta), July 25, 2009.

107. A drunk Pandey allegedly shouted: *Kya dikha rahe hain app? Vishwanath, thok de. Marva de.* (What are you showing? Vishwanath, shoot them. Get them killed.) See "Bihar MLA Threatens to Kill Reporters," *Times of India*, June 25, 2006.

108. "Jailed Bihar Legislator Gets Doctorate for Non-violence Thesis," Indo-Asian News Service, March 5, 2009, http://www.newindianexpress.com/nation/article43590.ece (accessed October 18, 2010).

109. Giridhar Jha, "Murder Accused Turns in to Fight Bihar Elections," *India Today*, September 23, 2010; K. C. Philip, "Gang War on Train Draws Blood in AC Coach," *Telegraph* (Calcutta), June 10, 2004.

110. Pooja Kashyap, "Widow Takes on Hubby 'Killer,'" *Times of India*, October 29, 2010.

111. Alok Mishra, "Danapur's Terror's Ads Anger Voters," *Times of India*, October 31, 2010.

112. Ramashankar, "Ganglord Jumps into Poll Ring from Jail," *Telegraph* (Calcutta), October 18, 2010. Ritlal Yadav's criminal rap sheet was so lengthy—20 cases in all—that he needed a separate annexure to detail them in his 2010 election affidavit submitted to the Election Commission.

113. Mishra, "Danapur's Terror's Ads Anger Voters."

114. "BJP Leader Killed in Patna," Press Trust of India, April 30, 2003, http://expressindia.indianexpress.com/news/fullstory.php?newsid=21003 (accessed October 2, 2010).

115. At the time of writing, none of these four politicians has been convicted. Just before Bihar's 2015 assembly election, Anant Singh was finally arrested on murder and kidnapping charges, prompting Nitish Kumar to expel him from the party. Singh, though lodged in jail and forced to contest as an independent, handily won reelection from Mokama without ever setting foot on the campaign trail. His party-mate Sunil Pandey was also arrested after being implicated in a January 2015 bomb blast case. Pandey too was dropped by the JD(U) and did not contest the election, although his wife ran (and lost). The RJD's Ramanand Yadav successfully won reelection from Fatuha, and Ritlal Yadav, who remains in jail awaiting trial, won election to Bihar's upper house of the assembly as an independent. See Amarnath Tewary, "JD(U) MLA Anant Singh Arrested," *Hindu*, June 25, 2015 (accessed November 15, 2015); Amarnath Tewary, "JD(U) MLA Sunil Pandey Ar-

rested," *Hindu,* July 12, 2015; Giridhar Jha, "Jailed Gangster Ritlal Yadav Wins Bihar Election against JD-U and BJP Rivals," *India Today,* July 10, 2015.

116. Ward Berenschot, *Riot Politics: Hindu-Muslim Violence and the Indian State* (New York: Columbia University Press, 2012).

117. Ibid.

118. Michelutti, "Wrestling with (Body) Politics," 60.

119. Ibid. Although the scholar Lucia Michelutti uses the term *goonda* to describe the criminal Yadav politicians she studies, they are arguably more akin to *dadas* given their political prominence and relative position in the local criminal hierarchy.

120. Hansen, *Wages of Violence.*

121. As Berenschot explains, there is a rationale underlying the violence employed by *goondas* in India that is grounded in the local political context. Violence and criminality are essential to cultivating an image of being "tough."

122. Hansen, "Politics as Permanent Performance," 21. Shiv Sena leader Bal Thackeray's role cannot be minimized in this respect; his "art of building up hysteria" and "very effective histrionics" are crucial to the Shiv Sena's politics of performance. See Suhas Palshikar, "Shiv Sena: A Tiger with Many Faces?" *Economic and Political Weekly* 39, no. 14/15 (April 3–16, 2004): 1497–1507.

123. Wilkinson, "Constructivist Model of Ethnic Riots."

124. Berenschot, *Riot Politics.*

125. Author's interview with BJP Rajya Sabha MP, New Delhi, July 2009.

126. Author's interview with senior representative of a national party, Patna, October 2010.

CHAPTER 6. THE SALIENCE OF SOCIAL DIVISIONS

1. "Lucknow Goes Blue for Chief Minister's Birthday," Indo-Asian News Service, January 14, 2008, http://www.dnaindia.com/india/report-lucknow-goes-blue-for-chief-minister-s-birthday-1145075 (accessed June 2, 2012). Mayawati's biographer reports that for her fifty-first birthday, Mayawati's birthday festivities included a 51-kilogram cake, 100,000 ladoos (Indian sweets), 60 quintals of marigolds, and around 5,000 flower bouquets. See Ajoy Bose, *Behenji: A Political Biography of Mayawati* (London: Penguin, 2009).

2. The allegation regarding the meteoric rise in Mayawati's personal assets was contained in a charge sheet filed by federal investigators looking into the former chief minister's "disproportionate assets," a euphemism for corruption. See "Mayawati Can Be Prosecuted in Corruption Case: CBI," Press Trust of India, August 27, 2010,http://www.ndtv.com/india-news/mayawati-can-be-prosecuted-in-corruption-case-cbi-429031 (accessed November 16, 2015).

3. In July 2012, the Supreme Court dismissed the CBI's probe into Mayawati's "disproportionate assets," claiming that the CBI had overextended its mandate in a separate corruption investigation it had opened against the BSP leader. The Supreme Court clarified in May 2013 that the CBI could open a new investigation into Mayawati's assets, but the CBI demurred. In January 2014, a private citizen filed a public interest suit with the Supreme Court demanding the CBI initiate a

fresh probe. The court agreed and ordered a new investigation, although the CBI continues to resist. "SC to Hear Mayawati's Disproportionate Assets Case," *Outlook,* January 28, 2010; Liz Mathew, "No Material Evidence against Mayawati: SC," *Mint,* July 9, 2012; J. Venkatesan, "CBI Free to Probe Mayawati Assets Case: Supreme Court," *Hindu,* May 1, 2013; "DA Case Comes Back to Haunt Mayawati," *Times of India,* January 18, 2014.

4. "Indian Dalit Icon Mayawati Attacked over Rupee Garland," BBC News, March 16, 2010, http://news.bbc.co.uk/2/hi/8570289.stm (accessed June 7, 2012).

5. Affidavit submitted by Mayawati to the Election Commission of India in advance of the Uttar Pradesh 2012 state assembly election; Ajoy Bose, *Behenji,* chap. 14.

6. "Mayawati Dalit Ki Beti Nahin, Daulat Ki Beti Hain," *Rediff,* January 6, 2015, http://www.rediff.com/news/report/mayawati-dalit-ki-beti-nahin-daulat-ki-beti -hain/20150106.htm (accessed November 17, 2015).

7. Sharat Pradhan, "Mayawati Spends Crores to Fulfil Her B'day Dream," *Rediff,* January 15, 2003, http://www.rediff.com/news/2003/jan/15up.htm (accessed November 15, 2015); Sharat Pradhan, "Mayawati Wants Cash on Her Birthday," *Rediff,* January 14, 2005, http://www.rediff.com/news/report/sharat/20050114 .htm (accessed November 15, 2015); Srawan Shukla, "Having Her Cake and Eating It Too," *Tehelka,* January 24, 2009.

8. Quoted in Steven I. Wilkinson, "The Politics of Infrastructural Spending in India," unpublished paper, Institute for Policy Studies and the World Bank, July 31, 2006, http://siteresources.worldbank.org/INTCHIINDGLOECO/ Resources/Wilkinson_ThePolitics_of_InfrastructuralProvision_in_India.pdf (accessed November 15, 2012).

9. Subash Mishra, "Film Flare," *India Today,* March 17, 2003.

10. Sharat Pradhan, "Engineer's Murder Sparks Off State-Wide Protests in UP," *Rediff,* December 25, 2008, http://www.rediff.com/news/2008/dec/25up-engineers -death-sparks-off-protest.htm (accessed June 10, 2012).

11. Sharat Pradhan, "I Take Money for Party Tickets: Mayawati," *Rediff,* June 5, 2006, http://www.rediff.com/news/2006/jun/05maya.htm (accessed June 10, 2012).

12. U.S. Embassy New Delhi, "Mayawati: Portrait of a Lady," diplomatic cable, October 23, 2008, https://wikileaks.org/plusd/cables/08NEWDELHI2783_a.html (accessed January 10, 2015).

13. Ibid. Somewhat colorfully, the same U.S. diplomatic cable described Mayawati as acting like "a virtual paranoid dictator replete with food tasters and a security entourage to rival a head of state. . . . In addition to this outsized security apparatus, she constructed a private road from her residence to her office, which is cleaned immediately after her multiple vehicle convoy reaches its destination."

14. Vibhuti Agarwal, "Mayawati: WikiLeaks Founder Should Be Sent to Mental Asylum," *Wall Street Journal India Real Time* (blog), September 6, 2011, http:// blogs.wsj.com/indiarealtime/2011/09/06/mayawati-wikileaks-founder-should-be -sent-to-mental-asylum-2/ (accessed December 1, 2015).

15. According to Shekhar Tiwari's affidavit submission ahead of the 2007 Uttar Pradesh assembly elections, only 2 of his alleged 14 criminal cases had formally commenced the judicial process.

16. "BSP Leader Manipulating Engineer's Murder Case, Says Witness," Indo-Asian News Service, October 14, 2009, http://twocircles.net/2009oct14/bsp_leader_manipulating_engineers_murder_case_says_witness.html (accessed June 3, 2012).

17. "BSP MLA Chargesheeted in PWD Engineer Murder Case," *Indian Express,* January 3, 2009.

18. U.S. Embassy New Delhi, "Mayawati Cancels Birthday Party, Cash Gifts Still Welcome," diplomatic cable, January 16, 2009, https://wikileaks.org/plusd/cables/09NEWDELHI108_a.html (accessed January 10, 2015).

19. Man Mohan Rai, "BSP MLA, Shekhar Tiwari Gets Life Imprisonment in PWD Engineer Murder Case," *Economic Times,* May 7, 2011.

20. U.S. Embassy New Delhi, "Mayawati Cancels Birthday Party."

21. Smita Gupta, "BSP at the Crossroads," *Economic and Political Weekly* 33, no. 26/27 (June 27–July 10, 2009): 20.

22. Author's calculations based on affidavits submitted to the Election Commission of India by candidates contesting Uttar Pradesh state assembly elections in 2007.

23. The corresponding share of candidates facing serious cases in unreserved seats was 17 percent. Author's calculations based on affidavits submitted to the Election Commission of India by candidates contesting Uttar Pradesh state assembly elections in 2007.

24. Incidentally, most parties typically do not field Dalit candidates in non-reserved constituencies.

25. Indeed, the BJP government of Narendra Modi and the preceding Congress-led government were noncommittal about setting a release date for the detailed caste enumeration, citing the "sensitivity" of the information.

26. Marc Galanter, *Competing Equalities: Law and the Backward Classes in India* (New Delhi: Oxford University Press, 1984).

27. Mona L. Krook and Diana Z. O'Brien, "The Politics of Group Representation: Quotas for Women and Minorities Worldwide," *Comparative Politics* 42, no. 3 (April 2010): 253–72.

28. For a brief history of India's legislative reservations, see Francesca Refsum Jensenius, "Mired in Reservations: The Path-Dependent History of Electoral Quotas in India," *Journal of Asian Studies* 74, no. 1 (February 2015): 85–105.

29. Sections 330 and 332 of India's constitution stipulate that seats in the state assemblies and the lower house of Parliament should be reserved for SCs or STs in proportion to their respective populations in the state as a whole.

30. In this section, I use *jati* as shorthand to refer to caste as well as tribal divisions within the larger umbrella groupings of SC and ST. Some research finds some support for the idea that internal divisions among SCs are less salient due to SCs' common bonds. See Thad Dunning, "Do Quotas Promote Ethnic Solidarity? Field and Natural Experiment Evidence from India," unpublished paper, Department of Political Science, University of California–Berkeley, September 2010, http://www.thaddunning.com/wp-content/uploads/2010/09/Dunning_Quotas.pdf (accessed April 20, 2016).

31. Even if one believes that jatis are electorally relevant to SCs and STs, divisions within the umbrella SC and ST are largely irrelevant to citizens from other caste groups.

32. Kanshi Ram, *The Chamcha Age (An Era of the Stooges)* (New Delhi: Self-published, 1982).

33. Bhimrao Ramji Ambedkar, *Mr. Gandhi and the Emancipation of the Untouchables* (Bombay: Thacker, 1943), 24–25.

34. It is important to note that Ambedkar's views were not consistent on the issue of separate electorates, as he later spoke out against their use.

35. Ram Vilas Paswan, "Dalit Politics in Contemporary India," *Roundtable India (blog)*, March 30, 2010, http://roundtableindia.co.in/index.php?option=com_content&view=article&id=1162:dalit-politics-in-contemporary-indiamr-ram-vilas-paswan&catid=61&Itemid=56 (accessed August 17, 2015).

36. Author's interview with a senior official from a major national party, October 2010, Patna.

37. For more on the political "styles" of Yadavs and the connection to criminal activity, see Lucia Michelutti, "Wrestling with (Body) Politics: Understanding Muscular Political Styles in North India," in Pamela Price and Arild Ruud, eds., *Power and Influence in South Asia: Bosses, Lords, and Captains* (Delhi: Routledge, 2010).

38. Steven I. Wilkinson, *Votes and Violence: Electoral Competition and Ethnic Riots in India* (New York: Cambridge University Press, 2006).

39. Christophe Jaffrelot, *India's Silent Revolution: The Rise of the Lower Castes in North India* (New York, Columbia University Press, 2003), 102. In another article, Jaffrelot wrote of Scheduled Caste reservations: "Not having received their mandate from their caste fellows—always a minority in the reserved constituencies—elected officials in these constituencies were not very keen to defend their interests in the assemblies to which they were elected." See Christophe Jaffrelot, "The Impact of Affirmative Action in India: More Political than Socioeconomic," *India Review* 5, no. 2 (2006): 173–89.

40. Galanter, *Competing Equalities*, 549.

41. Francesca Refsum Jensenius, "Power, Performance and Bias: Evaluating the Electoral Quotas for Scheduled Castes in India" (PhD diss., University of California–Berkeley, 2013).

42. Francesca Refsum Jensenius, "Development from Representation? A Study of Quotas for Scheduled Castes in India," *American Economic Journal: Applied Economics* 7, no. 3 (2015): 196–220.

43. Rohini Pande, "Can Mandated Political Representation Increase Policy Influence for Disadvantaged Minorities? Theory and Evidence from India," *American Economic Review* 93, no. 4 (September 2003): 1132–51; Timothy Besley, Rohini Pande, and Vijayendra Rao, "Political Economy of Panchayats in South India," *Economic and Political Weekly* 42, no. 8 (February 24, 2007): 661–66.

44. Simon Chauchard, *Why Representation Matters: The Meaning of Ethnic Quotas in Rural India* (New York: Cambridge University Press, forthcoming).

45. The creation of the state of Telangana, carved out of erstwhile Andhra Pradesh in 2014, increased the tally of Indian states to 29. Delhi and Puducherry,

though both union territories, not states, also possess elected assemblies. This takes the total number of elected assemblies to 31.

46. Statistical estimates are derived from a multilevel logistic regression of a binary measure of whether a constituency has at least one candidate standing with a serious criminal record on reservation status and other constituency factors. The model also includes random effects parameters for states, districts, and years. For more information on much of the regression evidence cited in this chapter, see Milan Vaishnav, "The Merits of Money and 'Muscle': Essays on Criminality, Elections and Democracy in India" (PhD diss., Columbia University, 2012).

47. To investigate the possibility of underrepresentation of SCs and STs among the "criminal" population, I accessed 2004 data from the Ministry of Home Affairs on the group-wise breakdown of convicts and those in jail while undertrial. The data are disaggregated by caste grouping and state, which allows for a comparison of the percentage of convicts and those in jail under trial who are identified as SC (ST) against the SC (ST) proportion of the state population. For the majority of states, there is no evidence that SCs and STs are underrepresented among the criminal population.

48. For a review, see Sonalde Desai and Amaresh Dubey, "Caste in 21st Century India: Competing Narratives," *Economic and Political Weekly* 46, no. 11 (March 12, 2012): 40–49.

49. Yogendra Yadav, "The Paradox of Political Representation," *Seminar* 586 (June 2008), http://www.india-seminar.com/2008/586/586_yogendra_yadav.htm (accessed August 17, 2012).

50. One study concludes its investigation of delimitation in two large Indian states by suggesting that "a politically neutral redistricting process can be implemented by a non-political body with a transparent and inclusive process." See Lakshmi Iyer and Maya Reddy, "Redrawing the Lines: Did Political Incumbents Influence Electoral Redistricting in the World's Largest Democracy?" Harvard Business School Working Paper No. 14–051, December 2013, http://www.hbs.edu/faculty/Pages/item.aspx?num=46005 (accessed August 20, 2015). Similarly, scholar Francesca Jensenius examines claims that past delimitation commissions have unfairly drawn the boundaries of SC reserved constituencies so as to include large numbers of Muslims who had no chance of standing for public office. She finds no empirical basis for such allegations. See Francesca Refsum Jensenius, "Was the Delimitation Commission Unfair to Muslims?" *Studies in Indian Politics* 1, no. 2 (December 2013): 213–29.

51. The seven states included in this analysis are: Andhra Pradesh, Chhattisgarh, Delhi, Karnataka, Madhya Pradesh, Mizoram, and Odisha. There is a small degree of switching between reserved categories. In the dataset, seven constituencies previously reserved for SCs became reserved for STs, and two former ST constituencies became SC reserved. But switches from one reserved category to another account for only 5.5 percent of all switches. For the analysis, I disregard these nine constituencies.

52. The analyses compare the longitudinal differences in criminality, or the changes over time, only in those constituencies that switched reservation status. The outcome of interest is the constituency share of candidates facing serious cases

and the key variable of interest is the reservation status, controlling for other constituency-level factors.

53. Author's analysis of affidavits submitted to the Election Commission of India from seven states that had two elections between 2003/4 and 2008/9. In statistical terms, I use a technique known as "matching." Matching uses an algorithm to "match" constituencies within the same district and state, which appear identical on all observable criteria, save for their reservation status. The next step is to see how criminality varies among these matched constituencies according to reservation status. This matching technique confirms that reservation is negatively associated with criminality at conventional significance levels.

54. The length of a Lok Sabha MP's term is five years, unless early elections are called or a government falls.

55. Rajya Sabha members are elected in accordance with the system of proportional representation by means of the single transferable vote. In addition, the president nominates up to 12 members for their specific expertise and contributions to the fields of art, literature, science, and social service.

56. If the Rajya Sabha does not return a money bill to the Lok Sabha within 14 days, the Lok Sabha version of the bill is deemed to have passed both houses.

57. There are a few additional differences between the two houses, regarding eligibility requirements (the minimum age for Rajya Sabha members in 30 versus 25 for the Lok Sabha) and permanency (the Rajya Sabha is a permanent body not subject to dissolution).

58. For instance, in the June 2010 Rajya Sabha elections held across seven states, all 30 members were elected unopposed to the upper house.

59. B. Venkatesh Kumar, "Election to Raya Sabha: Proposed 'Reform,'" *Economic and Political Weekly* 37, no. 4 (January 26, 2002): 292–93; Kautilya Kumar, "Just an Avenue to Dispense Patronage," *Times of India*, December 14, 2010.

60. Suchandana Gupta, "Rajya Sabha Row: Scholarly Debate Stifled in India?" *Times of India*, December 13, 2010.

61. "Camel-Trading, Rajasthan Style," *Economic and Political Weekly* 27, no. 29 (July 18, 1992): 1533–34.

62. Memorandum from the Election Commission of India to the Secretary of the Ministry of Personnel, Public Grievances, and Pension, "Biennial Election, 2012 to the Rajya Sabha from the State of Jharkhand," April 9, 2012, http://eci.nic.in/eci_main1/current/CBI_inquiry.pdf (accessed August 9, 2015).

63. B. Muralidhar Reddy and J. Balaji, "Rajya Sabha Poll in Jharkhand Countermanded," *Hindu*, March 30, 2012.

64. The entry of businessmen into the Rajya Sabha provides a new revenue stream for parties while satisfying the businessmen's desires for status and policy influence.

65. "Business In and Outside Rajya Sabha," *Financial Express*, November 20, 2002.

66. Kumar, "Election to Raya Sabha."

67. There are at least two procedural aspects of indirect elections specific to India that might dampen the presence of candidates facing serious criminal scrutiny in the upper house. First, India has an anti-defection law, which limits the frequency

of "cross-voting" and gives party leaders even more power in selecting candidates and ensuring their election. Party members risk being disqualified if they disobey a party whip. The ability to disobey party orders has been further weakened through a recent reform that allows for an open ballot in Rajya Sabha elections. Legislators can no longer hide behind the veil of secrecy when casting their votes, further strengthening party leaders' hands. Second, a 2003 constitutional amendment removed the requirement that Rajya Sabha members be residents of the state from which they are nominated. The removal of the residency requirement provided de jure recognition of a de facto reality: many parties had previously found numerous ways to circumvent the official residency requirements. The formal repeal gave parties even greater incentive to nominate influential individuals who do not necessarily possess strong local connections. To the extent such connections are positively correlated with criminality, one should expect to see fewer criminal politicians in the Rajya Sabha. See Kuldip Nayar, "Bringing Down the Upper House," *Indian Express,* April 20, 2004.

68. Radhika Ramaseshan, "Cong Elders Eye Lok Sabha Tickets," *Telegraph* (Calcutta), January 4, 2009.

69. Statistical estimates are derived from a multilevel logistic regression of a binary measure of whether the member of Parliament has a serious criminal record on the individual's status as a member of the upper or lower house and legislator characteristics. The model also includes fixed effects parameters for states.

70. See Neelanjan Sircar and Milan Vaishnav, "Ignorant Voters or Credible Representatives? Why Voters Support Criminal Politicians in India," unpublished paper (on file with author), Carnegie Endowment for International Peace, April 2015.

71. For instance, one study argues that criminal candidates begin at a disadvantage because their alleged criminality carries some degree of social stigma, which will have a negative effect on their vote share. Money, however, allows them to reduce this stigma among voters and hence recover at least some of this "lost" vote share. The authors also point to the resulting nexus between money and "muscle." See Bhaskar Dutta and Poonam Gupta, "How Indian Voters Respond to Candidates with Criminal Charges: Evidence from the 2009 Lok Sabha Elections," *Economic and Political Weekly* 49, no. 4 (January 25, 2014): 43–51.

72. One example is that of the convicted politician D. P. Yadav of Uttar Pradesh. See Rajesh Kumar Singh, "From Land of Milk and Money to Life-Term: Life of DP Yadav," *Hindustan Times,* March 16, 2015; Vineet Khare, "I Am DP, Don," *Tehelka,* May 4, 2010.

73. "Before Vyapam Scam, a Plunder of Fodder and Health Funds," *Hindustan Times,* July 9, 2015.

74. "Kushwaha Entry Not Hasty, but Move to Woo OBCs: BJP," *Indian Express,* January 7, 2012.

75. "Babu Singh Kushwaha's Membership Suspended: BJP," Indo-Asian News Service, January 8, 2012, http://indiatoday.intoday.in/story/kushwaha-bjp-leaders -suspend-membership-nitin-gadkari-nrhm-scam/1/167736.html (accessed September 1, 2012).

76. Pranab Bardhan, "Democracy and Distributive Politics in India," in Ian Shapiro, Peter Swenson and Daniela Donno Panayides, eds., *Divide and Deal: The*

Politics of Distribution in Democracies (New York: New York University Press, 2010).

77. Dan Morrison, "In Indian Politics, Crime Pays," *New York Times Latitude* (blog), February 1, 2012, http://latitude.blogs.nytimes.com/2012/02/01/in-indian -politics-crime-pays/?_r=0 (accessed February 2, 2012).

CHAPTER 7. CRIME WITHOUT PUNISHMENT

1. Sheela Bhatt, "Arvind Kejriwal: The Man the Govt Loves to Hate," *Rediff,* September 8, 2011, http://www.rediff.com/news/report/special-arvind-kerjiwal-the -man-the-government-loves-to-hate/20110905.htm (accessed September 5, 2014).

2. Nikhila Gill, "Lokpal Bill: Over Four Decades of Failed Attempts," NDTV, December 26, 2011, http://www.ndtv.com/india-news/lokpal-bill-over-four-decades -of-failed-attempts-567097 (accessed September 7, 2014).

3. "Politicians Don't Let Honest CBI Officers Work: Kejriwal," *Outlook,* July 2, 2012.

4. "Arvind Kejriwal Calls MPs 'Rapists, Murderers,'" *Times of India,* February 28, 2012.

5. Mehboob Jeelani, "The Insurgent," *Caravan,* September 1, 2011.

6. Ibid.

7. Abantika Ghosh, "Jan Lokpal a Frankenstein's Monster: Sibal," *Times of India,* June 30, 2011.

8. Pratap Bhanu Mehta, "Of the Few, by the Few," *Indian Express,* April 7, 2011.

9. Ibid.

10. "Hazare Appeals to Kejriwal to Call off His Fast," News18, April 4, 2013, http://www.news18.com/news/india/hazare-appeals-to-kejriwal-to-call-off-his -fast-600933.html (accessed April 20, 2016).

11. Sruthijith K. K., "Arvind Kejriwal Slams Government Representatives for Dilly-dallies," *Economic Times,* August 31, 2011.

12. "The Divide within Civil Society," NDTV, June 15, 2011, http://www.ndtv .com/india-news/the-divide-within-civil-society-458482 (accessed September 7, 2014).

13. "'A Jokepal Bill,' Says Team Anna; Plans 2nd Fast," NDTV, June 16, 2011, http://www.ndtv.com/india-news/a-jokepal-bill-says-team-anna-plans-2nd-fast -458642 (accessed September 8, 2014).

14. Jeelani, "Insurgent."

15. Bhatt, "Arvind Kejriwal."

16. Andrew Buncombe, "I Am an Anarchist, Says Delhi Chief Minister Arvind Kejriwal as He Causes Traffic Chaos with Protest in City Centre," *Independent,* January 20, 2014.

17. "Arvind Kejriwal Quits as Delhi CM after Jan Lokpal Fiasco," *Economic Times,* February 14, 2014.

18. Ibid.

19. "The One Lesson I Have Learned Is That I Will Never Resign, Says AAP's Arvind Kejriwal," *Indian Express,* November 21, 2014.

20. Pew Research Center, *Indians Reflect on Their Country and the World* (Washington, D.C.: Pew Research Center, 2014).

21. Public Affairs Centre, "The State of India's Public Services: Benchmarks for the New Millennium," April 2002, http://www1.worldbank.org/publicsector/pe/milleniumreport.pdf (accessed April 20, 2016).

22. Max Weber, "Politik als Beruf," speech delivered at Munich University, 1918. An English translation is available at http://anthropos-lab.net/wp/wp-content/up loads/2011/12/Weber-Politics-as-a-Vocation.pdf.

23. Nishith Prakash, Marc Rockmore, and Yogesh Uppal, "Do Criminally Accused Politicians Affect Economic Outcomes? Evidence from India," unpublished paper, Department of Economics, Youngstown State University, October 2015, http://yuppal.people.ysu.edu/criminal_mla_11_08_14.pdf (accessed January 23, 2016).

24. For instance, in the 2014 general election, 37 percent of candidates won a majority of votes cast in their respective constituencies. That number was actually a significant increase from 2009, when just 22 percent were "majority winners." See Milan Vaishnav and Danielle Smogard, "A New Era in Indian Politics?" Carnegie Endowment for International Peace, June 10, 2014, http://carnegieendowment .org/2014/06/10/new-era-in-indian-politics/hdc6 (accessed June 15, 2014).

25. Second Administrative Reforms Commission, Government of India, *Ethics in Governance (Fourth Report)* (New Delhi: Government of India, 2007), http://arc.gov.in/4threport.pdf (accessed March 18, 2013).

26. Diego Gambetta, *The Sicilian Mafia: The Business of Private Protection* (Cambridge: Harvard University Press, 1996), 25.

27. Ministry of Home Affairs, Government of India, *Final Report of the Vohra Committee* (New Delhi: Government of India, 2005), http://adrindia.org/sites/default/files/VOHRA%20COMMITTEE%20REPORT_0.pdf (accessed April 20, 2016).

28. National Commission to Review the Working of the Constitution, "Review of Election Law, Processes, and Electoral Reforms," Consultation Paper, January 8, 2001, http://lawmin.nic.in/ncrwc/finalreport/v2b1-9.htm (accessed January 16, 2012).

29. Second Administrative Reforms Commission, Government of India, *Public Order (Fifth Report)* (New Delhi: Government of India, 2007), 2, http://arc.gov .in/5th%20REPORT.pdf (accessed March 14, 2013).

30. This section draws on material which first appeared in Milan Vaishnav, "Resizing the State," *Caravan*, October 1, 2012.

31. Ila Patnaik and Ajay Shah, "Reforming India's Financial System," Carnegie Endowment for International Peace, January 2014, http://carnegieendowment. org/2014/01/29/reforming-india-s-financial-system (accessed February 1, 2014).

32. Asit Ranjan Mishra and Prashant K. Nanda, "How Policies Can Shape Make in India," *Mint*, February 15, 2016.

33. Karthik Muralidharan, Jishnu Das, Alaka Holla, and Aakash Mohpal, "The Fiscal Cost of Weak Governance: Evidence from Teacher Absence in India," National Bureau of Economic Research Working Paper No. 20299, July 2014.

34. Karthik Muralidharan et al., "Is There a Doctor in the House? Medical Worker Absence in India," unpublished paper, Department of Economics, Harvard

University, April 2011, http://scholar.harvard.edu/kremer/publications/there-Doctor -House-Medical-Worker-Absence-India (accessed February 10, 2015).

35. Jishnu Das and Jeffrey Hammer, "Money for Nothing: The Dire Straits of Medical Practice in Delhi, India," *Journal of Development Economics* 83, no. 1 (May 2007): 1–36.

36. Jishnu Das et al., "In Urban and Rural India, A Standardized Patient Study Showed Low Levels of Provider Training and Huge Quality Gaps," *Health Affairs* 31, no. 12 (December 2012): 2774–84.

37. Nazmul Chaudhury et al., "Missing in Action: Teacher and Health Worker Absence in Developing Countries," *Journal of Economic Perspectives* 20, no. 1 (Winter 2006): 91–116.

38. Sandip Sukhtankar and Milan Vaishnav, "Corruption in India: Bridging Research Evidence and Policy Options," *India Policy Forum* 11 (July 2015): 193–261.

39. Karthik Muralidharan, Paul Niehaus, and Sandip Sukhtankar, "Building State Capacity: Evidence from Biometric Smartcards in India," National Bureau of Economic Research Working Paper No. 19999, March 2014.

40. Sukhtankar and Vaishnav, "Corruption in India"; Muralidharan, Niehaus, and Sukhtankar, "Building State Capacity."

41. Sukhtankar and Vaishnav, "Corruption in India."

42. A 2014 study by the VV Giri National Labour Institute reportedly found that contract labor accounts for 55 percent of public sector jobs. See Yogima Seth Sharma, "Following Rajasthan, Centre to Revisit Contract Labour Law," *Economic Times,* July 3, 2014.

43. Ernst & Young LLP and Federation of Indian Chambers of Commerce and Industry, "Private Security Services Industry: Securing Future Growth," 2013, http://ficci.in/spdocument/20329/Private-security-services-industry-Securing -future-growth1.pdf (accessed April 20, 2016).

44. See, inter alia, Devesh Kapur and Pratap Bhanu Mehta, "Indian Higher Education Reform: From Half-Baked Socialism to Half-Baked Capitalism," *India Policy Forum* 4 (July 2008): 101–58.

45. This section draws on and, in some cases, reproduces material that first appeared in Devesh Kapur and Milan Vaishnav, "Strengthening the Rule of Law," in Bibek Debroy, Ashley Tellis, and Reece Trevor, eds., *Getting India Back on Track: An Action Agenda for Reform* (Washington, D.C.: Carnegie Endowment for International Peace, 2014). That chapter, in turn, grew out an earlier article in *Outlook* magazine. See Devesh Kapur, "The Law Laid Down," *Outlook,* January 7, 2013. I am grateful to Devesh Kapur, whose insights greatly shaped my own thinking on these issues.

46. World Justice Project, *Rule of Law Index 2015* (Washington, D.C.: World Justice Project, 2015).

47. Ibid.

48. Government of India, Ministry of Personnel, Public Grievances, and Pensions, Department of Administrative Reforms and Public Grievances, *Report of the Commission on Review of Administrative Laws* (New Delhi: Government of India, 1998), http://www.darpg.gov.in/sites/default/files/Review_Administrative_laws_ Vol_1.pdf (accessed April 19, 2016).

49. The situation is presumably even worse at the state level, which has far greater potential to affect the day-to-day lives of citizens and workings of business. The precise scope of the challenge remains unclear, however, because India lacks an inventory of state laws on the books.

50. Information on the "100 Laws Repeal Project" can be found at http://ccs .in/100laws?_ga=1.69967696.195209879.1397058421.

51. Devesh Kapur and Milan Vaishnav, "Rule of Law Reform: A Mixed Record," Carnegie Endowment for International Peace, May 26, 2015, http://carnegieen dowment.org/2015/05/26/modi-s-first-year/i8td#8 (accessed May 30, 2015).

52. Arvind Verma, "Police in India: Design and Performance," in Pratap Bhanu Mehta and Devesh Kapur, eds., *Public Institutions in India: Design and Performance* (New Delhi: Oxford University Press, 2005), 194–257.

53. David H. Bayley, "The Police and Political Order in India," *Asian Survey* 23, no. 4 (April 1983): 495.

54. A 2013 review claims there is "little doubt" that the absence of real police reform in India is the "most catastrophic point of failure of Indian security reforms." See Sarah J. Watson and C. Christine Fair, "India's Stalled Internal Security Reforms," *India Review* 12, no. 4 (November 2013): 289.

55. Reflecting on the poor morale within the ranks of India's police, the director general of police in Uttar Pradesh told an international NGO: "If you brought a US policeman here he'd commit suicide within one day." Human Rights Watch, *Broken System: Dysfunction, Abuse, and Impunity in the Indian Police* (New York: Human Rights Watch, 2009), 7.

56. Sandeep Mishra, "IPS Officers Slam Lateral Entry into Police Services from Armed Forces," *Times of India*, April 23, 2012.

57. Abhinav Garg, "Big Backlog, Staff Crunch Ailing Forensic Lab: Govt," *Times of India*, October 3, 2013.

58. S. K. Das, "Institutions of Internal Accountability," in Pratap Bhanu Mehta and Devesh Kapur, eds., *Public Institutions in India: Design and Performance* (New Delhi: Oxford University Press, 2005), 149.

59. Ibid., 149–51.

60. Ibid. According to Das, "In all cases investigated by the CBI, the government is empowered, even at the stage of investigation, to acquaint itself with details of evidence, which, in essence, means that the government can interfere at the stage of investigation itself and thwart the case." For contemporary examples, see Mihir Srivastava, "The Congress Bureau of Investigation," *Open*, April 6, 2013.

61. Bishwajit Bhattacharyya, *My Experience with the Office of Additional Solicitor General of India* (New Delhi: Universal Law Publishers, 2012).

62. Abhijit Banerjee et al., "Improving Police Performance in Rajasthan, India: Experimental Evidence on Incentives, Managerial Autonomy and Training," National Bureau of Economic Research Paper No. 17912, March 2012.

63. Commonwealth Human Rights Initiative, "Seven Steps to Police Reform," September 2010, http://www.humanrightsinitiative.org/programs/aj/police/india/ initiatives/seven_steps_to_police_reform.pdf (accessed August 10, 2015).

64. Pratap Bhanu Mehta, "India's Judiciary: The Promise of Uncertainty," in Pratap Bhanu Mehta and Devesh Kapur, eds., *Public Institutions in India: Design and Performance* (New Delhi: Oxford University Press, 2005), 159–60.

65. Government of India, Law Commission of India, *Arrears and Backlog: Creating Additional Judicial (Wo)manpower*, Report No. 245 (New Delhi: Law Commission of India, July 2014), http://lawcommissionofindia.nic.in/reports/Report245.pdf (accessed October 1, 2014).

66. Centre on Public Law and Jurisprudence, *Justice without Delay: Recommendations for Legal and Institutional Reform* (Sonipat: O. P. Jindal Global University, 2011). The report is available at: http://papers.ssrn.com/sol3/papers.cfm?abstract_id=1679350.

67. Between 2000 and 2010, the number of cases admitted to the Supreme Court doubled (24,747 to 48,677). In 2004, 7 percent of regular hearing matters had been pending for more than five years. In 2011, the corresponding figure stood at 17 percent. See Supreme Court of India, *Court News* 7, no. 2 (April–June 2012), http://supremecourtofindia.nic.in/courtnews/2012_issue_2.pdf (accessed January 3, 2015).

68. Rukmini S., "Two-thirds of Prison Inmates in India Are Undertrials," *Hindu,* October 30, 2014.

69. National Commission to Review the Working of the Constitution, "All India Judicial Service," Consultation Paper, January 8, 2001, http://lawmin.nic.in/ncrwc/finalreport/v2b1-15.htm (accessed March 21, 2012).

70. According to legal scholar Madhav Khosla: "The haphazard growth of tribunals has diverted attention from any serious reform of the high courts." See Madhav Khosla, "The Problem," *Seminar* 642 (February 2013), http://india-seminar.com/2013/642/642_the_problem.htm (accessed March 3, 2014).

71. Smriti Singh, "Fast-Track Courts Slow Down Justice," *Times of India,* September 20, 2013.

72. The list of committees and commissions includes, inter alia, the Goswami Committee on Electoral Reforms (1990), the Vohra Committee (1993), the Indrajit Gupta Committee on State Funding of Elections (1998), the National Commission to Review the Working of the Constitution (2001), the Election Commission of India's report on electoral reforms (2004), the Second Administrative Reforms Commission (2008), and multiple reports by the Law Commission of India.

73. Pratap Bhanu Mehta, "Citizenship and Accountability: The Case of India," paper presented at the World Bank Conference on New Frontiers of Social Policy, Arusha, Tanzania, December 12–15, 2005, http://unpan1.un.org/intradoc/groups/public/documents/apcity/unpan034373.pdf (accessed May 6, 2014).

74. In contrast, there is much less concern over false reporting of criminal cases given that these are a matter of public record, whereas one's financial holdings rely largely on private information sources.

75. Although the Supreme Court has clarified that incomplete affidavits provide a sufficient basis for disqualification, the ECI has appeared hesitant to enforce this regulation. Furthermore, even if it did, the penalties are quite light. Amending the Representation of the People Act to make this infraction the grounds for disqualification would raise the stakes. A report of the Law Commission has suggested exactly this remedy; see Government of India, Law Commission of India, *Electoral Disqualifications,* Report No. 244 (New Delhi: Law Commission of India, February 2014), http://lawcommissionofindia.nic.in/reports/report244.pdf (accessed April 22, 2016).

76. Association for Democratic Reforms, "Lok Sabha Elections 2014: Analysis of Criminal Background, Financial, Education, Gender and Other Details of Candidates," May 9, 2014, adrindia.org/download/file/fid/3565 (accessed January 3, 2016).

77. The politician who made this remark was Jaya Jaitly, former president of the Samata Party. See PRS Legislative Research, "Summary of Proceedings from the Conference on Effective Legislators," December 5, 2008, http://www.prsindia.org/uploads/media/conference/ConferenceSummaryFinancingElectionCampaigns.pdf (accessed January 12, 2013).

78. In 2003, the spending limit for the typical Lok Sabha constituency was raised to 2.5 million rupees (then $56,000), in February 2011 to 4 million rupees ($89,000), and in early 2014 to 7 million rupees ($115,000).

79. Association for Democratic Reforms, "Lok Sabha Elections 2014: Analysis of Election Expenditure Statements of MPs," August 1, 2014, http://www.adrindia.org/research-and-report/election-watch/lok-sabha/2014/analysis-election-expenditure-statements-mps-2014 (accessed June 10, 2015).

80. "Dangerous for Democracy," *Hindu,* March 21, 2013.

81. P. Sainath, "EC Can't Disqualify Candidate over Poll Accounts, Paid News: Government," *Hindu,* March 20, 2013.

82. "Ashok Chavan Gets EC Notice in 'Paid News' Case," Press Trust of India, July 13, 2014, http://timesofindia.indiatimes.com/india/Ashok-Chavan-gets-EC-notice-in-paid-news-case/articleshow/38328274.cms (accessed July 14, 2014).

83. The Supreme Court of India has previously ruled that a failure to maintain accurate accounts is not tantamount to engaging in corruption. See Abhinav Garg, "HC Dismisses Ashok Chavan 'Paid News' Case," *Times of India,* September 13, 2014.

84. One reform worth pursuing is to amend the Representation of the People Act to designate "paid news" an electoral offense and, therefore, make the practice grounds for electoral disqualification.

85. E. Sridharan and Milan Vaishnav, "India," in Pippa Norris and Andrea Abel van Es, eds., *Checkbook Elections? Political Finance in Comparative Perspective* (Oxford: Oxford University Press, 2016).

86. Association for Democratic Reforms, "Submission of the Association for Democratic Reforms to the Special Investigation Team on Black Money," December 12, 2014, http://adrindia.org/content/circulation-unaccounted-money-activities-related-electoral-process-adr-submits-memorandum (accessed June 1, 2015).

87. Some commentators have also questioned the notion that the remit for scrutinizing parties belongs to the CIC rather than to the ECI. See, for instance, Pratap Bhanu Mehta, "Party Fixing," *Indian Express,* June 6, 2013.

88. "CIC Summons Six Parties for Non-Compliance of Directives," *Outlook,* December 1, 2014.

89. Ruling of the Central Information Commission in the complaint filed by Subhash Chandra Agrawal, Jagdeep Chhokar, Anil Verma, and Shivani Kapoor, March 16, 2015, http://www.rti.india.gov.in/cic_decisions/CIC_CC_C_2015_000182_M_149924.pdf (accessed April 5, 2016).

90. "Parties under RTI: SC Sends Notice to Election Commission, Centre" *Indian Express,* July 8, 2015.

91. Election Commission of India, "Guidelines on Transparency and Account-ability in Party Funds and Election Expenditure Matter," August 29, 2014, http://eci.nic.in/eci_main1/PolPar/Transparency/Guidelines_29082014.pdf (accessed August 1, 2015).

92. The remaining sources pertain to income from known donors or from other known sources. See T. Ramachandran, "Most Funds of National Parties from 'Unknown' Sources," *Hindu*, September 29, 2013.

93. An alternative proposal is to mandate disclosure of donors if their *total* contribution, even if broken up into many discrete donations, surpasses 20,000 rupees.

94. An analysis by the Association for Democratic Reforms of income tax returns submitted by India's national parties between 2004–5 and 2012–13 found that the BSP declared receiving more than 3 billion rupees in voluntary contributions during this period. However, it allegedly did not collect any donations above 20,000 rupees during this eight-year period, eliminating the need to disclose the identities of individual contributors. See Association for Democratic Reforms, "Submission to the Special Investigation Team on Black Money."

95. "I-T Exemptions on Donations Lead to Birth of New Parties: CEC," *Indian Express*, January 16, 2011.

96. Association for Democratic Reforms, "Analysis of Pending Criminal Cases of Lok Sabha MPs from 2009," March 11, 2014, http://adrindia.org/content/analysis-pending-criminal-cases-lok-sabha-mps-2009 (accessed May 5, 2014).

97. Ibid.

98. Association for Democratic Reforms, "Comparison of Pending Cases and Convictions Declared by Elected Representatives," September 27, 2013, http://adrindia.org/content/comparison-pending-cases-and-convictions-declared-elected-representatives (accessed March 11, 2014).

99. Ibid.

100. The stipulation that charges must be framed by a judge is an important one because it suggests that a judicial agent has determined there is sufficient prima facie evidence for a trial. This is a more stringent threshold than the mere existence of charges. As the Law Commission of India notes: "When filing a charge-sheet, the Police is simply forwarding the material collected during investigation to a competence Court of law." It implies no application of a judicial mind. See Law Commission of India, *Electoral Disqualifications*, 30.

101. Following the Supreme Court opinion, union law and justice minister Ravi Shankar Prasad requested that high courts monitor ongoing cases against any sitting MPs and MLAs of a serious nature and where charges have been framed. See "Monitor Cases against MPs, MLAs: Law Minister to CJs," *Hindu*, September 6, 2014. The Supreme Court did not take a firm position on the issue of whether candidates could be restricted from contesting elections in the first place if they face serious charges, although it did say the proposal merits further consideration. See *Public Interest Foundation and Others vs. Union of India and Others* (2011) Writ Petition (Civil) No. 536.

102. In addition, any person who is convicted for a term of two years or more, irrespective of the law he or she was found guilty of violating, stands disqualified. See M.R. Madhavan, "Legislature: Composition, Qualifications, and Disqualifications," in Sujit Choudhry, Madhav Khosla, and Pratap Bhanu Mehta, eds., *Ox-*

ford Handbook of the Indian Constitution (New Delhi: Oxford University Press, 2016).

103. There are some interesting nuances buried within the Supreme Court ruling on convicted politicians that have yet to be fully understood. For instance, if an MP or MLA obtained a stay on his/her sentence, he/she would still face immediate disqualification. If, however, he/she obtained a stay on the conviction itself, disqualification would not pertain unless and until a higher court upheld that conviction. See Prianka Rao, "The Representation of the People (Second Amendment and Validation) Bill, 2013," PRS Legislative Research Brief, December 9, 2013, http://www.prsindia.org/uploads/media/Representation/Brief-%20RoPA%202nd%20%28A%29%20Bill%202013.pdf (accessed April 1, 2016).

104. Association for Democratic Reforms, "Analysis of Criminal Cases Declared by the Newly-Elected Lok Sabha MPs in View of the Supreme Court Order Dated 10th of March, 2014," June 20, 2014 (on file with author).

105. "Election Commission Lifts Ban on Amit Shah; No Relief for Azam Khan," *Economic Times,* April 18, 2014.

106. Abhijit V. Banerjee, Donald Green, Jennifer Green, and Rohini Pande, "Can Voters be Primed to Choose Better Legislators? Experimental Evidence from Rural India," unpublished paper, Department of Economics, Massachusetts Institute of Technology, October 2010, https://casi.sas.upenn.edu/sites/casi.sas.upenn.edu/files/iit/Can%20Voters%20be%20Primed.pdf (accessed April 20, 2016).

107. Raghuram Rajan, "Is There a Threat of Oligarchy in India?" speech to the Bombay Chamber of Commerce, September 10, 2008, http://faculty.chicagobooth.edu/raghuram.rajan/research/papers/is%20there%20a%20threat%20of%20oligarchy%20in%20india.pdf (accessed December 1, 2013).

CHAPTER 8. AN ENTRENCHED MARKETPLACE

1. "Modi Vows to Send Politicians with Criminal Background to Jail," *Times of India,* April 15, 2014.

2. Ibid.

3. "Modi Pledges to Rid Parliament of Criminals," *Hindustan Times,* April 21, 2014 (accessed April 22, 2014).

4. Ibid.

5. "Criminal-Free Parliament Top Priority, Says Modi," *Indian Express,* April 22, 2014; "Narendra Modi Vows to Send Criminal Politicians behind Bars," *Economic Times,* April 22, 2014.

6. Association for Democratic Reforms, "Lok Sabha Elections 2014: Analysis of Criminal Background, Financial, Education, Gender and Other Details of Candidates," May 9, 2014, adrindia.org/download/file/fid/3565 (accessed January 3, 2016).

7. In 2009, the last time India held a national election, there was just one politician with a Twitter account (with roughly 6,000 followers). When Narendra Modi went on social media to declare victory in the 2014 general election, he tweeted his announcement to 4.3 million followers. See Raheel Khursheed, "India's 2014 #TwitterElection," *Twitter India* (blog), May 15, 2014, https://blog.twitter.com/2014/indias-2014-twitterelection (accessed July 15, 2015).

8. Association for Democratic Reforms, "Lok Sabha Elections 2014."

9. "Will Ask SC to Expedite Cases on MPs with Criminal Charges: Modi," *Outlook,* June 11, 2014.

10. Association for Democratic Reforms, "Lok Sabha 2014: Analysis of Criminal, Financial, and Other Background Details of Union Council of Ministers," May 27, 2014, http://adrindia.org/research-and-report/election-watch/lok-sabha/2014/lok -sabha-2014-union-council-ministers-analysis-cr (accessed September 30, 2014).

11. P. R. Ramesh, "His Master's Mind," *Open,* April 11, 2014.

12. Aditi Phadnis, "Amit Shah, BJP's Master Strategist," *Business Standard,* August 2, 2013.

13. At the time of his 2012 reelection to the Gujarat assembly, Shah was named in two ongoing criminal cases according to the affidavit he filed with the Election Commission at the time of nomination. Following a Supreme Court order, these two cases—the encounter killing of extortionist Sohrabuddin Sheikh and his wife, Kauser Bi, and the alleged murder of the witness to the killing, Tulsiram Prajapati— were clubbed together. Although rumors swirled, Shah was never formally charged in a third case, known as the Ishrat Jahan case, which involved the encounter killing of four suspected terrorists. See Uday Mahrurkar, "CBI Chargesheet against Amit Shah a Blow to Narendra Modi," *India Today,* September 5, 2012.

14. See, inter alia, Human Rights Watch, *Broken System: Dysfunction, Abuse, and Impunity in the Indian Police* (New York: Human Rights Watch, 2009), 7.

15. The court's qualms were clearly not without some merit. In the run-up to the campaign, Shah became embroiled in a scandal that came to be known as "Snoop-gate." The scandal involved leaked audio recordings of top Gujarat officials alleg- edly discussing Shah's authorization of the secret surveillance of a young woman connected to Modi. The identity of the woman and her connection to Modi were shady, to say the least, but the BJP government, far from denying the allegations, openly acknowledged using the state machinery to surreptitiously track the woman "at her father's request." The operation was said to have been directed and over- seen by Shah himself. See Shantanu Bhattacharji, "All You Need to Know about Snoopgate," *Business Standard,* November 27, 2013.

16. Poornima Joshi, "The Organiser," *Caravan,* April 1, 2014.

17. Dean Nelson, "Fear and Loathing in India's Muslim Heartland Could De- cide General Election," *Telegraph* (United Kingdom), April 5, 2014.

18. Gyan Varma, "Amit Shah Chargesheeted over Muzaffarnagar Election Speech," *Mint,* September 11, 2014.

19. At a press conference announcing Shah's appointment as BJP president, his predecessor Rajnath Singh declared: "There is no need to introduce Amit Shah. He has enormous imaginative abilities, is rich in organizational skills and has tre- mendous management abilities to ensure victories." Andrew Macaskill and Kar- tikay Mehrotra, "Modi Aide Accused of Murders to Lead India Ruling Party," *Bloomberg Business,* July 9, 2014.

20. "Ishrat Jahan Fake Encounter: CBI Gives Clean Chit to Amit Shah," Press Trust of India, May 7, 2014, http://www.thehindu.com/news/national/other-states/ ishrat-jahan-fake-encounter-cbi-gives-clean-chit-to-amit-shah/article5985667.ece (accessed November 16, 2015).

21. Rashmi Rajput, "Amit Shah Discharged, Court Finds No Evidence," *Hindu,* December 30, 2014.

22. "Sohrabuddin Case: Why Didn't CBI Approach Higher Court against Amit Shah, Asks Congress," Press Trust of India, March 30, 2015, http://www.firstpost .com/politics/sohrabuddin-case-didnt-cbi-approach-higher-court-amit-shah-asks -congress-2180335.html (accessed July 30, 2015). A petition by the brother of one of the victims is still pending in the Mumbai High Court. "Rethink on Removing Plea against Amit Shah: HC to Rubabuddin," Press Trust of India, October 20, 2015, http://www.business-standard.com/article/pti-stories/rethink-on-removing -plea-against-amit-shah-hc-to-rubabuddin-115102001463_1.html (accessed No- vember 16, 2015).

23. At the time of his election to the Lok Sabha, Baliyan faced one pending crim- inal case linked to the Muzaffarnagar riots. According to the affidavit he submitted to the Election Commission, Baliyan was accused of violating prohibitory orders, using criminal force against a public servant, and wrongful restraint.

24. Ellen Barry and Suhasini Raj, "Amid Modi's Centrist Shift, an Aide with a Turbulent Past Rises," *New York Times,* July 5, 2014; and Sreenivasan Jain, "Mu- zaffarnagar: The 'Riot' Men for the Job," NDTV, April 3, 2014, http://www.ndtv .com/elections-news/muzaffarnagar-the-riot-men-for-the-job-556040 (accessed November 14, 2015).

25. "Muzaffarnagar Riots Accused Sanjeev Baliyan in Modi's Cabinet," *First- post,* May 27, 2014, http://www.firstpost.com/politics/muzaffarnagar-riots-accused -sanjeev-baliyan-in-modis-cabinet-1543867.html (accessed November 15, 2015); and "Sanjeev Baliyan: From Riot Accused to Central Minister," *Times of India,* May 27, 2014.

26. Imran Ahmed Siddiqui, "Ex-Vet at Service of Farmers: How Riot-Tainted Baliyan Rose to Be Minister," *Telegraph* (Calcutta), May 29, 2014.

27. Ashish Tripathi, "'Stains' Good for BJP, Blot for Rivals," *Times of India,* November 9, 2013.

28. Reflecting on the political capital he accumulated as a Thakur strongman, Sharan Singh once told a reporter: "I used to touch the feet of Brahmins. Today, young Brahmin boys touch my feet calling me *guru ji* [teacher]." Supriya Sharma, "In Uttar Pradesh, Big Dons Aren't Afraid to Cry in Public," *Scroll.in,* April 14, 2014, http://scroll.in/article/661744/in-uttar-pradesh-big-dons-arent-afraid-to-cry -in-public (accessed July 8, 2014).

29. "Muscling His Way to Power," *Tehelka,* October 2, 2004; S. Hussain Zaidi, "Power Shift in Gangster Land," *Open,* April 18, 2014. When the journalist Su- priya Sharma asked Sharan Singh directly if he was a strongman, the politician had this to say: *Kissi gareeb ko kissi shareef ko maine tang nahi kiya. Aur jo atatai hai maine kabhi sangarsh se apna kadam peeche nahi hataya.* (I have never troubled the poor and the decent. And I have never shied away from taking on those who oppress others.) See Sharma, "In Uttar Pradesh, Big Dons Aren't Afraid."

30. "Brij Bhushan Shares Space with Advani and Dawood in CBI Files," *Times of India,* May 4, 2014.

31. Ibid. According to his 2014 Lok Sabha election affidavit, Sharan Singh faced two pending cases in which charges had already been framed.

32. Sharma, "In Uttar Pradesh, Big Dons Aren't Afraid."

33. "I am not Gandhi, I am a Mafia Man: SP MP," News18 video, September 30, 2012, http://www.ibnlive.com/videos/politics/sp-mp-sot-512775.html (accessed April 20, 2016).

34. Charu Sudan Kasturi, "In Bellary, Bisleri Bath Is Bottled and Modi Is Risky," *Telegraph* (Calcutta), April 17, 2014.

35. Johnson T. A., "Despite 'Taint,' Sreeramulu Hopes to Win by Mining Modi Name," *Indian Express,* April 11, 2014.

36. Frank Jack Daniel, "In Indian Mining Town, Nexus between Politics and Crime Plays Out," Reuters, April 22, 2014, http://www.reuters.com/article/us-india-election-crime-idUSBREA3L0DQ20140422 (accessed April 10, 2016); Sriramulu disclosed eight pending cases in his 2014 Lok Sabha election affidavit. In a 2012 case involving an attempted murder charge, a Karnataka judge had already framed charges against the politician.

37. Mahesh Kulkarni, "Why BJP Bets on Sreeramulu despite Sushma's Opposition," *Business Standard,* March 17, 2014.

38. Vichare declared 13 pending criminal cases in his 2014 Lok Sabha election affidavit. In his 2009 election affidavit, he disclosed 11 ongoing cases. One media report claimed that at least 24 cases had been registered against Vichare in Maharashtra's Thane district over the course of the past 25 years. See "24 Cases in 25 Years against MP Rajan Vichare, Who Force Fed Maharashtra Sadan Staffer," *DNA,* July 24, 2014.

39. Thomas Blom Hansen, *Wages of Violence: Naming and Identity in Postcolonial Bombay* (Princeton: Princeton University Press, 2001), 111.

40. "Rajan Vichare Wins Hands Down in Criminal Cases Race," *Fourth Estate* (blog), April 12, 2014, http://web.archive.org/web/20141029234103/http://fourth estateonline.in/?p=1430 (accessed April 21, 2016).

41. Sandip Roy and Lakshmi Chaudhry, "Shiv Sena MP Force Feeds Fasting Muslim: A Curious Case of Communal Chapati," *Firstpost,* July 24, 2014, http://www.firstpost.com/politics/shiv-sena-mp-force-feeds-fasting-muslim-a-curious-case-of-communal-chapati-1630795.html (accessed April 20, 2016).

42. Alok Deshpande, "Shiv Sena MP Vichare Faces 8 Police Cases," *Hindu,* July 23, 2014 (accessed April 20, 2016).

43. According to the affidavit Taslimuddin submitted to the Election Commission in advance of the 2014 Lok Sabha election, he faced four ongoing criminal cases. In two cases, charged had already been framed.

44. Swati Chaturvedi, "Criminal on Bail in Manmohan Ministry," *Tribune,* May 26, 2004; Bhuvaneshwar Prasad, "Taslimuddin, the Undisputed Leader of Seemanchal Region," *Times of India,* October 20, 2010.

45. "Status Will Go Down If Charge Lower than Murder Slapped: Adhir," Press Trust of India, April 14, 2014, http://www.business-standard.com/article/pti-stories/status-will-go-down-if-charge-lower-than-murder-slapped-adhir-114041400748_1.html (accessed November 15, 2015).

46. Susenjit Guha, "Bengal PCC Chief Faces Criminal Charges," *Sunday Guardian,* February 15, 2014.

47. Affidavit submitted by Vitthalbhai Radadiya to the Election Commission of India in advance of the 2014 Lok Sabha election. See also Rohit Bhan, "Elections

2014: The Tainted Candidates of Porbandar," NDTV, April 25, 2014, http://www
.ndtv.com/elections-news/elections-2014-the-tainted-candidates-of-porbandar
-558822 (accessed November 15, 2015).

48. Rohit Bhan, "Who Is MP with a Gun, Vitthalbhai Radadiya?" NDTV, October 12, 2012, http://www.ndtv.com/people/who-is-mp-with-a-gun-vitthalbhai
-radadiya-501616 (accessed July 10, 2014).

49. "MP, Who Pulled out Gun at Toll Plaza, Won't Apologise; Refused Bail," NDTV, October 17, 2012, http://www.ndtv.com/india-news/mp-who-pulled-out
-gun-at-toll-plaza-wont-apologise-refused-bail-502058 (accessed July 10, 2014).

50. One advantage of the present study is that it relies on data covering all candidates who stand for election, not only the eventual winners. This is not true of all studies in the political selection literature.

51. One recent study of party selection in the Indian context used interviews with senior officials across major political parties to gain a better understanding of their deliberative process when it comes to selecting party candidates. See Adnan Farooqui and E. Sridharan, "Incumbency, Internal Processes and Renomination in Indian Parties," *Commonwealth and Comparative Politics* 52, no. 1 (January 2014): 78–108.

52. One innovative example is a study by a researcher who successfully convinced political parties in Benin to randomize clientelist platforms in a real (rather than simulated) election setting. See Leonard Wantchekon, "Clientelism and Voting Behavior: Evidence from a Field Experiment in Benin," *World Politics* 55, no. 3 (April 2003): 399–422.

53. Carlos Pereira and Marcos Andre Melo, "Reelecting Corrupt Incumbents in Exchange for Public Goods: Rouba Mas Faz in Brazil," *Latin American Research Review* 51, no. 1 (Spring 2016): 88–115.

54. Pablo Fernández-Vázquez, Pablo Barberá, and Gonzalo Rivero, "Rooting Out Corruption or Rooting for Corruption? The Heterogeneous Electoral Consequences of Scandals," *Political Science Research and Methods* 4, no. 2 (May 2016): 379–97.

55. Devesh Kapur and Milan Vaishnav, "Quid Pro Quo: Builders, Politicians, and Election Finance in India," Center for Global Development Working Paper 276, March 29, 2013, http://www.cgdev.org/sites/default/files/Kapur_Vaishnav
_election_finance_India-FINAL-0313.pdf (accessed April 1, 2013).

56. Daniel Gingerich, "Brokered Politics in Brazil: An Empirical Analysis," *Quarterly Journal of Political Science* 9, no. 3 (September 2014): 269–300.

57. Mariana Escobar, "Paramilitary Power and 'Parapolitics': Subnational Patterns of Criminalization of Politicians and Politicization of Criminals in Colombia" (PhD diss., London School of Economics and Political Science, 2013).

58. International Crisis Group, "Cutting the Links between Crime and Local Politics: Colombia's 2011 Elections," Latin America Report No. 37, July 25, 2011, http://www.crisisgroup.org/en/regions/latin-america-caribbean/andes/
colombia/37-cutting-the-links-between-crime-and-local-politics-colombias-2011
-elections.aspx (accessed September 1, 2014).

59. Atul Kohli, *Democracy and Discontent: India's Growing Crisis of Governability* (New York: Cambridge University Press, 1991).

60. According to one editorial in a local newspaper, when it comes to the criminalization of politics in West Bengal, "The only change that has come under the new regime is that the [Trinamool Congress's] writ has replaced that of the Communist Party of India (Marxist) at all levels of administration." See "State of Decay," *Telegraph* (Calcutta), July 2, 2014.

61. Soudhriti Bhabani, "Political Goondaism in Bengal: Was, Is, and Will Be," *India Today*, June 11, 2013. One Trinamool Congress MLA, confronted by a party worker over the party's decision to induct a suspected criminal syndicate leader previously associated with the rival Communist Party, justified the move by saying: "The party cannot be run with writers and bearded intellectuals. Bhojai [the controversial inductee] is our party's asset. The decision to take him in the party was taken at the highest level." Furthermore, the MLA argued, the presence of a feared *goonda* was a necessary evil that would help neutralize the threat posed by the Left: "To fight Pakistan, I am bringing in China. Do you have any objection? With China, I will take on Pakistan. If China swallows me up, that's my concern." See Subrata Nagchoudhury, "We Cannot Run a Party with Intellectuals: TMC MLA on Induction of Ex-CPM Goon," *Indian Express*, January 29, 2011; Aniruddha Ghoshal, "In the Boomtown, 'Syndicates' Hold Key to Pole Position," *Indian Express*, October 2, 2015.

62. Ruchi Chaturvedi, "'Somehow It Happened': Violence, Culpability, and the Hindu Nationalist Community," *Cultural Anthropology* 26, no. 3 (August 2011): 342–43; Paul Zacharia, "Conduct of a Perfect Murder," *Caravan*, June 1, 2012.

63. Ruchi Chaturvedi, "North Kerala and Democracy's Violent Demands," *Economic and Political Weekly* 47, no. 42 (October 20, 2012): 21–24.

64. Ibid.

65. Nahomi Ichino, "Essays on Ethnic Diversity and Political Instability in Sub-Saharan Africa" (PhD diss., Stanford University, 2008).

66. Daniel Jordan Smith, *A Culture of Corruption: Everyday Deception and Popular Discontent in Nigeria* (Princeton: Princeton University Press, 2008).

67. Omobolaji Ololade Olarinmoye, "Godfathers, Political Parties and Electoral Corruption in Nigeria," *African Journal of Political Science and International Relations* 2, no. 4 (December 2008): 67.

68. Richard L. Sklar, Ebere Onwudiwe, and Darren Kew, "Nigeria: Completing Obasanjo's Legacy," *Journal of Democracy* 17, no. 3 (July 2006): 100–115.

69. Smith, *Culture of Corruption*, 122.

70. Candidates and godfathers often collude in the deployment of thugs—sometimes called "area boys"—around election time to mobilize or suppress turnout, as circumstances warrant. Daniel Smith describes such collusion in fascinating detail. Before a local election, godfathers, politicians, and their hired goons would meet "secretly" to plot how they would deploy their "muscle" during elections. The politicians would actually intentionally leak news of the meeting so as to intimidate rival factions. See Smith, *Culture of Corruption*, 121–25.

71. Human Rights Watch, *Criminal Politicians: Violence, "Godfathers," and Corruption in Nigeria* (New York: Human Rights Watch, 2007).

72. Colin Clarke, "Politics, Violence and Drugs in Kingston, Jamaica," *Bulletin of Latin American Research* 25, no. 3 (June 2006): 420–40.

73. Clarke, "Politics, Violence and Drugs in Kingston, Jamaica."

74. Obika Gray, "Badness-Honour," in Anthony Harriott, ed., *Understanding Crime in Jamaica: New Challenges for Public Policy* (Kingston: University of the West Indies Press, 2003), 13–48.

75. Obika Gray writes of Jamaica's political dynamics: "An important claim to personal authority now relied on a capacity to deploy militant social identities that would cause others to pause and possibly concede respect." See Gray, "Badness-Honour," 19–20.

76. Ibid., 35.

77. Harriott, *Understanding Crime in Jamaica.*

78. Robert Hislope, "Crime and Honor in a Weak State: Paramilitary Forces and Violence in Macedonia," *Problems of Post-Communism* 51, no. 3 (May-June 2004): 18–26.

79. Robert Hislope, "Shaking Off the Shakedown State? Crime and Corruption in Post-Ohrid Macedonia," Woodrow Wilson International Center for Scholars Meeting Report 271, February 26, 2003, https://www.wilsoncenter.org/publication/271-shaking-the-shakedown-state-crime-and-corruption-post-ohrid -macedonia (accessed July 16, 2015).

80. Huma Yusuf, *Conflict Dynamics in Karachi* (Washington, D.C.: U.S. Institute for Peace, 2012).

81. Ibid.

82. Ibid.

83. Olarinmoye, "Godfathers, Political Parties and Electoral Corruption in Nigeria."

84. Clarke, "Politics, Violence and Drugs in Kingston, Jamaica."

85. Subrata K. Mitra, *Power, Protest and Participation: Local Elites and Development in India* (New York: Routledge, 2002).

86. D. N., "Landlords as Extensions of the State," *Economic and Political Weekly* 24, no. 4 (January 28, 1989): 179–83.

87. Charles Tilly, "War Making and State Making as Organized Crime," in Peter B. Evans, Dietrich Rueschemeyer, and Theda Skocpol, eds., *Bringing the State Back In* (New York: Cambridge University Press, 1985), 169–91.

88. In some cases, the criminals who became locally dominant political forces once served in the employ of powerful rural landlords propped up by the British Raj.

89. Abhijit Banerjee and Lakshmi Iyer, "History, Institutions, and Economic Performance: The Legacy of Colonial Land Tenure Systems in India," *American Economic Review* 95, no. 4 (September 2005): 1190–1213.

90. John T. Sidel, "Bossism and Democracy in the Philippines, Thailand, and Indonesia: Towards an Alternative Framework for the Study of 'Local Strongmen,'" in John Harriss, Kristian Stokke, and Olle Törnquist, eds., *Politicising Democracy: The New Local Politics of Democratisation* (London: Palgrave Macmillan, 2005).

91. Andrew Dawson, "The Social Determinants of the Rule of Law: A Comparison of Jamaica and Barbados," *World Development* 45 (2013): 314–24.

92. The Money, Politics and Transparency project, a joint initiative of Global Integrity, the Sunlight Foundation, and the Electoral Integrity Project, has created an interactive web portal with cross-country indicators of political finance. For more information, visit https://data.moneypoliticstransparency.org/.

93. Nicholas Carnes and Noam Lupu, "Do Voters Dislike Working-Class Candidates? Voter Biases and the Descriptive Underrepresentation of the Working Class," *American Political Science Review* (forthcoming); Nicholas Carnes and Noam Lupu, "Rethinking the Comparative Perspective on Class and Representation: Evidence from Latin America," *American Journal of Political Science* 59, no. 1 (January 2015): 1–18.

94. Nicholas Carnes, *White-Collar Government: The Hidden Role of Class in Economic Policy Making* (Chicago: University of Chicago Press, 2013).

95. Former World Bank president Robert Zoellick summed up this consensus in a 2011 speech: "Our message to our clients, whatever their political system, is that you cannot have successful development without good governance. . . . We [the World Bank] will encourage governments to publish information, enact Freedom of Information Acts, open up their budget and procurement processes, build independent audit functions." See World Bank, "Citizen Empowerment, Governance Key for Middle East-Zoellick," April 6, 2011, http://www.worldbank.org/en/news/press-release/2011/04/06/citizen-empowerment-governance-key-middle-east-zoellick (accessed January 3, 2015).

96. Matthew S. Winters, Paul Testa, and Mark M. Frederickson, "Using Field Experiments to Understand Information as an Antidote to Corruption," in Danila Serra and Leonard Wantchekon, eds., *New Advances in Experimental Research on Corruption,* vol. 15 of Research in Experimental Economics (London: Emerald Group Publishing Limited, 2012), 213–46.

97. The seminal study in this regard is Anthony Downs, *An Economic Theory of Democracy* (New York: HarperCollins, 1957).

98. Two studies, in particular, helped make the case that the identity of politicians matters both for electoral reasons as well as subsequent policy outcomes. See Timothy Besley and Stephen Coate, "An Economic Model of Representative Democracy," *Quarterly Journal of Economics* 112, no. 1 (February 1997): 85–114; and Martin Osborne and Al Slivinski, "A Model of Political Competition with Citizen-Candidates," *Quarterly Journal of Economics* 111, no. 1 (February 1996): 65–96.

99. A study by Abhijit Banerjee and Rohini Pande does explicitly look at how voter "ethnicization," or the preference for politicians from one's own ethnic group, produces political corruption. However, the study assumes that all citizens would like "high quality" or honest, noncorrupt representatives but often end up with "low quality," corrupt representatives because their preference for co-ethnic candidates overwhelms concerns about probity, etc. Although insightful, it does not quite capture what value added criminality provides over co-ethnicity. See Abhijit Banerjee and Rohini Pande, "Parochial Politics: Ethnic Preferences and Politician Corruption," unpublished paper, Harvard Kennedy School, 2007, http://scholar.harvard.edu/files/rpande/files/parochial_politics_0.pdf?m=1412891482 (accessed April 10, 2016).

100. Simon Chauchard, "Ethnic Preferences and Candidate Quality: A Vignette Experiment in North India," unpublished paper, Department of Government, Dartmouth College, 2015, http://www.simonchauchard.com/wp-content/uploads/2014/12/Chauchard_crim_091414.pdf (accessed April 11, 2016).

101. Francis Fukuyama, *Political Order and Political Decay: From the Industrial Revolution to the Globalization of Democracy* (New York: Farrar, Straus and Giroux, 2014), 37.

102. Madhav Khosla, *The Indian Constitution* (New Delhi: Oxford University Press, 2012), xii.

APPENDIX A

1. In addition, the database contains information on 226 members of the Rajya Sabha, as of 2010.

2. Hand checking was ever more vital because a common act of political treachery in India is for an underdog party to run a candidate with the same name as the favored candidate in order to confuse voters.

3. To my knowledge, there have been relatively few known instances of candidates failing to disclose or making false disclosures about their criminal antecedents. In one case, involving a local politician in Tamil Nadu, the Supreme Court ruled that concealing one's criminal antecedents was grounds for immediate electoral disqualification. See "Declaration of Criminal Antecedents Must for Candidates: Supreme Court," *Indian Express,* February 6, 2015.

4. Government of India, Law Commission of India, *Electoral Disqualifications,* Report No. 244 (New Delhi: Law Commission of India, February 2014), http://lawcommissionofindia.nic.in/reports/report244.pdf (accessed April 22, 2016).

5. The coding strategy I employ here is similar to the one used in Eric C. C. Chang, Miriam A. Golden, and Seth J. Hill, "Legislative Malfeasance and Political Accountability," *World Politics* 62, no. 2 (April 2010): 177–220.

6. Two examples illustrate why it is essential to code individual criminal charges. In May 2011, Congress MP Rahul Gandhi was arrested after participating in a peaceful demonstration to raise awareness about farmers' rights. Gandhi was charged with violating IPC sections 144 (joining an unlawful assembly with a "weapon of offence") and 151 (knowingly joining an assembly after it has been ordered to disperse). Gandhi's protest was nothing more than an attempt to woo support before elections. See "Rahul Arrested amid High Drama, Released," *Hindu,* May 12, 2011. Contrast this to the case of Shekhar Tiwari, an MLA from the same state, charged with extorting and killing a bureaucrat who refused to donate money to the MLA's party. Tiwari—charged with violating sections 302 (murder), 342 (wrongful confinement), and 364 (kidnapping)—was sentenced to life in prison. See Man Mohan Rai, "BSP MLA, Shekhar Tiwari Gets Life Imprisonment in PWD Engineer Murder Case," *Economic Times,* May 7, 2011.

7. Officials intent on maligning a politician are likely to have a harder time manufacturing a false case involving murder charges than one alleging unlawful assembly.

8. Indeed, an investigation of several prominent politicians' asset declarations found that, if anything, they underreported the market value of their assets. See Harinder Baweja and Aman Khanna, "Damning Self Disclosures: Top Leaders Lie on Oath," *Tehelka,* January 5, 2004.

9. There are four primary difficulties: lack of standardized reporting of candidate names; party switching among candidates; redistricting of constituencies,

which took place in 2007; and dynastic candidates (whose names are very close to those of their ancestors).

10. When one or both of these fields is not filled out or is difficult to decipher, I relied on supplementary information.

11. The government of Uttar Pradesh submitted the report in response to a request from the Allahabad High Court emanating from *Karan Singh versus State of U.P. and Others* (2006), Criminal Misc. Writ Petition No. 5695.

12. Elections were held early in 2002, and it is possible that many charges were actually filed after elections.

APPENDIX C

1. A brief description of the CMIE Consumer Pyramids Survey can be found here: http://www.cmie.com/kommon/bin/sr.php?kall=wcontact&page=consumer_pyramids.

2. The actual urban population of India is much larger than what the official statistics report, due to the idiosyncrasies of census definitions. For instance, if the census defined *urban* according to standard population thresholds, as much as 50 percent of India would be classified as urban.

Index

Note: Page numbers followed by "f," "n," or "t" indicate figures, endnotes, and tables, respectively.